ESCAPE FROM VICHY

ESCAPE FROM VICHY

The Refugee Exodus to the French Caribbean

ERIC T. JENNINGS

Harvard University Press

Cambridge, Massachusetts
London, England
2018

Figure 4, Josef Breitenbach, Martinique, 1941, © The Josef and Yaye
Breitenbach Foundation

Library of Congress Cataloging-in-Publication Data
Names: Jennings, Eric T. (Eric Thomas), 1970– author.
Title: Escape from Vichy : the refugee exodus to the French
Caribbean / Eric T. Jennings.
Description: Cambridge, Massachusetts : Harvard University Press, 2018. |
Includes bibliographical references and index.
Identifiers: LCCN 2017036661 | ISBN 9780674983380 (hardcover : alk. paper)
Subjects: LCSH: World War, 1939–1945—Refugees—Martinique. | World War,
1939–1945—France—Marseille. | Martinique—Intellectual life—20th century. |
Political refugees—Martinique—History—20th century. | Political
refugees—Europe—History—20th century.
Classification: LCC D809.M435 J46 2018 | DDC 940.53 / 1450972982—dc23
LC record available at https://lccn.loc.gov/2017036661

CONTENTS

UNITED KINGDOM

BELGIUM

Lille

Le Havre

Sedan   LUXEMBOURG

GERMANY

Roland Garros   Drancy

Marne

Meuse

Rhine

Strasbourg

Damigny   Paris

Seine

Moselle

Rhine

F R A N C E

Marolles

Occupied by Nazi Germany

Colmar

Loire

Saône

ATLANTIC
OCEAN

Bourges

Cher

Doubs

SWITZERLAND

Vichy

VICHY FRANCE/
FREE ZONE

Lyon

Loire

Bassens

Bordeaux

Dordogne

Isère

ITALY

Rieucros

Rhône

Garonne

Montauban

Nîmes   Durance   Manosque

Langlade   Arles   Aix-en-Provence   Nice

Gurs   Toulouse   Les Milles   Marseille   Fréjus

Le Vernet   Pamiers   Sanary-sur-Mer   Toulon

SPAIN

Rivesaltes
Saint-Cyprien

Mediterranean Sea

France in 1941

- - - - Demarcation line

▨ Occupied by Nazi Germany

▨ Annexed by Nazi Germany

▨ Vichy France / Free Zone

■ Internment camp

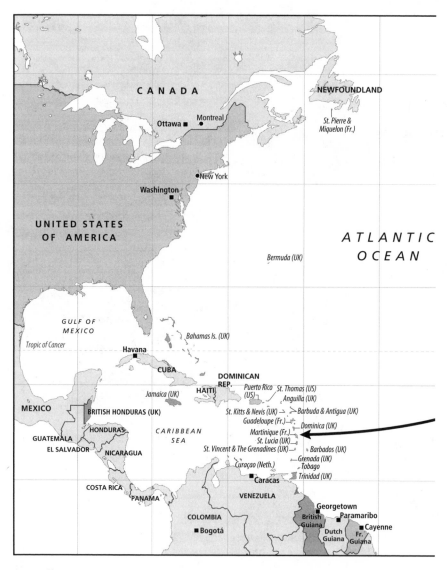

Marseille-to-Martinique route

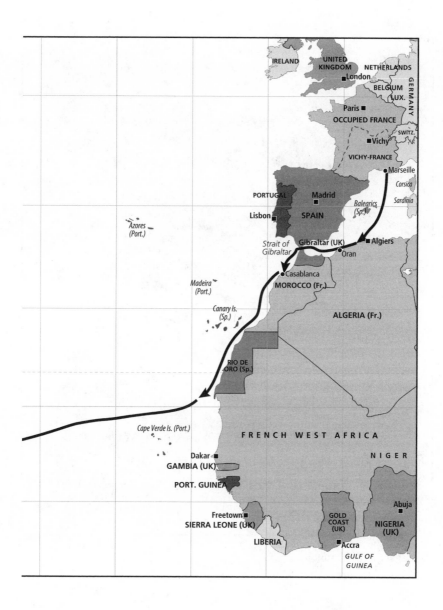

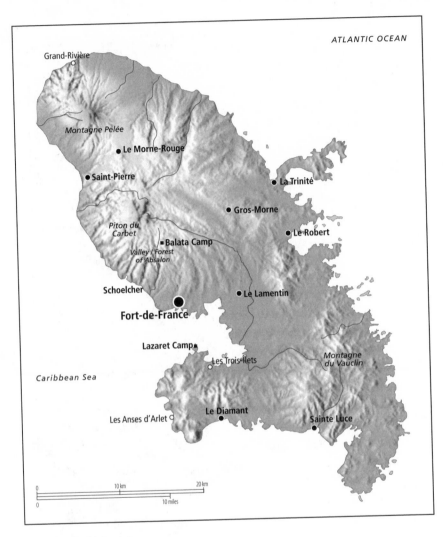

The island of Martinique

Introduction

I
N A JULY 17, 1941, report, the Red Cross took stock of the situation in
Vichy France's many internment camps, where desperate foreign refugees
were rounded up. The report's informants were Dr. Alec Cramer and Pastor
Pierre-Charles Toureille. Cramer worked for the Red Cross and had visited
a host of French camps in November 1940. Toureille was an expert on the
refugee crisis who operated in close relation with all major agencies concerned with aiding the migrants. He would tirelessly save Jewish children
during the war, would be arrested by Vichy and the Germans no fewer
than seven times, and would join the ranks of the Resistance.[1]

The thousands of refugees Toureille described in his report had come to
France to escape persecution from Adolf Hitler, Francisco Franco, and
Benito Mussolini. Some arrived in 1933, many more after the persecutions
of Kristallnacht (the November 1938 attacks on Jews), and more still in
the wake of Franco's victory in Spain. They included Spanish Republicans,
anti-Nazi Germans and Austrians, antifascist Italians, and Jews from all over
Europe, as well as patriots of many nationalities and faiths who wished to
continue the fight. Many were wanted by the Nazis. With few other avenues
available, their desperate quest to reach safer shores led them into the limbo
of Vichy-controlled Martinique. As an "old colony" of France, the Caribbean island of Martinique proved easier to reach and legally enter than in-
dependent nations of the Western Hemisphere. This is the biography of their
collective escape.

After France's calamitous defeat in June 1940, the collaborationist Vichy
regime first tried to facilitate emigration for these refugees. However, as one

overseas haven closed after another, and as one country after another in
the Americas refused to admit them, Vichy tightened the screws on the camps.
In August 1942, they became antechambers to Auschwitz. Between 1940 and
1942, the Red Cross, along with other humanitarian organizations, scrambled to extract as many refugees as it could. In the July 1941 document, it
calculated as follows on the basis of Toureille's numbers: "Currently, of the
360,000 foreigners declared undesirable, 7,000 have left to the Americas
via the following ships: *The Winnipeg, Wyoming, Mont Viso* and *Alsina*."[2]
These ships and many more, such as the *Paul Lemerle*, the *Ipanema*, and the
Carimaré, had left Marseille for Fort-de-France, Martinique, crammed
with refugees seeking the safety of the New World. They left in the nick
of time.

This book follows the short but sizeable migration that Toureille had identified: the wartime escape of thousands of European refugees to the French
Caribbean, and the myriad encounters and synergies that resulted. The
Martinique corridor's very existence, not to mention conditions of departure,
travel, and arrival, all shed light on the contradictions, breaks, and continuities at the heart of Vichy's treatment of refugees. The story also features
a remarkable cast of characters, some better known than others. Collectively,
their various experiences speak to many contemporary concerns, including
refugee crises, fears that potential enemies might be posing as migrants,
and themes of encounter, exile, and resilience.

This saga has not received previous attention, except at its fringes, for
instance by those interested in the efforts of Varian Fry's Emergency Rescue
Committee (ERC).[3] It is not uncommon to read or hear of some of the refugees considered in this book having reached either New York or Mexico from
Marseille, with Martinique earning no mention, not even a footnote. As
for the well-studied ERC, this American organization, like the Red Cross,
the Quakers, and the Jewish rescue organization HICEM (an acronym for
the merger of three Jewish emigration groups: The Hebrew Immigrant Aid
Society, The Jewish Colonization Association, and Emigdirect), undoubtedly played an important role in guiding some refugees to safety. However,
as I will show, none of these organizations actually hatched the Martinique
plan or controlled the maritime route.

Wartime Hollywood may have come closest to capturing elements of
this story: both *Casablanca* (1942) and *To Have and Have Not* (1944) touch
on aspects of it, focusing, respectively, on refugees leaving mainland France

only to find themselves agonizingly waylaid in a French overseas territory, and on wartime Martinique. The "yarn of war refugees in French Morocco," as *Casablanca* was initially billed, seems an apt depiction of the first stopover on the Martinique rescue route. Moreover, several of the migrants who transited through Morocco and Martinique in 1940 and 1941 ended up working in Hollywood studios. Indeed, so many actors and actresses in *Casablanca* were refugees themselves that one can identify a kind of "roll-call" effect in the film.[4]

And yet Tinseltown missed the heart of the matter, or rather it chose to focus only on one aspect of one route: the Casablanca-Lisbon connection. My focus lies elsewhere. On location in Martinique, the ambiguous rescue took on yet another dimension. Surrealist exile André Breton would stumble on the journal *Tropiques,* founded by Aimé and Suzanne Césaire and René Ménil, which ushered in a rich confluence between Surrealism and Negritude—an intellectual current dedicated to celebrating blackness and rejecting racism. In the French Caribbean, many refugees from Marseille forged lasting ties, among each other to be sure, but also with leading local dissidents, articulating their own liberation ideology at this very time. Various biographers have described the meeting of minds between the Surrealists and the apostles of Negritude, and several of those involved wrote of their experiences. But the striking story of transatlantic escape and synergy, with Martinique at its epicenter, has yet to be told. In other words, this book also helps illuminate the Second World War's intellectual impact, in particular its substantive mark on anticolonial dynamics.

This transatlantic story starts in Marseille. However, it is not one of diffusion but rather one of confluence. It is a deeply connected history.[5] As their freighter steamed from Marseille to Martinique in April 1941, professional revolutionary Victor Serge and anthropologist Claude Lévi-Strauss contemplated the ways in which the Americas and Europe were profoundly linked. During interminable discussions on board, they concluded that the Atlantic represented for the twentieth century what the Mediterranean had constituted to the ancients: "an inland sea."[6] Soon, Martinican thinkers Aimé and Suzanne Césaire would prompt the travelers to add Africa to their reconfigured shores.

The actors of this drama were involved in global North–South and transatlantic dialogue. It therefore stands to reason that it should relate to colonial and postcolonial studies. Historians in those areas have long debated the weight of the Second World War in the process of decolonization. Various dynamics have been advanced: Japanese occupations in Southeast Asia and the accompanying defeat and humiliation of former colonizers by an Asian conqueror; power inversions resulting from nonwhite contributions to the war effort and a push to desegregate army units in and across national contexts; the role of colonies in liberating metropoles; and the ultimate defeat and repudiation of Hitlerian racism.

This book offers a new lead on the last count, inasmuch as it identifies and analyzes a key intellectual turn on the sinuous paths of decolonization. In 1950, a Martinican intellectual would shock the world by drawing a direct parallel between Nazism and European overseas empires. He insisted that what appalled many about Hitler was "the fact that he applied to Europe colonialist procedures which until then had been reserved exclusively"[7] for the degradation and murder of the colonized. The author was none other than Aimé Césaire, and the book in which this argument appeared, *Discourse on Colonialism,* would become a touchstone for revolutionaries. Nine years prior, Césaire had begun testing a dual critique of fascism and imperialism. To deliver this first salvo, Césaire and his comrades had relied on a timely instrument brought over on the ships from Marseille: Surrealism. This epiphany involved a profound, yet deeply ambiguous, engagement with the ideas and aesthetics conveyed and relayed by the refugees from Marseille, against a precarious and shifting backdrop. The nature and texture of that engagement speak, I believe, to another way in which the Second World War shaped the processes of decolonization. That the impetus should have come from Martinique is not altogether surprising. As Michael Rothberg has noted, far from being somehow marginal to the global stage, in 1941 the island offered a "privileged perspective on the crosscutting events of war and colonialism,"[8] a perspective in which this meeting of minds needs to be situated.

This book also engages with other strands of migration, genocide, and conflict studies. Much historical attention has been devoted to singular characters such as Aristides de Sousa Mendes and Chiune Sugihara, who rescued Jews in occupied Europe. Protection within France constitutes a rich and prolific subject of investigation as well.[9] Collective relief schemes involving Jews setting off to the Dominican Republic and to China have also been the focus of excellent studies.[10] Another body of scholarship has considered the less coordinated flight from the continent of thousands of migrants ahead of the Holocaust. Others still have chronicled American "restrictionism" and, more broadly, North American reactions to genocide that ranged from indifference to callousness. This book contributes to each of these fields, without fitting neatly into any of them. Although Fry tapped into the Martinique route, he knew nothing of how and why it came about. The Martinique rescue path was actually cobbled together in 1940 for paradoxical reasons that involved equal doses of pragmatism, xenophobia, and humanitarianism. It closed in May–June 1941—immediately before Hitler's invasion of the Soviet Union and the beginning of mass industrialized extermination—not because of German insistence, nor even because of the threat of submarine warfare, but mostly because of US concerns about Germanic-sounding passenger surnames on board. In this sense, the book invites a reappraisal of early US and British reactions to the humanitarian crisis in France.

Nor, of course, were the refugees all Jewish, which means that the "rescue," if that term is appropriate, needs to be situated in a larger context. In addition to Jewish passengers, large numbers of Spanish Republicans, dissidents (German and Austrian leftists, Surrealist artists, and anti-Nazi intellectuals), non-Jewish French nationals, and Czechoslovaks and Poles wanting to continue the struggle against Hitler were all part of this exodus.

The scene is set at a critical moment, when emigration was still possible but was becoming increasingly challenging. The Martinique escape also highlights a series of complicated dynamics around exodus and diaspora. Walter Mehring, one of the German Jewish refugees long stranded in Marseille, crisply spelled out the contradictions of his condition when he underscored how fortunate he had been to be expelled from Vichy France to the Caribbean. In 1940 and 1941, he and his companions felt a clear and present danger. As I will show, although it is vital to avoid teleology, it is also important not to let the risk of it blind historical sensitivity. Such an overreaction could lead one to misattribute the ominous tone of contemporaneous testimonies from 1940 and 1941 simply to a presentist impulse to somehow "read history backward" and see the Holocaust looming before it began. Throughout, I have done my utmost to retrieve individual experiences of exile while tightly tethering them to chronology and context.

Within the field of migration studies, over a decade ago Nancy L. Green identified two opposing tendencies: one, which she termed "the new citizenship studies," emphasized the impact of the state on immigrants; the other, more transnational, centered on the experiences of migrants themselves, insisting on their agency. The fields in question are very dynamic, but the divide Green identified in 2005 seems to have persisted. One of the challenges I have set for myself with this study is to attempt to overcome the divide, by showing how migrants navigated administrative hurdles, sought out complicit functionaries, and shared information about administrative soft spots. I seek, therefore, to bridge some of the gaps that migration histories have featured, including the dichotomies of "citizenship vs. transnationalism and structure vs. agency." I take up Green's invitation to consider "the ways in which the states and societies of origin aided and abetted or fretted about and even obstructed the emigration movement."[11] Within the Martinique escape story, each of these impulses—abetting, fretting, and obstructing—appears in turn.

This is a portrait of transatlantic escape and confluence as the world unraveled. As such, it lends itself to multiple brushes. In order to shed light on migration and encounter, I have adopted a plural approach that is at once cultural, intellectual, political, and colonial. After surveying the refugee crisis in France, the book considers whether departure from Europe to the Caribbean constituted rescue or expulsion, or perhaps a blend of the two. It examines Vichy's policies and attitudes toward "undesirables," while also privileging the perspectives of migrants themselves. It then turns to the Martinique escape avenue, considering the scope of the refugee corridor and the experiences of European migrants to the French Caribbean between 1940 and 1941, as well as the Martinique route's ultimate undoing, and the reasons for it. Finally, it explores the intellectual and artistic connections that this encounter elicited, while bringing to life both the particular and the converging contexts of wartime Marseille and Martinique. It highlights unexpected connections born of a European calamity.

CHAPTER ONE

Undesirables

ALTHOUGH SEVERAL THOUSAND desperate people reached Martinique in 1940 and 1941, as Pierre-Charles Toureille's figures make clear, the vast majority of those endangered remained in France. Many met tragic ends. Some did find alternative paths to safety in the Americas, Africa, or Asia, via Spain or Portugal; others reached Switzerland; a great many survived the war in mainland France, protected by valorous local guardians. Before delving into the Martinique escape route itself in Chapter 2, it therefore seems fitting first to review the situation in mainland France between 1938 and 1942, the fate of migrants stranded in the limbo of the so-called unoccupied zone, and the handful of other emigration options available to them. Indeed, most refugees placed Martinique on a short list of possible departure avenues that included Lisbon and North Africa. Rankings and opportunities on those lists changed as circumstances shifted over the course of 1941.

The Camps

Even before the German invasion of France in May 1940, in November 12, 1938, a decree of the French republic had specifically mandated that "undesirable foreigners" be interned in "specialized centers" and subjected to "close surveillance."[1] Internment camps sprang up around France. They were soon bursting at the seams with foreigners deemed "undesirable." By 1938 they were full of Spanish Republicans who had fled across the Pyrenees as Francisco Franco's forces gained the upper hand. Then, as France prepared for war in September 1939, a slew of new measures called for the internment of the "stateless," as well as German and Austrian nationals, and of foreigners considered "suspicious, dangerous or undesirable."[2] A law dated November 18, 1939, granted French prefects the right to intern anyone suspected of posing a threat to national defense.

A great many of those targeted were leftists and other dissidents who had sought refuge in France, as well as Jews fleeing the Nazis. A blend of xenophobia heightened by the economic crisis, of anti-Semitism, and of mounting concern for a possible fifth column, be it German, Italian, or Spanish speaking, accounts in no small part for this backlash against refugees. And yet, paradoxically, the backlash occurred in a country that had been statistically "the foremost land of asylum in the world" over the course of the 1930s.[3] Indeed, in 1933, while the League of Nations, and individual countries, dragged their heels on plans to establish quotas for an equitable division of Jewish refugees in particular, France's doors remained relatively open, despite a surging anti-immigrant tide. Laurent Joly estimates that France admitted two hundred thousand Jewish immigrants between 1900 and 1940.[4] Despite an undeniable backlash that took shape between 1933 and 1939, France had also opened its doors to tens of thousands of Russian, Armenian, and Italian refugees between the two world wars.[5]

France's collapse at the hands of Germany in June 1940, and the chaos that ensued, further exacerbated the refugee crisis. France was unevenly carved in two, with an unoccupied zone (sometimes called the free zone) controlled by Vichy to the south, and a German-occupied zone to the north.

The camp archipelago that stretched across the unoccupied zone after July 1940 was certainly a legacy of the French Third Republic,[6] a republic that committed suicide in Vichy's casino on July 10, 1940, by handing full powers to octogenarian would-be savior figure Philippe Pétain. In the realm of camps, as in many others, the new regime inherited the republic's infrastructure. Some of the makeshift camp buildings, such as the former tile factory in the case of Les Milles, had served as repositories for so-called enemy nationals since 1939. Others, such as Gurs and Saint-Cyprien in southwestern France, had been constructed in haste to house Spanish Republicans that same year. In fact, the inmates themselves built the camp of Saint-Cyprien. Sometimes, waves of different refugees rolled into the camps in rapid succession. In May 1940, as Adolf Hitler's forces penetrated French defenses at Sedan, roughly ten thousand female refugees were tossed into the confines of Gurs, where they joined the 3,500 Spanish Republicans and 1,329 French Communists, as well as other "suspects" already present. Soon Gurs became one of the main internment centers for foreign Jews in the unoccupied zone. By the fall of 1940, some forty-five thousand individuals, approximately thirty-five thousand of them foreigners, were interned in Vichy camps in the unoccupied zone alone.[7]

Historians continue to debate to what extent Vichy marked a rupture from or represented continuity with the republic that preceded it, including in its treatment of foreign refugees.[8] Certainly, Vichy utilized preexisting camps, personnel, and decrees to further its ends, although none of the laws passed before 1940 had been explicitly anti-Semitic.[9] And, admittedly, the notion of refugees as a burden at best and dangerous undesirables at worst was nothing new in 1940, either. Yet the point remains that, until 1940, most refugees on French soil were not in mortal danger in the way they suddenly collectively became after the fall of France.

Concretely, the June 1940 armistice that Pétain sought and obtained from Germany, and the Vichy regime born from it, changed the refugee crisis on several counts. For one thing, thousands of refugees fled the German-controlled north for southern France. For another, the armistice's article 19 stipulated that Vichy would have to "surrender on demand" any German or Austrian national wanted by the Nazis. Up until the Germans invaded the unoccupied zone in November 1942, the number of such handovers proved relatively and mercifully limited (only twenty-one in total at that point, thanks in part to heel dragging on the part of some Vichy officials; however, as we will see, Vichy also aimed to satisfy German demands by bypassing the armistice commission altogether).[10] Yet it remained both a haunting menace for German exiles and a marker of Vichy's dishonor and subservience. Additionally, in the wake of the armistice, Vichy transferred the network of camps from the purview of the Ministry of War to that of the Ministry of the Interior. This led to a drive to consolidate camps, and to numerous transfers of already exhausted refugees.[11] Then too, to quote Anne Grynberg, Vichy "swept away the last barriers to arbitrary confinement" that had existed until that point, with an October 4, 1940, law that granted prefects considerable latitude to intern "foreigners of Jewish race" into camps.[12] Moreover, material conditions in the camps deteriorated significantly after France's defeat.

Last but not least, refugees, who up until then had been labeled "para-
sites" by xenophobic elements in France, now found themselves scapegoats
for the defeat of 1940. In the perverse logic of the day, France's collapse
had not been military.[13] Instead, France had fallen because of decay and
rot; the Germans had simply toppled an already crumbling edifice. To many,
the stateless, the anti-Nazi exiles, the Spanish Republicans, and especially
the Jews were the source of the rot; or, at the very least, they needed to be
cast aside as France regenerated.[14] The question then became how to get rid
of them; the answer would change over time, according to circumstance.
In April 1941, Vichy's first commissioner of Jewish affairs, Xavier Vallat,
declared in the press that the "veritable legions" of foreign Jews who had
caused "misery" to France would "likely be sent back" (refoulés).[15]

As Vicki Caron has shown, until July 1942, emigration remained Vichy's
tool of preference to resolve the refugee crisis, "preferably . . . emigration
abroad, but as a last resort colonial options were to be considered as well."[16]
In the Bouches-du-Rhône department, of which Marseille is the capital, the
Vichy regime elaborated a clear mechanism to deal with refugees seeking
asylum abroad. Already on October 10, 1940, the Ministry of the Interior
had contacted prefectures about ways of ridding France of foreign refugees
considered a burden to the nation (étrangers en surnombre). In a November 20, 1940, letter, the Ministry of the Interior instructed the prefect
of the Bouches-du-Rhône to place refugees "awaiting emigration," or in
the process of obtaining visas for countries outside Europe, in the camp
of Les Milles, outside Aix-en-Provence. The letter explicitly mentioned
that Les Milles had been chosen for this purpose because of its proximity
to the Spanish and Portuguese consulates in Marseille, consulates rightly
considered the most likely to provide transit visas.[17] Indeed, by March
1941, Les Milles even had its own designated emigration officer, Louis
Gaude, who tried to tap into a wide range of departure channels.[18]

Like most camps, Les Milles' function changed over time. First, in
1939, it was a camp to hold "undesirable foreigners"; then, by October–
November 1940, it became a "transit" center for emigrants;[19] and finally, by
August 1942, it turned into an antechamber to Drancy, outside Paris, then
to Auschwitz. Les Milles reflected the regime's successive impulses first to
isolate and marginalize, then to be rid of, and finally to deport refugees
desperate to escape Hitler's clutches.

Conditions in Vichy's camps varied considerably but were on average very grim. Already in September 1940, the Red Cross reported that at the camp in Saint-Cyprien, young guards relentlessly kicked some of the elderly refugees ousted from Belgium.[20] Local inhabitants sometimes proved no more charitable to the migrants. For instance, some of the Jewish refugees who reached the same camp in 1940 were greeted to cries of "Death to the German spies!"[21] To make matters worse, lice, fleas, and flies tormented the inmates.[22] Access to latrines was on average poor.[23] By November 1942, the Red Cross reported that "undernourishment" in the camps was rampant. It estimated that one-third of all interned foreigners in the Vichy zone no longer had the strength to stand for more than ten minutes. Dysentery, tuberculosis, meningitis, and typhoid fever were also raging in some camps.[24] A medic at Gurs observed that in addition to malnutrition, inmates suffered from the elements, as well as a lack of light and space.[25] Crowded, unsanitary spaces were taking a heavy toll.

Before the first wave of deportations in 1942, refugees nevertheless managed to create a lively cultural and intellectual universe at Les Milles, trying their best to overcome the camp's "soul-deadening" atmosphere.[26] They organized an orchestra and book-binding, photography, language, and history workshops; assembled a library; even put on a drag show; and practiced sports.[27]

Yet escape remained their enduring obsession, reflected in their art. Already in 1939, German inmate Max Ernst had drawn two haunting figures representing "stateless" refugees in the camp, companions of his whom he reduced to metal files, so overwhelming was their will to decamp (figure 1).[28]

In the guards' refectory at Les Milles, in 1941 an anonymous artist, most likely Karl Bodek, painted a curious mural detail, depicting sardines in the foreground and in the background a vessel that might spirit them away (figure 2). To the right, three stereotyped black "natives"—one bearing a spear—frolic in and around a pineapple. The scene, featuring a ship in the shape of a ham, likely evokes dual refugee fantasies: the dream of oceanic escape to some tropical haven (with the black characters in the pineapple as visual cues), together with culinary abundance. The ham may be of significance in its own right, considering both Jewish nutritional restrictions and the drawing's location in the guard's refectory. Bodek was a Jewish

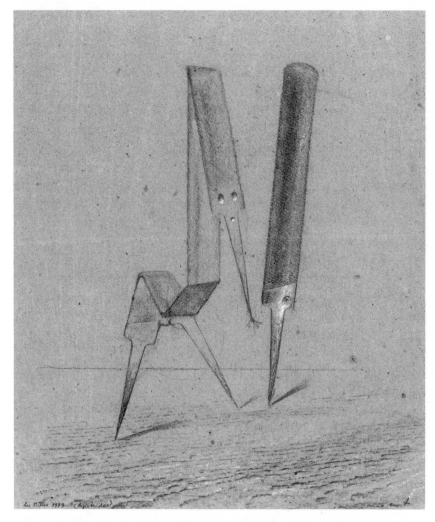

FIGURE 1. Max Ernst, *The Stateless* (Staatenlose), 1939. © Estate of Max Ernst/SODRAC (2017). Staatsgalerie Stuttgart, Graphische Sammlung, Inv.Nr. C 1970/1984 Bleistift-Frottage, 46.7×36.6 cm.

artist who had spent the interwar years in Vienna, before fleeing to Belgium. Like many expelled from Belgium during the German advance in 1940, he found himself interned at Gurs, before being transferred to Les Milles in April 1941. He was deported to Drancy on August 11, 1942, then three days later to Auschwitz, where he perished.[29]

FIGURE 2. Mural painting in the former guards' refectory of Camp des Milles, artist uncertain, ca. 1941 (detail, left). Fondation du Camp des Milles—Mémoire et Éducation (www.campdesmilles.org), all rights reserved, reproduction prohibited.

As Bodek's story suggests, the turning point for camp inmates came in 1942. It hinged largely on shifting attitudes in the halls of Vichy. At the end of April 1942, Pierre Laval returned to power as Vichy's second-in-command (with vast powers and control over both foreign and domestic affairs), to the delight of the Nazis, who appreciated his desire to anticipate and outperform their expectations.[30] The Vichy regime's emphasis shifted from emigration to deportation between July and August 1942. On July 17, Vichy's police chief René Bousquet informed all prefects that exit visas for foreign Jews were canceled, a measure that took effect the following day.[31] On July 29, Henri Cado, associate director of Vichy's national police, wrote to the prefects of the two Pyrenean departments where Gurs and Rivesaltes were located, ordering them to tighten camp surveillance, and to hide from inmates the news of their upcoming transfer to Drancy, in the occupied zone.[32] Then, on August 3, the camps of the unoccupied zone were locked. Two days later, Cado issued a telegram to prefects in the southern zone asking them to prepare all foreign Jews who arrived in France after January 1936 for deportation. Thereafter, even foreign Jews who secured emigration papers to the Americas were deported.[33] A first wave swept the camps of southern France in August and September 1942, with 10,614 foreign Jews deported from the unoccupied zone to Nazi extermination camps. Bousquet had committed to deporting

10,000 Jews from the free zone, but Vichy in fact provided more.[34] This tragedy took place at a time when Pétain's regime exercised full sovereignty over the southern half of France. These August 1942 convoys, writes Serge Klarsfeld, were the only ones ever to reach Auschwitz from territories with no formal German presence.[35]

On November 10, 1942, on the very eve of the German invasion of the so-called free zone previously controlled entirely by Vichy, the Red Cross reported that there were fewer than two hundred inmates remaining at Les Milles, and "no more than a few hundred" left at Gurs.[36] The Red Cross pleaded for medicine, as the healthiest refugees had been taken, leaving only the very ill. Ten months prior, in September 1941, there had been 1,354 interned at Les Milles and 4,764 at Gurs.[37] The camps had been emptied before German forces even reached the southern half of France.

Leaving the Camps

Even before July 1942, extracting refugees from these camps had been no easy task, although Mary Jane Gold of Varian Fry's Emergency Rescue Committee (ERC) proved up to the challenge in many cases. Fry's organization, supported by none other than Eleanor Roosevelt, Peggy Guggenheim, and Gold, would prove among the most active rescuers, focusing its efforts on European artists, writers, politicians, scientists, and scholars. In her memoirs, Gold relates her brazen entry into the camp at Le Vernet, south of Toulouse. She recounts sizing up the camp's director on the basis of his office décor (a portrait of Napoleon), asking him for a cigarette, accepting dinner with him, and along the way dropping the names of the four refugees he subsequently freed on her request: German Social Democrats Franz Boegler, Hans Tittel, Wilfred Pfeffer, and Fritz Lamm, the last of whom was also Jewish.[38]

Authorized releases like these became more and more challenging to obtain between 1941 and 1942. On June 25, 1941, Vichy's "head of government" Admiral François Darlan issued a circular to prefects instructing them not to free "foreigners of Jewish race" who had resided outside France before May 10, 1940.[39]

Rescue organizations and individual samaritans tried their best to keep up with evolving policies and procedures. How could one legally get out of the Gurs camp? Suzanne Ferrière of the Red Cross asked Marcelle Trillat of the Service social d'aide aux migrants in Lyon in July 1942, precisely as release from a camp was becoming impossible. The answer was complex, the waters murky. Up until then, Trillat reported, one required authorization from the prefecture, proof of 2,000 francs per month income and 15,000 francs in the bank, and the approval of the Ministry of the Interior at Vichy. In theory, nobody interned in France after May 1940 could be permanently released, she added; only health and other exceptional passes could be awarded. But now even this arduous process was called into question, Trillat added ominously.[40]

Unauthorized escapes also occurred in significant numbers before July 1942. Once again, timing mattered greatly. Shortly before the fall of France, German Jewish photographer (and former partner of novelist Alfred Döblin), Charlotte (aka Yolla) Niclas-Sachs was arrested at home in Paris without warning and interned as an enemy alien in the camp at Gurs. She quickly resolved to escape Gurs when she deemed that she no longer could stave off what she termed "internment psychosis." A friendly black cat's complete disregard for the camp's boundaries further emboldened her. In the confusion that followed the June 1940 armistice, she succeeded in darting out of the camp, thanks to a simple but efficient stratagem. A sympathetic Spanish Republican inmate drew the attention of the camp's guards because of a large medal he wore, no doubt a military decoration earned during the Spanish Civil War. When the camp guards demanded that he remove it, a kerfuffle ensued that tied up several guards. The distraction allowed Niclas-Sachs to abscond, running at "a speed that [she] would probably never attain again in [her] life." She then received assistance from a local family that provided her with food and shelter in exchange for her work in the fields. After months of a precarious existence marked by soup kitchens, bed bugs, and misery, Niclas-Sachs eventually managed to reunite with her husband, Rudolf Sachs. In Marseille, the two of them secured passage on one of the last ships bound for Martinique in May 1941.[41]

A great many escapes were foiled, however. Such was the case for Jakob Lahm, a German internee who was on the cusp of being handed over to the Nazis when he bolted from Les Milles in late 1940, only to be recaptured and reinterned at the same camp.[42] Similarly, German Jewish writer Lion Feuchtwanger (author of the 1925 novel *The Jew Süß,* which the Nazis would transform into anti-Semitic vitriol) escaped the Saint Nicolas camp outside Nîmes. After five days of struggling to make ends meet, he turned himself in, accepting the camp commandant's "invitation" to return.[43] Fry's ERC ultimately shepherded Feuchtwanger and his wife to America, via Spain and Portugal.

In Nice on May 29, 1941, Vichy's police arrested a fifty-four-year-old divorced German Jewish woman named Meta Heymann. Heymann was born in 1887 in the East Prussian town of Nikolaiken (modern-day Mikolajki, Poland). She was booked for "escaping an internment camp." Her first trial took place in Nice on June 10, 1941; her appeal was held in Aix-en-Provence on September 3, 1941.[44] There she was handed a ten-month prison sentence, which she served at the Présentines women's jail in Marseille.[45] Heymann's married name, Meta Rennemann, appears, with her proper birth date, on the list of those deported to Auschwitz on a May 30, 1944, convoy.[46]

The Aix-en-Provence appeals court at which Heymann stood trial was overcrowded, its judges working long hours. In the fall of 1941 they processed unusually large numbers of cases of illegal entry into France and of trafficking of all sorts, especially in food tickets (on top of the usual stream of cases of absinthe possession, assault, robbery, exhibitionism, illegal hunting, and fishing with dynamite). They were also busily enforcing new Vichy laws on alcoholism, abortion, and insults to the head of state Pétain.[47]

One can also identify semiauthorized releases, such as that of German Jewish dissident poet and satirist Walter Mehring. Vichy's police caught him trying to flee France over the Pyrenees and interned him at Saint-Cyprien in early September 1940. At the time he penned a poem that included the line, "Four thousand Jews are slowly rotting here," in what the author termed "Pyrenean Hell."[48] Nearly a decade later, Mehring would recall, "I once had thought I would never forget the horribly grinning buck teeth of the police chief in Perpignan who had caught me preparing to escape across the Franco-Spanish frontier."[49] Somehow, Mehring managed to cable Fry, who responded with a "We received your message, keep your confidence up" that was accidentally transcribed as "We received good news, keep your confidence up."[50] Despite this muddled exchange, Fry's pressure worked. Within two days, the camp's director handed Mehring unsigned liberation papers. Unsigned, specified the camp's commander, because the whole procedure was shady, and this way he was less likely to be reprimanded should Mehring be caught again.[51]

Elena Frank's case illustrates the hurdles faced by inmates filing requests for legal exit from camps. She wrote to Fry's ERC from the Rieucros camp in Lozère in November 1940. Frank was the spouse of German expressionist and pacifist Leonhard Frank, who was interned in a separate camp. She believed that she had been denounced in Paris. She was in any event manifestly weary, having first emigrated from Russia to Germany in 1920, then to Switzerland in 1933, and then, in a case of terrible timing, to Paris in June 1939. To Fry she invoked her friendship with *All Quiet on the Western Front* author Erich Maria Remarque and with Thomas Mann. She thanked Fry in advance for his help, but "remained skeptical about how effective it could prove." Nevertheless, she outlined to the American the steps required for leaving the camp, as explained by the prefecture in Mende: prefectorial authorization, written statements of loyalty drafted by two French nationals, a dwelling certificate, and, "last but not least,"[52] a guarantee of means of subsistence. As she pointed out, not knowing anyone in the Lozère rendered it all but impossible to obtain local statements of loyalty. Frank was evidently determined. By January 1941, Fry was writing to his New York offices, "I wish you would break your necks to get Madame Frank some kind of a visa before we break hers. She is the worse pest yet." The pestering worked, and Fry arranged, with the help of HICEM and the Unitarian rescue services, not just for Frank's departure from Marseille to America via Lisbon but also for her to be reunited with her young son, who had been left behind in Switzerland, before setting off.[53]

The Quest to Emigrate

Frank's case shows how exiting a camp and emigrating could be procedurally linked, dependent once again on both context and chronology. Thus, the ERC's Daniel Bénédite (real name Daniel Ungemach) relates that in the fall of 1940, the commander of the camp of Langlade in the Gard assured him that he would immediately release any refugee who obtained a visa allowing him or her to leave France.[54] This also reconfirms that Vichy's policy at that juncture was to encourage emigration.

And yet it was not always easy to obtain a visa. The files assembled by relatives and others to rescue refugees in Vichy camps shed light on the complexity and the arbitrariness of the multilayered process involved in gaining freedom from the camps via emigration. In order to leave for the United States, one needed to produce not only proof of funds and livelihood but also an affidavit from an American contact (later, this requirement was increased to two affidavits). In addition to the American paperwork, an exit visa was required from Vichy, and a transit visa as well if a third country was involved.

In other words, in theory, proof of admission to a foreign country was a necessary but not a sufficient condition for safe legal departure from Vichy's camps. Indeed, even a solid US sponsorship file was sometimes not enough. Consider the case of Max and Meta Strauss, German Jews whose families hailed from Michelstadt and Karlsruhe, and their children Margot and Edith. The Strausses had sold manufactured goods; Max had served in the First World War. Max's New York cousin, Benjamin Weil, enthusiastically supported the family's application. Weil, who worked in and owned real estate, as well as boasting considerable assets in and around Manhattan, vouched to support his cousin and family once they reached America.[55]

In short, the Strausses were among the few to have a valid and enthusiastic American guarantor. After weathering the storms of Kristallnacht, the family had been expelled from Germany. Their expulsion was tied to the infamous decision made by the gauleiters of Palatinate and Baden on October 22, 1940, to "dump" more than seven thousand Jews onto defeated France (the gauleiters were deliberately and abusively extending the armistice agreement's clause concerning Jews from Alsace and Lorraine).[56] Vichy detained the family at Gurs on October 25, 1940, a camp where men and women were routinely separated from one another. From there, the Strausses were transferred to the camp of Rivesaltes on March 12, 1941. Conditions proved so harsh that the parents decided to hand their daughters to the children's relief organization L'œuvre de secours aux enfants (OSE). The OSE, supported by other aid groups, managed to save 623 children from camps in the unoccupied zone before June 1942, and many more in August 1942. Parents and children bade heart-wrenching farewells.[57]

The Strausses' files reveal that Meta and Max were then transferred to Les Milles, whence they hoped to emigrate. Of all the camps in the south, Les Milles was rightly reputed to provide the best platform for emigration, and so hope was rekindled for a time. Yet the couple languished in Les Milles until August 1942, when they were sent to Drancy, outside Paris. On August 19 and 28, 1942, respectively, Max and Meta were deported from Drancy to Auschwitz, where they were immediately murdered. Margot and Edith survived, protected by strangers in Annecy. After the war, the two girls took the ship from Marseille to America, the very route on which their parents had pinned their hopes.[58]

Why had Weil's sponsorship failed? Without intense local lobbying for individual refugees, and for refugees who were not celebrities on a rescue list, it proved extremely difficult to escape the camps of southern France. Furthermore, the Strausses had reached Les Milles just as the various emigration channels were being blocked, in rapid succession. That being said, lobbying and the influence of sponsors are hard to measure, and in the end frustratingly little seems to separate cases of refugees who made it out, via Martinique or other channels, and those like the Strausses who did not. "Leaving France is a titanic task," reflected Germaine Krull after having managed to do so herself via Martinique.[59] The comment generally proves to have been spot on, although chronology mattered: 1940 did not present the same challenges for departure as 1941, and especially 1942.

In some instances, between 1940 and 1942, when emigration remained the Vichy priority, French officials promoted departures within the framework available to them. Take a September 17, 1940, letter from an anonymous official at the third division of the prefecture in Perpignan to the Ministry of the Interior at Vichy. It concerned thirty-four German and Polish Jews who had been expelled from Belgium. Eighteen of them were in possession of papers to leave for the United States or South American nations (Bolivia, Paraguay, Argentina, and Chile), three for China, one to Canada, one to Mexico, one to Cuba, one to Morocco, and one to New Caledonia. The refugees had been interned at Saint-Cyprien in accordance with Interior Ministry instructions dated July 7 and 15. The Perpignan official then recommended liberating all of the refugees in question, who were certain not to want to linger in France. He even gave a special "favorable" mention to his own plan.[60] More than just personal initiative was at work here: the camps were chronically overcrowded, and the Ministry of the Interior wished to close some of them. In November, it asked prefects not to intern more foreigners unless they were indigent; a month later it requested a temporary halt to the internment of new "nondangerous" foreigners in camps.[61] Why continue to detain those who intended to leave France?

The Perpignan prefecture would put forward another list of thirty-two individuals with exit papers one month later, on October 19, 1940. However, this time the Interior Ministry's response scolded Perpignan for trying to expedite procedures and reminded them that all Germans and Austrians on the list needed first to be vetted by the Nazi commission led by Ernst Kundt, which looked after the application of article 19 of the armistice convention ("surrender on demand").[62] Repeated German delays in drafting, updating, and transmitting the Kundt Commission lists to Vichy officials certainly contributed to bogging down emigration files.[63] Thus, the "surrender on demand" clause did more than instill terror; it also slowed refugee files, even for those who did not feature on the famous wanted list. The Kundt Commission did not stop at drawing up lists of Germans that Vichy must hand over: it also visited the camps in the southern zone and promised rehabilitation and a second chance for "good Germans" with no criminal record who opted to return to the Nazi national community (via a specially designated reeducation camp set up in Strasbourg, no doubt conceived as a kind of decontamination chamber before reentry into the German national community or *Volksgemeinschaft*).[64]

At this juncture, escape to French colonies or by other routes remained feasible. Indeed, it was still possible to leave camps in southern France, at least until August 1942. Yet the process was increasingly arduous, the challenges more numerous over time. A Red Cross document from December 1941 related how a wide range of organizations had cooperated on the goal of "reemigration" for refugees. The American Joint Distribution Committee funded and supported HICEM, which endeavored to secure papers and passages to safety for Jewish inmates in Vichy's camps. The Quakers, the YMCA, the Unitarian Service Committee, and a host of other organizations tirelessly endeavored to improve conditions in the camps. Other groups, such as Fry's ERC, likewise toiled to try to get select internees out.[65]

These organizations built bridges between the crisis epicenter and possible safe havens. It bears emphasizing that the course of events was also largely dictated by what transpired in receiving nations. Despite the American government's steps taken in July 1941 to limit passage to the United States by eliminating the special emergency visitor visa,[66] many continued to gain safety in 1940 and 1941 via Morocco, Portugal, or Martinique. Moreover, the United States was not the only possible destination: Mexico represented an option, thanks to the sympathy of both its president and the Mexican consul in Marseille. Mexico and Vichy reached an agreement in August 1940 that facilitated the reemigration to Mexico of Spanish Republicans and of foreigners involved on the Republican side in Spain. Mexican president Lázaro Cárdenas was a staunch opponent of Franco's who had also allowed Leon Trotsky safe passage to his country and had welcomed many Spanish Republicans. During Cárdenas' mandate, the Republican rescue organization JARE (Junta de Auxilio a los Republicans Españoles; Board of Aid to the Spanish Republicans), along with Vichy France and the Red Cross, coordinated the departure of Spanish Republicans to the Western Hemisphere, most notably aboard the *Winnipeg* and the *Wyoming,* between August and November 1940.[67]

However, Cárdenas' replacement by the conservative Manuel Avila Camacho on December 1, 1940, dampened Mexico's willingness to admit large numbers of refugees. While massive rescue schemes were shelved, thousands of refugees nonetheless continued to gain safe passage to Mexico, including Anna Seghers, Victor Serge, and hundreds of Spanish Republicans who made their way there via Martinique. In Marseille, meanwhile, Mexican consul Gilberto Bosques, who had been appointed by President Cardenas in 1938, expanded the August 1940 agreement with Vichy by extending it to international brigade members. He also arranged for the lodging and subsistence of many and signed tens of thousands of visas, until the Germans shut down Mexico's consular services in France in November 1942.[68]

Daniel Bénédite identifies the winter of 1940 as the golden window of opportunity for refugees to depart unoccupied France: the embassies of Chile, the Dominican Republic, Columbia, and Venezuela briefly became more receptive at this time, and the United States unfroze quotas on central Europeans, as well as allowing visitor visas.[69] Thereafter things soured. Already in January 1941, the Red Cross noted that with the exception of the Dominican Republic, most Latin American nations were refusing refugees.[70] Then, over the course of 1941, the Red Cross observed, a host of factors gradually conspired to render emigration all but impossible. The Martinique route unraveled in May. In June the United States passed the Russell Act, which by July led Washington to restrict immigration. The Russell Act stipulated that stringent investigations were to be conducted in both Washington and foreign consulates, and that refugees were to be rejected if they had relatives still living in zones under German control. By November, the Germans were refusing to grant exit papers to Jewish emigrants wanting to leave for Spain or Portugal (they also blocked the exit of Spanish Republicans, whom they rightly perceived as determined anti-Nazis who might try to join the British ranks). Then Portugal sealed its only land border to migrants and ceased delivering transit visas altogether. Lastly, the US entry into the war in December 1941 led the Red Cross to despair that the numerous American aid agencies would close shop in France.[71]

In November 1941, Fry, who had been expelled from France and was writing from New York, bemoaned that on the American end, "the visa situation is despairing. The requirement of two affidavits of support is alone enough to make it almost impossible to get visas for people who have no rich and close relatives here."[72] By August 1942, the ERC's Bénédite observed in a letter to Fry, "The visa situation is grim indeed. A few rare American visas are still reaching us (including for some people who had lost all hope), but they are drops in a bucket, and there have not been any Mexican or Cuban visas for a long time now. And yet the need is there."[73]

This chronology largely accounts for Vichy's gradually giving up on emigration. It also overlaps, without completely coinciding, with a period of hesitation in German policy. Indeed, from 1933 to October 1941, emigration still constituted the officially endorsed Nazi solution to the so-called Jewish problem. That said, within the span of those eight years and under the umbrella logic of emigration, German policy evolved swiftly. As Debórah Dwork and Robert Jan Van Pelt have shown, it went from encouraging individual departures of Jews to "pressure on the community as a whole to emigrate, to a 'territorial' solution: a reservation [around Lublin in Poland]."[74] Christopher Browning has examined how, with the radicalization brought about by the Battle of Britain and the invasion of the Soviet Union, the Nazis abruptly reversed their policy on promoting Jewish departures. On October 18, 1941, Heinrich Himmler sealed German borders to Jewish emigration.[75] Before this watershed date, the Nazi modus operandi had been emigration; thereafter, it switched to extermination for the Jews.

Outside the Camps

We have seen how some escaped from Vichy's camps and others were released from them; others still managed never to set foot in them at all. Many German dissident artists sought refuge in 1940 in locales like Sanary-sur-Mer, near Toulon. Marseille's Jewish population increased some 50 percent after the fall of France and the first roundups of Jews in Paris.[76] Other refugees, especially Spanish ones, found shelter in estates made available by the consul of Mexico in Marseille. Countess Marie-Louise (Lily) Pastré, whose family fortune came from Noilly-Prat Vermouth, lodged many other artists at risk, including the painters Rudolf Kundera and André Masson, as well as numerous writers and musicians, including Edith Piaf's Jewish songwriter Norbert Glanzberg. Finally, and most famously, Fry's ERC fostered a community of artists in exile at the Villa Air-Bel in Marseille, a magical place found by Bénédite and paid for by Mary Jane Gold. Serge dubbed it the Villa Hope-for-a-Visa.[77]

After the fall of France, refugees in and around Marseille faced desperate times. Many perils loomed for these migrants at large: being handed over to the German authorities, being denounced to Vichy officials, or landing in jail or in a camp.[78] Even poverty presented new dangers. Indeed, the Interior Ministry's November 1940 instructions to the prefecture of the Bouches-du-Rhône specified that foreigners who could not "meet their own financial needs" should be interned at Les Milles while awaiting emigration.[79] Reading between the lines, this social category found itself at special risk, because without sufficient funds, visas and other necessary departure papers could never be secured. This meant waiting at Les Milles as it shifted from being a transit camp to serving as the antechamber of Auschwitz.

Police raids increased over the course of 1941: between April and July, Vichy dragnets in the Var, the Alpes-Maritimes, and the Bouches-du-Rhône led to the arrest of dozens of foreign Jews. Then, on December 10 and 11, the French police conducted large raids in the hotels, cafés, and bars of Marseille, examining the identity papers of some 20,000 individuals over the course of those two days. Of these, 535 individuals were held on the floating prison ship *Providence,* and another 1,970 were transferred to police headquarters for interrogation. Seventy-six of those arrested were foreign Jews, and 293 were "Spanish subjects."[80] Then, in 1942 came the threat of deportation, even from the unoccupied zone.

The Alfred Neumann case is especially chilling. A prolific German Jewish novelist reviled by the Nazis, Neumann had initially found refuge in Italy, before Benito Mussolini enacted his 1938 racial laws.[81] He then migrated to Nice, where he spent all of 1940. Distress evidently did not necessarily translate into solidarity among refugees: the diary of the six-foot-tall Neumann refers to fellow German in exile and future passenger to Martinique Mehring as a "sardonic dwarf," prone to fits of pessimism, whose stay at

Marseille's Hôtel Splendide had gone to his head. Mostly, Neumann's diary describes the multiple and simultaneous escape channels he attempted. These corridors of potential aid constituted a veritable labyrinth. They included Swedish and Danish diplomatic leads; Spanish, American, and Portuguese consular efforts; and Fry's ERC, not to mention the various channels through which he sought exit papers from Vichy. On October 16, 1940, Neumann reflected, "How much time I have passed in the last three months, in offices and consulates! And yet, I must say I have been lucky, even with bureaucrats."[82] This turned out to be an understatement. Three months after his January 1941 escape to New York via Barcelona and Lisbon, his name appeared on the Bouches-du-Rhône prefecture's "supplemental" list of "foreigners who are to be refused an exit visa," likely at the request of the German authorities.[83] Neumann had absconded with little time to spare.

Neumann's many rescue channels speak to a profusion of possible leads, some more fruitful than others. Among the more active organizations were the American Quakers, who spared no effort in assisting foreign Jews trying to leave Marseille for safer shores. To give but a handful of examples, in February 1941 they attempted to pull out of prison one Edouard Hirsch, who was in possession of papers to immigrate to Palestine. They asked the Service des étrangers that Belgian refugee Antoine Descamps be spared the cost of new identity papers before his slated departure to Angola. They appealed for new papers for Margaret Bloch, who had been allowed to leave the Gurs camp. And they asked for residence permission for former Berliner Charlotte Meyer, Rose Levy, Boris Goldenberg, and Bruno Kaiser (the last just released from Gurs) to stay in Marseille while waiting for their files to be processed by the US consulate. In some cases, the Quakers requested assistance only with the final step, as was the case for one Toulon-based Peter Gluck and his spouse, who needed only transit papers from Vichy, having already secured US authorization and purchased their tickets. The Quakers also brought certain refugees to the attention of HICEM in some cases, and to that of Fry in others.[84] In short, the Quakers did not control or even influence an emigration route per se, but they served as valuable go-betweens and advocates for refugees in interactions with the sometimes prickly local French administration.

In his summary of his organization's activities in Marseille for the year 1941, the head of refugee questions for the Quakers in France, Howard

Kershner, wrote that his offices "see the daily stream of visitors who come with reference to their hopes of emigration. In spite of restrictions becoming more and more severe, an important number of people are leaving the country steadily, mostly for countries in North or South America."[85] This was an apt depiction of the year 1941 from the standpoint of refugees: we know in retrospect that it constituted a last window of escape.

As these different cases suggest, life for uninterned refugees in Marseille in 1940 and 1941 revolved around endless meetings with aid agencies, interminable queues at consulates, months of anguish over visa procedures, and constant rumors about boat departures and possible new exit avenues, be they via Spain or North Africa. Three refugees who ultimately escaped via Martinique shed light on this waiting pattern. Poet and literary critic Mehring's October 1940 verses from Marseille evoke "a tipsy straggler" "in search of ship and pier." He then follows the forlorn refugee, "only to join a lineup long and grim."[86] Belgian former Bolshevik Serge recalls of the migrants and their mood, "Our crowd of refugees includes great minds of all classes . . . among them are so many doctors, psychologists, engineers, teachers, poets, painters, writers, musicians, economists and politicians that we could have built the soul of a great nation. Among this misery lies as much talent and ability as there was in Paris at its zenith. And yet, all we see are people subjected to manhunts, infinitely tired, at the end of their emotional rope."[87] German Jewish writer Seghers also brilliantly conveys the anguished wait in Marseille in her semifictional novel *Transit*. One character despairs,

> My visa hasn't arrived yet. . . . The little official assured me it was just a question of days, but the departure of the *Paul Lemerle* is also a matter of days. They're now saying at the Martinique Line that the ship will be leaving sooner than scheduled because of a special government order. The little Mexican [consular] official was very polite, actually he was more than just polite. You probably know him too since you go there so often. He's a strange little devil. At every other consulate they make you feel as if you're nothing, a nobody; the consuls all talk as if they were talking to a nobody with a phantom dossier.[88]

Collectively, such testimonies speak both to the desperation on the docks and in the offices, consulates, and cafés of Marseille, and to the city's role as a dissident global capital in 1940 and 1941, an ersatz Paris, to paraphrase

Serge. Marseille, of course, had always been a mosaic: already in the 1930s, nearly a quarter of its inhabitants were foreigners.[89]

On another occasion, Seghers' keen eye captures the tragic competition that pitted wary refugees against one another. One of her characters aptly describes the waiting area at the Marseille prefecture:

> Each of these ready-to-leave souls has experienced as much as a whole generation of humankind normally might. One will start telling another next to him how he escaped sure death three times already, but the man next to him has also avoided death at least three times himself. He listens only superficially, then he elbows his way into a gap in the line, where another man will tell him how he has escaped death. . . . And if you can't wrangle yourself forward with trickery and pure meanness to be among the first ten who can then race over to the *Transports maritimes* with their exit visas, you'll find the passenger list will already be closed. Nothing can help you then.[90]

Such competition also sneaked its way into diaries. For instance, Neumann jotted on November 4, 1940, "I bumped into Kurt Wolff at the Kuoni travel agency. He is fighting far behind me, with no passport and no visa for the United States. I like him."[91] Every quest for escape was relative; every would-be migrant struggling behind was one less in front. The "battle for visas" described by Serge and others in wartime Marseille was multidirectional, and not just waged between Vichy officials on one hand and refugees on the other.[92]

However, not all refugees were busy elbowing one another out of lineups. A sense of fraternity also emerges from many files. In some instances, refugees became advocates for others or were asked to do so. Consider the letter that Serge received from former Italian Communist Leo Valiani, alias Paul Chevalier. On the basis of correspondence from a friend of his, Valiani asked whether Serge might help Andrea Caffi obtain a visa for Mexico, which Caffi ultimately did. There was a common antifascist thread to this request, Valiani and Caffi having both previously fled Mussolini's police state for France. Caffi was living in Toulouse, and he was threatened with reinternment at Le Vernet. After all, Valiani mentioned, as a Russian-born anarchist who had been in communication with Lenin, Caffi must have crossed Serge's path at some point. If not, then perhaps Serge had read his work on Byzantine history? Such was the tenor of rescue correspondence among refugees in unoccupied France.[93]

Beyond writing heaps of letters to each other and to rescue organizations and queuing in interminable lines for exit and entry visas, those fortunate enough to avoid internment in Vichy's camps also played a sinister game of cat and mouse with Vichy, and even with German officials. Upon registering in hotels, many of them showed their actual identification papers, perhaps ignorant of the fact that registration lists all found their way to police headquarters. Such was the case of the German Jewish art historian John (Gustav) Rewald, who registered under his own name at the Hôtel de Bordeaux in Marseille as a "German man of letters"—which he undoubtedly was, as the world's leading authority on French impressionist painter Paul Cézanne. Rewald would ultimately join painter André Masson and his family, as well as hundreds of others, aboard the *Carimaré* bound for Martinique in April 1941.[94]

Other refugees crossed paths with their nemeses. In Marseille, where he sought to secure safe passage from consulates and aid organizations on August 6, 1940, Neumann unwittingly stayed in the same high-end hotel—the Splendide—as Philippe Henriot, a Catholic former deputy who had thrown his full support behind Pétain.[95] Coincidentally, Fry's ERC was setting up shop at the same time in another room on the fourth floor of the very same establishment. Space was scarce: Gold remembers the organization's secretary balancing a typewriter on her lap while sitting on the room's bidet. Soon, patrons complained to management about the long queues forming in front of Fry's door.[96] As for Mehring, the ERC paid for his lengthy stay at the Splendide, until he was thrown out to make room for the German Armistice Commission, which commandeered an entire floor of the hotel.[97]

The Eye of Vichy

Vichy's General Commissariat for Jewish Affairs kept a close watch on Jewish refugees as they sought to escape the unoccupied zone by any means possible. A May 6, 1941, note from this unit took stock of recent developments as follows: "Based on information obtained from reliable sources, we have learned that Jews no longer want to leave for Palestine, as they fear a possible German advance in the region. We hear many are leaving for Martinique."[98] In other words, Erwin Rommel's advances in North Africa, combined with German support for Vichy in Syria and Lebanon, had persuaded many would-be migrants that Palestine had become a less safe, and certainly a less accessible, destination than Martinique. Tragically, this memo was drafted precisely as the Martinique route was about to unravel—it ended with the Dutch interception of the *Winnipeg* bound for Martinique, crammed with refugees, in late May 1941.

By the end of October 1941, Vichy's spy network was reporting that Cuban officials were overrun by immigration requests from Jews in France (both French and foreign, presumably). The requests ran at a concomitant pace with German advances in Russia, contended this source. It specified that would-be migrants were members of social categories hit hard by Vichy's anti-Semitic laws: they included large numbers of lawyers and doctors. Pétain's secret service added, rightly it turns out, that Cuba had significantly curtailed the number of visas it was issuing, and that "the passenger traffic" that had been so intense just a few months earlier "between Lisbon and the Americas has now ground practically to a halt." Cuba, like many other countries, was henceforth admitting refugees only "on an exceptional basis."[99]

By November 30, 1941, Vichy's intercepts of correspondence from would-be migrants revealed first that the tone of letters from Jews in France to international relief organizations was growing increasingly desperate due to the "interruption of maritime routes" between Europe and the Americas. Second, the intercepts showed the mounting difficulties refugees faced in obtaining US affidavits for entry into America. Third, they exposed the growing desperation to secure Spanish transit visas for Cuba. Finally, they registered a Spanish crackdown on refugees using Spanish shipping lines to emigrate, and observed that Portugal remained one of the few avenues left. The end of the Martinique route had marked the first of several doors to be slammed shut in rapid succession on increasingly forlorn people.[100]

Remaining Routes

Some, who watched in despair as their comrades left for Martinique in 1941, still found their way out of Marseille that year and even the following year. Let us consider maritime departures first. In September 1941, a small number of Jewish refugees reached Shanghai aboard vessels from Marseille bound for French Indochina, which was, and would remain, loyal to Vichy even after the regime's disintegration in France. In late 1941 and early 1942, a considerable number of Jewish refugees managed to find refuge in Morocco. Louis Gaude, who had operated as the emigration specialist at Les Milles, even visited Morocco to convince local authorities to allow them entry.[101] The other main escape routes were overland, and they involved considerable risk of capture. Still, Michael Marrus and Robert Paxton estimate that some ten thousand Jews managed to cross the Alps to Switzerland and another twelve thousand the Pyrenees to Spain in 1943.[102]

For French Jews too, the process of leaving Marseille was becoming more arduous over the course of the war, although the physical threat to them was less immediate until the Germans invaded the unoccupied zone in November 1942. For French nationals as well, colonial channels remained important, if only as pretexts. For instance, leading Free Frenchman Jean-Louis Crémieux-Brilhac recounts how during the summer of 1942, his wife, Monique Crémieux, left Marseille to join him in London. She departed Marseille for Portugal, armed with a promise of a job in Portuguese Angola and aided by the connivance of a French policeman who knowingly asked her if she knew the way to Angola as he approved her exit to Spain.[103] However, on balance, all of these late departures by boat, including the one we are about to follow, were the exceptions that proved the rule. Leaving Marseille by sea after the Martinique route unraveled in May 1941 became an even greater challenge.

The countless hurdles faced after that date are perhaps best encapsulated by the experiences of novelist Jean Malaquais. Born Wladimir Jan Pavel Malacki, Malaquais was a secular Polish Jew, the son of a classics teacher. He immigrated to France in 1926 and inauspiciously spent his first night in the City of Light sleeping on the Austerlitz Bridge. He then proceeded to teach himself French at the Bibliothèque Sainte Geneviève.[104] A mere thirteen years later, he beat out Jean-Paul Sartre for the prestigious Renaudot Prize for his novel *Les Javanais,* inspired by his experiences in a coal mine in the Var. A fervently anti-Stalinist Marxist and friend of André Gide's, he served in the French army during the Battle of France in May and June 1940 but never acquired French citizenship.

Thereafter, he found himself in the unoccupied zone with an artist partner eight years his junior, Galina Yurkevich (born in 1915). She was the orphaned daughter of an officer in the czar's army. Both were technically illegals (Malaquais describes Yurkevich as officially "stateless")[105] and could have been deported on a whim.

Malaquais' war diary is a jewel of clairvoyance and insight: In it he predicts Hitler's invasion of the Soviet Union six months before it occurs, the downfall of colonial empires, and the Nazis' eventual defeat in the east. He theorizes on the origins of Hitler's racism and also observes the suddenly restrained and subdued nature of normally effusive southern French people around him. Mostly, the diary, even more than his famed novel about the period, *Planète sans visa,* provides a faithful reconstitution of the travails of refugees hanging by a thread to any hope of escape.

Malaquais' journal recounts the tribulations of his peers: He learns with horror of Walter Benjamin's suicide on October 10, 1940, after his failed escape across the Pyrenees to Spain. Two weeks later, Malaquais pays a visit to the Villa Air-Bel outside Marseille, where Serge, Jacqueline Lamba, Victor Braumer, Hans Bellmer, Max Ernst, Wifredo Lam, and others congregate while awaiting visas through Fry's ERC. He writes, "There is much speculation about transit visas, exit visas." He describes the ERC's offices, located at 60 rue Grignan in Marseille, as follows: "All along the stairwell, from the ground floor to the second, one finds a multilingual crowd seeking salvation."[106] Salvation, of course, is departure from France. In these narrow halls Malaquais witnesses the shared experiences of visa seekers. Others are less charitable to the place. Neumann describes it as exuding a "revolting atmosphere of emigration."[107]

The Malaquais-Yurkevich couple settles first in Banon, in the hinterland of Manosque, then in the Marseille suburb of Saint-Barnabé. Like many others in France at the time, with provisions scarce, they eat rutabaga in every imaginable form.[108] Malaquais sells a typewriter for food. Money is evidently in short supply, with Fry providing occasional cash. Malaquais gambles on his own chess games, and he and Yurkevich sell espadrilles that they craft with their friends.[109]

The couple also experiences a number of close calls. On March 23, 1941, Malaquais is asked for his papers; he produces false ones that dupe the police. On June 22, 1941, Yurkevich is imprisoned in Marseille on board the prison ship *Providence,* and she is rescued by Malaquais, who poses as a doctor. Even more brazenly, out of "bad conscience at having swum with impunity in a shark-infested cesspool," in other words at having stayed out of the camps when so many have not, on April 4, 1942, Malaquais approaches Les Milles with "the crazy hope of coming in aid to some of [his] comrades rotting there."[110] According to another testimony, he actually entered the camp, trying, in vain, to rescue "one of his Belgian comrades."[111] Malaquais' experience closely mirrors that of Serge, although the two did not see eye to eye. Serge too recollects being thrice apprehended in Marseille, twice as he simply walked about town, and again when he was briefly interned aboard the *Providence*.[112]

Malaquais and Yurkevich cling to every escape lead. As he writes in *Planète sans visa*, "Britain, Africa, the Americas all beckon on the other side of the shimmering, salutary water. There is just the small matter of striding over it."[113] A professor Justin O'Brien at Columbia University's French Department seems prepared to sign an affidavit for the writer; later an American literary agent and translator named Madeline Boyd offers her support through the ERC. Trying to help in his own awkward way, André Gide writes a letter of recommendation to the Mexican consulate, alluding to the couple's complicated (that is, unmarried) matrimonial status. Yurkevich even draws a portrait of the Mexican consul Bosques' son in a subconscious or conscious effort to ingratiate herself to him. However, each lead seems to result in a dead end. On April 2, 1941, Malaquais notes, "The Bretons, the Serges, Wifredo and Helena Lam, Claude Lévi-Strauss and a bunch of other lucky souls set sail for Martinique. . . . As for us, not a visa on the horizon." By May 9, 1941, he gives up on the American consulate after "countless" visits there. On June 4, 1941, he lunches with Fry, and he soon becomes persuaded that the American humanitarian is testing him or his politics.[114]

Ultimately, multiple factors allow the couple to leave for Venezuela in the nick of time, or even past it. Most are purely fortuitous. In June 1942, faced with the refusal of the prefecture to deliver exit papers and that of the Mexican and Portuguese consulates to issue transit papers, Malaquais receives advice from Bénédite of the ERC (Fry has by then been expelled by Vichy). By June 24, thanks to Mexican intervention, Venezuelan visas are promised at last, but exit papers are still required. Malaquais proceeds to bribe a French doctor to sign a document falsely attesting that he suffers from syphilis, gambling that this will help rather than hinder his odds of obtaining exit papers. Even this fails. Malaquais then observes with sheer horror the mass deportations in the unoccupied zone in August 1942.

With everything but the exit permissions in place, but having also run out of ideas on how to obtain them, the couple decides to confront the beast in its lair and daringly heads to Vichy. They arrive in the spa town that has been converted into the makeshift capital on September 16, 1942. Serendipity then strikes again when Malaquais bumps into his former military officer, who offers to help. He arranges an interview with a brusque but high-ranking visa official who proceeds to test Yurkevich's artist credentials by asking her to "draw something, anything . . . right away." Galina passes the improbable test in speed art.[115] Upon returning to Marseille on September 20, she heaves a sigh of relief in her diary at being "one foot in Marseille, the other in Mexico,"[116] which the couple does eventually reach after Venezuela. They cross the Spanish border on September 26, 1942, and set sail from Cadiz to Caracas on October 4, 1942.[117]

Their departure took place long after most conventional exit routes had been shut. Indeed, starting in May 1942, Vichy's new commissioner of Jewish affairs Louis Darquier de Pellepoix insisted on reviewing each emigration file. In September 1942, Pierre Laval declared that "it would be a violation of the armistice to allow Jews to go abroad for fear that they should take up arms against the Germans." As a result, only some six hundred Jews received authorization to leave in the second half of 1942.[118] Malaquais and Yurkevich had absconded only weeks before Vichy ceased to issue exit visas altogether on November 8, 1942.[119] The Germans invaded the unoccupied zone three days later. They rapidly set their sights on cosmopolitan, multicultural Marseille. Hitler would call it the "canker of Europe," an urban "asylum for the international underworld."[120]

A few weeks after reaching Caracas, Yurkevich began a painting titled *The Wait*.[121] Yurkevich's Penelopean patience, and that of Malaquais, finally paid off in the end. Yet even this resourceful couple had not managed to find their way onto the boats to Martinique; they watched enviously as Breton, Lévi-Strauss, Lam, and Serge took the route. Salvation for the Malaquais-Yurkevich couple came fortuitously at the very last minute. One can well imagine that refugees without the military contacts, the wherewithal to endure administrative stonewalling, the goodwill of multiple guarantors and organizations to back them, the support of the Mexican consul, or the turns of phrase necessary to prevail in multiple showdowns with French bureaucrats would have failed where this resilient and resourceful couple succeeded.

It bears remembering, therefore, that many more missed the boats than made them. As for the optimal boats to take, rescue organizations readily admitted that the Martinique corridor afforded refugees in southern France the best remaining chance in 1940 and 1941.

CHAPTER TWO

Opening the Martinique Corridor

AT THE BEGINNING OF *Tristes tropiques,* the famous anthropologist Claude Lévi-Strauss recalls being stranded in Marseille in 1941, "already feeling like a potential concentration camp victim." Armed with only an invitation from New York's New School for Social Research, he "knew he must leave, but how?" Here, the ethnographer's writings on the subject become terse, even cryptic: "From conversations in Marseille, I learned that a boat was to leave soon for Martinique. . . . Finally I obtained my ticket on board the *Paul Lemerle.*"[1] Even with an invitation from America, could it have been this straightforward for a French Jewish academic to leave the free zone for Martinique in early 1941? Or could Varian Fry's Emergency Rescue Committee (ERC) or some other network have abetted his departure? In 1997, Lévi-Strauss responded graciously but categorically to my written query: "I found out about the boat thanks to my old contacts at the shipping company, and without any other help whatsoever. . . . Why Vichy would allow . . . this boat to leave, I have no idea. [At the time] I thought it might be transporting clandestine material."[2] Fifty-six years after the fact, Vichy's motivations for allowing refugees to depart remained unclear to the anthropologist. Indeed, given the dreadful conditions on board, none of the participants quite knew what to make of their exodus at the time: Was this renewed persecution and deportation, part of a vast diaspora begun in 1933, or was it rescue?

The *Capitaine Paul Lemerle,* it turned out, probably carried dissident refugees as its only contraband. (I have found no corroborating evidence for passenger Ruth Davidoff's claim that the ship was secretly transporting

German mines).[3] The passengers included Lévi-Strauss, the revolutionary Victor Serge and his son; surrealist poet André Breton; his partner, artist Jacqueline Lamba, and their daughter; avant-garde photographer Germaine Krull; painter Wifredo Lam and his scientist partner, Helena Holzer (later Benitez); novelist Anna Seghers; her spouse and their two children; Dr. Minna Flake and her family; Austrian trade-unionist Harry Kriszhaber and his wife; German lawyer Alfred Kantorowicz and his spouse; film writer Jacques Rémy; and cinematographer Curt Courant, among many others. The vessel was not alone in traveling from Marseille to Martinique in the early months of 1941. Between October 1940 and May 1941, fifteen ships left the Mediterranean port bound for Fort-de-France, crammed with refugees. Four more would follow in May 1941, only to be caught in a kind of no-man's-land before finally reaching a safe haven.

Even Fry seemed taken aback by the sudden rate and scope of departures. He could hardly believe this good fortune, even less account for it. He later underscored the importance of this moment: "It was the ships to Martinique which really kept us busy. We couldn't have thought up anything better if we had the power to arrange the route ourselves. They not only eliminated the trouble with the transit visas—they also removed the danger of the trip through Spain. For they went directly from Marseille to Martinique, and from there it was possible to go straight to New York. They were almost as good as the much advertised but never realized rescue ship which was to have gone to Marseille to take refugees [directly] to New York."[4]

Clearly, Fry's ERC helped many refugees exploit this unanticipated opportunity. But to humanitarian organizations like Fry's, the opening itself seemed almost providential, and its eventual closure equally arbitrary. As this closure approached, on May 18, 1941, Fry issued the following telegrammed appeal to prominent US samaritans: "Break now imminent between Vichy-Washington means end hope of rescue for 300 men women anti-Nazis all European nationalities wanted by Gestapo now in possession complete emigration papers and awaiting evacuation Marseille. Fear momentarily announcement Vichy decree interrupting Marseille-Martinique shipping thus cutting *best avenue of escape*."[5] May 1941 thus marked the closing of this long-overlooked window of opportunity for European refugees seeking to flee Adolf Hitler's Europe. We know in hindsight that it would constitute the last major avenue out of France for thousands of antifascists, Jews, and Spanish Republicans.

Origins of the Martinique Plan

The idea of sending refugees to Martinique was hatched by a leading Vichy government official in 1940. The significance of such a genesis is multifold. First, along with the Dominican Republic, the French Caribbean route was one of very few government-endorsed tropical emigration schemes ever made operational, out of a host of earlier expulsion or rescue projects, be they Nazi, Polish, French, or Zionist. Second, this window of opportunity sheds light on the Vichy regime's stance on emigration. Third, the inception and course of the Martinique plan, followed all the way to the treatment of the refugees upon their arrival in the Caribbean, betrays a range of competing agendas. The Martinique route, then, illuminates the contradictions, tensions, breaks, and continuities inherent in Vichy's treatment of refugees.

Vichy's interior minister Marcel Peyrouton stands at the origin of the Martinique escape route. As a young man, he lived for a time in Martinique. A colonial official by training, before the war, Peyrouton was closely tied to the centrist Radical Party. He became Vichy's second minister of the interior on September 6, 1940. Thereupon, he undertook a sweeping purge of the prefectorial corps, as well as applying and implementing Vichy's anti-Semitic laws.[6] However, he also opportunistically helped plan the December 13, 1940, arrest of the leading advocate of collaboration with Germany, Prime Minister Pierre Laval—a move that was conditioned in large part by internal rivalries at Vichy. In many ways Peyrouton embodied the mainstream of an early Vichy.[7] More importantly, as former French secretary general in Tunisia, having also served in Tahiti, Cameroon, Madagascar, and Togo, Peyrouton boasted numerous colonial contacts, which no doubt contributed to shaping the Martinique scheme. As Vicki Caron has shown, Peyrouton emerged as an advocate of Jewish emigration—even urging administrators to bend financial requirements so as to facilitate Jewish departures.[8]

Peyrouton was responding on a very basic level to overcrowded refugee camps in southern France. On another front, Peyrouton was also involved in transferring Communist detainees to camps in Algeria, which reflected a similar impulse to be rid of undesirables by dispatching them overseas. Although Peyrouton's motives were evidently complex, as they were couched in alternately discriminatory and humanitarian terms, his objectives were clear. On November 29, 1940, he sent a remarkable letter to Vichy's Ministry of the Colonies. It reads,

> I have the honor of informing you that I am considering practicing a policy of massive emigration of foreigners who are overrepresented in the French nation and economy. Taking their fill of consumer goods without producing any themselves, sometimes suffering from the rigorous treatment that has been by necessity imposed on them, such foreigners cannot remain in this current limbo. A sense of social responsibility, a concern that we not falter on the rules of humanity, give us an imperious obligation urgently to arrange the departure of the greatest number of them to warmer climes. . . . I have the honor of asking you—given the urgency before us, for the aforementioned reasons, to distance these people from the metropole—whether it would be possible to direct a certain number of them to the French Caribbean. The stay of these said foreigners would be temporary in nature, and motivated purely by the exceptional circumstances through which we are living.[9]

The ambiguity of Peyrouton's language lies at the heart of this emigration project. Peyrouton borrowed from two prevailing discourses: on the one hand that of xenophobia and scapegoating, which had only been sharpened by the defeat of May–June 1940, and on the other hand that of a vague sense of humanitarianism blended with colonial paternalism. This humanitarianism, however, was actually employed to turn on their head previous notions of France as a land of asylum. In this instance, Vichy's interior minister contended, the "rules of humanity" mandated emigration, not hospitality. Here was an implied recognition of a looming threat, even though half of France remained unoccupied.

Peyrouton ordered his administration to move forward with his proposal. Just two months after Peyrouton's initial letter, on February 1, 1941, Vichy's colonial minister cabled the governor of Martinique, "The Ministry of the Interior informs me of the departure of fifty Jews, mostly German, for the USA via Martinique. I have granted rights of transit."[10] This particular message will be discussed in greater detail later. What matters here is that the movement of migrants to Martinique began in earnest under Peyrouton's mandate; only two weeks later, he would resign his portfolio. But the Martinique proposal, which he had first advanced, opened the last sizeable avenue out of Vichy France in the winter of 1940 and spring of 1941, despite countless attempts to thwart it.

The extant records do not allow me to draw a single straight line between the vessels crammed with refugees and Peyrouton's scheme: a letter to the shipping company or some other kind of incontrovertible evidence is missing. What is more, some fifty European refugees made their way from Casablanca to Martinique aboard the *Charles Dreyfus,* which set sail for Martinique even before Peyrouton's memo was issued.[11] In addition, the *Cuba* brought Spanish Republicans to the French Caribbean five months before Peyrouton's plan was hatched. However, it is also clear that the trickle of refugees leaving somewhat haphazardly for Martinique before Peyrouton's instructions increased to a coordinated stream thereafter. And, as we shall see, there is convincing evidence that prefectures, which answered directly to the Ministry of the Interior, played an active role in making the Martinique escape passage known to refugees. One thing is evident from Peyrouton's directives: emigration was still the order of the day in 1940 and 1941. The Martinique route was certainly timely in this respect.

Invoking a curious blend of humanitarianism and xenophobia, Peyrouton's letter of November 1940 had in reality rescripted earlier emigration plans to French colonies. These previous schemes included the ill-fated Madagascar project, but also a more overlooked plan hatched between 1934 and 1939, to create a safe haven for Jewish refugees in French colonial Guinea. Then too, French colonial authorities had agreed to the establishment of a Jewish refugee settlement in France's South American colony of Guiana in 1938–1939, and they likewise pondered the possibilities of settlement in New Caledonia. The South American scheme had been floated by a revealingly titled "research center for solutions to the Jewish problem" and had even received the verbal support of France's Ministry of the Interior in April 1939. Such emigration and colonization fantasies, located somewhere on the spectrum between rescue and expulsion, were nothing new. And, interestingly, Jewish organizations had long played a part in their elaboration, be it in the case of the Madagascar scheme or of a previous bid to settle in Angola. Emigration and colonization had in fact been major concerns of Jewish philanthropic organizations since the turn of the century. A group loosely defined as the territorialists, presenting themselves as the true heirs to Theodor Herzl's movement, tended to reject what Zionism had become as overly idealistic, focusing instead on a series of possible alternative Jewish homelands, be they in Uganda, Angola, Australia, or Madagascar.[12]

Of all the emigration schemes put forward before October 1941, it was precisely that of Madagascar that seems to have most captured the attention of contemporaries and historians alike. The origins of this outlandish project to send Jews to the antipodes can be traced to 1885, although it was rooted in much earlier theories linking the inhabitants of Madagascar to the Jews. The idea subsequently gained currency throughout Europe, and it came to fascinate individual humanitarians, Zionists, and anti-Semites alike. The Polish government advanced the project officially in 1926 and continued to press it in the 1930s. Leading Nazis soon warmed to the idea, which would become their idée fixe until August 1940, only scrapping it definitively in October 1941. Interestingly, as late as August 1941, Admiral François Darlan was still countenancing the scheme. The plan was of course never realized for a host of reasons. Its meanings remain contested to this day. To some historians, it was a "fictional device" par excellence. To others it was tantamount to a "death sentence" or a "super ghetto" for Jews. Christopher Browning, while denying any teleology between the Madagascar plan and the Holocaust, concedes that "Madagascar implied a murderous decimation of the Jewish population." Crucial though the Madagascar project was on the tortuous path to genocide, it remained a dead letter, a case of "what if" history.[13]

The Martinique route also drew from the precedent of other rescues that were successfully undertaken in 1939. Indeed, the *Winnipeg,* one of the very same ships that would be employed to rescue refugees in 1941, had been used at the very outset of the Second World War to transport Republican Spanish Civil War veterans to Chile. The organizer of that contested rescue initiative (contested because of allegations that Trotskyites were left behind) was none other than the Nobel Prize–winning Chilean poet Pablo Neruda. Another one of these ships, the *Ipanema,* had been requisitioned to bring Spanish Republicans from France to Mexico.[14]

There existed, in other words, a long legacy of rescue and emigration schemes. To be sure, the Martinique route was itself something of a hybrid fallback solution. Even in its boldest configuration, Martinique constituted a point of transit, not permanent settlement, though it was never clear how long transit might last, and certain refugees did file for asylum once in the

Caribbean. But in November 1940 Peyrouton had turned to the Ministry of the Colonies as a last resort. He had first approached ambassadors of North and South American countries for assistance, in vain.[15] Only then did he zero in on the French West Indies. Peyrouton knew well that Martinique constituted a more feasible exodus option as the doors of other countries closed, precisely because Martinique was a French territory, and foreigners consequently did not require an additional visa to reach it.

The only major hurdles to the Martinique plan were maritime (the sea war was raging) and internal to Vichy. In order to achieve his goals, Peyrouton would require the cooperation of the hardline Pétainist minister of the colonies, Admiral Charles Platon.[16] Although they certainly allowed the occasional refugee to gain passage to Martinique, Platon and his subordinates, down to governors of individual colonies, would prove resistant to large-scale emigration initiatives, slowing them without ultimately managing to block them completely.

Conflict within Vichy

In this sense, the course of the Peyrouton plan at once confirms and challenges conventional historical wisdom concerning Vichy's outlook on emigration. Whereas a few historians, such as Susan Zuccotti, have called into question the earnestness of early emigration plans under Vichy, Caron has established that Vichy undertook genuine efforts at emigration, only to be "thwarted on several fronts," most notably by immigration restrictions in the Americas.[17] Nonetheless, she argues, emigration remained the officially endorsed Vichy solution to France's so-called refugee problem until the beginning of deportations in 1942. Indeed, Michael Marrus and Robert Paxton show that Laval reminded his commissioner of Jewish affairs as late as May 1942 that Vichy policy was "to facilitate in every possible way the emigration of foreigners and Frenchmen superfluous to the national economy."[18]

In the case of the Martinique route, however, the struggle lay not so much between Vichy leadership and the increasingly fanatical Commissariat général aux questions juives but rather between Peyrouton's Interior Ministry and Platon's intractable colonial administration. That the Colonial Ministry constituted a bastion of Pétainism is not altogether surprising. I have shown elsewhere how Pétainist colonial officials insisted on exporting Vichy's anti-Semitic legislation wholesale to the French overseas empire.[19]

The "bureaucratic obstruction" to emigration described by Marrus and Paxton certainly did take place.[20] But in this instance, it pitted one Vichy agency against another. This illustrates the nuances and complexities of Vichy responses, or, if one prefers, the plurality of Vichys. Ultimately, what is most notable about Peyrouton's scheme is that in spite of major opposition, it did materialize, unlike hosts of previous emigration and colonization dreams.

Peyrouton's November 1940 letter did not explicitly refer to Jewish emigration; it employed the umbrella term "foreigners," alluding to Jewish refugees, no doubt, but including Spanish Republicans, non-Jewish anti-Nazi Germans, and other now-endangered groups as well. As specifics began to make their way into Colonial Ministry correspondence concerning Martinique, however, the emphasis shifted to Jewish emigration.

Evidence clearly shows the Ministry of the Interior forcing the Martinique plan through, overcoming opposition from the Ministry of the Colonies. The most compelling example came early, in January 1941, when Vichy's notoriously anti-Semitic police chief in Marseille, Maurice Rodellec du Porzic, announced to the Ministry of the Colonies that he had placed fifty "mostly German Jews" on board a vessel to Martinique. Someone in the Ministry of the Colonies scrawled on the freshly received notice, "Who are these passengers? Are they traveling on their own funds? Who will pay for their stay in Martinique? Where are they from?" To allay these concerns, Du Porzic phoned the Ministry of the Colonies on January 31, assuring his interlocutor that the refugees would only pass through Martinique in transit. Platon was left little choice but to warn Fort-de-France that the fifty refugees were en route.[21]

The Ministry of the Colonies did fight back, as did colonial governors. Pushback came early, even before Peyrouton's memo was issued in fact, in the form of Vichy governor Henry Bressoles' reaction to the very first ship that reached Fort-de-France from Marseille and Casablanca since the fall of France, in October 1940. The governor expressed concerns to Vichy that the foreign refugees, some of whom were purportedly "suspect," would only "sow discord" in Martinique. Should these events recur, Bressoles warned, future vessels would be kept offshore to be searched before docking.[22]

By early 1941, the governors of each colony singled out in Peyrouton's plan—Martinique, Guadeloupe, and French Guiana—responded unfavorably to Peyrouton's initiative. Martinique's governor Bressoles telegraphed on January 3, 1941, "The United States claims to worry about the arrival of foreigners in these parts, especially about Central Europeans."[23] By March 3, 1941, Bressoles' successor, Yves Nicol, cabled Vichy just as bluntly, "I can only admit travelers in transit armed with visas. . . . I would like to underscore the risks of accumulating in Martinique often dubious individuals who could sow trouble and become subject to foreign influences."[24]

French Guiana's governor Robert Chot proved no more receptive. The arrival of "Israelite families bearing German-sounding names" could be used as a pretext for American officials seeking any excuse to dislodge Vichy from the Caribbean basin.[25] The governor of Guadeloupe, Constant Sorin, showed equal contempt for the scheme, even as refugees were arriving in nearby Martinique. On March 19, 1941, he cabled Vichy, "I deem it appropriate henceforth to refuse all requests for Israelites to settle in Guadeloupe. . . . There are serious drawbacks . . . to establishing a tide of Jewish immigration capable of becoming a beachhead and then a community, which would be facilitated by the proximity of the USA, their religious pole."[26] In this flourish of mixed metaphors, the specter of America was employed in a radically different way from Bressoles' and Chot's messages, but for identical ends. Whether as an agent of an imagined Zionist invasion or as a paranoid and overzealous enforcer of the Monroe Doctrine, the United States was invoked as a prime motive for discouraging further Jewish arrivals from Marseille.

There existed, of course, a basis for fearing that the United States would react unfavorably to news of German-speaking refugees in the Caribbean. But this should not cloud the fact that French colonial governors used the US reputation for sensitivity on such issues as a pretext to try to refuse Jews entry. Based on extensive correspondence with the governors of all colonies concerned, Platon replied to Peyrouton on January 8, 1941, "Admiral [Georges] Robert [Vichy high commissioner to the Caribbean] informs me that the Antilles can only receive four hundred people. But I must underscore that first, local conditions and lack of supplying, and second, possible American shows of concern over foreign arrivals in these islands—dictate that it is preferable to shelve this project altogether."[27]

In spite of these objections, immigration to the Antilles continued until late May 1941. The quota of four hundred individuals was no doubt respected in principle by keeping passengers in transit for short periods only, before sending them off to the United States, Cuba, Mexico, the Dominican Republic, and other destinations. What appears striking is, first, the insistence with which colonial officials sought to scuttle Peyrouton's plan, and, second, its surviving as long as May 1941 in light of this hostility. In Guadeloupe, for instance, Sorin followed his initial unfavorable report with two subsequent refusals to allow Jewish immigration. On May 2 1941, he "maintained his decision to refuse any further Jewish settlement in Guadeloupe."[28]

This being said, Sorin was under pressure to do so. On March 4, 1941, the president of Guadeloupe's chamber of commerce complained that many Jews had just arrived in Pointe-à-Pitre from Marseille via Martinique aboard the *Wyoming*. He evidently feared the competition of newcomers. Why would Guadeloupe take these migrants when they were being refused everywhere else, he asked? And precisely as Martinique was beginning to tighten restrictions? The chamber of commerce president "asked" the governor to prevent future Jewish arrivals and to "send back" those who had already reached the isle.[29]

Barring any permanent settlement, then, refugees were considered migrants in transit. They thus never figured into the census of Jews in the French West Indies, ordered by the anti-Semitic colonial authorities. An April 22, 1941, local police report in Martinique illustrates the status of these refugees: "Out of the 222 passengers on board the *Paul Lemerle*, which arrived here on April 20, 1941, only three will be settling here in Martinique. . . . All the other passengers have either been interned at the Lazaret camp, or have been authorized to reside here [in Fort-de-France], while awaiting their departure."[30] A former leper colony, the Lazaret was one of two camps in which Vichy interned foreign refugees who reached Martinique. The other was Balata.

By April 17, 1941, the Ministry of the Colonies was persuaded that the "French Caribbean is currently threatened by a large number of stateless people and Jews wanting to settle there." It drew a clear distinction between those wanting to stay permanently and those in transit. The first scenario was out of the question unless the would-be settlers were French and had received authorization from the governor. However, refugees in transit continued to be allowed so long as they could prove their admission to a nation in the Americas and means of subsistence.[31] The next day, Vichy's Colonial Ministry put its foot down, establishing strict conditions on those wanting to stay in Martinique permanently. And yet it clearly remained beyond the Ministry of the Colonies' purview to completely interdict passengers in transit.[32]

The strongest reactions to the Jewish refugee flow tended to come from the authorities in Martinique. In late July 1941, shortly after the Martinique line was compromised by Allied ship seizures, Platon still gave approval for Jules Levy and his family to be allowed to leave France for Martinique. The Levys were Alsatian Jews from Colmar, part of a region annexed by Germany in 1940. Platon's motivations are unclear: he may have felt sympathy for the Levy family as Alsatian patriots. In any event, in Fort-de-France, Admiral Robert answered that he was categorically opposed to the Levys' voyaging to the French Caribbean.[33] There is no sign in the archives that the Alsatian Levys ever reached the Caribbean.

Jewish passengers were not the only ones involved in this vast refugee flow. In March 1941, Platon cabled Martinique that he had granted transit visas to 135 Spanish Republican refugees bound for Mexico via Fort-de-France.[34] These Spanish refugees were also caught up in the tug of war between Vichy agencies. Admiral Robert in Martinique proved far more receptive toward the Spaniards than he did toward Jewish refugees, only to be rebutted by the French foreign ministry. Indeed, in May 1941, Robert floated the idea of a former Mexican representative to France serving as Mexican consul in Martinique, where he could "handle the transit of Spanish refugees coming through our colony en route to Mexico." However, Admiral Darlan, who by then had taken over Peyrouton's portfolio, as well as that of the foreign minister, responded unfavorably. He expressed two concerns: that the Mexicans would only serve to stir up revolutionaries, and that a Mexican consul might act as an American Trojan horse.[35] While under Peyrouton Vichy had pleaded with the governors of colonies to admit foreign refugees, and Jewish ones in particular, by May 1941 governors were the ones receiving negative responses from Vichy on a proposal designed to aid Spanish Republicans to gain safe passage to Central America.

And yet, for all of these hesitations, shifts, and bickering, the fact remains that until May 1941, Vichy allowed a large wave of refugees to depart for Martinique. A generic acceptance letter drafted by the Ministry of the Colonies, intended for officials in prefectures, constitutes an especially revealing document. It reads,

> The transit visa for a non-stop voyage to Martinique formulated by Mr./Mrs. X who is bound for X has been accepted and given number X. It is contingent on the passenger obtaining exit papers from France and on proof of admission to X, as well as the consignation of a sum of nine thousand francs by the person to the navigation company, and when appropriate, the funds necessary to be lodged temporarily in Martinique, as well as those necessary to sail from the Antilles to their final destination. Finally, could you kindly specify, as you hand the pass to the individual, that they are personally responsible for finding a place on board the ship, and that the shipping company has received strict orders concerning those bound for the Antilles.[36]

In short, Vichy at once asserted its authority and ensured that refugees only pass through Martinique, without lingering there. But it also outlined the path for those so desperate to leave France. It is worth noting that although the letter stressed that passengers required both an exit visa and an entry visa to a non-French territory in the Western Hemisphere, some migrants managed to depart without the latter.

Scope

How important an escape corridor was the French Caribbean? It was certainly incommensurate with the scale of the refugee crisis facing France. At the heart of the matter was the fact that the United States and other Western Hemisphere nations granted few visas. Another problem was that, with the exception of the *Cuba* and the *Ipanema,* the ships involved were not regular passenger liners but freighters, or so-called *paquebots mixtes,* featuring limited passenger capacity. In an April 1942 report, the Jewish emigration society HICEM labeled the route "a small outlet for a few of our refugees, that the international situation has now rendered unusable."[37] Limited though it might have been, given the turn of events in 1941 and 1942, it undoubtedly saved thousands of lives.

Vichy's hardline rear admiral Pierre Rouyer kept meticulous notes during his time in the French West Indies. One of his tables, reproduced here, lists the civilian vessels that reached Fort-de-France from unoccupied France (including French North Africa) after the armistice of June 22, 1940, with their date of arrival in Martinique:

Charles L. Dreyfus from Marseille via Casablanca, October 19, 1940
Belain d'Esnambuc from Casablanca, December 11, 1940
Capitaine Paul Lemerle from Marseille via Casablanca, January 2, 1941
Fort Richepanse from Casablanca, January 27, 1941
Mont Angel from Casablanca, February 6, 1941
Winnipeg from Marseille via Casablanca, February 15, 1941
Wyoming from Marseille via Casablanca, February 24, 1941
Ipanema from Marseille via Casablanca, March 14, 1941
Arizona from Marseille via Casablanca, March 31, 1941
Mont Angel from Marseille via Casablanca, April 7, 1941
Capitaine Paul Lemerle from Marseille via Casablanca, April 20, 1941
Carimaré from Marseille via Casablanca, April 29, 1941
Fort-de-France from Marseille via Casablanca, May 9, 1941
Arica from Marseille via Casablanca, May 10, 1941[38]

The majority of the ships listed here, most notably the *Winnipeg, Carimaré, Paul Lemerle, Ipanema, Arica,* and *Wyoming,* were crammed with refugees. In some cases, figures are readily available. The Jewish refugee organization HICEM recorded 230 refugees aboard the Martinique-bound *Paul Lemerle* on its second crossing in April 1941, and Vichy officials on arrival counted 222 passengers on board the same ship, of whom all but three were refugees (the small discrepancy between the two figures may have to do with the fact that a few people disembarked in Casablanca).[39] HICEM further indicated that the *Carimaré* transported 400 refugees, of whom roughly a quarter were Jews.[40]

Manuel Siegel, who wrote the report for HICEM in Havana entirely on the basis of his interviews with passengers on the last ships, erroneously suggested that only three boats had reached Martinique from Marseille before April 1941, and that each one had carried only thirty to forty refugees.[41] In March 1941, the German American exile newspaper *Aufbau* would also wrongly describe the *Ipanema* as the "first ship that it was possible to take directly from the unoccupied zone to Martinique"; this may suggest that *Aufbau* tapped into the same source.[42] From Rouyer's table, we know the number of ships Siegel lists, and *Aufbau*'s calculations, to be grossly incorrect.

There is therefore much uncertainty about refugee numbers on the early crossings. One hypothesis is that because the first vessel predated Peyrouton's memo, fewer refugees found their way on board. However, even some of the ships arriving in January 1941 seem to have transported modest numbers of refugees. We learn from a report issued by the US consulate in Martinique that the *Fort Richepanse,* which reached Fort-de-France in January 1941, carried only 248 passengers, "mostly demobilized soldiers." The US consular report further complicates matters, though, because it also refers to another ship that does not figure on Rouyer's table: the *Guadeloupe,* which reached Fort-de-France on January 16, 1941, with "110 passengers from Marseille."[43]

The ships listed here were the ones that departed from Marseille or Casablanca for Martinique. Rouyer cites another three that sailed to the French West Indies between June 1940 and May 1941, from the ports of Bordeaux and Nantes in what became occupied France. Historian Léo Elisabeth indicates that the first of these three, a passenger liner named the *Cuba,* which reached the French West Indies from Bordeaux on July 13, 1940, carried many hundreds of Spanish antifascists to the French Caribbean.[44] The ship had likely set sail just before the Germans entered Bordeaux on June 30.

In addition to these ships and the *Guadeloupe,* we also need to add four more vessels to the bottom of Rouyer's list, some of which were undertaking their second wartime crossing from Marseille to Fort-de-France: the *Alsina* embarked for Buenos Aires via Martinique in January 1941, only to be blocked, then rerouted to Dakar, then to Casablanca, where it remained in limbo. The *Winnipeg* also embarked on one more fateful voyage to Martinique, before being intercepted by a Dutch vessel off Trinidad on May 26, 1941. The *Alsina* was packed with some six hundred refugees;[45] although waylaid, the refugees on board both vessels eventually gained safe shores. Two more ships, the *Mont Viso* and the *Wyoming,* both crammed with refugees, also left Marseille bound for Martinique shortly before the boarding of the *Winnipeg.* After the interception of the *Alsina* and the *Winnipeg,* the *Mont Viso* and the *Wyoming* were left stranded in Casablanca. HICEM estimated that each one carried four hundred passengers.[46]

We know from the French naval archives, moreover, that on its second 1941 crossing, the *Winnipeg* alone carried 732 passengers, nearly all of them refugees.[47] Of these, 345 held valid travel documents for North America, 15 had the necessary papers to continue to South America, and 59 to Central America. Three hundred and thirteen did not hold visas to any nation of the Western Hemisphere and had still been allowed to board for Martinique, a sign that departing officials were turning a blind eye to the regulations instituted by the Ministry of the Colonies.[48] Vichy subdivided the German contingent on board as follows: 155 German nationals, 17 ex-Germans (denaturalized), 53 stateless people born in Germany, and 23 refugees coming from Germany.[49]

To further complicate matters, some of the vessels picked up additional refugees in Morocco, where many migrants were left stranded in conditions far grimmer than Hollywood depicted in the film *Casablanca*. Thus, the *Charles L. Dreyfus*, the first vessel to reach Martinique from Marseille after the advent of Vichy, carried on board fifty European refugees from Morocco. The governor of Martinique soon complained that these refugees could not pay for their own internment.[50]

Without reliable passenger data on some of the vessels, with wide variations in passenger numbers for those we have (between 110 and 732 travelers—and bearing mind the *Ipanema*'s capacity of roughly 1,000), and with the additional complication of passengers boarding in both Marseille and Casablanca, it is impossible to determine exact totals for the Martinique escape route. HICEM's indication that the earliest vessels contained few refugees, as well as the important caveat that the number of passengers does not equal the number of refugees, dictates the selection of a conservative average per ship, one well below the *Winnipeg*'s 732 and the *Alsina*'s 600. Taking a cautious average of 250 refugees per vessel, multiplied by the twenty crossings identified here (the fourteen listed by Rouyer plus those of the *Guadeloupe*, *Cuba*, *Winnipeg*, *Alsina*, *Mont Viso*, and *Wyoming*), brings us to a total of 5,000 refugees who embarked on the Martinique lines between June 1940 and June 1941. This conservative estimate falls short of Pastor Pierre-Charles Toureille's estimate of 7,000 but still represents a very considerable refugee flow.

Networks

How did one join the ranks of those bound for Martinique? Leaving for the French Caribbean in 1940 and 1941 involved more than merely good luck, a tip, or an exit visa from a prefecture, although we will examine each of these in turn. It was above all an administratively challenging and financially expensive proposition, especially for foreigners. The process was complicated by Vichy's restrictions on foreign currency, which made it virtually impossible for refugees to pay for transportation—a cost usually levied in US dollars.[51]

On this same financial score, any refugee wishing to leave for Martinique was required to pay a hefty deposit. We have seen that 9,000 francs were required by the shipping company just to transit through Martinique. In addition to this sum, the company requested the following amounts as deposits for the second leg, depending on the final destination: United States, 13,000 francs; Mexico, 15,000 francs; Cuba, 10,000 francs; Columbia, 13,000 francs; and Venezuela, 10,000 francs.[52] And this did not even begin to cover the expensive administrative fees to be levied in the French Caribbean itself (for those interned), nor the cost of a visa to a country in the Americas. At the Vernet camp in 1941, the Martinique "deposit fee" was erroneously demanded even of refugees slated to depart through Lisbon[53]—an indication of bureaucratic incompetence, corruption, or a willingness to prioritize the Martinique route.

In addition to these hurdles, there existed a well-documented hierarchy of rescue, entirely dependent on American or Latin American visa policies. Hence, it was often easier for a German exile to obtain a US visa than for a stateless East European refugee; conversely, if a German exile happened to be on the Kundt Commission list, his or her odds of being allowed to leave in the first place were much reduced. Stereotypes that proved deadly for one group of people on one side of the Atlantic could be flipped on their head on the other, admittedly far safer, shore. Thus, Fry lamented in December 1941 that the Cuban authorities "were busily engaged in rounding up all non-Jewish German refugees in the quaint belief that, not being Jews, they must be Nazis."[54] We shall see that in the case of Martinique, it was the American obsession with wolves in refugee clothing that ultimately doomed the escape route. Obstacles thus proved as innumerable as they were complex.

Fry's ERC made the most of the Martinique route. Yet even Fry readily admitted, "The regulations were shrouded in mystery, but we were told that every prefecture in the unoccupied zone had been provided with lists of persons to whom visas were to be refused."[55] Still, Fry's network helped some 1,200 refugees in total to leave for safer horizons.[56] There was much to do: cover the transit fees, arrange exit visas, and secure places on board.

One of those assisted by Fry's services was Wilhelm Herzog. A German playwright and journalist, he had authored a play on the Dreyfus affair and a biography of Louis Barthou. Barthou was the would-be architect of a co-alition against Nazi Germany. Herzog left promptly after Hitler's election to chancellor. After being denaturalized by the Nazis, Herzog was left state-less and therefore especially vulnerable, despite the impressive names he could invoke as sponsors in America: Albert Einstein and Thomas Mann. As France fell, Herzog and his Swiss wife found themselves in Sanary-sur-Mer, part of a community of exiles already infiltrated in the 1930s by a German intelligence agent. On November 28, 1940, Fry warned Herzog of an additional danger: the Swedish government might be unable to issue papers to him without authorization from Berlin. Furthermore, despite having cabled the United States no fewer than seven times regarding Her-zog's request for a visitor visa, the ERC had received no response. Fry wrote to Herzog that he was persuaded that "the delay is due to the State De-partment and not to any negligence on the part of [Herzog's] committee of friends." This must have come as cold comfort. With US permission finally obtained, in February 1941, the Var prefecture advised the Herzog couple to file for exit visas with the Bouches-du-Rhône prefecture in Marseille. Fry wrote to the Bank of France asking for dollars for the couple's passage to the United States via Lisbon; he then liaised with HICEM to secure pas-sage through Portugal. Finally, however, Herzog ended up on one of the last ships to Martinique in 1941, the *Winnipeg,* only to see the boat inter-cepted and commandeered to Trinidad. Herzog eventually gained passage to the United States four years later.[57] Without the dogged determination of Fry's ERC and a solid network of supporters, as a stateless anti-Nazi, Herzog would undoubtedly have had little chance of escape.

HICEM too proved very active, and it was in fact overwhelmed by demand. The organization contributed to assisting the Herzogs, for in-stance, as did the Quakers. Over the course of April and May 1941 alone, HICEM's Marseille offices drew up nearly 2,000 emigration files in the camps of the unoccupied zone and made 939 visits to consulates in an effort to secure departures.[58] By the end of May 1941, HICEM's Marseille offices had received thirty-five thousand requests for departure from would-be Jewish exiles. The organization was able to help some, but certainly not everyone concerned: it arranged for 1,568 successful departures between January and June 30, 1941, then another 3,000 in the first half of 1942.[59]

Timing was everything. Renée Poznanski chronicles the case of the Rosenfeld family, who transited from Gurs to Les Milles. Their daughter who lived in the United States had obtained a tourist visa for them, and they were set to leave for New York via Lisbon in July 1941. However, the family learned of a Martinique-bound ship that was scheduled to leave earlier. The very same thing happened to the Seghers-Radvanyi family, who were initially slated to leave via Lisbon. Convinced that Martinique represented an earlier passage to safety, the Rosenfelds canceled their passage to Lisbon, only to see the Martinique route suddenly suspended in May 1941. With Maria Rosenfeld gravely ill, HICEM intervened and solicited aid from countless sources, including the Red Cross, the rail companies, and the camp authorities at Les Milles, before finally prevailing.[60]

Transatlantic dialogue also counted in making the Martinique route known. The German American émigré newspaper *Aufbau* ran an article on March 7, 1941, titled "Via Martinique to New York." It reads, "A new opportunity for reaching America from unoccupied France has emerged, according to information from American Lloyd, in the form of steamer service from Marseille to Fort-de-France, Martinique. On February 15, a number of German refugees left Marseille on the *Winnipeg*. The next ship is set to sail mid-March and the French authorities are allowing those with an exit visa to take these ships. From Martinique, the French Line offers many transfers to New York."[61] Two months later, the same newspaper announced that "people in camps would be given first priority" to embark to Martinique.[62] Proof of transatlantic information sharing between families and friends in America and refugees in France can be found in the May 30, 1941, issue of *Aufbau*, in the form of an advertisement from Paul Tausig's travel agency. It offered to arrange safe passage from Marseille to New York via Martinique. Tragically, the ad ran just as the Martinique line had been interrupted.[63]

Finally, operating at once in Morocco, in France, and through contacts in the French Caribbean, Guadeloupe's deputy Maurice Satineau also aided

refugees to secure passage to the French Caribbean through official channels. A January 16, 1941, note from embarrassed staff at the Ministry of
the Colonies reveals that a letter from Satineau asking for multiple passages
to Guadeloupe had been inadvertently mislabeled and lost.[64]

Evidently, at Vichy as elsewhere, the left hand did not always know what
the right hand was doing. Dominique Chathuant has shown that Vichy's
police services suspected Satineau of bringing one Richard Meyer and his
family, as well as the Rotbluht and Lederberger families, to Guadeloupe,
under the pretext of needing personnel for a pineapple juice venture in the
first case and of requiring a chauffeur in the second case. The police further
believed that Satineau secured passage for a Claude Lubinsky and her mother
to the Dominican Republic. It followed its leads as far as Lyon, where a
certain Mrs. Witmann had purportedly liaised with a "Mr. Sapino" to create
a veritable network through which Jews could reach Guadeloupe, presumably
via Fort-de-France.[65]

Some elements do, however, cast doubt on Satineau's motives and even
on his actions. Few are more damning than documents held in Vichy inspector
Emile Devouton's files. In one March 7, 1941, statement in particular, Rear
Admiral Rouyer purported to have received a complaint from a Polish
Jew named Rotebliss. He had arrived in Martinique without a visa for the
Americas and risked being sent back at the very least to Casablanca. The
desperate refugee then allegedly learned through Meyer that Satineau could
help obtain departure from Martinique to Brazil via Guadeloupe, in exchange for 32,000 francs. Rotebliss allegedly paid the sum to Satineau, only
to wait in vain for a ship to Brazil. According to Rouyer, Jules Lederberger
found himself in the same situation after Satineau had helped him reach
Guadeloupe.[66]

Also intriguing is an April 18, 1941, telegram in which Minister Platon
indicates that he is granting a transit visa for the Dominican Republic to
Mrs. Lubinsky, "to whom he had previously denied a visa to Martinique."
The same holds for Meyer and Lederberger, whose passages to Guadeloupe
were authorized by Platon in person on January 21, 1941. All of this casts
some doubt on Satineau's actual role in securing passage to the French Antilles for Lubinsky, Lederberger, and Meyer.[67] Had the former parliamentarian pressed Platon to accept the refugees? A March 6, 1941, letter in
which Satineau complained of all administrative doors being slammed in
his face casts some doubt on his actual sway at the time.[68]

The Satineau case is complex, and certainly Rouyer's status as a diehard Pétainist wanting to curb the flow of refugees needs to be considered. Nevertheless, it seems improbable that the two complaints he received were entirely made up, and equally likely that Satineau proved unable to deliver entirely on what he had promised. Indeed, refugees trapped in the purgatory that was the French Caribbean in 1941 still did not feel entirely out of harm's way. Yet none of this, even the hefty payments he received, detracts from the fact that Satineau had clearly brought several Jewish refugees, including Lederberger, from southern France to the safer shores of the French West Indies.

Last but not least, some refugees lent a helping hand to others. Thus, Vichy suspected pilot and captain Marcel Delorme and his wife, Maria de Englander, of having financially assisted passengers Bloch and Philipsohn, helping them reach New York from Martinique.[69] In short, it was thanks to networks small and large, formal and informal, that most refugees learned about, then navigated, the Martinique escape corridor in 1940 and 1941.

Of course, all the help in the world would not do the trick if one of the many formalities went awry or bureaucratic obstructions became insurmountable. German Jewish musician Frida Kahn makes this very observation in her memoirs. She writes with gratitude of the work of Fry and his team, as well as the many friends who supported her and Erich Itor Kahn, before adding, "All the moral support we received . . . did not protect us from becoming victims of the bureaucracy and the unhappy coincidences caused by ill will and unfortunate delays." Some pages earlier, Frida Kahn makes clear that French bureaucracy seemed especially adept at creating such victims: "Something seemed to happen to the minds and souls of civil servants in France. Perhaps something had already happened to their minds and souls to make it possible for them to choose this career."[70]

German national Helena Holzer (later Benitez) felt much the same way as she contemplated emigration prospects. During the Spanish Civil War, she had been in Catalonia, where she worked as a scientist in a tuberculosis clinic. She headed for France as Francisco Franco's forces triumphed and was imprisoned in Gurs as an enemy alien. She managed to leave Gurs after the fall of France and joined her partner, Wifredo Lam, in Marseille, at the Villa Air-Bel. There she and Lam received the support of Fry's ERC. And yet, many decades later, she still vividly remembered sitting terrified before two French police officials as they grilled her with a series of questions during her exit visa interview.[71] She evidently answered them to the police's satisfaction and was able to board the *Paul Lemerle*.

These subsequent attempts by refugees to grapple with contingency, with how and why they had managed to leave while others had not, may betray a measure of survivor's guilt. They certainly speak to the confusion and apparent arbitrariness surrounding maritime departures from Marseille in 1940 and 1941. For our purposes, they also set the stage for a historical discussion of the Martinique corridor's meanings and an examination of refugee profiles.

CHAPTER THREE

Understanding the Martinique Route

THE FRENCH CARIBBEAN WAS certainly not the only option. However, by 1941 it had emerged as the best one, so much so that Varian Fry, HICEM, and even the camp director at Les Milles all recommended it to would-be migrants as the route to take posthaste. This does not mean that choices were obvious. This chapter begins with four individual stories of how foreign refugees either stumbled on or were directed to the Martinique corridor. It then considers the cases of a number of French migrants who left via Martinique, contemplates why some refugees succeeded while others did not, and searches for the broader meanings of this escape passage.

Minna Flake

German Jewish refugees Minna Flake, Josef Breitenbach, Anna Seghers, Erich Itor Kahn, and their families all wound up aboard the ships for Martinique, as did the Spanish politician Luis Fernández Clérigo. Their stories shed considerable light on refugee conditions in southern France leading up to their departures, not to mention the ways in which they came on the Martinique route. For them at least, there was nothing foreordained about passage to the French Caribbean.

Flake (née Margareta Mai) was born into a German Jewish grain merchants' family in Würzburg in 1887. She moved to Paris to follow university courses in 1910 before graduating in medicine from Humboldt University in 1915.[1] After a stint in Switzerland, she joined the German Communist

Party in 1919–1920, only to be expelled from it in 1927 for political "deviation."[2] While practicing medicine in Berlin, she contributed to the *Socialist Physician (Der sozialistische Arzt)*. Flake's work, especially in pediatrics, was sufficiently recognized for her to be named medical supervisor of Berlin schools. Her American visa sponsor described her position in pre-1933 Berlin as follows: "Chief Medical Officer at the Public Health Department, Berlin, Prenzlauer Berg in charge of school hygiene and supervising the various child care institutions."[3]

The Gestapo arrested Dr. Flake and her daughter Renata (aka Renée, born 1917) within months of the Nazi seizure of power in 1933. During interrogations, the authorities sought, but failed to uncover, evidence that Dr. Flake had performed abortions.[4] The family was also tormented by the SA (Sturmabteilung); the brownshirts rifled through their personal library. Finally, Flake managed to leave for France. There she opened a practice, remained militantly anti-Nazi, and mingled with German opposition members in exile, including Paul Frölich, a founding member of the German Communist Party and biographer of Rosa Luxemburg.[5] Renée and her family found an affordable flat to rent in the Paris suburb of Montrouge, and she took a variety of jobs, first in a bookstore, then as a translator. Dr. Flake's attempts to secure a US visa began in September 1939, when France declared war on Germany. Under the "political affiliation" box on the application form, she listed "Socialist."[6]

Like so many others, after having opposed the Nazis in Germany, Renée's husband, Walter Barth, was interned as an enemy alien by French authorities in 1939. By 1940, the family, composed of Minna Flake, Renée, Renée's husband, and their baby Katrin (born in 1939), had fled to southwestern France, near Montauban, where they would stay until their departure to Martinique via Marseille.[7] Montauban was a historically Protestant town; many historians have stressed the networks of support extended to Jews in Protestant sections of France after the fall of the country.[8]

Dr. Flake secured a US affidavit from Los Angeles–based Dr. David Brunswick, who attested to her outstanding work in the field of pediatrics. Brunswick and his wife, Dorothea, listed their worldly possessions, as well as their gross annual income, in their affidavit in support of Dr. Flake.[9] She could also count on the goodwill of German émigré doctor (and later Berkeley professor) Walter Friedlander, who wrote to Fry's Emergency Rescue Committee (ERC) in the strongest possible terms, noting that Flake and her family "are in great danger when the Gestapo gets hold of [them]." No doubt Friedlander's confusion of the German *wenn* (meaning "if") with the English "when" rendered the threat even more imminent. Friedlander added that the family represented "a real asset for democracy" and pleaded with Fry's office to do what it could. However, Friedlander and others mistakenly sent their testimonies directly to Flake in France, when they actually needed to reach the State Department. Weeks passed as the letters were rerouted to their proper destination.[10]

Renée Barth recalls, "We were in the mouse trap and tried desperately to get out. We tried everything." China and South America came up in conversation as possible destinations. In fits of depression, Minna Flake professed to want to "go down with Europe," only later to relent on account of the baby. A small community of German exiles did provide moral support. Barth mentions on several occasions mingling with the Cohn-Bendits (Erich and Herta), and their son Gabriel, all of whom were also on the ERC's protégé list.[11] In 1945, the Cohn-Bendit couple would have another child, Daniel, who would go on to become the leader of the May 1968 movement in France. The Flake-Barths also likely encountered other refugees who would follow their path from Montauban to Martinique. Among them were the Kriszhabers, as well as Dyno Löwenstein. Just demobilized from the French army after the defeat, Dyno was the son of secular Jewish German Social Democrat Kurt Löwenstein.[12]

Meanwhile, the Flake-Barth family was living on a shoestring, though the Quakers did provide cornmeal and milk powder on which to survive.[13] On October 10, 1940, Dr. Flake wrote to the ERC in Marseille. She described "a desperate situation," Renée having spent 900 francs in vain on an exit visa in Marseille, Walter Barth having twice failed to leave via Lisbon. Ten days later, she gratefully acknowledged receipt of 750 francs from the ERC. However, on November 16, 1940, a stunned Flake wrote the ERC upon receiving the lesser sum of 350 francs. "I remind you," she admonished the ERC, "that I am on the list of people to save by all means possible, and that I have a family of five people here." By December 4, 1940, she wrote to the ERC that the checks were arriving irregularly, but that she had followed their advice and succeeded in obtaining an exit visa at the Montauban prefecture.[14]

Once the family reached Marseille, Renée Barth recalls being asked by the throngs of people waiting outside the US consulate, "What are you doing here? You are not famous." The US consul then proceeded to pose a very similar question to her: "Is your husband famous?" In Barth's rendition, the consulate was overrun with celebrities being rescued by a range of organizations, especially Fry's, and "the consuls were offended in their loss of autonomy. They did not like to be told by Washington who could get the visas."[15] If anything, relative anonymity helped in this instance, Barth contends. Or perhaps another way of looking at it is that Flake was just famous enough. Finally, after overcoming a host of complications surrounding passports, Flake and her family obtained visas from the United States. Barth describes the stunned look of other refugees as the US consul plucked her out of the waiting crowd to give her the good news.[16]

The next piece of evidence from Dr. Flake's file at the German Exile Archives in Frankfurt involves a heart-wrenching undated note from the ERC, requesting passage for Lisbon on April 15, 1941, for the Flake-Barth family, "because the boat to Martinique does not take children." However, either the news was false or the shipping company relented, because Flake and her family left for Martinique aboard the *Paul Lemerle,* the same vessel that would carry to safety André Breton, Claude Lévi-Strauss, Victor Serge, Anna Seghers, Dyno Löwenstein, Jacques Rémy, and many more. Barth recalls the anguished moments before setting sail, when Vichy's police came on board and dragged the Spanish Republicans off the ship, on Francisco Franco's request.[17] The Flake-Barth family reached New York, via Martinique, on May 29, 1941.[18]

Josef Breitenbach

Photographer Josef Breitenbach was born in Munich in 1896 to a Jewish couple working in the wine trade. As a young Socialist, he was implicated in the Bavarian revolutionary movement of 1918. The Nazis stripped him of his German citizenship, and he fled for Paris in the wake of their 1933 takeover. In Paris, he honed his photographic skills and rubbed shoulders with Man Ray and the Surrealists, including Breton. Soon he was experimenting with Surrealist montage and superimpression.

As an "undesirable" and stateless foreigner in France, in 1939 he was interned in a number of makeshift camps, including in the Colombes stadium outside Paris. From there, he and thousands of others were transferred to Bourges, and then on to the camp at Bengy-sur-Craon, before another convoy brought him to southwestern France as France fell to the German advance in 1940. Near Bourges, Breitenbach wrote that he and 95 percent of his companions of misfortune would gladly have enrolled in the French army to fight the Germans, but that the commission in charge of vetting such requests vanished or temporized without pronouncing verdicts. As the summer of 1940 turned to fall, Breitenbach noted that discipline regimes grew harsher: "internees" were gradually turning into "prisoners."[19] Soon he was assigned to a work camp near Agen, in southwestern France. Meanwhile, his son Hans Breitenbach managed to find his way to Britain, where he would serve as a glider pilot for the British armed forces.

Josef Breitenbach was released from internment on November 18, 1940, as Vichy's Interior Ministry sought to ease the pressure on the camp system. In February 1941, he reached Marseille. From his base at the Hôtel Méditer-ranée, he made the quest for emigration his full-time job. In his few moments of respite from this task, he took photographs of the port city.[20]

Like the Flake-Barth family, in 1940 Breitenbach obtained support from Walter Friedlander in America, as well as numerous other contacts, and especially from the Quakers, who helped him secure his affidavits.[21] Initially, Breitenbach had a spot booked on a ship running from Lisbon, paid for by American contacts. On February 19, 1941, the American Export Lines in Marseille wrote the US consulate indicating that the bill for Breitenbach's passage to America had been settled. However, the photographer ultimately opted to leave via Martinique instead, likely because the Portuguese channels were beginning to close and Martinique could be reached directly from Marseille. The Breitenbach papers in Tucson include a receipt from the ERC dated April 15, 1941, showing that the organization paid 4,300 francs for his voyage to Martinique aboard the *Winnipeg*.[22] Breitenbach boarded the *Winnipeg* on May 6, 1941, only to have the ship intercepted by the Dutch twenty days later. Like all other passengers on board, he was then sent for "triage" to Trinidad—where the British hoped to filter out possible Nazi spies—and made his way from there to New York on June 13.

Anna Seghers

Novelist Anna Seghers (née Netty Reiling) was born into a German Jewish family in 1900. She joined the Communist Party in 1928, after training at the University of Heidelberg in history, Chinese, Russian and French literature, and art history. Her PhD thesis focused on representations of Jews and Judaism in the work of Rembrandt. In 1925 she had married the Jewish Hungarian philosopher Laszlo (Ladislaus) Radvanyi. The couple left Germany for Paris one year after the Nazis were elected into power. They were, after all, to borrow Susan E. Cernyak's phrase, "twice enemies of the Reich," as Jews and Communists. In Paris, they raised their two children, Pierre and Ruth. In 1940, Laszlo Radvanyi was interned as an "undesirable foreigner" at Roland Garros tennis stadium, which had been transformed into a makeshift internment center. Like famed writer Arthur Koestler, he was transferred from Roland Garros to the Vernet camp in May.[23]

Seghers and her two children returned to Paris after having first joined the chaotic mass exodus of civilians who took to the roads of France as the French army crumbled. Knowing that the Nazis would hunt her, she and her children prudently stayed in a hotel, then in a small room on the Rue Saint-Sulpice, then near the Porte d'Orléans. However, she asked her son and her Polish friend Else to check whether it was safe for her to return to their apartment just for a matter of minutes so as to save some cherished belongings. Thereupon, the neighbor informed Pierre and Else that the "German police" had already searched the apartment. As a precaution, Else then burned the manuscript of Seghers' legendary novel *The Seventh Cross,* which the police had failed to uncover. It dealt, appropriately, with escape from a German concentration camp, and with the reaction of ordinary people to the seven escapees asking for shelter. Fortunately, Seghers had already dispatched a copy to her contacts in America, and the novel would appear to great fanfare in the United States in 1942, one of the few depictions of German internment camps at the time. Now persuaded that Paris was unsafe, Seghers and her two children fled to the unoccupied zone, crossing the demarcation line in a farmer's field that straddled the freshly created internal border.[24]

They finally reached Pamiers, the closest town to Le Vernet. Seghers signed Pierre up at the local school, as she would in Marseille later. That year he was the Odysseus of the French school system, leaving Louis le Grand in Paris for a school in Pamiers, then attending the Lycée Thiers in Marseille. The family then managed to obtain assistance from Fry's ERC, from the League of American Writers, from the Quakers, and most importantly from Mexico. Once they received a Mexican visa from Consul Gilberto Bosquez, Laszlo was transferred from Le Vernet to Les Milles, to await emigration. This is when Seghers and Pierre recall obtaining help from the Marseille prefecture to obtain exit visas. The family was warned, however, that if Laszlo failed to leave for Martinique, he would have to return to Les Milles. All four boarded the *Paul Lemerle* in Marseille in April 1941 after passing what Pierre Radvanyi recalls as a double or even triple set of passport controls.[25] Given their shared languages and politics, and the way toddlers tend to generate attention, it seems hard to believe that the Seghers-Radvanyi family would not have encountered the Flake-Barths on board.

Erich Itor Kahn

Composer and pianist Erich Itor Kahn was the youngest of these four German Jewish exiles. He was born in 1905 in the Odenwald. He trained at the Hoch Conservatory in Frankfurt. During his formative years, Anrold Schönberg, whom the Nazis would label a "degenerate artist," emerged as one of his leading creative influences. This promising phase of Kahn's life came to an abrupt end in 1933. The gifted musician was fired from his position at Radio Frankfurt after the Nazis were elected into office.[26] He and his musician wife, Frida (née Rabinowitch, born in Russia in 1905), fled to Paris in November 1933, where they joined Frida's parents, who had come there from Palestine in 1928. Erich and Frida thrived in the French capital, despite the political tensions and their precarious situation as refugees.[27] In Paris, Erich composed a "Hassidic Rhapsody" for a choir and organ ensemble.[28] Through their friend, the female art deco sculptor Chana Orloff, with whom they first stayed, Erich and Frida socialized with Marc Chagall, Georges Braque, and Paul Clemenceau, the last of whom was the brother of the former French prime minister.[29] While in France, Erich played alongside and befriended some of the classical music titans of his time, men also engaged in the struggle against fascism. Among them were the Spaniard Pablo Casals, widely considered the world's greatest cellist at the time, and Bronislaw Huberman, a renowned German Jewish violinist.[30]

Beginning in 1939, Erich was interned in one French camp after another (Marolles in the Loir-et-Cher and Tence in the Haute-Loire), with only a brief respite of freedom between December 1939 and May 1940. In 1939, Frida was still free and lobbied tenaciously to have her husband liberated. However, as German forces invaded France in May 1940, she and Erich were both detained for seventeen painful days at the Vélodrome d'Hiver before being sent to Gurs.[31] Two years later, over eight thousand other Jews would be crammed into the same Vélodrome d'Hiver before being deported to Auschwitz.

As of May 1940, Erich and Frida were frequently separated by virtue of Gurs' camp rules, but they tirelessly explored different emigration options via correspondence and the occasional meeting. One of the more surprising leads arose in late November 1940. A New York–based international lawyer named Albert F. Coyle cited a freshly signed American executive order number 8430. In Coyle's understanding, President Franklin D. Roosevelt's order could amount to "permission for selected immigrants from Europe to come to the [US Virgin] Islands until they obtain their American Immigration visas." Coyle considered this option "much preferable to the obtaining of a temporary visitor's visa." Due to backlogs at European consulates, Coyle insisted, "If we can get the Kahn family out of Europe, I can obtain their American immigration visas within thirty days; whereas if they come to the United States as visitors they lose the two years' priority which they now have on the quota waiting list." This was because the Kahns had initially applied for US visas in 1938, and therefore held an early spot in line, so to speak.[32] From the standpoint of the Kahns and their US counsel, the US Virgin Islands, like Martinique, constituted a sort of safe house in the form of a stopover in the New World before reaching the United States.

Nothing ultimately came of the US Virgin Islands scheme, which was blocked by none other than President Roosevelt.[33] And so the Kahns tapped into multiple networks closer to them in France. Fry's ERC delivered care packages and obtained Erich's liberation from Gurs and transfer to Les Milles. The Unitarian Service Committee paid for the couple's way to America via Lisbon, a trip that Fry arranged, although the Kahns ultimately did not take that route. On Erich's behalf, in November 1940 Countess Lily Pastré lobbied not only Fry but also her friend Sabine Charles-Roux, who was active in protecting prisoners of all stripes. With Fry and Charles-Roux heading to Vichy, Pastré expressed hope that these twin efforts would succeed in having Erich released outright. Pastré also signed paperwork for Erich, probably the letter attesting to his fine moral conduct that was required to leave a camp.[34]

The tender and compelling correspondence between Erich and Frida in 1941 speaks to the dangers they faced and the ways they weighed various emigration options. Erich was still interned at Les Milles, while Frida remained free in Fréjus. On April 8, 1941, he wrote her with palpable anxiety about "a new source of stress for us." He was referring to the arrests and dragnets around Marseille. He explained to Frida, in case she had not heard of these events, "There are currently many raids in Marseille, in restaurants, hotels and on the streets, Jews are being picked up (including women) and taken to the police where they stay sometimes 24 hours, and people are then thrown out of Marseille." He also mentioned rumors of a change in attitude toward refugees on the part of Portugal. He added more hopefully that the couple's Spanish visas had arrived, and asked if Frida had received her exit visa.[35] The letter shows doors slamming in the couple's face as persecution of Jews intensified.

On April 17, 1941, Frida wrote Erich. Her tone was more frantic than usual. "We can no longer hesitate and must leave as soon as possible by any available route," she opined. She had also received advice from Marcel Chaminade (born Moskowski), a member of Fry's team. Chaminade had told her that it was "easy" to change routes; one was not locked into the Lisbon channel onto which they had initially pinned their hopes. She concluded that all administrative hurdles were out of the way: "Everything is ready, may the Good Lord think of us."[36]

That very day, Erich responded. He worried about Frida's sudden desire to change plans and jettison the Iberian channel altogether in favor of the Martinique one. He noted that the Martinique option presented drawbacks of its own: "A long wait over there seems inevitable." The pianist had been rightly informed that foreign migrants were held in camps in Martinique as well. He reasoned, "Naturally we must leave as soon as possible, but there is no point in swapping Martinique for Gurs, right?" Here Frida's and Erich's approaches clearly differed, Frida considering even internment in the Western Hemisphere a far safer bet, Erich seeing little difference between being cooped up in the Pyrenees and in the Caribbean. The musician's pessimism toward the Martinique option did not end there: all first- and second-class cabins were taken and even dormitories were full, he observed. Then there were the rumors that only men would be allowed on the ships to Martinique, not women or children (this part of the story is of course corroborated by the Flake-Barth case). Last but not least, with payment already made for departure via Portugal, could they transfer the funds to the Martinique line? Peggy Guggenheim apparently held out hope that the shipping companies could reach a deal among themselves.[37] Two days later, Erich wrote to Frida with more hopeful news that the "next ship to Martinique will in fact take women and children."[38]

The Martinique option carried the day. Thanks to HICEM's work on the reservation front, on May 10, 1941, the couple boarded the *Mont Viso* for Martinique.[39] However, two weeks later the Dutch intercepted the *Winnipeg* and took it to Trinidad. This was the ship ahead of them on the same route that carried Josef Breitenbach. The *Mont Viso* was consequently waylaid in North Africa, and all other rescue ships to Martinique were suspended. The Kahns remained in limbo in Morocco for a time, but they eventually did reach New York. Most importantly, they made it across the ocean, escaping from France in the nick of time. Their story, like Breitenbach's, shows the mutability of escape plans. Only a few weeks before setting sail, they had imagined departing via Spain and Portugal. Contingency clearly played an important role in the Martinique escape route.

Luis Fernándes Clérigo

With its close calls and multiple departure options, the case of Luis Fernándes Clérigo bears some similarities to the ones we have just seen. However, it also reminds us of the diversity of refugees; in addition to German Jews, the cargo ships to Martinique carried a great many Spanish dissidents. It further suggests the key role played by low- to mid-ranking French government officials, a role that will be explored at greater length in the second part of this chapter.

Clérigo was born in Madrid in 1883. He studied law at the Universidad Central of the Spanish capital and was elected a deputy in parliament in 1931. By 1936, he had emerged as a leading figure of the Socialist Spanish Popular Front. He held the position of president of the national tourist board.[40] His influence in government rose proportionately as the Popular Front fell at the hands of Franco: by the time of the republic's defeat, he found himself close to the top of the governmental summit. As the republic crumbled, he obtained asylum in Paris, securing a deal for other parliamentarians to leave as well.[41]

Clérigo fled to the unoccupied zone ahead of the German advance in May–June 1940. He then managed to obtain a ticket aboard the *Alsina*, which was due to leave Marseille in January 1941. However, Vichy's police prevented him from boarding, as his papers were not in order.[42] He was then interned. The menace that Clérigo and his compatriots faced should not be minimized. Franco had submitted a list of some two thousand Spaniards—Clérigo included—that he wished to see returned to Spain to face reprisals.[43] However, Vichy did not feel as much pressure to negotiate with Spain as it did with Germany, and it sought to send these political "undesirables" to Central and South America whenever possible.

In this instance, Vichy's Ministry of the Colonies, which stonewalled plans for Jewish departures, appears to have been at the heart of the scheme to send Clérigo to the Western Hemisphere, a mere month after Vichy police had blocked his first attempt. On February 12, 1941, the Ministry of the Colonies contacted the Bouches-du-Rhône prefecture, as well as colonial services in Marseille, to coordinate the safe passage of Clérigo and a party of five to Fort-de-France, with the expectation that from there they would sail on to Buenos Aires. Two days later, Vichy's colonial office in Marseille reported that, thanks to the diligence of Marseille's prefecture, it had obtained exit papers for Martinique for Clérigo and his entourage.[44] They would indeed reach Martinique from Marseille aboard the *Ipanema*. From Fort-de-France, Clérigo would find his way to Mexico, rather than Argentina.

In Mexico, before his death in 1948, Clérigo passed his time translating Machiavelli's *The Prince*, editing Spanish-language translations of Soviet laws, and watching bullfighting, even befriending matadors. Meanwhile, Clérigo's son, Carlos Fernández Valdemoro, who had reached Mexico a year before his father, had swiftly enrolled in the local offices of General Charles de Gaulle's Free French press services. He brought with him the knowledge he had gained as a member of the propaganda ministry of the Spanish Second Republic. Carlos too became a leading bullfighting enthusiast and chronicler.[45]

Those Who Made It, and Those Who Did Not

How did one make the boat to rebuild one's life overseas? Germaine Krull mused in a French-language manuscript that three elements were required to leave unoccupied France safely in 1941: luck, money, and courage (in addition to bravery, *courage* in French also conveys a sense of determination). We should add at least three more pieces to the puzzle. Many of the cases we have just examined, including those of Seghers, Kahn, and Flake, make clear that connections and networks mattered just as much as Krull's three elements. And, of course, timing proved another key ingredient, which some refugees became keenly aware of as Europe's departure gates gradually creaked shut. Last but not least, the centrally conceived, albeit ambiguous, Martinique plan became absolutely crucial for the escape of thousands.

Beyond networks and serendipity, how did one find one's way onto a ship bound for Martinique? Some of the fortunate ones managed to tap into family or government connections. This proved easier for French nationals than for foreigners—indeed, a number of French Jews targeted by Vichy's discriminatory measures also took the Martinique route, among them Claude Lévi-Strauss. Such was also the case of French Jewish nuclear scientist Bertrand Goldschmidt, who reached Martinique aboard the *Carimaré* in 1941. Goldschmidt had left the occupied zone in 1940. He ignored the siren calls of his laboratory directors André Debierne and Irène Joliot-Curie (daughter of Pierre and Marie Curie) to return to Paris and instead took up a teaching position at the University of Montpellier. Vichy promptly fired him in December 1940 on the basis of its new quotas on Jewish professors. Goldschmidt's mother was already in New York by 1941; there she "knocked on all doors" to get her son to America. She was able to cook up some fictitious positions for him. However, Goldschmidt ultimately found more reliable planks on which to pass to the French Caribbean: he was introduced to the American consul in Marseille through a family friend. He also benefited from a high-level contact at Vichy's Ministry of the Interior, a certain Mr. Bernard. All of these leads came together to enable his departure. After setting sail for Fort-de-France, he learned that Vichy had tightened restrictions, banning the departure of any man under the age of thirty who was not on government business (he was twenty-nine). Vichy was concerned that these men might serve in foreign armies. Goldschmidt had left in the nick of time.[46]

In Goldschmidt's case, as in many others, word of mouth played an important role. Tips came from various sources, although many turned out to be bogus. The famous *bobards,* or false news, spread like wildfire in wartime France, kindled by the fact that the tightly controlled press could no longer be trusted.[47] Escape avenues that seemed open one week closed the next, if they had ever really existed at all. Rescue organizations, other refugees, and prefectures all were involved in grasping at emigration straws and distributing them. Escape remained an agonizing exercise in drawing straws.

One case stands out in particular. Jacques Assayas was born in Istanbul in 1911, and then raised in Milan by Sephardic Jewish parents. His mother hailed from Thessalonica and spoke Ladino, a language derived from Old Spanish that is spoken in Sephardic communities. Assayas and his family acquired French citizenship in 1932 after France emerged as a protégé power for Ottoman subjects; he wrote that his parents chose France because of its reputation as a land "of liberty, generosity and sensitivity." And so the family moved to Paris. As Assayas entered the film industry, for which he would write many scripts, he was advised by colleagues to change his name to Rémy. In an era when anti-Semitism and xenophobia were rapidly gaining ground in France, this was a calculated decision to fit in, to avoid drawing unwanted attention as an outsider.[48]

One of the Vichy regime's foundational obsessions involved stripping French Jews of their citizenship: the process began in 1940, when all Jews naturalized since 1927 suddenly risked losing their citizenship.[49] The denaturalization commission that Vichy established proved particularly efficient over the course of the sixteen months commencing in September 1940. (Although Rémy did not know this, Jews born in Istanbul, like him, stood a far greater chance of being denaturalized than those born in Belgium, Italy, or Germany.)[50] Vichy's denaturalization frenzy, as well as other anti-Semitic measures, not to mention the fact that he had visited Germany on the eve of the Nazi takeover in 1933, meant that Rémy saw the ominous clouds gathering on the horizon and surmised what the storm could bring.

Here is how Rémy describes boarding the *Paul Lemerle,* bound for Martinique, in 1941: "One leaves any way one can. Between France and Martinique, it's done by cargo ship. One such cargo ship is about to leave for Fort-de-France. Take it or leave it. There are ten would-be candidates for every spot on board. So long live the cargo!" He also relates his parting experience: "The police officer handed me my passport with its exit visa. He was smiling. Every day, he saw the gloomy lines of people hoping for a favorable answer. The answer was always no. For me it was yes. Why? Luck, chance, resourcefulness [*débrouille*]. In any event, I was leaving."[51] Rémy's insights perfectly encapsulate the combination of good fortune, timing, and determination required to gain passage on the vessels bound for Martinique in 1940 and 1941.

Like Goldschmidt, Rémy managed to leave without tapping into Fry's ERC. Young French Jewish anthropologist Lévi-Strauss also fit into this category. His biographer Emmanuelle Loyer underscores the importance of contingency in his case as well. Indeed, Lévi-Strauss thought of remaining in France for a time. He faced multiple options. He hesitated in deciding whether to accept his post in Paris at the prestigious Lycée Henry IV, lie low in the rural Cevennes, or teach in Perpignan and Montpellier. Some suggested he make a formal request of exception to Vichy's Jewish statutes.[52] When he wisely decided to decamp, his visa was denied at the last second at the Brazilian embassy—the ambassador had been suddenly stripped of his power to deliver visas. Lévi-Strauss ultimately succeeded in leaving via Martinique, thanks to an invitation from the New School for Social Research in New York and contacts at the shipping line in Marseille. But, as Loyer notes, whether one left, and, if so, where one ended up, turned on the smallest twists of fate.[53]

Fry's papers also contain chilling tales that underscore how departure to the safety of Martinique could hinge on seemingly inconsequential details, and could be variously interpreted as prearranged or fortuitous. They also remind us that Vichy was no monolith. The cases of the two Rudolfs fit all of these patterns. Rudolf Breitscheid was the former president of the German Social Democratic Party and delegate to the League of Nations. Rudolf Hilferding had served as minister of finance under the Weimar Republic. The Nazis actively sought the two men, and they denaturalized Hilferding in June 1935. Indeed, as a Jewish Social Democrat, Hilferding earned an additional dose of Nazi hate. Joseph Goebbels's propaganda showcased an image of him in a 1938 Berlin exhibition titled "The Eternal Jew"; Adolf Hitler's regime further claimed that Hilferding was responsible for Germany's suffering during the Great Depression. Hilferding, meanwhile, continued to publish in the Socialist German-language press, first from Czechoslovakia, then from Paris. He deemed Nazism "the deadly enemy of the German people and of humanity" and began enumerating points of commonality between Hitlerism and Stalinism.[54] Fellow refugee Kurt Kersten recounts that Breitscheid carried poison upon reaching France, which he intended to take should the Nazis get hold of him.[55] Although they were not aware of it, in late August 1940 Vichy had included Breitscheid and Hilferding on a list of foreigners who should not be allowed to leave France. This document circulated to all prefectures at the time.[56]

The situation was fluid, and the following year brought an about-face. After many fruitless attempts to obtain visas in Marseille and Arles, on January 27, 1941, the two men and their spouses, Tony Breitscheid and Rose Hilferding (the latter of whom was to follow subsequently), were at last granted *titres de voyage* by the Marseille prefecture, as well as letters of introduction to the shipping companies. Fry relates how both prefectures and subprefectures suddenly proved willing to process paperwork for refugees bound for Martinique. Why had the August 1940 instructions been rescinded? Had Marcel Peyrouton's instructions trickled down to the Mediterranean shore? Or did this administrative effort not come from the summit at all, but rather from local initiative? In any event, at the prefecture the two statesmen were "given recommendations to steamship companies and were forbidden to cross Spain, but told . . . to take the route via Martinique."[57] In other words, the Martinique route was recommended to them. However, with no individual cabins remaining in any class aboard the *Wyoming*, the management of the shipping company "very strongly advised them not to" accept the alternative, bunks in the group dormitory (Rose Hilferding was apparently in poor health). To Fry's horror, they resolved to wait for the next ship instead. Hilferding subsequently had a change of heart, but it was too late. Both Breitscheid's and Hilferding's visas were abruptly rescinded on January 30 by "order of Vichy," a mere three days after their departure had been approved.[58]

On February 8, Vichy extradited both Rudolfs to Paris. Two days later, they were handed to the Nazi authorities in the occupied zone, after empty promises of protection. The high court records of the National Archives in Paris reveal that a shortcut had been used to accelerate their handover. Philippe Pétain's regime had allowed the creation of a Gestapo office at Vichy (led by the Alsatian-born and totally bilingual SS captain Hugo Geissler). This bureau in essence streamlined and accelerated "surrender on demand" requests, including the two that concern us here, effectively bypassing the Wiesbaden commission. These records reveal not only German requests for the two Rudolfs and other dissidents but also Vichy's eagerness to satisfy such German requests. In other words, while some at Vichy's prefectures had tried to save the two men, others within the same regime resolved to hand them over to their tormentors.[59] The two Weimar statesmen stayed for a short time at Santé Prison. The Gestapo murdered Hilferding in Paris shortly thereafter. Breitscheid perished at Buchenwald near the end of the war.[60]

Next to such tragic foiled escapes, one finds remarkable accounts of near misses. German Jewish poet and translator Walter Mehring recounted just such a saga to Fry.[61] According to Fry, Mehring would end up taking one of the spots on board intended for Breitscheid and Hilferding. In late January 1941, Mehring happened to cross paths with the two Social Democrats, who informed him of the arrival of the *titres de voyage*. At the Arles prefecture, Mehring was told by "the old lady of the *Bureau des Passeports* . . . that [he] must try to find a place aboard the ship for Martinique; and she gave [him] a special visa for Martinique beside the Vichy visa."[62] Mehring also seems to have received assistance from another bureaucrat in Marseille. The ERC archives contain an original handwritten note from Mehring to Fry on a Marseille hotel's letterhead, dated February 3, 1941. It reads, in English, "I have seen once more Madame Esmiolle at the Prefecture. She has changed my *visa de sortie* for the Antilles. I have got it already."[63]

Mehring no doubt got the spelling wrong: Esmiolle is not a common last name, while Esmiol is, at least in southern France (and is pronounced the same way). An Anna Esmiol appears in the Bouches-du-Rhône prefecture personnel records. Born Anna Chabran in Marseille in 1892, she rose through the ranks of state officials. She was hired at the start of the First World War as a typist before becoming a head clerk (*commis principal*) in December 1941. Unlike some of her colleagues, she was listed as speaking no foreign languages.[64] Might this Anna Esmiol be the same bureaucrat who assisted Anna Seghers and many others? Her file photo in no way matches the description provided by Seghers (that said, *Transit* is semifictional). This might suggest complicity on the part of multiple female employees at the Marseille prefecture. However, when Seghers' son Pierre Radvanyi was kind enough to look at her file photo seventy-five years after the fact, he deemed that she might well have been the functionary who helped his mother and him.[65]

Whatever the case may be, Mehring was truly fortunate, for he experienced yet another amazing instance of administrative complicity. This one flew in the face of German orders. As he prepared to board the Martinique-bound *Wyoming*, the police looked over Mehring's papers. Mehring continues,

Examining my papers, the Chief took out of the shelf a card, so that I could read it, running this way:

Walter Mehring, Interdit de sortir de France, Décision de la Kundt Commission (Walter Mehring, banned from leaving France by decision of the Kundt Commission).

He called the prefecture, and ten minutes later, he gave back to me my papers and said smiling: *"C'est peut-être un autre Walter Mehring. Partez!"* (Maybe it's another Walter Mehring. Go!)[66]

In his memoirs, out of either a flair for the dramatic or the channeling of a personal recollection that does not appear in Mehring's account, Fry depicts the police officer winking as he says, "Go!" to Mehring.[67] Wink or no wink, this police chief appears twice to have made deliberate efforts to convey to Mehring that he, as a French official, was willfully infringing the rules—first by conspicuously displaying his order to Mehring, and then by concocting an improbable double of the Jewish poet. The fact that he called the prefecture is equally significant, as Breitscheid, Hilferding, and others learned of the Martinique vessels through this route, and one can therefore deduce a level of complicity within prefectures.

Alfred and Friedel Kantorowicz's experience closely mirrors Mehring's. Alfred Kantorowicz was a German Jewish lawyer, writer, and publicist. A day before boarding the *Paul Lemerle,* the couple went to the *police maritime* with their valid visas for America. The Seghers-Radvanyi couple had just completed the task and assured the Kantorowiczes that it constituted a "mere formality." However, the police officer reviewing the Kantorowiczes' papers promptly found Alfred's name on a list (no doubt the Kundt list) and announced that he was under arrest. "This is the end, they will throw me in jail then deliver to me to the Gestapo," Alfred despaired. He then gathered his courage to utter a last-ditch name drop: "Colonel Riverdi said he spoke of us to you." The officer raised his eyes, responded with an enigmatic "Ah, so it's you," stamped their visas, and told them to "scram."[68] Clearly, as in the Malaquais-Yurkevitch case, contacts had helped the Kantorowicz couple immensely.

Meanings

Beyond this, how can one account for the acts of administrative disobedience or complicity we have just encountered in the Mehring and Kantorowicz cases? One answer hinges on bureaucratic obstruction as a kind of "art of resistance." In this scenario, a high-ranking police officer, perhaps the very same person, was turning a blind eye to both Mehring and Kantorowicz on the basis of connections and perhaps convictions. The main challenge to this theory is that ignoring the Kundt Commission's wanted list represented no small infringement of the rules. Was this a risk the police would knowingly run multiple times?

That individual Vichy bureaucrats like Esmiol and the anonymous policeman were taking personal risks in letting some refugees go seems evidenced by Ministry of the Colonies correspondence from April 7, 1941. On that day, Minister Charles Platon complained that some refugees were reaching Martinique with unsigned exit visas. Platon fumed that all such paperwork needed to be signed by both the prefect and the subprefect of the department from which the traveler had departed (in this instance, the Bouches-du-Rhône in Marseille).[69] As in the case of Mehring, who was given an unsigned release from Le Vernet, this seems likely to have constituted an oppositional bureaucratic practice. Indeed, more evidence of deliberately lax passport controls at the point of departure can be found in a March 2, 1941, telegram from Admiral Georges Robert in Martinique. He complained that some passengers on the Marseille–Casablanca line continued to arrive in Fort-de-France with the intention of reaching the United States, but without any US authorization in hand.[70]

The profiles of people being allowed to board for Fort-de-France in Marseille in 1941 also point to either negligence or complicity. Victor Serge provides an obvious example. Richard Greeman reminds us that as the revolutionary desperately sought to leave Stalin's clutches in 1935 and 1936, "Serge was [already] considered an undesirable subversive by all the chancelleries of Europe."[71] His subversiveness had not diminished four years later. Indeed, in September 1940, Serge's American sponsors even hinted that Fry's ERC might be dragging its heels on the Serge file because of his politics.[72] As Rosemary Sullivan has chronicled, Serge contacted his benefactors in February 1941. His letter was tantamount to an about-face: he no longer required authorization to enter the United States, as he would be departing for Martinique, and hopefully, from there, he would continue on to Mexico.[73] This came to pass, as Serge left Marseille aboard the *Paul Lemerle*. However, in theory at least, the German authorities had no say over a Belgian national like Serge leaving Vichy French territory in 1941.

It was quite another matter for German refugees. At least in principle, their departure was subject to Nazi approval.

As it happens, many prominent anti-Nazi German refugees were being exfiltrated to Martinique under Vichy agents' eyes. Let us consider four of them in turn. Lothar Popp (1887–1980) definitely fits in this category. He was a Marxist revolutionary and coleader of the famous Kiel mutinies that rocked Germany days before the end of the First World War. When the Nazis were voted into office in Germany in 1933, Popp left for Prague; after they entered Czechoslovakia in 1938, he decamped to Paris; after they invaded Paris, he headed to the unoccupied zone. It is believed that in 1940 he herded sheep in southern France before finding his way onto one of the last ships from Marseille to Martinique, the *Winnipeg*, in 1941. According to family history, Popp made his way on board through contacts with French sailors—an intriguing point if one thinks of his past role leading naval mutinies in Germany during the First World War.[74]

Josef Weber (1901–1959) presents a somewhat similar profile and was likewise wanted by the Nazis. A leading Trotskyite, he was part of the exile group known as the International Communists of Germany, a splinter revolutionary organization founded in November 1918. Weber fled for Paris in 1933, where he published in the exile press under the pseudonym Johre—one of many noms de plume he would adopt over the course of his life. He fought the Nazis with his pen, even advocating a break from Marxist orthodoxy when he recommended supporting German religious groups that were standing up to Hitler. Weber managed to escape a French internment camp and made for Marseille after the fall of France. From there, he too found his way onto one of the last cargo ships to Martinique in 1941.[75] Popp and Weber would both try to spirit the legacy of Rosa Luxemburg overseas (with varying success: Weber would wield influence in US anarchist and ecological circles, while Popp settled into the educational toys and sweets trade). The point here, however, is that as militant German anti-Nazis, they were both marked men, but they were nevertheless allowed to board for Martinique.

Erika Biermann provides a third example of someone the Nazis would have preferred to capture than see leave for safer shores. Biermann was the daughter and sole surviving child of Hermann Müller. A Social Democrat, Müller had served as foreign minister of the Weimar Republic, and he was one of the men who signed the Treaty of Versailles on behalf of Germany.

Hitler considered the treaty to be an ignominious stab in the back and its German signatories traitors. Biermann managed to flee Paris for the South of France in 1940. In Arles, she worked for a time as Breitscheid's secretary. Unlike her employer, she was able to board the *Winnipeg* in 1941.[76]

Last but not least, German Social Democratic parliamentarian Emil Kirschmann had fervently fought the Nazis during their rise to power. He fled first for autonomous Saarland in 1933, then, after its absorption by Germany in a 1935 referendum, he left for France. There he pursued his activism in the German exile community. In Marseille in March 1941, Fry paid Kirschmann to bribe an official to get hold of the famous Kundt Commission list of wanted Germans—Fry was desperate to know which refugees featured on the list. In all likelihood, Kirschmann experienced the unpleasant feeling of finding himself on it. What happened next remains hazy. Friedlander relates that in 1941 Kirschmann was initially denied an exit visa by Vichy, but that a mysterious French colonel had him discreetly ushered aboard the *Paul Lemerle,* bound for Martinique. Another source claims that Kirschmann was helped on board the *Paul Lemerle* by Fritz Heine, the German Social Democrat who worked for Fry's ERC.[77]

All of this seems to point in the direction of individual Vichy officials choosing to turn a blind eye. Or perhaps, as Fry has hinted, it betrays the limits of German knowledge of German opposition members in the free zone?[78] The many cases just listed, especially that of Lothar Popp, also raise the possibility that these desperate people eluded not only German authorities but Vichy ones as well. Simon Kitson suggests that access to Marseille's dock perimeter was far easier than the regime would have liked, although he adds that "stringent security identity controls" awaited passengers immediately before boarding.[79]

An alternative, and not necessarily contradictory, theory runs as follows: Vichy's police agents in Marseille, perhaps even Esmiol, were acting in accordance with Vichy's Interior Ministry, and were actually obeying rather than disobeying their superiors at Vichy. The notion seems to be supported by the phone call Mehring describes. If one combines that phone call with the undisputed fact that prefectorial agents were the ones directing many of the refugees onto the ships for Martinique, and that the Interior Ministry championed the Martinique route, one is tempted to see in the departures the realization of Peyrouton's memorandum. This theory is strengthened by the fact that in 1940 and 1941, Vichy successfully consolidated police forces under a national, prefectorial purview (historian Jean-Marc Berlière has noted the pushback from police chiefs loath to finding themselves ordered around by prefects).[80]

Perhaps the most compelling evidence for a clear and direct continuation of Peyrouton's plan comes from the files of Harry and Maria Kriszhaber. Both were Austrian Jews. Although little is known of Maria's trajectory, Harry was a leading trade unionist who had spent time on a kibbutz in Palestine. His ERC file indicates that his work brought him in direct conflict with the Nazis.[81] Like the Barth-Flake family, the Kriszhabers found refuge in Montauban in 1940. There they contacted Fry's ERC. Early in 1941, the organization learned that the Montauban prefecture was asking who, among the refugees with visas for the Americas, would be willing to participate in a "collective departure" via Martinique. On February 18, 1941, the Montauban prefecture wrote to Harry Kriszhaber directly. The phrasing is worth quoting: "I have the honor of informing you that in view of an imminent collective departure of emigrants, you are to be sent to Marseille with your family. . . . Please present yourself to the Montauban train station on February 25 at 11 am. An escort will await you, holding your passport and your exit visa."[82] The letter was signed and stamped by the prefecture of Tarn-et-Garonne.

Anne Klein has taken this correspondence to mean that the couple was *expelled* to Martinique in February 1941.[83] There is the rub. In many ways, the letter does sound like a notice of expulsion. It stipulates that papers will be retained by the authorities until the last minute, that an escort is to accompany the couple, and that they are to "be sent" to Marseille rather than travel of their own volition. In fact, correctional conditions prevailed until they left: Harry was interned briefly at Les Milles (which drew protests from the ERC), while Maria was allowed to stay at the Hôtel Terminus.[84] This was typical of the different treatment that Vichy meted out to male and female refugees. The point is, however, that if this was expulsion, it was also timely and welcome. Indeed, the couple no doubt greeted news of their departure to Martinique with leaps of joy, for they had of course asked to leave, and Fry had explored multiple options for them. The couple finally sailed to Martinique at the end of March 1941, on the *Paul Lemerle*. That the Tarn-et-Garonne prefecture sent them a detailed notice clearly points to the Ministry of the Interior's ongoing involvement in directing migrants to Martinique. Quite apart from that, however, this case once more raises the question of whether the Martinique route constituted rescue or expulsion, or perhaps a blend of both, a point to which I will return.

To the many examples of prefectorial complicity listed here I should add the case of the Seghers-Radvanyi family. Both Anna Seghers and her son Pierre Radvanyi were persuaded that a female bureaucrat at the Marseille prefecture had deliberately assisted them in their exit procedures.[85] Seghers recounts this woman's role as follows in *Transit:*

> At the prefecture there was a woman, an official, who was working on my documents, she helped me. She was odd-looking, small and fat, but her eyes were kind, the sort of kindness I've never encountered before in this country. And she helped everybody. She gave them advice and helped them solve their problems. No file was too complicated for her. You sensed immediately that this woman was ready to help anyone and everyone, that she wanted to make sure we could all get out in time so that no one would fall into the hands of the Germans or end up in some concentration camp and die there for no reason at all. . . . You see, she was one of those people because of whom an entire people will be saved.[86]

Clearly, to Seghers, this functionary was acting of her own volition in going beyond the call of duty. Her son adds that this female official was "discreet and sympathetic."[87] Discretion also seems to imply transgression. And yet, one registers similar cases of aid and support in other prefectures, such as Arles' and Montauban's. Cumulatively, the many cases of complicity across multiple prefectures, and the dummy form that Vichy sent to officials to grant exit visas, lend credence to the idea of a continuation of Peyrouton's plan.

One problem with this theory is that it fails to account for why Breitscheid and Hilferding were then arrested and handed over to the Nazis. Another is that it flies in the face of one of Fry and Daniel Bénédite's recollections: they concur that German Jewish production engineer Heinz-Ernst Oppenheimer first brought the Martinique boats to the ERC's attention. Fry adds that "the prefecture gave him the visas . . . on the solemn promise that he wouldn't tell a soul about it."[88] Bénédite remembers Oppenheimer stating that the ships were in theory reserved for Vichy personnel, both civilian and military, heading to the French West Indies.[89] Allowing a refugee on board was therefore conceived as a favor, granted on an individual, exceptional basis. All of this is more consistent with the idea of individual initiative, in keeping with Seghers' account.

Another problem with the complicity thesis involves multiple allegations, including one by Serge, that Vichy officials pocketed money from an illegal traffic in exit visas to Martinique. The contention runs completely contrary to Pierre Radvanyi's recollections.[90] Of course, it is possible that some were asked for bribes and others were not, and it is also conceivable that Serge simply considered the 9,000 franc deposit a swindle.[91] However, Krull too mentions a "shady scheme" (*combine*) involving payment for the Martinique line. In her words, "I had to hand out a considerable number of thousand franc bills, left and right, before being able to board the boat. Finally, I got a place on a freighter that left Marseille for Martinique." She adds that "exploitation" of helpless refugees was occurring "on a large scale."[92] Then again, in some instances venality could also prove to be a godsend, as when a friend of ERC liaison officer and German Socialist Bedrich Heine succeeded in purchasing the Kundt Commission's list of wanted German nationals from the prefecture in Pau (Kirschmann did the same, of course, but the list evolved and the ERC needed to stay on top of additions to it).[93]

Expulsion or Rescue?

Regardless of whether it was collective or individual, venal or voluntary, complicity in aiding departures certainly was not in itself a marker of humanitarianism. Consider the following tirade that a Marseille policeman directs at the narrator in Seghers' semifictional *Transit,* a harangue that rings particularly true: "In a grim fury he told me that the Bouches-du-Rhône *département* was overpopulated, and the regulations required me to leave the country as soon as possible, and that I could retain my freedom only on condition that I at once book passage on a ship, any ship whatsoever. I should understand, he said, that French cities aren't there for me to live in, but for me to leave from."[94] Here the exclusionary part of Peyrouton's scheme resurfaces. Just as the Kriszhabers were directed to Marseille by an escort, so too did this policeman do more than merely "invite" refugees to depart.

For all of the help that he received from Esmiol, Fry, and others, including the port policeman, Mehring also believed that he had been expelled. Although he perceived the irony in this, he did not necessarily view the two logics as contradictory. He described having to turn in all of his existing paperwork in Marseille—his *carte de séjour* request and even his fake passport with a visa for the Belgian Congo—in exchange for a "little slip of paper with a number in blue ink, the purple stamp of the 'Sureté Nationale' and the machine typed visa: 'Valid for one departure.'" He wrote of then boarding the *Wyoming* with "the soggy paper of '*Refoulement*' on me, an expulsion that was the object of jealousy of thousands." He added, "It is true, I almost envied myself the chance to be expelled."[95]

In fact, one finds this exclusionary thread running through the Martinique route from start to finish. The situation on board the cargoes to Martinique, as well as the prevailing conditions upon arrival, only serves to confirm that this was both a convoy of "undesirables" and a relief effort, at once an expulsion and a rescue. In other words, to many officials, and in Vichy's rhetoric, how and where the "undesirables" went was a matter of little concern, so long as they left mainland France.

One of the passengers on the Martinique-bound *Winnipeg* in 1941—the ship that the Dutch would intercept off Trinidad, bringing an end to the Martinique corridor—also used the language of expulsion. Raymond Sallé was no refugee; he was bound home for Vichy-controlled Indochina from metropolitan France. Seeing his stay in France unduly extended because of the war, Sallé paid a personal visit to minister of the colonies, Rear Admiral Platon. Platon proved helpful, placing him on board the *Winnipeg*, which, in his own words, "would transport to Martinique . . . 700 Jews who had been *expelled* from France" (emphasis mine). If Sallé accurately remembered Platon's phrasing, this would constitute additional proof of the project's exclusionary nature.[96]

On the opposite side of the ideological spectrum, the reflection of the ERC's Bénédite on the Martinique route yields two central points: first, that it was a deliberately planned Vichy outlet, and, second, that it was largely designed as a way of ridding France of undesirables. His memoirs interpret the Martinique-bound vessels as follows: "Vichy thought it over and decided that there was no point in keeping in France foreigners who could leave it." He adds that, admittedly, those who got to Martinique "only represented a small percentage of those Vichy considered to be 'extra mouths to feed' but it would not be so bad to get rid of a few of them so long as they wanted to leave." Besides, Bénédite reasoned, so long as Vichy officials were not granting exit visas to German nationals listed by the Kundt Commission, the entire project did not violate the rules of the armistice agreement.[97]

Does the fact that Vichy's Ministry of the Interior saw in the Martinique route a divine opportunity[98] to rid France of undesirables alter our perception of Seghers' complicit prefecture employee, of Esmiol, or of Mehring's winking policeman? Assuredly not. They can certainly be seen in the same light as some of the low-ranking administrative heroes identified by Julian Jackson, such as Auguste Boyer, the camp guard at Les Milles who helped inmates escape in 1942.[99] The point here is that at the entry point of the Martinique corridor, motivations varied, while moral imperatives both collided and coalesced.

Ultimately, polyglot avant-garde photographer Krull may have best explained the range of reactions would-be emigrants encountered from Vichy authorities. As a Dutch-Franco-German Communist bisexual artist who sought to join de Gaulle's Free French, Krull was especially keen to leave France. She succeeded in obtaining a Brazilian visa and passage on board the *Paul Lemerle* to Martinique. She wrote, "Marseille resembles an immense fairground where suspect scams and the hope of mutual aid seem to coexist. Everything is possible here: one policeman risks his career to help you leave, while another does not hesitate to hand an escaped French soldier over to the Germans. . . . There are those who do everything to help young people leave to freedom and those who toss young Poles and Belgians in jail for wanting to reach England."[100] To Krull, at least, the vast gamut of human behavior distilled in Marseille during this time of crisis exerted a greater influence on the fate of refugees than any orders issued from above.

Serge, who also boarded the *Paul Lemerle* for Martinique with his half-Jewish son Vlady, reached a slightly different conclusion in May 1941. Where Krull saw individual agency as the decisive factor, Serge perceived a vast bureaucracy divided into two camps. He wrote that Fry "earned the dangerous hostility of the Gestapo and of Nazified [French] officials." "Fortunately," he added, "an opposite current also exists in the [French] administration."[101] Like many others in the crosshairs, Serge painted a Manichean picture: he perceived one clique of bad Vichyites, another of good ones. However, the evidence given here suggests that shades of gray might be more aptly used to depict the episode. Certainly, some officials helped while others did not, but the point remains that Vichy's Interior Ministry encouraged and even organized refugee departures to Martinique, and that inciting departure was not necessarily a sign of benevolence, despite what we now know to be the fate of refugees left behind in southern France in 1942.

An Ambiguous Plan

This brings us to the case of Jacques Schiffrin. Born in Baku in 1892 to secular Jewish parents of Portuguese and Alsatian ancestry, he emigrated in the wake of the Russian Revolution. Schiffrin arrived in Paris in 1922 and a year later founded what would become one of the most influential book series in France, the Pléiade. Schiffrin obtained French citizenship in 1927.[102] By 1931, the Pléiade was publishing handsomely bound classics that became its trademark, as well as new works, most notably those of André Gide. Five years later the Russian-speaking Schiffrin would accompany Gide on his eye-opening visit of the Soviet Union. In 1935, Gallimard publishing house purchased the Pléiade. Under German pressure, on November 5, 1940, Gaston Gallimard summarily fired Schiffrin.[103] Schiffrin and his family then fled the occupied zone and found refuge on the Riviera. On February 19, 1941, Schiffrin requested exit visas and his family's entry to the United States. In his application, he indicated that he had lost his only means of subsistence—his book series—and wished to join his sister and friends in New York.[104]

This sets the stage for Schiffrin's May 2, 1941, letter to Gide. He recounts having been summoned to Marseille's prefecture so as to take the scheduled May 15 boat for Martinique. However, upon arrival in Marseille, he encountered "a new kind of torture." He elaborates, "Things get done, then they are undone the very same day: which is to say that when one administrative hurdle has been passed, and one is lucky enough to gather all the paperwork necessary to take the boat (visas, tickets, passports etc), the very next hurdle topples everything achieved up to then, and all is lost!"[105] Leaving for Martinique seemed a Sisyphean test. And yet Schiffrin, his wife, and his son, did finally board the Martinique-bound *Wyoming,* as planned, on May 15, 1941. Schiffrin's son André recalled longshoremen hurling anti-Semitic slurs at the departing travelers. Lévi-Strauss shared similar memories of boarding the *Paul Lemerle.*[106] The *Wyoming* would subsequently be waylaid at Casablanca after the Dutch intercepted the *Winnipeg.*

The Schiffrin saga suggests once more a combination of factors at work: he was aided by Fry's ERC, but he also surfed on the prefectorial wave that carried so many to Martinique via Marseille.[107] And yet, even as one administrative branch opened doors, others seemed to slam them shut, in a classic case of bureaucratic chaos. As far as escape corridors go, this one proved supremely tricky, with setbacks and pitfalls at every turn. And, as it happens, Schiffrin took the very last wartime boat from Marseille bound for Martinique.

The risk of teleology is particularly acute when considering escape from unoccupied France before the Holocaust. The fact is that few knew what to make of the Martinique route at the time. Beyond luck, connections, and determination, refugees themselves were unclear as to how precisely they gained safe passage while many others did not. Did they know what missing the boat could mean for them?

Avoiding drawing historical straight lines that lead inexorably toward the Holocaust is certainly important. Yet it would be preposterous to contend that the refugees who committed suicide after being blocked at the Spanish border, or who threw every name they knew in the balance to leave for America, or who handed their children over to relief organizations, and, for that matter, the Vichy officials who evoked an epic humanitarian crisis, were somehow unaware that ominous threats loomed for Jewish and antifascist refugees alike even in southern France in 1941. The crowding of refugees and competition among them in Marseille also intensified feelings of panic. Everyone seemed to understand that the stakes were high. German Jewish lawyer Alfred Apfel died of a heart attack in Fry's office in February 1941, minutes after the American warned him that he should keep a low profile in Marseille given that he "had been an outspoken" critic of Hitler's.[108] Nazi representatives of the armistice commission visited Vichy camps and demanded that German émigrés be transferred to their custody; rumors abounded that Vichy would hand Spanish Republicans over to Franco. Vichy also denaturalized Jews at a breakneck pace, rendering them stateless and intensely vulnerable. French scientists aiding the Rockefeller Foundation to rescue their colleagues in October 1940 had already drawn up contingency plans in the event that the Nazis invaded the southern zone.[109]

And so those who could leave let out a huge sigh of relief as they boarded for Martinique, despite and perhaps partly because of the invective directed at them as they departed. Helena Benitez registered the following emotions among her fellow passengers as they embarked on the *Paul Lemerle:* "There were some tears among the refugees, but mostly joyful exuberance. They had managed to outwit Hitler."[110] Ultimately, thanks to this unexpected and tragically short escape window, thousands made it to what they rightly considered safer shores.

Yet things were not always as they appeared. Frida Kahn, who lambasted French bureaucrats, wrongly believed that Fry and the Joint Distribution Committee "had persuaded the French authorities to make a few freighters available to transport those with American visas to Martinique, where they could board a ship for the United States."[111] In fact, Fry and the committee understood neither the Martinique route's origins nor the Ministry of the Interior's promotion of it, and they were certainly in no way responsible for it.

Meanwhile, the officials who pressed for the Martinique route within the ministry in question in 1940 and 1941 couched their plan in humanitarian terms, to be sure, but also in xenophobic ones. To them, the Martinique route represented a relief valve designed to rid France of undesirables that had swarmed the nation. Here we may have an institutional-level equivalent of Renée Poznanski's point that for many individuals in wartime France, anti-Semitism and Jewish rescue were not necessarily incompatible.[112]

The invective directed at the Schiffrins as they departed, much like the cold welcome that awaited the migrants in tropical Martinique, would confirm to many that this was more of a mass expulsion of undesirables than a concerted rescue effort. To say that the escape route lacked clarity would be an understatement. Itself the embodiment of an early Vichy, or at least an early Vichy solution to a refugee crisis, the Martinique route simultaneously displayed the tropes of racist expulsion and rescue, professed humanitarianism and manifest indifference.

CHAPTER FOUR

The Crossings

W HO PRECISELY WERE THE MEN, women, and children so desperate to set sail from Marseille in 1940–1941? We have seen that the motley group of refugees defies simple categorization. They included anti-Nazi Germans and Austrians, Spanish Republicans and International Brigade members from Spain bound for South or Central America, European Jews, and dissident artists and intellectuals, not to mention "regular" patrons of the Marseille-to-Martinique line. Many travelers fit into more than one of these categories, of course.

One such overlapping example can be found in the Masson family. Hierarchies of danger are easier to determine in hindsight. Obviously, both Jewish refugees and prominent anti-Nazis found themselves at special risk even in unoccupied France in 1941. Again, some families appeared in both columns. Diego Masson, son of Surrealist painter André Masson and his Jewish wife, Rose Masson (née Maklès), recalls feeling, rather counterintuitively, that the whole family fled, first to Marseille in 1940, then to Martinique aboard the *Carimaré* in early April 1941, more on account of the devastating caricatures that André Masson had done of Adolf Hitler, Francisco Franco, and Benito Mussolini than of the family's partially Jewish descent.[1] Indeed, all Surrealists considered themselves at risk because the movement had been at war since the 1920s with ultranationalists such as Action Française militants. After all, Surrealism promoted revolt and insubordination among its core values, as well as the desire to "let the subconscious speak." Surrealists also sought to challenge notions of obscenity and to topple bourgeois conventions.[2]

Then again, Diego Masson casts doubt on his father's political instincts when he relates that André Masson had chosen to live in Spain in the 1930s because it seemed a land that neither war nor fascism could ever reach.[3] In any event, Varian Fry's ERC appears to have shared André Masson's logic concerning the prime reason for their leaving Europe. A November 14, 1940 letter from the ERC's Ingrid Warburg to American authorities reads, "Because of his courageous attitude against Fascism there is no doubt that [Masson] would be in real danger were he caught by the Nazis. Therefore I hope that a visitor's visa may be granted to Mr. Masson as soon as possible."[4] One thing is clear: the Masson family, especially Rose, were doggedly persistent. Fry complained of what he called the "tantrums" (*crises de nerfs*) that she and especially family friend and famed psychoanalyst Jacques Lacan threw in the ERC's Marseille offices to ensure the Massons' eventual departure for Martinique.[5]

As the Masson example suggests, the constellation of people on board the ships to Martinique was nothing short of remarkable. The politically committed Germano-Franco-Dutch modernist photographer Germaine Krull has left a vivid recollection of her passage to Martinique, and of the refugees on board the *Paul Lemerle:*

> Almost without exception, all of the passengers are cultivated people, learned and occupying important social ranks: doctors, lawyers, a professor of philosophy, famous authors like André Breton with his wife and young daughter, Victor Serge and his son. Painters like the renowned Cuban Fernandez Lam [*sic;* should read Wifredo Lam], two German archeologist celebrities, well-known German writers, the son of a Mexican ambassador, an elderly German gentleman who is the sole specialist in his branch of medicine . . . a former Catalan minister with his wife and children, Jacques Rémy, a French filmmaker, the famous operator of the Curt Courant cinema,[6] a German ex-banker and his wife, the former owner of a factory in Bavaria, and a series of young people of all nationalities.[7]

Krull's observations give a sense of the mix of people on board, and especially of the elitist dimension of this route to freedom.

Art specialist John Russell has dubbed the crossing on the *Paul Lemerle* a "Who's Who of a European elite that might otherwise have perished in German custody."[8] This elitist aspect should come as no surprise. After all, migrants underwent more or less formal vetting procedures in order to leave unoccupied France: interviews with consulates, visa acquisition, deposits, the purchase of expensive permits, and, for some, passage through the filters of Fry's ERC, whose mandate involved rescuing celebrities. Moreover, departure was expensive. Daniel Bénédite relates the existence of a Marseille black market in tickets to Martinique; in the back alleys of the Vieux Port, passage to Fort-de-France sold for a fortune.[9] Even on the regular market, transatlantic voyages cost upwards of four times more after the fall of France than they had previously.[10]

Also uniting many of the passengers was their common victimization by Fascists and Nazis. Revolutionary Serge described his shipmates on board the *Paul Lemerle* as follows:

> We arrived in Martinique in the last days of April 1941. . . . Us: that is to say three hundred refugees from Europe. A little over two hundred [of them] reduced to fleeing the old continent only because they belong to the people who gave the world Christ, Spinoza, Marx, and Freud: the Jews. Many reactionaries amongst them, incidentally. . . . A little under a hundred revolutionaries filled with the memories of their grand struggles and all their defeats, full of hope nonetheless. Heroic defenders of Madrid, fighters of Teruel and of the Asturies, militants from Barcelona, the first soldiers of this Second World War and of the European Revolution; German and Austrian socialists who leave behind them working houses in Vienna attacked by Dollfuss [Engelbert Dollfuss], Hitler's concentration camps and the tombs of comrades decapitated with axes or hanged in Dachau's cells; survivors of the purges in Russia and of murders everywhere, doggedly faithful and clairvoyant towards the Russian Revolution. Together, we know all totalitarian regimes, in a sense, all of the jails, all types of suffering and death, all of their plans for global domination.[11]

To Serge, the boat was nothing short of a microcosm of anti-Nazi, antifascist, and anti-Stalinist defiance. Interestingly, Serge suggests that of the roughly 230 refugees on board the *Paul Lemerle,* some two-thirds were Jewish. Serge further portrayed the ship as "an ersatz concentration camp of the sea,"[12] referring no doubt at once to the stark accommodations and the fact that so many Jewish refugees and Hitler opponents were on board. Similarly, describing the recently arrived refugees in Martinique, an informant of US journalist Nicol Smith insisted that "most of the refugees are Jewish."[13] Pierre Radvanyi, conversely, remembers a majority of Spanish political refugees on the *Paul Lemerle.*

For his part, satirist and poet Walter Mehring, aboard the *Wyoming,* which set sail for Martinique on February 1, 1941, divided passengers into political, rather than national or religious, typologies. He broke down the Spanish refugees on board as follows: "Republicans, Communists, POUM [Trotskyite] people, Anarchists, Royalists, Catalan separatists, all of them noble."[14] Another testimony considered passengers by profession, noting the high number of doctors and dentists (sixty, if this testimony is to be believed) aboard the *Winnipeg* in May 1941.[15] Multiple narratives afford additional insights into the diversity of nationalities aboard the *Paul Lemerle.* Breton counted "Germans, Austrians, Czechs, Spaniards and only a few French people."[16] Film writer Jacques Rémy entered into greater detail on the same crossing. He identified "German refugees who had just left concentration camps and who preferred France to Germany, and America to France."[17]

Next Rémy turned to the tragic cases of those who boarded only to be refused passage. He described "Spanish women who saw, on the demand of Franco's embassy, their husbands prevented from joining them at the last minute." He added, "They left alone, their kids in tow, desperate and brave at once."[18] The *New York Times* covered the same sorry episode, relating that "many of the refugees, who all had passports with valid exit visas, sobbed as they were ordered ashore. Only seventeen women and fifteen men escaped the ban."[19]

Of course, Spanish Republicans had been allowed to sail on other boats to Martinique. Aboard the *Wyoming,* which set sail in February 1941, René Hauth wrote his family, sharing details about his fellow passengers. Hauth was an Alsatian journalist and member of the French intelligence services who sought to reach the New World so as better to serve the anti-Nazi cause. In a letter dated February 6, 1941, he described the *Wyoming* coming within sight of Barcelona. The ship drew close enough to shore that passengers were able to make out the city's statue of Christopher Columbus. At that point, many of the Spaniards on board who had been "ruthlessly chased out" of Spain by Franco showed signs of bearing a "heavy heart."[20]

Hauth established typologies of his own in a subsequent letter to his loved ones, dated February 12, 1941. He explained that there were "two categories of people on board" the *Wyoming:* "first those who were told to leave, next those who had to move heaven and earth to leave." He added that the two groups "do not mix." To Hauth, the first category, interestingly, included only French officials being sent to the Caribbean. Among the second category, of course, he listed Jews seeking the safety of the Americas, but also Venezuelan and Columbian families that had been waiting to return home since the fall of France in 1940, as well as people like him who were wishing to continue the struggle.[21]

Another group aboard the *Paul Lemerle* Rémy labeled "Czechs and Poles who had left their countries to fight in France." These people were seeking to pursue the war from Canada or South Africa. Like Hauth, Rémy also pointed out South Americans who had long resided in France and decided that the time had come to leave, as well as Belgians and Dutch nationals, and "finally a handful of Frenchmen like myself." Rémy believed the oldest passenger on board the *Paul Lemerle* to be eighty-two years old (Krull estimated that he was eighty-three): this retired doctor "was German and had known Kaiser Wilhelm's court." Rémy drew individual portraits as well: one of them was a Jewish theology professor from Silesia who spent the trip reading a massive Hebrew tome. Rémy provided another snapshot, of a Czech engineer who had worked in the armament sector and now wished to bring his knowledge across the Atlantic to help Canada or the United States. The engineer "was much admired on board," specified Rémy, for he won all of the chess tournaments organized during the crossing.[22]

Of all these accounts of the crossing, Claude Lévi-Strauss' is among the most detailed, chronicling everything from the overcrowding of the *Paul Lemerle* to its lack of sanitary facilities. The anthropologist's eye affords some attention to a handful of fellow passengers, drawing remarkable portraits of Breton and Serge in particular. As one of only four men to be granted a bunk in a proper cabin, Lévi-Strauss was clearly conscious of being among the privileged. But he was largely mute on the rest of the passengers, save for a wealthy Martinican Creole, an Austrian industrialist, and a North African Jew traveling with a Degas painting (although he does not name him, this appears to have been Henri Smadja, the future director of the resistance newspaper *Combat*).[23] Lévi-Strauss also does not much delve into the mood on board. Given that the crossing took weeks and in several cases more than a month, one would have assumed that passengers would have had ample time to mingle. When I queried Lévi-Strauss about this silence, he explained, "So as to overcome the promiscuity around us, we created small, inward-looking groups, rather than make outside contacts."[24]

This instinct to form groups may also have reflected a certain amount of suspicion on board, for there was no certainty about having escaped harm's way. Indeed, one had to tread carefully before bringing up politics on the deck. In Anna Seghers' novel *Transit,* one character relates being warned by the lady in Marseille's prefecture that Vichy spies lurked on board. In this rendition some Spanish Republicans were even yanked off the ships in Casablanca after their presence was detected. In the tale Seghers relates, a mere smile from one Spaniard's sister had confirmed to a spy that her Republican sibling had boarded.[25]

Fear was everywhere. Even some of the refugees who made it on board still felt tracked, hunted, or followed. A decade after his escape via Martinique, Mehring wrote of "the name of the tyrant which had echoed from every radio and every headline and had pursued [him] from country to country, from dream to dream, all the way across the ocean to the Antilles and the American continent."[26] Conversely, in 1997, Lévi-Strauss remembered feeling as if he was "out of harm's way" as soon as his ship left Marseille's harbor in 1941.[27]

A document preserved in the Martinique archives lends further credence to the notion that passengers on the Fort-de-France line were routinely spied on, or at least denounced. Emerci Parthos (or Parkos; the name appears with both spellings) was a Rumanian Jew, traveling from Marseille back to his home in Tahiti via Martinique aboard the *Paul Lemerle* in December 1940. Tahiti had recently joined General Charles de Gaulle's Free French, and passengers heading there attracted suspicion as a matter of course. What is interesting about the Parthos case is that he was prevented from leaving Fort-de-France, on the basis of testimony provided by at least one fellow passenger on the *Paul Lemerle.* Parthos was accused of having uttered "tendentious" opinions about Vichy. The naval report recommending his internment, signed Colonel Quenardel, added that he and his wife were not only Jewish but also Freemasons. It concluded that they were also favorable to General de Gaulle.[28]

To genuine spies we should add amateur or even fanciful ones. Breton recounts that on the vessel that followed his, the *Carimaré,* the ship staff, with no better entertainment available, had decided to pose as German secret policemen so as to terrify and torment the migrants on board.[29] Of course, Seghers' story is semifictional, and Breton's is secondhand, possibly conveyed by André Masson. What is more, Breton's anecdote needs to be read against other evidence. A May 1941 document from Martinique, for instance, shows two of the sailors of the *Carimaré,* both hailing from Le Havre in Normandy, being severely punished for having aided one of their comrades to desert to the Allies.[30]

Whether the spies were real or imagined, fear of them, the condition the French call *espionnite,* was alive and well on board, as well as on shore. There was in fact good reason for discretion. Bertrand Goldschmidt was one of the passengers aboard the *Carimaré* in 1941. From Martinique, he would reach the United States, then, in 1942, Montréal. There, as part of an Anglo-Canadian team, he would become one of a handful of Frenchmen to work on an aspect of the Manhattan Project that created the first nuclear bombs. Later he would spearhead the Centre d'énergie atomique and France's own nuclear program. In his memoirs, he recounts being denounced in 1941 by a fellow traveler on the *Carimaré*. The denunciation had nothing to do with secret nuclear projects, or with anything scientific for that matter. Upon arrival in Fort-de-France, Vichy's police thoroughly searched him and his belongings, insisting that he had in his possession a copy of former French prime minister Léon Blum's 1907 progressive marriage manual. He did not, and in fact he had never owned one. Goldschmidt deduced that he must have been denounced, one can surmise perhaps out of anti-Semitic association with Blum, or maybe for reading some other book on board.[31] The winds of freedom did not exactly sweep the decks of these ships, nor wartime Martinique for that matter.

Meanwhile, Serge's and Rémy's wonderfully detailed accounts of the *Paul Lemerle*'s crossing confirm Lévi-Strauss' point that passengers congregated in small groups. Arguably, it was Rémy who most profoundly reflected on the social experiment that the crossing constituted. Despite its chaotic layout, "the deck belongs to everyone," noted Rémy optimistically. He promptly realized, however, that "instinctively people immediately formed into groups according to tastes, tendencies and origins." Despite sharing food, experiences, and fates, despite the soot covering everyone on deck, thereby "discouraging elegance," despite the fact that there was nothing to purchase on board, "differences have surfaced just as they do on shore." Rémy's verdict was unequivocal: "Even for an instant, a community of equals has proven impossible."[32]

According to both Rémy and Serge, the penguin-like clusters of passengers were divided according to gender, generation, occupation, and social rank. Mothers with children occupied the front of the deck. Another group was composed of card players and chess players. Those whom Rémy calls "snobs" and those Serge terms *Wirtschaftsemigrenten* (economic migrants) congregated by the captain's quarters on a part of the ship soon named the "Champs Elysées." Businessmen gathered in the ship's center. Among them, Rémy singles out a diamond dealer from Antwerp. High atop the boat, near the chimneystack and the lifeboats, German exiles fleeing Hitler congregated at "Montparnasse." At the back of the ship, Serge describes "jolly and boisterous Spaniards," in an area dubbed "Belleville."[33] Travelers reproduced Paris' socioeconomic divisions to a T, cloning its geography of power.

Serge chronicles how difficult it was to build bridges across these spaces. He attempted to engage a "touching bourgeois couple" in conversation. Harmless chitchat seemed to go well until formal introductions began. At that point, the gentleman proceeded to present himself as a Catholic Austrian banker protected by the Vatican, heading to Brazil. Serge responded with the short version of the truth: "I am a friend of Mr. Trotsky's." As Serge relates the episode, an "ah" of acknowledgment accompanied by round, saucer eyes were the Austrian's sole responses.[34]

The "intellectuals" congregated around the only available table on deck, adjoining the smokestack, in the heart of "Montparnasse," a reference to Paris' bohemian artist quarter. Rémy alludes to Breton, Lévi-Strauss, and Serge forming what sounds like an informal onboard seminar. He listened in wonder to "distant and so poignantly relevant memories of the Soviet Union" (Serge's), and to the "prodigious adventures of a man who relived the first hours of human history and of the stone-age among the primitive peoples of Oceania" (Lévi-Strauss').[35]

Meanwhile, Lévi-Strauss recollects exchanging letters on board with Breton about the relationship between "aesthetic beauty and absolute originality"—an incongruously old-fashioned and rather astonishing undertaking when one considers the size of the ship and their ongoing verbal dialogue.[36] Serge's notebooks mention reading Walter Benjamin's essay on Baudelaire on board and lamenting the German philosopher's recent death, which occurred while he was trying to escape France for Spain.[37] Serge also describes a litany of other discussion topics between Lévi-Strauss and himself: peculiar policing techniques in São Paulo that involved grafting animal characteristics onto criminal types; what Lévi-Strauss allegedly called the weighty "natural fatality" that purportedly caused Latin America to lag behind; the labor movement in the United States of America. Lévi-Strauss and Wifredo Lam conversed about Brazilian culture and especially Afro-Brazilian beliefs and rituals. Others joined in, such as a young German specialist of prehistory who presented his findings.[38] In short, one of the finest free universities ever assembled seemed spontaneously to convene on board.

Curiously, few if any women appear to have been invited into this academic coterie, despite the presence on board of famed novelist Seghers, of pioneering photographer Krull, of Surrealist painter Jacqueline Lamba, of anti-Nazi pediatrician Dr. Minna Flake, and of laboratory scientist Helena Holzer (later Benitez). Krull recalls forming a group with "an elderly female German medical doctor, her daughter a young lawyer, her engineer son and their daughter Kateninette, two years old, as well as a Belgian student, a young Luxembourger woman, and a large and kindly still breast-feeding Spanish woman, who also has two older boys aged six and eight."[39] The first four were undoubtedly Flake, Renée and Walter Barth, and their daughter Katrina. Meanwhile, Seghers seems to have sought some time alone so as to begin her novel *Transit*, which indeed she commenced drafting on board the *Paul Lemerle*.[40]

In short, the female artists, doctors, and authors on board seem to have been decidedly less cliquish than their male counterparts, or perhaps they were simply kept out of their coterie. Lamba's biographer, Alba Romano Pace, makes the case that for all of his antibourgeois iconoclasm, Lamba's then-husband Breton adhered to very traditional gender roles. He never took Lamba seriously as an artist, and within his circle women and men tended to take part in separate conversations. Perhaps for this reason, Mexican painter Frida Kahlo's coldness to Breton in the 1930s had morphed into contempt, even hostility. She only had time, and eyes, for Lamba.[41]

This said, Renée Barth does remember Serge's exposé on the constellations of the Southern Hemisphere aboard the *Paul Lemerle*, and his tales of fighting for the Bolsheviks. So perhaps the groupings were more permeable than some testimonies allow.[42] Despite his point about tightly knit groupings on deck, Lévi-Strauss suggests that individual connections were certainly being established. He distinctly remembers flirtation leading to many "rapprochements" aboard the *Paul Lemerle*. He adds that there were "young and attractive women on board."[43]

Visualizing the Crossing

Thankfully, many snapshots of the crossings have survived. Dyno Löwenstein's group photo (figure 3) immortalized a scene on board the *Capitaine Paul Lemerle*. It too appears to show passengers mingling, at the very least congregating for the camera. It features Serge on the far left, and Lam, but also Walter Barth and his daughter Katrina (one of the young children at the back), along with many other passengers. All appear decidedly pleased to be heading westward. As we will see, Czech artist Antonin Pelc also took precious photo evidence aboard the same ship.

Although we are fortunate to have photos from the *Paul Lemerle*, the ship of photographers, so to speak, was without doubt the *Winnipeg*. On its final crossing to Martinique in May 1941, it carried Fred Stein, Josef Breitenbach, Ilse Bing, celebrity portraitist Chaim (aka Boris) Lipnitzki, Yolla Niclas-Sachs, Charles Leirens (also a gifted musician), and Ylla, a nom de plume of Camilla Koffler.[44] Many of these accomplished photographers, including Breitenbach, Stein, Niclas-Sachs, and Bing, had thrived in interwar Paris, rubbing shoulders with Man Ray and the Surrealists.

FIGURE 3. Photo taken aboard the *Capitaine Paul Lemerle* en route to Martinique, 1941. United States Holocaust Memorial Museum, courtesy of Dyno Löwenstein, photographed (photo 34443).

Bing and Stein had become masters of the lightweight Leica camera. Koffler had specialized as well in animal and pet portraiture, which would remain her area of interest long after the war.

Avant-garde photographers Bing, Niclas-Sachs, and Breitenbach have all left behind pictures of the crossing, whereas famed portrait photographer Stein sadly did not travel with his camera.[45] One of Breitenbach's photos shows the deck of the *Winnipeg* over the course of the May 1941 voyage, as it neared Martinique (figure 4). His camera is trained on the bow. The mixed-cargo status of the *Winnipeg* is readily apparent; this was no passenger liner. Only some ten travelers can be discerned, most of them passing the time either sunbathing or sitting in deckchairs. Some of the chairs lay strewn, collapsed on the deck. One passenger leans on a ship stack and may be sheltering a cigarette or a pipe from the wind. Several passengers are wearing colonial hats or helmets. One man gazes at the horizon, mesmerized by the ocean. The woman at the front of the picture may be passing the time knitting.

Bing was born in Frankfurt in 1899. In 1924, she undertook a doctorate in the history of art in that same city. Five years later, she acquired her first Leica, which would become her signature camera. Krull had recently uncovered the potential of that very device. Bing likened it to a musical instrument on which "one must play . . . sympathetically." Bing reached Paris even before the Nazi seizure of power. There, she published in a number of popular magazines, including *Vu* and *Le Monde Illustré*. She and musicologist Konrad Wolff wed in 1937. In May 1941, the pair sailed the Atlantic aboard the *Winnipeg*.[46] Her photos of the vessel leaving Marseille are held at the National Gallery of Canada. In several of them, one can identify Marseille landmarks, including Notre-Dame de la Garde Basilica and the Château d'If. One photo shows passengers finding their bearings and mingling with sailors (figure 5). The many ships in the background of this snapshot suggest that Marseille's port remained a beehive of activity in May 1941. Another shows a boy posing for the camera as four adult passengers seem to bid farewell to Europe (figure 6). Yet another centers on a dog on deck bearing a luggage tag.[47]

FIGURE 4. Photograph by Josef Breitenbach, Martinique, 1941. The photo was taken aboard the *Winnipeg* as it sailed toward Martinique. Courtesy the Josef Breitenbach Archive, Center for Creative Photography, the University of Arizona Tucson.

FIGURE 5. Photo by Ilse Bing, *On Board Ship*, 1941. View from the deck of the *Winnipeg* as it prepares to leave Marseille. Ilse Bing Photographic Fonds, National Gallery of Canada, Library and Archives, 2002.0196.39. Copyright Estate of Ilse Bing.

FIGURE 6. Ilse Bing, *Dockyard*, 1941. Passengers aboard the *Winnipeg* as it prepares to leave port in Marseille. Ilse Bing Photographic Fonds, National Gallery of Canada, Library and Archives, 2002.0196.40. Copyright Estate of Ilse Bing.

Convicts, Explorers, Defeated Exiles,
Pilgrims, Slaves, or Cargo?

Beyond these visuals, it is the comparative gaze of outsiders and insiders that jumps out from written testimonies. Vichy officials, interrogating him upon arrival in Fort-de-France, told a bewildered Lévi-Strauss that he was Jewish, not French.[48] Elite survivors of Europe's epic bonfire in their own eyes, Vichy sympathizers viewed them instead as boatloads of undesirable, stateless Jews. Lévi-Strauss quipped that the French crew considered all passengers to be Jewish, anarchist, or foreign, save for a wealthy Creole from Martinique.[49] How did the migrants perceive their passage to the Caribbean? Was it seen as the last migrant flight from charred Europe? Or was it instead a departure of virtual convicts, of political prisoners exiled by a French state that had reneged on earlier humanitarian promises?

There was no shortage of reflection on the condition of exile and refugee. Adolf Hoffmeister, who accompanied his anti-Nazi Czech compatriots Pelc and Alen Divis on the Bordeaux-to-Casablanca leg of their journey (the latter two would go on to Martinique, while Hoffmeister would leave Morocco via Lisbon), recalled rancorous debates on deck over just how the migrants should define themselves. "A refugee is an unwilling tourist," mused one traveler in the middle of the Mediterranean. No, opined another, "the refugee is the one honest man whose papers can never be in order, and, therefore, the police constantly demand that he show them." Another offered insight into loss of dignity: "A refugee is a man who embarrasses only those who have not yet been refugees."[50]

For his part, Serge used a revealing allegory to describe the voyage. He wrote of being in a similar boat to that of "seventeenth century Protestants, chased out of France and England by religious intolerance, who crossed the Atlantic to found the first North American colonies." Of course, like these religious minorities before him, Serge seemed implicitly to deny any pre-European significance to the Americas. He also stumbled on the limits of his own comparison with European pilgrims. While their future lay in the Americas, his and that of his comrades centered obsessively on "returning to a liberated Europe."[51] Serge's optimism needs to be underscored. In April 1941, as he wrote these words, few signs presaged any such liberation: his once beloved Soviet Union was still locked in a treaty with Nazi

Germany. The United States remained stubbornly uninvolved. France had been defeated. Britain and its colonies stood alone against Hitler.

Serge was not alone in deploying a colonial trope. At least three other passengers—Seghers, Mehring, and Lamba—drew direct parallels between their crossing to Martinique and Columbus' travels. In a mix of French and English, Lamba wrote Fry after reaching New York, "The voyage was about the same as his [Columbus'], don't remember how long [his] was, but ours was two months and a half, and it was pretty disgusting and bruitiful [sic—brutish? Or perhaps noisy?]."[52] Meanwhile, Seghers described her route to New York as more circuitous than Columbus' travels.[53] As for Mehring, he wrote from the Wyoming, as he approached Oran, "As concerns the comfort of the cabins, it recalls the one of Christopher Columbus' ship."[54] He also evoked Columbus twice in his poem "Love Song à la Martinique."[55] That Lamba, Mehring, and Seghers should all have resorted to the allegory of discovery is all the more surprising considering that they wished to convey the discomfort and the complexity of the westward journey.

Indeed, to others the fate of these desperate refugees bound for the New World seemed more evocative of the plight of convicts than that of explorers, of a middle passage than a mission to terra incognita. In this sense, Lamba's, Mehring's, and Seghers' telescoping back to Columbus denies the vaster context of successive diasporas. From a wider angle, of course, the migrants of 1941 represented a relatively small and recent movement—a mere ripple among the countless migratory waves to the Caribbean: indigenous, European, African, and Asian.

Interestingly, Lévi-Strauss refers to the departure on the Paul Lemerle as that of a shipload of "convicts." This he asserts, at least partly, on the basis of his experience on the docks of Marseille: he recalls machine-gun-toting guards rudely shoving along those who were trying to bid farewell to loved ones.[56] And, of course, French Guiana, to which many ships sailed from Fort-de-France, was home to probably the world's most notorious penal colony: Devil's Island, where the innocent Captain Alfred Dreyfus had been deported in 1895 on trumped-up charges of treason.

The passenger most haunted by the penal colony allegory was certainly Divis. This Czech artist who had worked in Paris since 1926. Along with his compatriot Pelc, he was wrongfully arrested in 1939 on charges of espionage, in the wake of the Soviet-Nazi nonaggression pact, when fears of a fifth column were reaching their zenith in France. The pair was initially jailed in spartan, unheated cells at the notorious Santé Prison. Upon their release, they were promptly transferred to internment camps, first at Roland Garros, then at Damigny in Normandy. Then, on May 27, 1940, as German troops advanced in France, the pair was relocated to the camp of Bassens near Bordeaux. They gained freedom when camp personnel panicked during a German air raid and released all inmates. In late June 1940, Divis and Pelc managed to escape to Morocco, where they were interned once more until early March 1941. From Casablanca they sailed for Martinique in April 1941 aboard the *Paul Lemerle*.[57] One series of Divis' drawings, inspired by graffiti on the walls of Santé Prison, features recurring images of a female figure and crossed-out bars used to signify the passing days of incarceration.[58] It was published after the war in a Czech article whose title can be translated as "Kaleidoscope of Prison Dreams."[59]

In figure 7, which was part of that series, the 1939 miscarriage of justice, combined with the anticipated departure to the colonies, shapes Divis' reading of his exodus, leading him to tie it to Dreyfus' fate. In this 1941 work typical of Divis' melancholic and idiosyncratic style, one discerns an obvious allusion to Dreyfus in the form of a date: 1894, the year of Captain Dreyfus' wrongful conviction on charges of espionage for Germany and his sentencing of deportation in perpetuity by a military tribunal. No doubt Divis correctly deemed the espionage charges against him to be as spurious as those against the Jewish captain. For Divis, the parallel does not end there. In addition to reflecting graffiti he spent endless hours contemplating in prison, the forlorn female figure may constitute an allusion to the indefatigable Louise Dreyfus, the captain's wife. The words "for life" echo Dreyfus' life sentence and hint that Divis saw little hope of returning to Europe since the Nazi tide showed no sign of ebbing. The mention of Nouméa is also intriguing, as New Caledonia, of which Nouméa is the capital, served as France's other penal colony. The piece may also reflect the influence of Franz Kafka's short story "In the Penal Colony," about the *bagne*'s nightmarish disciplinary mechanisms—a story itself informed by popular literature about the colonies.[60] The allusion to murder remains more enigmatic and may have come directly from Divis' prison cell wall. In the background, a steamer, whose silhouette bears an uncanny resemblance to the *Paul Lemerle*, prepares to take the convict away.

A. Diviš, Doživotní nucené práce

FIGURE 7. Alen Divis drawing that first appeared in the journal *Kytice* (year 3, 1948, page 265) to illustrate his book *Kaleidoscope of Prison Dreams*. Reproduction courtesy of Archiv výtvarného umění, Czech Republic (CC-BY-NC-ND).

Aboard the same ship, the *Paul Lemerle*, Rémy used the equally charged metaphor of escaped slaves to describe his fellow passengers.[61] Indeed, slavery references and even the notion of a middle passage and triangular trade (after all, the same vessels that brought the refugees returned to France laden with bananas and rum) are implied in several of the reflections on the crossings.[62]

What of morale? In his memoirs, Serge muses about his revolutionary comrades on board being defeated but not destroyed. He pays special attention to those who had wielded power in Spain and the Soviet Union and the multiple challenges they had faced in elaborating economic plans, enhancing production, and protecting cities from aerial attacks. Admitting "short term defeat," Serge claims that they are unbowed. In short, to Serge, the departure to Martinique aboard the *Paul Lemerle* constituted a tactical retreat.[63] Yet Serge was not immune to second-guessing the decision to leave. Unsurprisingly, bouts of homesickness and nostalgia frequently overcame the people on board these freighters: before even passing the Straits of Gibraltar, Breton apparently disclosed to Serge that he would prefer to be sitting on the terrace of the Deux Magots in Paris, where, as recently as 1939–1940, he had held court with his fellow Surrealists.[64] Meanwhile, Benitez recalls teaming up with Breton's spouse, Lamba, to try to lift their partners' spirits: "Jacqueline . . . and I had to work hard to generate enthusiasm and diversions to keep things under control."[65]

In stark contrast to the ethnographic, revolutionary, and literary gaze, a bizarre contemporaneous travel account presents the crossing to Martinique from the perspective of an inveterate anti-Semite devoted to Vichy. Replete with grotesque racist stereotypes, the text in question was penned by Raymond Sallé, a colonial trapped in France who boarded the *Winnipeg* to return to Indochina on a rather circuitous westward journey.

Sallé's text is laced with foul and incessant references to allegedly nomadic "passengers whose names remind one more of the Vistula than the Loire," or to "passenger business cards . . . which give one the impression of a quick tour of Central Europe." He employs entomological metaphors in his depiction of the deck, where he hears "swarms" of foreigners droning on in their foreign tongues and then suddenly experiences the pleasure of hearing one or two words spoken in French. In a classic anti-Semitic trope, he purports that passengers were adorned with so many jewels that "the slightest ray of sun proved blinding." Sarcastically, Sallé recalls how a rumor had spread on board that once in Martinique, "foreigners would all be placed in concentration camps—this seemed to scare them greatly. [They complained as follows:] 'these French, what tyrants.'" The author of these words did not realize how accurate both observations would prove.[66]

More interesting perhaps is the language Sallé uses to describe the entire enterprise. Elaborating on the fact that the *Winnipeg* had been a "mixed freighter," he rails, "The *Winnipeg* . . . used to carry 60 passengers . . . the rest was cargo. In place of the cargo, now 700 foreign migrants have squeezed in there, 95% of them Jews; this is alas the only freight that France can currently export."[67] To Sallé, the men, women, and children cooped up in the dark holds of the *Winnipeg* were nothing more than shady merchandise.

The Vessels

Passengers could at least agree on one point: welcome though they were, the ships failed to impress. Even their silhouettes disappointed. Karl Bodek's sardines painted on the walls of Les Milles would prove an augur for others. Serge enlisted the same image to describe the miserable freighter that would take him to Martinique in 1941: "Imagine a can of sardines on which someone stuck a cigarette butt."[68]

The ships that undertook the 1940–1941 crossings to Martinique belonged to several companies: the *Capitaine Paul Lemerle,* the *Alsina,* and the *Mont Viso* to the Société générale des transports maritimes à vapeur; the *Ipanema* to the Compagnie de Navigation France-Amérique; the *Wyoming,* the *Winnipeg,* the *Carimaré,* and the *Arica* to the Compagnie Générale Transatlantique, also known as the French Line; the *Charles L. Dreyfus,* which Vichy officials tended only refer to as the CLD because of the name Dreyfus, to Louis Dreyfus and Co. All of the ships were freighters or mixed cargoes, save for the *Cuba* and the *Ipanema,* both of which were designated as passenger liners.

Bénédite of the ERC rightly hypothesized that in addition to ridding France of unwanted foreigners, and rescuing harried refugees, the Martinique crossings no doubt served to make the shipping companies a pretty penny. The companies listed here owned old military transport and freighter vessels that were rusting away in Marseille's back docks. Converting them into rudimentary refugee transports would be easy ("passengers would content themselves with summarily appointed dormitories"), and, after all, "why should all the money go to the Portuguese [shipping companies]"? Bénédite was no doubt correct, although extant archives do not, unfortunately, give precise figures with which to determine the profit margins from these voyages.[69]

Bénédite does slightly miss the mark on one point. Although they were for the most part converted or mixed freighters and certainly not luxury liners, these ships had routinely transported passengers in the past, some of them celebrities. For example, in May 1938, Consuelo de Saint-Exupéry (a friend of the Bretons who would end up at the Villa Air-Bel, outside Marseille, in 1940) embarked on the *Wyoming* from France to her native El Salvador to meet with her aviator husband, author Antoine de Saint-Exupéry.[70]

Similarly, Lévi-Strauss had previously sailed aboard the *Capitaine Paul Le-merle,* which he indicates as the reason for his preferential treatment on board. Indeed, he was one of the very few to benefit from a proper cabin.[71]

The vessels' blueprints reveal minimalist infrastructures and facilities. Unlike the more spartan *Paul Lemerle,* the *Wyoming* at least featured a dining hall, a smoking room, and some twenty private cabins (although, on an earlier voyage from Vancouver in September 1939, it had carried mostly cargo—7,706 tons of it—and only ten passengers for sixty-five crew members).[72] Indeed, in February 1941 Hauth wrote of conditions aboard the *Wyoming* being quite crowded but decent enough: he mentioned the smoking room, the library, the bar, board games, and even an outdoor swimming pool. He termed the vessel a proper passenger liner.[73] The *Winnipeg,* conversely, had been designed to take only eleven passengers besides its crew. The ship's blueprint reveals only four small cabins, all located on the top deck.[74] And yet, already in May 1940, before the fall of France, it transported ninety-one passengers to Fort-de-France. In the report on that May 1940 crossing, unfortunately the last one available for the *Winnipeg,* the captain noted that the staff was strained, exhausted at having to cook and clean for 156 people instead of the usual 76. The crew scrubbed the long-neglected passenger cabins for some fifty days to render them "acceptable" for paying travelers. Indeed, the ship had previously been leased to another company that had brought Spanish Republicans to South America, and the French Line complained bitterly of the poor condition in which it had been returned. The vessel was hardly prepared to receive the four hundred passengers who would take it to Martinique in 1941. In 1940 at least, it counted only four life rafts.[75] By December 1941, several months too late for the migrants that concern us, plans were drawn up in Le Havre, the French Line's headquarters, for the *Winnipeg* to be equipped with more passenger cabins, at the expense of storage space.[76]

For the most part, conditions on board these ships were austere and cramped, to say the least. Breton dwells on the thin hay bedding and the "rolling" kitchen on the deck of the *Paul Lemerle.*[77] Lévi-Strauss specifies that the freighter had only two cabins, containing seven bunks in all. All other travelers were heaped onto hay mats in windowless storage compartments in the ship's bilge, piled into the hold like "cattle."[78] Aboard the same cargo ship, Pierre Radvanyi remembers sleeping on the deck, weather permitting, to avoid the dark confines below.[79] Rémy relates identical fea-

FIGURE 8. Photo showing Alen Divis, Antonin Pelc, and Max Kopf passing in front of the women's latrines on board the *Capitaine Paul Lemerle,* 1941. Photograph in the Antonin Pelc Archive, © National Gallery in Prague 2017.

tures, as well as a tiny sink and shower area on deck for all passengers to wash, and a collective bowl from which they ate, by groups of eight, "as in the army."[80] Renée Barth recollects that the *Paul Lemerle's* latrines were located on deck, "built towards the outside so everything would fall into the water right away; this meant we couldn't use it for the children."[81] A photograph in Pelc's archives shows these very facilities. The picture (figure 8) features Czech refugee artists Divis, Pelc, and Maxim Kopf about to walk past the women's latrines. On the right, one female and two male passengers can be seen washing clothes.

Mehring described traveling in "the basement of a steamer"—the *Wyoming*—which he called "a dirty ship."[82] Of the *Winnipeg,* Stein's wife, Liselotte Salzburg Stein, later remembered, "it had been a boat for oranges," before adding that many passengers now traveled in the former citrus-holding tanks, which still "smelled like rotten oranges."[83] In such cramped, uninviting quarters, intimacy of any kind was in scarce supply. Serge recounts in his notebooks that couples sometimes slinked into the life-boats to have sex.[84]

The same conditions could be found aboard the *Carimaré,* where the hold was transformed into a gigantic living quarter. Diego Masson recalls at once the freedom he enjoyed as a six-year-old aboard the ship (all the greater because his mother suffered from seasickness and could not follow him around) and the fact that food supplies were running fairly low by trip's end. Indeed, like most others that concern us, the ship took a staggering amount of time to reach Martinique from Marseille. Masson recollects it being "over a month," but different records suggest it took just under that time (leaving Marseille on April 2 and reaching Fort-de-France on April 29). Like the other vessels, it zigzagged along the west coast of Africa. Masson even recalls it twice crossing the equator, a considerable distance south of the most direct route between Marseille and Martinique (he was six at the time; might he have confused it with the crossing of the Tropic of Cancer?).[85] The *Paul Lemerle* similarly took twenty-eight days to reach Martinique from Marseille.[86]

A month-long crossing implies decent allowances for food. The quality of sustenance on board, or lack thereof, constitutes a recurring theme across testimonies. Krull describes the staple menu of the first weeks aboard the *Paul Lemerle:* a mystery soup, one square centimeter of meat per person with noodles or dry peas, a glass of wine, and a slice of bread, as well as an apple or an orange. She also provides insight on the origin of the meat: she describes cows and sheep being loaded in Casablanca, and then slaughtered for meat during the Atlantic crossing.[87] Before this turn of events, the precociously artistically gifted six-year-old Aube Breton drew some of the sheep, no doubt captivated by the uncommon seafaring livestock. The girl, or her parents, then offered the sketch to Lam and Holzer, who brought it with them from Martinique to Cuba.[88]

The sheep could not have been very numerous because meat remained something of a rarity on board. Renée Barth remembers a diet consisting mostly of lentils, dried beans, and dried peas.[89] As for Serge, he mentions an intriguing meeting of minds, when Flake and Breton jointly complained to the ship captain about the poor quality of the food.[90] As she would at the camp in Martinique, Dr. Flake no doubt brought her medical and hygienic expertise to bear in formulating this grievance.

All of this being said, conditions varied from ship to ship, and, of course, from class to class. There were at least three classes aboard the ships that concern us. Aboard the *Wyoming,* Hauth described quite decent meals, a real break with Vichy France, where restrictions conditioned every bite. He accounted for this by explaining that the *Wyoming* had previously stocked up on supplies in New Orleans: hence, the wines on board were Californian (they pleasantly surprised Hauth), and many of the tinned cans (including corned beef) were American as well.[91] In other words, experiences differed greatly based on one's ship's previous port of call, the quality of the shipping line, one's class on board, and so on.

Despite tensions and generally difficult conditions, passengers honored rituals and sea cultures, even in these squalid quarters, even in a time of war. The traditional festivities marking the crossing of the Tropic of Cancer were held aboard the *Paul Lemerle* in April 1941. Serge recalled select passengers, and even the captain, being dunked into basins of seawater by a crewmember disguised as Neptune, aided by a young seaman ringing a bell. Rémy remembered that another person was dressed up as Amphitrite, Poseidon's sea-goddess wife. Pelc captured part of this maritime ritual aboard the same ship. In his photo, one can discern improvised crowns and togas (figure 9). Rémy added that some on board had taken the precaution of changing into swimming trunks beforehand, anticipating what was about to happen.[92] Indeed, this rite of passage was commonplace. Aboard the *Cuba,* one of the French Line's regular passenger liners that sailed to Martinique, passengers in the 1930s had received a diploma, adorned with a smiling Neptune, to mark their first crossing of the Tropic of Cancer.[93]

Although these were certainly not cruise liners, entertainment was not limited to good-natured dunking. Gifted musicians paced the decks: the *Mont Viso,* for instance, carried accomplished German Jewish pianist Erich Itor Kahn to Martinique, and the *Winnipeg* Belgian musician Leirens, former Berlin Symphony Orchestra conductor Edvard Fendler, and pianist and musicologist Wolff. It is therefore not surprising that an impromptu concert took place aboard the *Winnipeg* in May 1941.[94] Hauth specifies that there was no pianist aboard the *Wyoming* in February 1941, but that passengers assembled to hear the Spanish Republicans on board sing and play the guitar. Serge mentions a Polish refugee interpreting a moving melody on the accordion aboard the *Paul Lemerle.*[95]

FIGURE 9. Photo showing the ceremonies marking the crossing of the Tropic of Cancer on board the *Capitaine Paul Lemerle,* 1941. Photograph in the Antonin Pelc Archive, © National Gallery in Prague 2017.

In another genre, Rémy attests that a theatrical soirée was organized aboard the *Paul Lemerle.* Skits were presented in Spanish, French, German, and even Viennese dialect. Some of them dealt with the terrible food on board, others revisited the anguish and difficulties involved in the struggle for visas. Other sketches anticipated arrival at Ellis Island, a vision of freedom and peace far more idyllic than the scene in Charlie Chaplin's *The Immigrant* in which passengers are roped in under the shadow of the Statue of Liberty.[96] Serge mentions fellow passengers staging a Marx brothers skit aboard the same ship.[97] Some of the migrants boasted more theatrical talent than others. Lysiane Bernhardt, granddaughter of virtuoso Sarah Bernhardt and an actress in her own right, took the *Winnipeg* to Martinique in 1941.[98]

As for the Surrealists, they created their own fun aboard the *Paul Lemerle.* Breton had his group play a tried and tested Surrealist game in which sets of answers and questions were advanced blindly and separately.[99] As Breton's biographer has remarked, the objective of these games involved "revelation, not relaxation."[100] In that vein, Serge beamed when he unwittingly answered, "A defeat that we will turn into a luminous victory," to the question, "What is historical materialism?"[101] Here Serge used a game aimed at making new meaning, or even at producing a kind of oracle, to instead reinforce his idée fixe. Such was his mind-set. In a sense, the question mattered little; he would likely have provided an identical response had he been asked about his favorite drink. The ultimate victory over fascism was all that counted.

Ocean Hazards

The mood was decidedly not lighthearted for the whole passage. Those who undertook it considered the voyage to be perilous, and certainly any wartime crossing included major risks. A simple perusal of the insurance instrument *Lloyd's Register* for the war years gives a sense of the percentage of cargoes that found their way to the seabed. Historians have tabulated a staggering total of 4,786 Allied merchant ships sunk over the course of the Second World War, not counting military vessels.[102] Of course, the freighters that concern us were not Allied ships, at least not yet.

Before delving into the many wartime menaces that faced freighters, a brief plunge into Martinique's turquoise coastal waters is in order. The maritime history of Martinique in 1940 is both complex and troubled. French warships faithful to the authorities in France converged on Martinique and Guadeloupe in late June 1940.[103] Among them was the rapid cruiser *Emile Bertin*, capable of sailing at a remarkable forty knots. It had used its speed to good effect, slipping out of Halifax Harbor as relations between Britain and the new Vichy regime soured. It carried on board a substantial portion of the gold of the Bank of France that the dying republic had managed to keep out of German hands. Off Fort-de-France, the *Bertin* joined the aircraft carrier *Béarn*. The cruiser *Jeanne d'Arc* and its crew dropped anchor in nearby Guadeloupe. Of course, the United States was not yet at war, and Vichy's admiral Georges Robert—as high commissioner to the French Antilles—did his utmost to placate American interests, at least for the time being (he even tried to have the *Béarn*'s aircraft dispatched to French Indochina, until the German Armistice Commission blocked the project).[104] Still, the warships remained a dissuasive force that Robert used to enforce Vichy's putative neutrality. In addition to that role, the assembly of warships also served as a powerful instrument of intimidation over French West Indians.

The decision of the authorities in Fort-de-France to side with Philippe Pétain's Vichy regime in July 1940 spelled sudden short-term maritime isolation: Britain first imposed a relatively flexible blockade in August 1940, hoping to bring the islands to side with de Gaulle. It nearly worked, for Martinique's situation was already precarious as France fell. Indeed, on June 17, 1940, before the blockade even began, officials in Martinique cabled France to announce that the island only had enough food supplies to last between forty-five days and two months.[105] The island had long been dependent on imported goods, making the situation all the more dire.

By July 27, American officials reported that "the situation at Martinique has quieted down," with British warships moving farther offshore.[106] Britain decided to further relax the blockade a few months later. Indeed, on October 18, the freighter *Charles L. Dreyfus* reached Fort-de-France from Casablanca and Marseille. Two days after that, Vichy's Ministry of the Colonies cabled Martinique indicating that orders could once again be placed for North African and French goods, now that the "a certain amount of traffic from France and Morocco" had resumed.[107] A month later, the French press reported that the cordon of British warships that had previously surrounded the French West Indies had completely vanished. No doubt it had gone to protect transatlantic convoys from German U-boats.[108]

Still, potential British threats to the Martinique line continued to weigh on Vichy minds. Thus, General de Gaulle's Free French in London learned that Captain Yves Le Carrères had been imprisoned at the Fort Napoléon in Guadeloupe in November 1940. Le Carrères was the captain of the *Charles L. Dreyfus,* which had docked in Fort-de-France in October 1940. A month later, however, as the *Dreyfus* prepared to return to Marseille via Casablanca, Le Carrères apparently refused to sign a document swearing that he would scuttle his ship in the event that it was boarded. Given Franco-British tensions in the wake of the British sinking part of the French fleet at Mers-el-Kebir in July 1940, as well as the fact that Great Britain controlled the high seas at the time, this measure clearly targeted Britain. Le Carrères' refusal to sign the document earned him the enmity of Vichy officials in the Caribbean, who had him detained.[109]

Some Vichy officials also worried about the lack of secrecy surrounding the passages. Indeed, refugees slated to depart from Marseille routinely liaised with family members and friends who had already gotten to Martinique. Because some of this mail traveled by air and consequently reached the isle faster than the migrants did, Vichy officials in Martinique fretted that the British might uncover ship coordinates and departure details from refugee correspondence. The fragments that Vichy's postal censors reproduced also provide a glimpse into the hopes and uncertainties elicited by the boats to Martinique. One reads, "We will leave on the *Carimaré* on the 31st"; another, "We have managed to book spots on the April 25 departure, it will probably be the *Winnipeg*."[110]

Britain was not the only impediment to Vichy's maintaining shipping to the French Caribbean and therefore its hold on the islands. Initially suspicious that Pétain might play a double game, the German authorities had seriously restricted shipping lines between France and its colonies. On September 10, 1940, Vichy finally cabled Fort-de-France, informing Admiral Robert and Governor Henry Bressoles that the German Armistice Commission had agreed to reestablish commercial and passenger traffic between France and the French West Indies, as well as between the French Caribbean and the Americas.[111]

Thereafter, the Marseille-to-Martinique ships represented a fragile economic lifeline for Martinique, one regularly threatened by both German and British, and soon American, concerns. It is no doubt ironic that, had the islands opted for General de Gaulle in London, rather than Marshal Pétain at Vichy, the ships that refugees took to safety would never have been allowed to leave port. The refugees gained passage aboard a line that was essential for Vichy to maintain its contested sovereignty and control over France's Caribbean holdings.

Beyond the threats inherent in the broader geostrategic context, individual crossings featured menaces both small and large. Renée Barth recalls two particular difficulties with the voyage to Martinique aboard the *Paul Lemerle:* a whooping cough epidemic on board, and the limited protection from falling overboard provided by a single slender, 1.5-foot-high cable running all around the deck. This was hardly the safest environment for her toddler daughter Katrina (nor for anyone or anything else: Serge tells the story of a passenger's cat that fell or jumped overboard). Yet Barth, like many others, saw even greater dangers lurking below. She noted that French and British vessels had recently exchanged fire in the Mediterranean. She also found out that the crew took active measures to avoid submarine attacks.[112] This certainly accounts for some of the zigzagging that passengers described.

Aboard the *Wyoming*, Hauth described a "general state of nervousness" that was stoked by one passenger in particular who had survived a torpedo attack on a previous voyage and compulsively shared his story with other passengers. Then, after the *Wyoming* left Oran, it joined a convoy that was escorted by a French destroyer.[113] Like Barth, Hauth also described other challenges. Specifically, he chronicled in detail the effects of a hurricane whose path the *Wyoming* crossed in the Atlantic. It struck at lunch, and passengers shrieked as plates landed on their laps and red wine carafes poured on them. Outside the dining hall, some passengers were injured by their own suitcases, others in their bathtubs.[114]

Still, U-boats remained the most serious source of angst. Serge had evidently read up on their capabilities. In 1942, shortly after the crossing, he drafted a manuscript on the war at sea. In it, he wrote with perceptible anguish about how difficult it was to detect military submersibles at dawn and dusk. He stressed their durability, providing the example of one submarine that had purportedly survived no fewer than fifty-seven attempts to sink it. And he noted their lethal effectiveness in temporarily freezing tanker traffic to and from Venezuela. Finally, Serge mentioned the then widely rumored possibility that U-boats might have found secret bases, or refueling stations, in Vichy's overseas possessions.[115] Although Serge seems to have been unaware of them, these rumors were heightened in February 1942 when a German U-boat dropped a seriously injured sailor off in Martinique who was none other than the son of German vice admiral Kurt von dem Borne.[116] The incident took on international significance immediately, with US undersecretary of state Sumner Welles berating Vichy's ambassador in Washington over it that very month.[117]

In reality, however, Vichy had taken precautions to protect its commercial vessels, including the ones that concern us, from U-boats. Indeed, the same ships that left Marseille for Martinique returned packed with bananas, sugar, and rum. The shipping line was therefore invaluable to the French Caribbean, and it constituted a key for the region remaining in Vichy's orbit. The records of the armistice commission show Vichy having to clear every ship passage to its loyal colonies, in a bid to reassure the Germans that these territories were neither receiving nor exporting Gaullist sedition. As a result, the Kriegsmarine knew in advance each Vichy vessel's movements to and from Fort-de-France, although not its passenger manifests. As long as Vichy remained a satellite of Nazi Germany, its vessels were safe from German submarines.[118]

In addition to clearing the voyage with the German authorities beforehand, the shipping companies ensured that each boat was clearly identified as a neutral vessel. Thus, in 1941, the *Winnipeg* bore blue, white, and red stripes along its side, with yellow trim, the color of neutral ships. This peculiar rainbow was lit by the ship's own projectors.[119] In addition, by rule the ship's name had to appear far larger than in peacetime. Finally and less ostentatiously, each of these ships had obtained a "navicert," which is to say a certificate of nonbelligerent status that theoretically ensured safe passage.[120] However, not all passengers were versed in neutral vessel signals, let alone attuned to the fact that Vichy had cleared the ships with Germany beforehand. The crossing consequently elicited anxieties of all sorts.

Ultimately, the threat that doomed the Martinique line came from Britain's Dutch ally and involved maritime commandeering. Its root causes had to do both with mounting tensions between Vichy and the British and Americans and with the tremendous appeal of French ships in the wake of France's defeat. As Michael Miller has shown, the fate of Norwegian, Greek, Dutch, and French ships after the defeat of these nations at the hands of Germany became a source of intense competition between belligerent nations but also among the crews themselves. Radio wars, "brawls[,] and intrigues" accompanied this ongoing contest for neutral shipping.[121] Countless ship entries in *Lloyd's Register* feature a small piece of corrector ribbon reassigning provenance and ownership.[122]

The ships that concern us here were not immune to such seizures on the high seas, most notably the *Charles L. Dreyfus,* the *Winnipeg,* the *Wyoming,* the *Mont Viso,* the *Alsina,* and the *Arica,* all of which eventually switched to US, British, or Canadian flags. Some of them (the *Mont Viso,* the *Winnipeg,* and the *Wyoming*) would be sunk by U-boats after having changed over to Allied ownership. Two German torpedoes struck the *Wyoming* on March 15, 1943.[123] We will see later how the transfer of ownership in the form of a veritable hijacking on the high seas marked the end of the Martinique route for refugees in May 1941.

Luggage and Cargo

Some travelers brought precious baggage with them. We saw that Henri Smadja carried a Degas painting to New York. Serge traveled with his own masterpiece, the manuscript of *The Case of Comrade Tulayev,* his chronicle of Stalin's terror.[124] Others, on the contrary, grieved their lost libraries as they crossed the gangplank. Such was the case of Mehring, who later wrote of the knowledge and comfort his father's vast collection of books had once brought him, and of the incredible, but ultimately vain, efforts of different people, including Jewish Czech diplomat Camill Hoffmann, to save it.[125]

Another singular character probably carried valuable documents with him aboard the *Wyoming.* Szajko Frydman (nom de plume Zosa Szajkowski) had by now begun his self-proclaimed task of compulsively rescuing Judaica from Europe. Called the "archive thief" by his biographer Lisa Moses Leff, Frydman had left his native Poland for Paris in 1927. In 1939, after France's declaration of war on Germany, he volunteered in the French Foreign Legion. On June 15, 1940, on the front in Franche-Comté, a German bullet pierced his body from left to right. He was then transferred south, to a hospital in Carpentras. This city with a long Jewish history became the first site of Frydman's larceny. Although he had shipped most of the precious documents and artifacts separately through other channels, he likely carried at least some historical mementos as he boarded the *Wyoming* in Marseille's harbor.[126]

Beyond this valuable luggage, and the passengers themselves, of course, the freighters carried other items in their holds. Since these ships constituted Martinique's link with the colonial metropole, all manner of mail, propaganda, and documentation was dispatched from Marseille to Martinique, while pineapples, sugar, bananas, and rum returned on the voyage back. In January 1941, Vichy's Ministry of the Colonies entered into negotiations with the French Line for it to transport Pétainist propaganda reels to Fort-de-France. Commercial films were also available, added Vichy, although a cost would be involved for entertainment movies.[127] That same month, Martinique's governor requested the "very urgent" dispatch of fifteen thousand portraits of Marshal Pétain to Fort-de-France on the next available boat from Marseille.[128] No doubt the refugees were unaware that they traveled in such company.

The return traffic proved critical for Vichy, at a time when Germany was siphoning off vast quantities of food from France. It is entirely possible that some of the goods from Martinique and Guadeloupe ended up making their way from Marseille to Germany in this era, as did many other colonial resources. In fact, in 1941 one Martiniquais planter, Marraud des Grottes, took pride in having only shipped 20 percent of his production to France, arguing that most of what reached the motherland was seized by the Germans.[129]

Quite apart from the German question, Vichy desperately wanted to ensure that produce continue to be shipped, in part to keep Martinique's economy running, and also to nourish the metropolitan population, whose potatoes, flour, and wine were all being seized by a voracious Third Reich. It was not always smooth sailing: at the end of January 1941, Vichy complained that of the 21,600 banana bunches that had just reached France from Martinique, 16,500 had arrived rotten.[130] Still, the majority of the foodstuffs seem to have reached mainland France in good shape. Given the food scarcity that Martinique soon faced, a surprising amount of produce was packed in the hold of Marseille-bound ships, such as the vegetables, bananas, and banana flour that enterprising Martiniquais shipped to Marseille aboard the *Winnipeg* in 1941.[131] Amazingly, as Martinique struggled to feed itself, it continued to export foodstuffs to the colonial motherland.

The authorities in Martinique also found much to gain from this maritime line. In February 1941, they negotiated to obtain three months' worth of deliveries in salted and canned fish from Morocco, grain from France, peanut oil from French West Africa, and wine from Algeria.[132] The ships from Marseille to Martinique via Morocco thus served the key purpose of supplying the islands with foodstuffs that had been wanting since the outbreak of war.

Nevertheless, trade had certainly not returned to prewar levels. In some instances, the authorities in Martinique balked at sending rum on some of the ships to Marseille, for fear that it might be confiscated as contraband should the ships be inspected. Serge's experiences nicely encapsulated the contrasts and ironies he detected between Marseille and Fort-de-France. In the former, he had drunk disgusting ersatz coffee that tasted more of sawdust than java. Once he arrived in Fort-de-France, however, he learned to his astonishment that sugarcane and other exports (presumably coffee, cocoa, and vanilla, all produced in small quantities on location) were rotting

in storage hangers for lack of ships to take them to France, and that refin-
eries were on the verge of closing shop.[133]

Ports of Call

Casablanca served, at the very least, as a stopover for all of the ships that
concern us here. For two of the last boats to leave Marseille for Martinique
on their second wartime crossing in May 1941, the *Wyoming* and the *Mont
Viso,* the Moroccan port city became an unintended terminus. Some of the
ships also stopped in the Algerian port city of Oran.

In some instances, refugees undertook the passage to Martinique in two
distinct phases, first reaching Morocco and then finding their way to the
Caribbean. This was the case of German dissidents Kurt Kersten and Lucien
Friedlander, who reached Casablanca after the fall of France in 1940. Kersten remembers that non-French travelers were forced to stay on the ship
for an additional seven days after it docked in Casablanca. They were then
transferred to a camp bursting with other European refugees. Kersten describes a tense atmosphere in Morocco: Jewish shops were vandalized,
and refugees looked on one another with deep suspicion. Finally, the two
German dissidents found their way to Martinique aboard the *Charles L.
Dreyfus.*[134]

Other ships, such as the *Capitaine Paul Lemerle,* merely stopped over in
Casablanca, as part of a Marseille-to-Martinique line. Barth, who held
French citizenship through her Alsatian father, recollects being one of only
two passengers, along with Breton, to be allowed to disembark from the
Paul Lemerle in North Africa in 1941 (Barth had forgotten Lévi-Strauss,
who was French as well, of course). All foreigners were uniformly considered "undesirables" by the local authorities and were kept on board.[135]
Serge confirms this. He confided to his notebook that only the French were
permitted to leave ship in Oran. He then launched into an impassioned
critique of the xenophobia implied in such a decision, a discrimination he
considered "moronic" given France's low birthrate and reliance on foreign
manpower, not to mention the "composite" nature of French ethnicity. In
Casablanca, an officer came on board to explain that foreigners could not
disembark "because we are at war." "With us," added Serge defiantly.[136]

Stranded aboard, Serge counted on Breton, one of the few allowed to
disembark, for his impressions of the cities of the Maghreb. To call the Sur-

realist judgmental would be an understatement. Oran he deemed "a mediocre French provincial town," and Casablanca "vomit-inducingly bourgeois." In Casablanca, merchants and middlemen came on board to offer their wares and services to the passengers left on board. Friends paid visits as well: an Italian Socialist, a French Socialist, and a Freemason—in other words, local subversives in the eyes of Vichy.[137]

Toward Fort-de-France

Serge's notebook describes the last hours of the *Paul Lemerle*'s voyage. As they neared Martinique, passengers stared in wonder first at flying fish and then at dolphins dancing with the boat's bow.[138] Other, more mundane and pragmatic considerations also crossed the minds of refugees. After interminable weeks at sea and in port, Lévi-Strauss remembers longing for a proper shower on land. However, within minutes of docking in Fort-de-France, he would come to realize that the "crammed and filthy" ship he and his companions were leaving was "idyllic" next to the treatment they now faced. It was as if Vichy officials had deliberately "sent these gentlemen a cargo of scapegoats on whom they could unload their bile," wrote the anthropologist.[139]

Vichy found itself between a rock and hard place in the Caribbean; the Marseille–Casablanca–Fort-de-France route constituted one of its few lifelines. Colonial officials no doubt realized this, yet they also treated the migrants who took the line on the insistence of the Ministry of the Interior—and against their repeated pleas—as a fifth column of undesirables, or even as the very cause of France's recent defeat. As we will see, wartime Martinique was exposed both to tectonic international pressures and to oppressive Vichy rule.

CHAPTER FIVE

Wartime Martinique

As they approached Fort-de-France, the refugees no doubt distinguished the massive Savane public space and the two-hundred-foot spire of the city's late nineteenth-century cathedral. They were mesmerized by the island's luxurious vegetation, especially the swaths of color provided by abundant bougainvilleas and the strikingly vivid royal poinciana *(flamboyant)* trees. Victor Serge dwelled on Fort-de-France's "splendid bay" and the surrounding "caiman shaped hills that sink into the sea."[1] After docking in what Minister Albert Sarraut had designated as one of the French empire's top four ports,[2] travelers may have discerned some architectural jewels, including the impressive covered market and the magnificent Schoelcher Library. City hall, completed in 1901, was adorned with images representing the final abolition of slavery in 1848.[3] Since 1940, the republic's slogan "Liberty, Equality and Fraternity" had been replaced on the building's façade with a declaration of the regime's new values, "Work, Family, Fatherland."

Fort-de-France had actually played second fiddle to Saint-Pierre until a volcanic eruption annihilated that rival town in 1902. Now Fort-de-France had taken over as the French Caribbean's commercial hub, which had previously been Saint-Pierre's function, as well as continuing to serve as its administrative capital. Population increases reflected the town's new stature, as it tripled between 1894 and 1931, going from a mere 16,056 inhabitants to 46,326. By 1940, it reached 60,000.[4]

Martinique's immigration law was generally aligned with that of France's other so-called old colonies, including Guadeloupe and Réunion

Island. The island's governor, appointed by Paris, held the right to expel any foreigner. However, in one respect Martinique did differ from the "old colony" rule. The legal mechanism by which slavery's successor had been put in place was discarded in Martinique in 1884. This is to say that *engagisme*, the long-term contracts signed mainly with South Asians brought over to toil in the sugarcane fields, was formally ended in Martinique in 1884–1885, while the practice remained enshrined in law in France's other old colonies until the end of the Second World War. In that respect, Martinique constituted something of an exception.[5]

The 1930s had seen Fort-de-France suffer from the Great Depression and its accompanying long-term social consequences. Sugarcane workers filed through its streets on a "hunger march" in 1935; the following year, the city's dockworkers walked off the job; in 1937 bakers and workers in the printing sector took to the picket lines. At the same time, Martinique began, very modestly, attracting migrants from the Middle East and Europe, as well as from neighboring Caribbean islands. While Martinique counted only 617 registered foreigners in 1927, that figure rose to 1,507 in 1938. Some locals began complaining of competition for scarce jobs and denouncing the arrival of Italians and Syrians in particular (earlier waves of immigrants from South Asia were no longer the scapegoats at this point).[6] The immigration figures of the 1930s would be dwarfed by the migratory wave of 1940–1941, which brought 5,000 refugees to the isle, admittedly on a shorter "in-transit" basis.

What did these refugees see as they landed in Martinique in 1940 and 1941? How did officials receive them? How did they relate to local inhabitants in a time of even greater shortages than the 1930s? Claude Lévi-Strauss already provided a hint on some of these scores. Serge came straight to the point: "Fort-de-France . . . welcomed them poorly."[7] However, before fully answering these key questions, it seems essential to provide details on the context of wartime Martinique, an island considered by many as a Vichy thorn in the Western Hemisphere's side between 1940 and 1943.

Stakes

When France fell to Nazi Germany in May and June 1940, French colonies, the French fleet, and the gold of the Bank of France emerged as three major international cards still out of German reach. The Vichy regime initially succeeded in securing most of these assets, although the United Kingdom launched a controversial preemptive strike on the French Navy in North Africa, and several French colonies did side with General Charles de Gaulle over the summer of 1940.[8] However, the vast majority of French overseas holdings, including Martinique and its sister island Guadeloupe, remained "loyal" to Philippe Pétain's authoritarian government, which initially held the edge in credibility. In the winter of 1940, Vichy continued to hold sway from Fort-de-France to Algiers and Dakar, and from Damascus to Hanoi.

How did this come about? In reality, local populations had little choice. To be sure, some of Martinique's and Guadeloupe's leading elected officials boldly attempted to join de Gaulle's Free French. However, French naval authorities reined them in. Ultimately, in the Caribbean, the decision to follow Vichy hinged on a June 1940 power struggle within the highest echelons of the local French naval unit. Between June 27 and June 29, it saw Pétain supporters—Captain (and soon rear admiral) Pierre Rouyer and Commandants Robert Battet and Yves Aubert—win over their still hesitant and wavering superiors, Admiral Georges Robert and Rear Admiral Henri-Paul Chomereau-Lamotte. Within this group, the most ardent advocate of remaining faithful to the British alliance was Chomereau-Lamotte, whose origins were Martinican. He suffered a fatal stroke on July 1. Rumors of foul play circulated thereafter, no doubt stoked by Rouyer's remark that the death had come eight days too late. Once High Commissioner and Admiral Robert swung over to Rouyer's pro-Pétain line, the civil administration, led by Governor Henry Bressoles in Martinique, quickly followed suit.[9]

Nevertheless, Vichy officials still deemed their position fragile that fall. In September 1940, Rouyer described the atmosphere in the French West Indies as symptomatic of the weakness and "sickness" that had supposedly plagued the French Third Republic. He implored Vichy to cable "any law that could help clean up this unfortunate land" and to dispatch new personnel to the islands that would be "healthy" and loyal to the new regime.[10] Despite important naval assets, Vichy's representatives never felt completely at ease in the Caribbean. For one thing, a gulf separated the navy, primarily composed of sailors from mainland France, from the army, made up largely of local black recruits. In September 1941, Admiral Robert cabled Vichy indicating that many of his best units were tied up guarding the gold of the Bank of France, leaving other areas vulnerable. To make matters worse, he doubted the loyalty of some in the military and saw cracks forming in the morale of reservists. He therefore implored Vichy to send ten lieutenants from France, eight for the infantry and two for the artillery.[11]

After the Netherlands fell to the German blitzkrieg in May 1940, first French and British, then later US, troops landed in the Dutch West Indies. The Dutch islands were thus kept out of the hands of the Nazis.[12] By July 1940 French Guiana, Saint-Pierre and Miquelon, Martinique, Guadeloupe, and their possessions (Saint Martin and Saint Berthélemy) thereby emerged as the only satellites of the Axis in the Western Hemisphere. As such, they would become a growing fixation of British and American attention. From 1940 through 1943, inhabitants of Martinique would pay the price for this gradually mounting isolation.

International and Trade Contexts

As Kristen Stromberg Childers has recently shown, after the fall of France, American attention became riveted on French territories in the Western Hemisphere. The Robert-Greenslade agreement of August 1940, which maintained Vichy's control over Martinique and Guadeloupe in exchange for considerable US oversight, completely transformed the relationship between Martinique and the United States. The latter vowed to keep supply lines open to Martinique in exchange for assurances that Vichy's warships would be kept on location, and that the United States would be granted unprecedented access to information.[13]

At this juncture, trade continued, including along the Marseille–Casablanca–Fort-de-France route so critical for the refugees. Local lines also ran unabated from Fort-de-France to destinations that included New York, the Dominican Republic, and Brazil. Indeed, in March and April 1941 Vichy even submitted requests for spare parts for its commercial and war vessels to the United States and received everything from ball bearings to radio equipment and projector lights from New York and Chicago.[14]

The period of accommodation and even cooperation between Vichy and the United States in the Caribbean can be interpreted in different ways. Most obviously, it coincided with relatively cordial relations between

Washington and Vichy; it bears repeating that on November 8, 1942, Vichy broke off diplomatic relations with Washington, rather than vice versa. Washington was also eager to ensure that the Vichy warships docked in the French West Indies remain there, and it deemed this possible via negotiation. Moreover, some have suggested that Washington wished to ensure stability in French Guiana so as to thwart Brazilian ambitions.[15]

However, one source at the British Foreign Office offered a different explanation for the seemingly lenient US position on the French West Indies. William H. B. Mack, the France expert at the Foreign Office, wrote in January 1942, "The State Department have surely made it clear for over a year that it is their policy to keep these islands going economically in order to prevent trouble with the coloured population which the U.S. would probably have to help to put down."[16] If Mack was correct, then fears of racially charged unrest, rather than the threat posed by an aircraft carrier and three cruisers, or a desire to maintain Vichy neutrality, drove Washington's stance on this matter.

This was no isolated case of US-British divergence on the Vichy Caribbean. In 1942, the British Foreign Office again attempted to persuade Washington to adopt a harsher line, drawing on the testimony of Félix Eboué, the black former governor of Guadeloupe and now leading Free Frenchman in Africa. Eboué estimated that a plebiscite would show 97 percent of French West Indians in favor of de Gaulle's Free French. He added that Britain and the United States must intervene, for Admiral Robert had implemented a police state that had systematically jailed opponents. On this last score, British notes reveal tellingly, "State Department have been informed of the substance of [Eboué's] remarks. They were not much impressed and observed that the majority of the islanders were illiterate negroes without political views." Eboué's addendum, which featured a list of internees at the Fort Napoléon in Les Saintes and at the Balata internment camp in Martinique, seems not to have swayed the State Department either.[17]

Yet it would be an error to suggest that the United States merely enabled Admiral Robert. In effect, the screws on Vichy's Caribbean islands were tightened incrementally. By the middle of 1941, Washington and London had narrowed their differences on how to treat Vichy-controlled Martinique. Already in January 1941, the United States warned that it might refuse to refuel French freighters on the Marseille–Martinique line that had previously stopped to refuel in Saint Thomas (a US territory since 1917); this refusal ultimately occurred on March 22, 1941, with the *Ipanema* docked in the US Virgin Islands. Washington demanded that Vichy henceforth make all passenger manifests to Martinique available to it.[18] By April 1941, Admiral Robert was telegraphing Casablanca about new US sensitivity to merchandise aboard the vessels reaching Fort-de-France, and suggesting that henceforth all goods should be labeled as originating from Morocco rather than France.[19]

Ultimately, the coup de grace came from Britain and its Dutch ally. In May and June 1941, a Dutch warship brought an abrupt end to the shipping line that concerns us here. It did so by seizing on the high seas two French freighters: the *Winnipeg* on May 26 and the *Arica* on June 1.[20] Also in 1941, the United Kingdom convinced Dutch authorities to suspend all service from Dutch isles to Martinique and Guadeloupe.[21] Vichy's rear admiral Rouyer interpreted this turn of events as a reaction to Admiral François Darlan's visit to Adolf Hitler at Berchtesgaden.[22] Much more was at stake in point of fact, but clearly Vichy rule over the French West Indies was tributary to tectonic forces well beyond the control of its henchmen in the Caribbean.

The Vichy Caribbean was increasingly caught between a rock and a hard place.[23] In April 1943 all official dialogue ceased between Vichy officials in the Caribbean and their US interlocutors. The United States implemented a "complete blockade" of the French West Indies.[24] This was the nail in Vichy's coffin in the French West Indies.

Autarky and Its Consequences

The gradual isolation of the French West Indies caused penury to set in, despite the Robert-Greenslade agreement. Imports to Martinique dropped spectacularly from 109,842 tons in 1938 to 78,673 tons in 1941, 46,213 tons in 1942, and a meager 19,313 tons in 1943 when the American blockade was enforced.[25]

Given these new shortages brought about by the war, Vichy officials in the French Caribbean tried to open trade with Canada. After all, connections abounded: the cod fishery was still thriving off Canada's maritime provinces, and the Royal Bank of Canada represented a major player in most of the Caribbean, including Martinique and Guadeloupe. However, London's Dominion Office stood firm and "sought to dissuade Canada from doing any trade with the islands at all."[26] Still, on occasion Ottawa defied London on this matter. Thus, early in 1943, a boatload of Canadian codfish was bartered for Martinique rum.[27] Ever resourceful, Admiral Robert even made overtures to French Indochina, asking authorities there to dispatch rice to the French West Indies, in vain.[28] More successfully, beef was imported from the Dominican Republic.[29]

Reduced trade was not the only challenge facing Martinique's economy. After the French West Indies sided with Vichy, the once lucrative tourism sector dried up overnight. Previously, the island's magnificent interior, its beaches and mineral springs, had attracted a number of loyal American, Canadian, and Guianese tourists and, most importantly, cruise ships that already in the 1930s had deposited throngs of visitors for short stays between December and March. In October 1940, Admiral Robert approached the American consulate in Martinique indicating that since Martinique was no longer at war, "he would like to see the American tourist vessels resume their calls at Martinique." Robert boasted "that Martinique is one of the most beautiful islands of the Caribbean." He even added that tourists would be welcome to take photographs, except in specifically designated sites.[30]

In addition to attempting to rekindle tourism and opening new trade routes, efforts were undertaken to produce locally, thereby diminishing reliance on imported goods. As soon as France fell, Martinique and Guadeloupe looked toward new food sources. On August 24, 1940, the pro-Vichy Martinican mouthpiece *La Paix* evoked a typically Vichyite "return to the soil," exhorting islanders to "abandon an artificial economy" and to forage for food locally. That same month, the head of Martinique's agricultural services, Henri Stehlé, broadcast a rather academic radio presentation on fruits, vegetables, and the island's cultivation potential.[31] Every Sunday at noon, Radio Martinique also advocated local production in a radio program entitled simply the "Martinican Effort." Whatever merits it had were likely expended undoing the damage of a program presented the day before. On Saturdays, the same station aired a segment entitled "Pierre's Culinary Chronicles"; given the paltry food supply, it must have fostered envy, resentment, and gastronomic nostalgia for the days of plenty.[32]

By 1942, in Martinique as in mainland France, the quest for food had become the perennial everyday occupation. Ersatz materials became the rule: Martinique's press from 1942 is replete with ads urging people to keep rabbit pelts or asking the public to utilize larger bottles of rum so as to save on glass.[33] Naturally, the public grumbled as it faced restrictions. British officials got wind of reports from refugees in Martinique suggesting that administrators and the military, as well as Vichy sympathizers, were hoarding food.[34] Vichy's zealous postal censorship, which avidly opened and read all correspondence, reported in April of that year on the abundance of letters complaining of the high cost of meat, fish, and oil. Some suggested that Vichy's important naval presence was compounding the problem with extra mouths to feed.[35] However, such candid complaints were becoming rare, not because the situation in Martinique was improving but because, by Vichy censors' own admission, many letter writers complained bitterly of their letters being opened. They were evidently worried that they would face consequences for their political views. Consequently, the censors saw "people . . . stopping in the middle of a sentence so as not to offend" them.[36]

Difficulties extended far beyond shortages in food and excesses in censorship. Vichy's inspector Emile Devouton conceded in an April 1941 report that the naval clique represented a burden on the local cost of living: "The presence in the French West Indies of an important number of naval officers and their families, as well as the influx of populations from rural into urban areas . . . has resulted in an extreme shortage of places to rent, and a constant hike in rent rates."[37]

Interestingly, another source placed the responsibility for inflation not on the navy but on incoming refugees. In May 1941, the head of Martinique's customs services complained that refugees who had recently arrived aboard the *Paul Lemerle* and the *Carimaré* were making "large purchases of gold and precious stones." Because these transactions were completed by check, rather than cash, the official worried of future currency troubles. He also voiced concern that refugees were purchasing clothing items at a time when they were scarce. His solution was to try to dissuade shopkeepers from selling clothes to newcomers, and to demand that incoming migrants declare their valuables.[38]

Repression and Racism

The regime's repressive instincts were of course directed at locals as much as they were at migrants. Vichy quickly set about jailing local opponents, by virtue of new measures dated September 1940 that concerned "individuals considered a danger to national defense or public safety."[39] Among those whom Vichy interned in camps such as Balata in Martinique, one counts the black journalist for *Le Clairon* Jean Toulouse, suspected of sharing information with US journalist Frank Gervasi, and the young sugar heir Joseph de Reynal de Saint Michel, imprisoned for having painted a V for victory on his car. Police found another "Gaullist inscription," presumably a cross of Lorraine, when they searched Reynal's house.[40]

Coercion, incarceration, and violence went hand in hand. After the war, a purge commission determined that gendarmerie commandant Pierre Delpech had committed acts of violence on at least one victim. So had Captain Marie-Joseph Castaing, policeman Maréchal, and the naval captain Géraud Marche, with the added mention that Castaing had supplemented beatings with racist insults. One of the victims, Georges Minatchy, was tortured with his hands behind his back, before being sent to the penal colony in Guiana. The archives suggest he was left a broken man.[41]

In the realm of symbolic violence, the new order systematically replaced markers of liberty with symbols of the Vichy regime. Thus, in Fort-de-France, it renamed Jules Grévy Square, named after the first openly democratic leader of the French Third Republic, Marshal Pétain Square.[42] Similarly, in 1941 in the town of La Trinité on Martinique's Atlantic coast, Victor Hugo Street was rebranded Marshal Pétain Boulevard.[43] No doubt as an ardent advocate of the republic who had gone into exile after Napoleon III came to power, Hugo was now persona non grata. However, locally, Hugo's resonance would have centered on his first novel, *Bug-Jargal*, a story set during the 1791 slave revolt in Saint-Domingue (later Haiti).[44] Renaming Victor Hugo Street was therefore tantamount to snubbing not only a great advocate of the republic but also an admirer of the Haitian Revolution. When he visited Martinique once more after the war, it was these 1941 changes to street names that André Breton provided as proof of Vichy's authoritarian agenda.[45]

Within this new political climate, between 1940 and 1943 those sympathetic to the democracies followed Hugo's path by choosing exile. A thirty-five-year-old fisherman from Martinique named Frédéric Bouvil left for Saint Lucia. From Castries he reported to British colonial authorities on November 26, 1940, "The people at Sainte Luce [in southern Martinique] are all de Gaulle sympathizers, also it is the wish of the people to serve under de Gaulle for the liberty and freedom of their mother country. At present, all the districts are governed by mayors but it is rumored that at any time they will be ejected from their office and administrators will be appointed by the Admiral to replace them."[46]

In Martinique, democracy and civil society came under sustained attack between 1940 and 1943. This backlash ushered in renewed and intensified racism. It, in turn, needs to be situated within the context of a heavily stratified colonial society, in which sugar magnates and the white so-called *béké* class already held disproportionate sway before 1940. Although a shortcut, novelist Daniel Maximin's pithy phrase is probably not far off the mark. He states that in 1940 "the békés savored their revenge over the Republic by sipping overly sweetened rum punch."[47]

It would nonetheless be a mistake to see in Martinique a society divided only by race. In fact, none other than Frantz Fanon has suggested that in Martinique in the 1930s, class trumped race. Social relations, he writes, were "not altered by skin color." To Fanon, "racial stories" constituted the mantle or "superstructure," not the prime movers. The liberation theorist suggests that all of this changed during the Vichy period, when the metropolitan sailors, who used to spend all of eight days per annum in the French West Indies, were suddenly left in Martinique for three straight years. Fanon clearly labels these sailors, and the regime they served, "authentic racists."[48] In other words, Fanon saw the advent of the Vichy regime in Martinique as marking a major break in terms of the rise of explicit and unabashed racism. Fanon went on to elaborate that racism was never static; for the most part, "vulgar, simplistic" racism of this type was historically on the decline (making way, alas, for a new "cultural racism"), he contended, and the Vichy period marked one of many periodic "resurgences."[49]

What was the connection between this racist turn and Vichy's drive to "cleanse" democratic institutions in Martinique? Already in November 1940, the US consulate had been warned by an anonymous source that the regime was poised "to place white Frenchmen in government positions which are now held by colored citizens."[50] To be sure, this was a shortcut, one tinged by US perspectives as well. In Martinique, people of color had occupied important positions in government, agriculture, trade, and business for decades, indeed centuries. Nor were color boundaries in any way hermetic in the French Caribbean. Yet it seems clear that Vichy targeted both blacks and figures it saw as politically suspect. However, given how entangled these two categories proved to Vichy officials, agendas can prove almost impossible to disassociate.

Perusing the *journaux officiels,* or registers of laws and decrees, from this era, one does indeed find mention of removal after removal of democratically elected officials. To replace them, Vichy nominated notables who shared the new regime's values, many of them from the white planter class. In 1941, Vichy inspector Devouton wrote, "Political men who occupied the position of mayor have mostly been replaced by notables, who are being asked to run municipalities as good family fathers might."[51] But the question remains: Was this paternalism explicitly racist?

Dominique Chathuant has shown persuasively that in neighboring Guadeloupe, legally elected black mayors were replaced by designated white ones in thirteen of the twenty-four municipalities on the two butterfly-shaped halves of the Guadeloupe, known as Basse-Terre and Grande-Terre (excluding the isles of La Désirade, Les Saintes, and Marie-Galante). On the sugar-producing island of Marie-Galante, interestingly, the three new mayors named in 1941 were black. To explain this exception, Chathuant hypothesizes that either Vichy failed to find ideologically suitable local white candidates or it might have sought to avoid offending the local population.[52]

The latter theory seems validated by internal Vichy discussions of the situation in Martinique. In February 1941, Devouton wrote, "Given the touchiness of the colored population, and particularly the mixed-race element, the Admiral [Robert] and myself have endeavored to limit to a strict minimum the designation of white creoles as mayors. Some excellent candidates had to be ruled out as a result."[53] Devouton's balancing act yielded the following results. Of the twelve newly named mayors in Martinique, four were white Creoles; of the nine existing mayors whom Vichy deigned to keep, three were white Creoles. Paternalism, authoritarianism, and racism were all undergoing careful calibrations in the halls of power at Fort-de-France. The regime was conscious, in other words, that its nominations were being watched closely and that a purge that could be perceived as both racist and powerfully undemocratic was likely to create a backlash.

Under the circumstances, Admiral Robert, Devouton, and consorts decided to rein in their racism in their nomination process in order to achieve their authoritarian agenda. Historian Léo Elisabeth has concluded that Vichy proved ambiguous in matters of race in Martinique. To demonstrate this, he points to the number of white sailors who married local black women—which on its own seems a dubious marker of antiracism—and to the high percentage of local black West Indians incorporated into the ranks of the navy at this time "to replace white dissidents" who left for Saint Lucia (another odd point, for the majority of dissidents were black). As for Vichy's naming békés to replace elected mayors, Elisabeth cautions, "Their color has been the focal point, but we should not lose track of the fact that they were rural notables . . . that three of them had already served as mayors, and that the remaining ones were veterans."[54] This last contention makes sense: it proves hard to distinguish racist motivations from paternalist, antidemocratic ones. Nevertheless, on balance, Fanon's point has not been fundamentally overturned. Revocation figures and internal Vichy documents both point to a whitening of the political class under Vichy.

In addition to mayors, municipal councils also experienced a purge. According to Camille Chauvet's calculations, only 30 of the 201 named municipal councillors in Martinique in 1941 had been in office before the fall of France a year prior.[55] The island's general council (or island legislature) experienced similar treatment. Some councillors were singled out explicitly because of their political orientation. Thus, on April 8, 1941, Vichy removed Marie Joseph Angelo from the Conseil Général. Governor Yves Marie Nicol had denounced him as the instigator of strikes back in 1935, and as the purported leader of a clique of disaffected politicians from the era of democracy.[56]

Admiral Robert and his entourage further introduced Vichy's witch-hunts to the French West Indies, including the persecution of the islands' thirty-six Jews in November 1941 (the figure excludes incoming refugees), as well as local Freemasons. The persecutions involved firings and property confiscation, enumeration by census, and other vexations and humiliations. The process also elicited denunciations.[57] On November 13, 1940, Governor Nicol sent out an urgent message to all administrative branches, asking for the names of Jewish officials. An ensuing pile of declarations of non-Jewishness was signed by legions of functionaries; it now fills a carton in Martinique's archives. Nicol personally oversaw the timetable for firings of Jews from certain professions in late 1941. Among those fired was a Jewish teacher named Ilija Salanski.[58] On the basis of British debriefings of Czechoslovakian and French officers who reached Saint Lucia from Martinique, Fitzroy Baptiste claims that a mysterious Comte de Cerezy was at least partially responsible for stoking the anti-Semitism of Vichy officials in Martinique (the sources specified that Cerezy operated for the French secret services).[59] The colonial archives in Aix-en-Provence reveal that the regime at Vichy was also micromanaging the introduction of anti-Semitic legislation from afar. Regardless of the precise mechanisms at work, it is clear that the refugees from Marseille had landed in an anti-Semitic satellite of Vichy in the Caribbean.

The purges also affected gainfully employed women, as well as people deemed hostile to the new order. The replacement of Martinique's governor Bressoles with Nicol in January 1941 was part and parcel of this incremental process. Vichy's inspector Devouton had requested that the planned retirement of Bressoles be hastened because of his purported residual sympathy for some former elected officials in Martinique. Nicol, a Pétain stalwart who had rejected Free French rule in French Equatorial Africa, was deemed more loyal.[60]

The troubled climate under Vichy also led to significant tensions between the white sailors loyal to Admiral Robert and the rest of the population, including black infantry personnel. Cases of white sailors behaving badly took on an especially problematic dimension for the authorities, precisely because sailors constituted the core of Vichy's repressive arsenal and were expected to embody the values of the new order. On August 7, 1942, for instance, a drunk sailor zigzagged into the Gaumont cinema in Fort-de-France, then collapsed in a deep sleep on several black audience members. This was clearly no isolated case, for the navy reported that such "degenerate" behavior was beginning to stir animosity from locals.[61]

An October 1942 naval patrol through the streets of Fort-de-France netted the following observations. First, a report alleged that "too many sailors can be seen arm in arm with local black women [doudous]." Second, it revealed a telling incident that took place around ten o'clock at night on October 4, 1942. That evening, three local black soldiers harassed a white petty officer. After the petty officer made it clear that he did not understand what the men were saying in Creole, the soldiers hurled insults at him in French, the most polite of which was "damned Frenchman." Brandishing his club, the petty officer tried chasing them, but he was blocked by local citizens who deliberately held him up. The report concluded that petty officers needed to be armed with more than mere clubs.[62] Clearly, Vichy's forces sensed that they were in a minority situation and that the population could turn against them at any time. It was into this fragile and fraught context that boatloads of "undesirable" refugees arrived.

The Case of Mayotte Capécia

None of this is to suggest that Martinicans of color were unanimously opposed to Admiral Robert and his cabal. A small number of Martinicans outside the wealthy planter and béké class threw their support behind Admiral Robert and the Vichy regime. In many instances, they did so for pragmatic reasons.

An academic skirmish has taken place over one such figure, novelist Mayotte Capécia (real name Lucette Céranus Combette). This Martinican woman of humble origins, who had been working at a Fort-de-France chocolate factory since the age of thirteen, drew the ire of Fanon. Fanon saw her as a black female throwing herself at a white male, and interpreted this as a denial of her blackness. Albert James Arnold recently added to these charges of alienation by implying that Capécia was also a literary fraud who perpetuated stereotypes and was a plagiarist to boot. Conversely, an effort at rehabilitation or at least at recontextualization has been spearheaded by Christiane Makward, Myriam Cottias, and Madeleine Dobie. Their feminist rereadings have emphasized Capécia's agency and her strategies and options within the limited room to maneuver available to her.[63]

The Vichy years in Martinique lie at the heart of the Capécia debate. In the spring of 1941, Capécia began a relationship with Max Salmon, a white Protestant naval aviator and lieutenant in Admiral Robert's forces. They first met at the Fort-de-France bar Au Vieux Logis, run by her sister. As Capécia wrote in one novel, "The presence of the *Emile Bertin* in Fort-de-France's harbor represented a significant increase in the male population."[64]

Vichy's sailors, as we already know, spent their idle time in the city's bars, where they met local women.

Dobie and Cottias perceive Capécia's relationship as part of a broader strategy to attain upward social mobility in a notoriously stratified setting.[65] This view seems confirmed in a passage from Capécia's novel *Je suis Martiniquaise,* in which she wrote of elation at being invited in 1941, by Lieutenant Salmon, "to one of those little villas that I had admired since my childhood." However, an Eliza Doolittle–like moment of frustration ensued. She realized that she was "not dressed as one should be," and that her heavy layers of makeup were drawing sneers, unless of course it was the color of her skin itself, she added.[66]

Capécia was caught in a social no-man's-land, rejected by the island's elite but also by Salmon's black maid, who looked at her with contempt. There was, of course, reason for envy to be directed at Capécia. All Martinicans tightened their belts, and Capécia admittedly complained of the price of fish and vegetables, and that breadfruit and avocadoes were being picked unripe because of unrelenting demand. Yet through her partner, Capécia at least had rabbits and chickens at her disposal, as well as a garden full of yams.[67]

Political disparities compounded economic ones. While Fanon left Martinique to join the Free French forces, Capécia attended Vichy gala events. At Fort-de-France's municipal theater, she watched as the regime made a spectacle of itself. An actor played Father Jean-Baptiste Labat, the seventeenth-century chronicler of the French Caribbean, in a scene in which he fired on British vessels. Admiral Robert's propaganda services were harnessing the local past so as to bolster their present Anglophobic case. Capécia clearly sided with Robert in his showdown with both the United Kingdom and the United States. She also heaped scorn on the local black infantry units that would eventually topple the white navy's grip on the island in July 1943.[68]

Capécia would pay for her choices and her opinions. She was admittedly not publicly humiliated by having her head shaven after the war as were so many women accused of "horizontal collaboration" with the Germans in mainland France. However, once Vichy rule ended, Capécia felt the "ostracism" of her compatriots.[69] This contempt even became a factor in her decision to leave for Paris. Again, if one were to project metropolitan categories onto the situation in Martinique, Capécia's attitude would probably be located on the "accommodation" part of the spectrum that runs between resistance and collaboration.

Rumors of Slavery's Return

The Vichy regime's ideology and agenda fostered a tense atmosphere in which all rights acquired under the French Republic seemed jeopardized. As an "old colony," along with Réunion, Guiana, and Guadeloupe, Martinique had enjoyed a special status markedly different from that of most colonial territories. While elsewhere the iniquitous *indigénat* served as a legal code, French laws were generally extended to Martinique. While most people in French colonies were French subjects, those of the old colonies were full-fledged French citizens. In this sense, the inhabitants of old colonies such as Martinique stood to lose more from Vichy's abrogation of civil liberties and voting rights than did those in most other colonial lands. Vichy marked a clear step backward, reminding French West Indians of other such moments in their history.

The fact that slavery had initially been abolished in French colonies in 1794 only to be reintroduced in 1802 under Napoleon also lent credence to the possibility of another terrible step backward. In 1848, the Second Republic had definitively abolished slavery in French colonies. Yet, as we have seen, it was replaced by coercive forms of contract labor. Moreover, its memory endured; during the second half of the nineteenth century, for instance, the hardening of controls over workers in Martinique and Guadeloupe under Napoleon III had fanned fears of reenslavement. Now, in 1940, the advent of an unabashedly authoritarian regime evidently conjured up the legacy of slavery. Indeed, departure to Saint Lucia and Dominica between 1940 and 1943 was often experienced as a form of modern-day *marronnage* (the term for escaped slaves).[70]

The rumors began early. Already on July 24, 1940, the church mouthpiece *La Paix* reported whispers of a special status for colonial people that might augur a return to slavery.[71] The murmur soon turned into a roar. A report from Martinique on March 9, 1942, bluntly conveyed these fears, relaying in particular "rumors in Gros Morne announcing the return of slavery."[72]

These rumors of a return to slavery were also connected to economic circumstance and Vichy's ways of dealing with it. The new regime passed laws severely punishing the destruction of crops. Productivity became an official priority, indeed the key to the survival of a besieged Vichy regime in an otherwise hostile Caribbean Sea. In an especially candid set of instructions dated May 30, 1941, the head of the gendarmerie in Martinique, Captain Delpech, outlined ways of returning agricultural workers to the fields. "Alas," he regretted, "no law requires cane workers to work." However, he suggested to his staff a series of measures they could adopt to achieve precisely such an end. "Use vagabondage laws as scarecrows," he urged. He then added, "This, along with the verification of people's identification . . . usually suffices to achieve the results that the government so keenly desires at present."[73] Here is precisely where fears of a return of slavery and new Vichy imperatives met. Vichy's police and gendarmerie utilized intimidation and vagrancy laws to foster a climate of fear in which any person of color could be brought in for questioning.

Resistance

Some of the first acts of resistance in September 1940 included the widespread distribution of Gaullist leaflets. Vichy's authorities responded swiftly, firing mayors and local police officers in communities where the pamphlets had circulated.[74] In addition to spreading information, inhabitants of the French West Indies mastered or recast forms of resistance that James Scott has termed "weapons of the weak."[75] Anonymous nocturnal singing offered rare opportunities for public expression under the cover of darkness. On the evening of June 14, 1943, the following defiant verses rang through the streets of Martinique's capital: "We don't have anything to eat, but we aren't afraid of you."[76]

The most radical course of action involved leaving Martinique altogether to join General de Gaulle's Fighting French. Interinsular connections played an important role in shaping escape routes. Some of the earliest *passeurs* to assist those wanting to leave Vichy-controlled Martinique in late 1940 were British nationals from Dominica with French West Indian kinship connections. In December 1940, Vichy authorities arrested one Strasfort Didnoit, hailing from Dominica, on charges of vagrancy. They soon discovered that he had assisted French sailors escaping for neighboring British islands. Vichy police rightly suspected another individual from Dominica, fisherman Herman François Gachette, known under the pseudonym Amant, of leading another ring.[77] Indeed, a document dated November 2, 1940, preserved in the Saint Lucian police archives, confirms that Gachette was "pro-de Gaulle" and was "a Dominican who [was] married to a native of Martinique." It also features lengthy reports by Gachette on conditions in Martinique, including dwindling food stocks, the distribution of Gaullist pamphlets, the state of public opinion, coastal battery locations, and the cost of living.[78] Evidently, interisland information gathering, passages, and ties proved essential for resistance activities in the French West Indies. Here we see a potent demonstration of Matthew J. Smith's argument about the Caribbean's profound interconnectedness through exile.[79]

A former Socialist municipal councillor named Maurice des Etages proved instrumental in organizing crossings from Martinique to Saint Lucia. He traveled personally to Saint Lucia to liaise with British military authorities to organize nocturnal departures by boat. In February 1941, he further provided British authorities in Saint Lucia with a wealth of information about conditions in Martinique. His report included estimates of support for Pétain and de Gaulle in different segments of society. Des Etages even considered the profile of new arrivals in Martinique from Marseille on board the vessels that interest us. He noted, "There are . . . some German Jews in Martinique who appear to be harmless. They came on troop ships arriving from Casablanca."[80] He discussed plans to use fishermen to bring more volunteers from Martinique to Castries. However, a month later des Etages was denounced after returning to Martinique. He attempted suicide aboard the Vichy vessel where he was interrogated, before being condemned to fifteen years' hard labor in Guiana on charges of treason. At his trial, des Etages spoke of his ardent patriotism and his desire to defeat Nazism.[81] After his arrest, his wife remained active in the resistance. She circulated from one fishing village to another, trying to convince fishermen not to denounce dissidents fleeing to nearby British islands.[82]

Notwithstanding setbacks like the arrest of des Etages, the flow of exiles and volunteers from Martinique and Guadeloupe to Saint Lucia and Dominica increased steadily between 1940 and 1943. On February 20, 1941, Captain Noël set about coordinating coastal defenses for Admiral Robert; rather than focusing on the possibility of US or UK landings, he mainly sought to prevent departures. Noël organized two watch posts in

Martinique. He raised the possibility of seeking "the voluntary collaboration of a certain number of people along the coast, especially along vulnerable and unsupervised stretches of coastline."[83] While Vichy's police, navy, and gendarmerie succeeded in foiling many departures, it could not stem the growing tide. Dissidents, as they called themselves, managed to reach Dominica from several locations in Martinique, including Grand-Rivière, where a plaque in their memory now stands. Several sites in southern Martinique lent themselves to departure to Saint Lucia.[84]

Dissidents were a heterogeneous bunch. Many women crossed as well as men, having no doubt heard through word of mouth that the Free French had established female units. The Free French trained these West Indian women and sent some of them to serve in Africa, others to the European war theater.[85] However, a number of women reached Saint Lucia with young children in tow,[86] which suggests that the Saint Lucian authorities were probably correct in labeling those individuals "refugees" rather than future combatants. Nor were West Indians the only ones to leave for Dominica and Saint Lucia. A significant number of Vichy's own white forces deserted, not to mention many of the Czechoslovakian troops stranded in Martinique.[87]

The sizeable Czech military contingent on Martinique was stuck in a Kafkaesque situation. By a bizarre twist of circumstance, they were as stranded as the stateless refugees from Marseille. Indeed, a 1939 French law passed in the wake of the Munich agreement had rendered Czech soldiers French in the eyes of the law, and the armistice of 1940 forbade French troops from leaving French territory. As a result, the Czechs were legally bound to remain on location in Martinique until 1943, although many absconded to join the Allies.[88]

Some in Vichy's service left cheeky notes behind as they left for Saint Lucia or Dominica. In June 1941, the captain of the tanker ship *Motrix* discovered a message left by Henri Vanhuysen. It explained that Vanhuysen was Belgian and not French, and signed off with the words, "I am now going to sail for the British nation, my second country. You won't be able to find me."[89]

The crossings proved both risky and expensive. Jean Massip, the Free Frenchman responsible for coordinating escapes and then the voyage onward to the United Kingdom or the United States, recalls that passage from Martinique to Saint Lucia or Dominica cost somewhere between 2,000 and

3,000 francs.[90] Des Etages mentions a lower but still significant price of 1,000 francs per crossing.[91] Volunteers rightly worried about the trustworthiness of boat owners offering the service, especially in the wake of a string of spectacular arrests following denunciations. Indeed, a deserter from Vichy's navy who reached Saint Lucia in 1941 explained to British authorities that two hundred of his comrades likewise wished to join Free France. He depicted the obstacles in their way as follows: "The only difficulties are 1) money—the men have not the funds to pay for transport, 2) they do not know with whom to make contact in Martinique to arrange their escape as they are afraid to approach persons there for fear they will be betrayed to the authorities."[92] Suspicion was such that many dissidents simply stole boats in their effort to reach Saint Lucia. This further heightened tensions with local fishermen.[93]

Other perils lurked at sea. Indeed, the roughly twenty kilometers separating French from British isles were treacherous, especially by night, for they featured both dangerous currents and sharks. German refugee Kurt Kersten resisted the overwhelming temptation to flee to Saint Lucia largely because of the dangers involved. He who had survived the trenches of the First World War described a "violent, hungry channel between the islands, howling and foaming, thirsty for human flesh."[94] Those who did brave the waters used a variety of small vessels for the clandestine crossings. Sailboats were on average only between five and seven meters (between sixteen and twenty-three feet) long.[95] Many also arrived by canoe.[96]

Czech soldiers, whose incredible wartime odyssey took them from Marseille to Martinique and then illegally on to Saint Lucia, provide interesting testimony. They describe the boat that carried them from Martinique to Saint Lucia as follows: "a native dugout . . . propelled by rough hewn oars and sails made of handkerchiefs. It took them ten hours to reach St. Lucia."[97]

An archival file from the Saint Lucian police services allows us to reconstruct part of the wave of departures from Martinique to Saint Lucia between 1940 and 1943. Although the file features some major gaps for the year 1942, it nonetheless permits identification of some one thousand individuals having undertaken the crossing. Total estimates from both Martinique and its sister island Guadeloupe to Saint Lucia and Dominica vary, some reaching five thousand (Massip, who helped send on the volunteers from Dominica and Saint Lucia, puts the figure at four thousand).[98] The Saint Lucian file mostly reveals an incredible sociological diversity among the exiles. They included the cast of characters we have already encountered: Czech soldiers stranded in the French West Indies who wished to resume the fight against Nazi Germany; sailors from Vichy's navy; European refugees who had managed to reach Fort-de-France in 1940 and 1941; and of course a great many French West Indians from diverse social backgrounds, all wanting to fight in the ranks of de Gaulle's Free French.[99] On location in Castries, Free French officials made these volunteers pass medical and military exams, before incorporating them into Free French ranks.

The migration clearly bore consequences for inhabitants of Saint Lucia and Dominica, whose accommodations were strained by this wave of dissidents. A calypso song from Dominica tells the story of "building the [French] resistance in Dominica" and of feeding these additional mouths.[100] This serves as a potent reminder of the remarkable ties that bound the Lesser Antilles. It also suggests the ways in which these connections enabled resistance to Vichy rule.

One hundred and fifty of the dissidents who reached Dominica from both Martinique and Guadeloupe were still minors and therefore required legal consent from their parents, at least in principle. Sixteen-year-old Henry Joseph fit into this category. Given the challenges involved in obtaining such consent from Dominica at a time of extreme tension between French and British isles, Free French general Henri Jacomy decided, "on an absolutely exceptional basis," that "this category of volunteers would be dispensed from providing proof of consent."[101] The fact that so many were not yet adults may reveal something about the kinds of rumors that swirled in the French West Indies, specifically surrounding what it meant to join the Free French ranks.

Given that youngsters were involved, what precisely motivated these spectacular escapes? Beyond the question of maronnage and its legacies, many departed out of patriotic and democratic sentiment, as well as out of anti-Nazi idealism. However, structural reasons also played a role: as Lucien-René Abenon and Joseph have underscored, many dissidents cited hunger and privations as reasons for leaving, while others invoked a sense of daring and adventure.[102]

Perhaps the most famous dissident to leave Martinique may himself have been underage, and was none other than Fanon (one biographer states that he was seventeen at the time of his departure, the other eighteen).[103]

In January 1943, Fanon seized the textile ration tickets that his father had been accumulating to eventually constitute a suit, sold them on the black market, and used the money to pay for his passage to Dominica. He met up with his illegal *passeur* in Morne-Rouge en route to the island's north coast, whence they set sail for Dominica. There, he answered the mandatory questions on his motivations for joining de Gaulle's Fighting French. However, Vichy rule in the French West Indies was overthrown shortly thereafter, and Fanon rather anticlimactically returned to Martinique and to school. With the new authorities in Martinique raising a military unit that would fight to liberate France, Fanon finally joined the fifth bataillon de Marche des Antilles in 1944.[104]

As he sailed the Atlantic in the hold of the transport ship *Oregon,* Fanon drew direct parallels with the conditions of slaves. He experienced the everyday discriminations that black troops endured in the Fighting French ranks (even Antilleans, who were in theory lumped into the "European" military category). In December 1943, for instance, six months after the end of Vichy rule, black noncommissioned officers (NCOs) training in Saint-Pierre (Martinique) complained bitterly that they were forced to sleep in hay strewn on the floor, while white NCOs were given individual beds.[105] Fanon's disillusionment grew toward a war that he had once perceived in binary terms as a vast common battle against Nazi racism. Meanwhile, in Martinique, some of the refugees who had arrived in 1940 and 1941 were likewise pursuing a fruitful dialogue with West Indian intellectuals over identity, racism, and empire.

Vichy's West Indian Demise

Ultimately, a combination of factors led to Vichy's downfall in Martinique in 1943. We saw that the United States' decision to strangle the island economically played a major role. So too did the thousands of departures of mostly young men and women to Saint Lucia and Dominica, which stripped the island's sugar sector of the good part of a generation of workers.

On June 3 and 4, 1943, revolt broke out in Guadeloupe, where a committee of national liberation briefly seized power, jailing Vichy's representatives, before the navy gained the upper hand.[106] The movement soon spilled over to Martinique. There, word spread of an unauthorized march at Fort-de-France's war memorial, to protest the third anniversary of the

1940 armistice. Arrests ensued, which only further fanned discontent. It is then that an infantry officer, Henri Tourtet, and his third company, stationed in Balata, entered the fray. On June 29, 1943, Tourtet officially proclaimed his unit's allegiance to General de Gaulle. He added, "We will defend our decision to the end." Robert then attempted to reach a mediated settlement, suggesting that he would allow Tourtet's men to sail for Dominica. But the Martinique National Liberation Committee urged Tourtet to stay. An uneven civil war was narrowly averted, uneven because Tourtet's unit only counted 425 men against the roughly 2,500 sailors still loyal to Robert.[107] Rear Admiral Rouyer explained Robert's reticence to attack Tourtet's unit as follows: "An operation against Balata . . . was recognized to be impossible, for it would have triggered a battle between the navy and the army, and consequently, between whites and blacks." Moreover, the civilian population was determined to be rid of Vichy. Rouyer described a charged and even "revolutionary atmosphere" in the streets of Fort-de-France.[108]

On June 30, 1943, Admiral Robert released a communiqué in which he announced that "in order to avoid bloodshed between Frenchmen and so as to end the merciless blockade," he had asked and obtained from the United States a guarantee of continued French sovereignty over the Antilles. Without explicitly referring to Free France or to General de Gaulle, Robert added that he would work to "set the modalities of a change of French authorities, after which I shall depart."[109]

While Tourtet was no doubt correct to suggest that the delicate negotiations could have broken off at any time, the fact is that the changeover from Vichy to Fighting France had also been meticulously prepared from the outside. The United States now reneged on the Robert-Greenslade agreement and finally supported de Gaulle's Fighting French, exerting considerable pressure on Robert. On July 12, 1943, the United States and de Gaulle's movement agreed to take stock of the gold held in Fort-de-France: the United States was welcome to send a technical adviser to help with the inventory process, but the gold would stay on location in Martinique.[110] On July 3, 1943, US admiral John H. Hoover landed in Fort-de-France, where he concluded his negotiations with Admiral Robert.[111]

In short, a combination of internal and external pressures, of coordinated civilian and Free French military action, had toppled Vichy rule in Martinique. Free French general Henri Jacomy used the following quite sensible formula to describe how Martinique switched allegiances in June 1943: "This was a military movement, in which the . . . infantry, after having proclaimed its disobedience towards the cowardly inaction of its superiors [in the navy], supported civilian leaders and succeeded in neutralizing simply through threats, those hostile to [de Gaulle's] cause." Jacomy lauded the efforts of a handful of infantry officers and NCOs. Alongside Tourtet, a small clique of disaffected European NCOs played key roles in leading the Balata revolt. One of them was Captain Franco. Already in October 1942, Franco, then posted in Cayenne, had bitterly complained to his superiors. His spouse, Rouffe Kleiman, had been targeted by Vichy's Jewish statutes. Franco was livid, and while explaining that his wife was actually Orthodox Christian, he took aim at his superiors. Was this any way to treat the spouse of someone who had fought the Germans in 1940 and had been released from a German stalag after having volunteered to serve for Vichy's army in Syria, he asked? Now posted to Martinique, this same Captain Franco played an essential role during the Balata revolt; Tourtet depicted him as the NCO having shown "the most resolve" during Martinique's June days.[112]

Understanding Vichy in Martinique

In December 1943, five months after Vichy had been dislodged from the French West Indies, the cruiser *Emile Bertin* returned to haunt Fort-de-France. This vessel had served as one of the main instruments of power of Admiral Robert and his Vichy cabal. It now returned for a short visit, nominally under Fighting French command. Yet its sailors seemed bent on exacting revenge on Martinique's black population. The new governor of Martinique complained that during the ship's five-day stay in port, "part of the crew came to shore and made hostile political pronouncements, molesting and hitting isolated civilians in the streets. We counted eight wounded civilians, one seriously." The new governor acidly described the "unspeakable actions of sailors who had supposedly rallied to the Free French side." He demanded that no other vessel previously posted in the French Caribbean under Vichy be allowed to return there. He added, "Conversely, it would be desirable for a Free French vessel with the Cross of Lorraine flag to be sent here with a propaganda mission as soon as possible. We need to show another side of the navy than the one that for three years maintained the population in forced neutrality by means of violence and police terror. We must demonstrate this to a population that is Gaullist at heart."[113]

Vichy's afterlives were many in the French Caribbean. In June 1944, some inhabitants of the French West Indies remained frustrated at the limited purges that had occurred since Robert was dethroned. The press joined the chorus demanding that justice be served. For instance, the June 10, 1944, edition of the Martinican newspaper *Justice* published a list of volunteers for Vichy's vanguard legion of volunteers for the National Revolution. It betrays remarkable social diversity: school teachers, a mechanic, a hairdresser, a cobbler, a woodworker, "industrialists," and a purveyor of bras were all listed as leading legionnaires. In keeping with the discourses of the dissident movement, they were now all deemed undifferentiated "henchmen . . . of Nazi supporters of slavery."[114]

Slavery had clearly become one of the main historical lenses used for comprehending a period of privations, denunciations, and political regression. The fraught context of wartime Martinique sets the stage, and contributes to explaining, the multiple reactions of authorities and West Indians alike to an unprecedented wave of political refugees landing in Fort-de-France.

CHAPTER SIX

Snake Charmers in a Viper's Nest

WHILE SOME FIVE THOUSAND Martinicans and Guadeloupeans were setting off from Vichy's Caribbean bastions to join Charles de Gaulle's Free French, approximately the same number of Spanish Republicans, European dissidents, and Jews were landing at Fort-de-France, escaping Adolf Hitler's, Benito Mussolini's, and Francisco Franco's clutches. André Breton would title his book chronicling his time in the French Caribbean *Martinique, Snake Charmer*, after Le Douanier Rousseau's 1907 painting set in the ill-defined tropics. The painting depicts a hooded figure drawing two serpents toward it with a flute. It evokes Surrealism's fascination with nature, the spectacular, and the irrational, the snake charmer himself constituting an apt allegory for Surrealists. In many ways, however, the parts of Breton's book dealing with his arrival in Martinique would better have been titled "The viper's nest." For the duration of their time in Martinique, the exiles would grapple with venomous authorities as best they could, sometimes outwitting them and outflanking them.

A Rough Landing

To most migrants, the French West Indies turned out to be a short-lived and disappointing haven. No sooner did passengers disembark than the vexations and persecutions began. More loyal to Philippe Pétain than were many of their counterparts in France (more royalist than the king, goes the French expression), the Vichy colonial administration was doubly disdainful of incoming refugees, as not only were they anathema on ideo-logical and racist grounds but they also seemed to bring only trouble, be it unwanted American attention or simply added expense. Claude Lévi-Strauss eloquently describes the arrival of the *Paul Lemerle:* "No sooner had we docked than [we were harangued] by an army possessed by a form of collective insanity which would have deserved to be studied by the eth-nologist, were he not busy using all of his intellectual resources towards escaping its terrible consequences." The anthropologist then provides de-tails on his tormentors: "The troops in shorts, helmeted and armed, who settled in the commandant's offices, seemed not so much to be conducting an interview . . . with each of us, so much as pouring out a slew of insults which we had to endure. Those who were not French were called enemies; those who were French were stripped of their Frenchness through the ac-cusation that they were cowards leaving their country: a reproach that was not just contradictory, but galling, coming from the mouth of men who, since the declaration of war, had in reality been sheltered by the Monroe Doctrine."[1] Among the next in line was Breton. He chronicled in horror the harassment of Lévi-Strauss: "A very distinguished young scientist, called upon to continue his research in New York was told: *no you are not French, you are Jewish, and the so-called French Jews are worse for us than the foreign ones.*"[2]

Like Breton and Lévi-Strauss, Germaine Krull commented on the harsh interrogation that refugees underwent upon arrival: "We are treated like prisoners. The fact that we left France freely with all of our papers in order, and visas from Vichy for the countries where we are headed, does not matter. The case of French writer André Breton, a former French officer having fought in the wars of 1914 and 1939, the case of some ten foreign comrades who volunteered on the [French] side and fought the Battle of the Somme, all of these cases seem more of a drawback than an asset. We wonder if we are dealing with French authorities or German ones."[3]

The interchangeability of Vichy and German officials was a recurring theme. Renée Barth mentioned, "We were met by a boat of French gen-darmes. However, they didn't look French at all. They all had what the French call *têtes carrées* (square heads, with a fold of fat in the neck). They wore brown uniforms, and incredibly, had a German accent when they spoke French." Barth subsequently discovered that some of the men were

Alsatians (this no doubt explained the accents, although it did not account for their purportedly brown uniforms).[4] Interestingly, many Antillean resisters likewise remarked that the most recent arrivals among the Vichy police and troops on the island "looked" or "sounded" suspiciously Germanic. Frantz Fanon has explained this displacement or state of denial with the following syllogism: Vichy's minions in the Caribbean were racist; France could not be racist; therefore, these Vichyites must be German.[5]

Refugees and French West Indians used such varying frameworks to explain the inexplicable: police inspectors blaming Breton and Lévi-Strauss for the defeat, hurling anti-Semitic invective at Lévi-Strauss and Bertrand Goldschmidt. How can one more convincingly account for the rude welcome the refugees experienced? The "collective insanity" Lévi-Strauss offered as an explanation may have betrayed a dissonant relationship with a motherland that was at once revered in the colonial context and now reviled as part of a new masochistic mood following France's sudden collapse. For his part, the anthropologist theorized that colonial officials felt free of blame for the defeat of 1940, and that their distance from mainland France had led them to substitute a faraway enemy—Germany—for a closer one in the United States.[6]

The hatred of incoming refugees was also connected to the penetration of Vichy ideology in select colonial milieus. We saw that in Martinique and Guadeloupe, the new regime was welcomed with open arms in some circles. To them, the advent of Vichy seemed a blessing, signaling the end of perceived political abuses and scandals, and of "unnatural" racial equality before the law.

More directly, the harsh treatment reserved for refugees was of course due to the chain of command within the naval forces that controlled Martinique. Breton was perfectly correct to suspect that an order along such a chain had gone out to treat all incoming refugees as prisoners.[7] On March 23, 1941, Admiral Georges Robert asserted that, "given the multiplication of false passports and identities," he must advocate a policy of jailing first and asking questions later. He cabled his subordinates, "I ask you to reinforce the surveillance of all the passengers arriving in our colony; I would see no inconvenience, in cases where . . . identity is not absolutely established . . . for passengers to be placed under forced and controlled residence."[8]

Already a March 11, 1941, memorandum instructed customs and police officials in Martinique on how to handle two distinct categories of refugees: the French and the foreigners. The French were to be discreetly watched, while foreigners were automatically subjected to forced residence. Those who were deemed unlikely to ever receive a visa for the Americas were to be "sent back" to Morocco. The same instructions also granted Lieutenant Marie-Joseph Castaing the right to decide in cases in which refugees might be considered a risk.[9] Castaing boasted in correspondence of the zeal he deployed in ridding Martinique of "rot," depicting himself as a "ruthless" intelligence gatherer.[10]

An elaborate questionnaire, rigidly structured along Pétainist lines, asked refugees their religion, who paid for their trip to the French West Indies, whether they had ever belonged to a secret society, and whether they "had ever taken part in any revolutionary activity whatsoever, in France or abroad." The form also made refugees swear not to "engage in any political activity" while in the French Caribbean. Curiously, the crucial question of one's final destination figured eighteenth, no doubt revealing how greater was the fear of subversion.[11]

The Lazaret

Following these instructions, nearly all foreign refugees, even some French ones (initially Barth and Breton), were imprisoned in two distinct internment camps outside Fort-de-France: Balata, in the cooler heights overlooking the city, and the Lazaret, a former leper colony by the ocean on the Pointe du Bout—slated today to become the grounds for a hotel. The Pointe du Bout site had been utilized for decades: in 1863, it shifted functions from a convalescence center to a lazaret.[12] It and Balata first served as internment camps in 1939, initially to intern enemy aliens: Germans in 1939 and, after Mussolini declared war on France on June 10, 1940, Italians as well.[13] Then, with the advent of Vichy, local German and Italian nationals poured out as refugees from mainland France poured in. This trend was a nearly exact reflection of what happened in camps in southern France.

US vice-consul in Martinique William Boswell provided considerable detail on the treatment and sorting of refugees recently disembarked from the *Wyoming:*

French citizens, whether coming to Martinique to establish permanent residence or in transit, are, of course, permitted to circulate freely on the island and to reside wherever they can find accommodations. Refugees of other nationalities fall into one of three categories: 1) those having visas from other countries and sufficient funds are not allowed to stay in Fort-de-France itself but must go to one of the nearby towns 2) those having visas from other countries but who lack sufficient funds are sent to the detention camp at Lazaret across the bay from Fort-de-France. 3) those who do not have visas from another country are [also] sent to the camp at Lazaret.[14]

The vice-consul then specified, "Immigration authorities state that if such persons do not find some means of proceeding to their destination within a month or six weeks after their arrival, they will be sent back to their port of departure, i.e. Marseille or Casablanca."[15] We will return to this threat of expulsion shortly.

Before each boat's arrival, the police arranged logistics for "welcoming committees"—one of which greeted Lévi-Strauss and his companions. Before the docking of the *Carimaré*, for instance, it was already ascertained that of its 174 passengers in transit, 150 were to be interned at Balata.[16] To add insult to injury, upon arrival, refugees were required to pay a hefty sum to cover their own internment (a 9,000 franc deposit and a further 1,500 francs to defray internment costs).[17]

Isaac Fontaine, a Martiniquais witness from the period, recalls the refugee presence on the island in the following terms: "In the camps, the first Martiniquais political dissidents joined the Polish, Yugoslav and German Jewish refugees brought by the *Winnipeg* and other vessels, and who were interned [at the Lazaret]. These families, chased from their homelands by the German invaders, had hoped to find refuge in Martinique. Very quickly, the camp conditions revealed themselves to be inadequate, driving many of them to leave for neighboring islands or the USA."[18] Incoming refugees, then, rubbed shoulders with local dissidents in makeshift camps.

In many ways these spaces were reminiscent of the camps the migrants had left in southern France. The only difference, Breton seemed to suggest, was the clever substitution on placards of the term "internees" with that of "guests."[19] As Breton implies, the nuance was strictly semantic. He did not know it, but Vichy officials used a similar euphemism in their internal correspondence: they referred to the Lazaret as a "welcome center."[20] Some refugees played along with this charade, asking, no doubt ironically, that friends and family write them at "the Foreigners' Hotel, Pointe du Bout, Martinique."[21] And yet the Lazaret bore all of the hallmarks of an internment camp, reminiscent, for instance, of those that the United States used to intern Japanese Americans. Martinique's archives show that by 1941, roll call took place twice a day at the Lazaret.[22] Still, as we will see, security tended to be considerably laxer in Martinique's camps than in those of unoccupied mainland France. Moreover, inmates themselves disagreed over just how harsh or lax conditions were.

Krull described how she was interned in the Lazaret camp in the middle of the night: "A concentration camp in Martinique under the very eyes of the USA, French gendarmes who act like Nazis. Not only are we under the control of Vichy and the boot of the Gestapo, but besides, we whites are now being guarded by Negroes."[23] Krull's own racial hierarchies added to her sense of humiliation rather than leading her to reflect on the nature of Nazi or Vichy racism.

The following day, Krull recounted,

> Our baggage was systematically searched. The search concerns only publications and letters; books and other publications authorized and printed in France are banned. Letters are examined from all angles, if one is in an envelope it is usually confiscated. Cameras are naturally confiscated, yet I was able to hide mine under my arm. We learn from the authorities that we will stay here until a French boat sets sail from here to either New York or South America. How long might that take? No one knows. Only the next day, when the US Consul comes to see if our visas are in order, do the authorities consent in his presence to give us courteous replies, and they end up promising that we will be allowed rotating visits [into Fort-de-France]. But that is all that the American Consul's requests and insistence managed to yield.[24]

Krull's concealed camera served her well. Her remarkable photographs, which today are held at the Folkwang Museum in Essen, Germany, complement her unpublished account of her exodus on the *Paul Lemerle* and her experience in Martinique, held in the same collection. They reveal scenes of everyday life at the Lazaret camp and include pictures of Wifredo Lam and his spouse, Helena Holzer; Minna Flake; Victor Serge; Vlady Serge; and Jacques Rémy (figures 10 and 11). One picture shows a little

FIGURE 10. Germaine Krull, photo showing Wifredo Lam and Helena Benitez (née Holzer) in the Lazaret camp, Martinique, 1941. Artist's rights: © Nachlass Germaine Krull; photo: © Museum Folkwang Essen—ARTOTHEK.

FIGURE 11. Germaine Krull, photo showing some inmates at the Lazaret. Krull's own caption reads, "Left to right seated: Jacques Rémy, French cinema producer. LT a Belgian law student; Victor Serge, Russian writer. Standing: Mrs. MB 20 years old, from Luxemburg; HP German engineer, Wlady Serge, son of Victor Serge, also a painter." Artist's rights: © Nachlass Germaine Krull; photo: © Museum Folkwang Essen—ARTOTHEK.

blond girl (perhaps Kristen Barth?) on hay bedding. Another photo reveals the camp's spartan conditions: it shows inmates queuing for precious drinking water (figure 12). The legend reads, in English, "Each morning at 11 am, 100 bottles of mineral water arrive and the inmates (some 200 usually) line up like this to get it."[25] In the relatively orderly queue, one can discern a child, a dog, some men in bathing suits, a woman in a long skirt, and an older man in suspenders, as well as the water containers the inmates carried. Precisely because of the ban on cameras, the photographs in the Folkwang Museum in Essen, combined with the Antonin Pelc photos in Prague, constitute, to my knowledge, the only surviving snapshots of life in the Martinique refugee internment camps in 1941.

Other visual materials, however, complement and sometimes contradict Krull's grim verdict and photo evidence. For instance, one of German refugee Carl Heidenreich's intriguing watercolors shows the camp building against the luxurious green vegetation and the blue Caribbean Sea

FIGURE 12. Germaine Krull, photo showing the water queue at the Lazaret camp, 1941. Artist's rights: © Nachlass Germaine Krull; photo: © Museum Folkwang Essen—ARTOTHEK.

(figure 13). The inmate's lively, romantic, but rather conventional landscape paintings done at the Lazaret contrast jarringly with both Krull's photographs and Heidenreich's much more somber and challenging abstract work done before his departure from Europe and after his arrival in America. Gabrielle Saure sees in Heidenrich's Martinique watercolors the influence of Raoul Dufy, and she rightly adds that the landscapes "convey almost romantic notions of travel, of a tranquil and orderly world that contrasts with Heidenreich's actual situation." Several of his watercolors depict vistas looking away from the camp's grounds, onto the Bay of Fort-de-France, and toward the Anses d'Arlet, reflecting perhaps the temptation of escape. Another shows the Mont Pelée, which, then as now, dominates the horizon to the north of the Lazaret.[26]

While, for Heidenreich, Martinique marked a stylistic rupture, for Czech artist Antonin Pelc the month-long stay in Martinique (April 20, 1941, to May 21, 1941) seems to have constituted something of an apotheosis.[27] Cockfighting soon enraptured Pelc, as he devoted a series of paintings to the popular activity, as well as painting and drawing landscapes and portraits of Martinicans. Calling cockfighting popular in wartime Martinique

FIGURE 13. Carl Heidenreich, Martinique watercolor showing one of the camp buildings and the Bay of Fort-de-France. Courtesy Karla Lortz, Carl Heidenreich Estate.

would be an understatement. In May 1941, Vichy's local gendarmerie reprimanded the lead police officer in Trois-Îlets, the closest town to the Pointe-du-Bout, for his all-consuming poultry obsession. "If only this were edible fowl," griped an anonymous gendarme in the margins. It would seem the officer, named Bernard, had transformed his police post, down to its jail cell, into the quarters for his prized combat roosters. This feathered hobby left scant room for official police business.[28] Given the proximity of Trois-Îlets to the Lazaret, Pelc may have rubbed shoulders with this very character and his winged combatants. In any event, Pelc's Martinique cockfight scenes would remain a recurring motif in his work long after his departure from the Caribbean.

Evidently, Pelc was able to leave the camp to ply his craft. Nor were inmates limited to painting outside the walls. None of the Czech artists at the Lazaret—Pelc, Alen Divis, or Maxim Kopf—put down their brushes in the camp. In other words, there seems to have been no ban on canvases. Divis painted a beach scene that seems likely to have been executed at the Pointe du Bout. German artist Heidenreich did the same, executing a re-

FIGURE 14. Drawing by Antonin Pelc, *The Camp of the Pointe du Bout, Martinique.* Reproduced from author's collection. Rights © National Gallery in Prague 2017.

markable watercolor showing the Bay of Fort-de-France with a Lazaret camp building in the foreground. The scene is rather idyllic, featuring neither walls nor even a hint of surveillance.

Pelc, for his part, kept a camera, and his evocative drawing of the Lazaret camp may well be based on a photo or perhaps a mental snapshot. Indeed, on June 26, 1941, about a month after leaving the island, Pelc completed a piece entitled *The Camp of the Pointe du Bout, Martinique.* The drawing focuses on a camp building—a typical Martiniquais dwelling or *case*—and the gracefully gnarled trees that surrounded it (figure 14). The lounge chair seen under the patio resembles the one that Serge took with him from the *Paul Lemerle,* a detail conveyed by Krull. The foliage at the image's center, and the execution of the piece itself, exudes a serene atmosphere far removed from Krull's bleak description of the same camp. She writes of "four or five shacks, the whole ensemble surrounded by walls

FIGURE 15. Photo by Antonin Pelc, showing the Lazaret camp from the sea, 1941. Photograph in the Antonin Pelc Archive, © National Gallery in Prague 2017.

guarded by black sentinels."[29] Perhaps because Pelc, unlike Krull, had endured the Santé Prison, as well as internment at Roland Garros, and then the camp at Damigny in northern France, his 1941 drawing of the Lazaret seems downright rosy, even magical, by comparison.[30]

Pelc's photographs of the Lazaret are no less noteworthy. He too evidently managed to introduce, then keep, his camera in the camp. One of his pictures (figure 15) shows the camp as seen from the sea, which prompts the question of whether it was taken on initial approach or subsequently. In it, one can make out several typical sheet-metal roofs, as well as the large trees Pelc rendered in his drawing. The wall that surrounds the camp resembles more of a retaining structure than the imposing barbed-wire-topped barriers that enclosed metropolitan French camps. Pelc's photo also highlights the Lazaret's seaside location.

Two more of the photos in Pelc's collection provide hints of everyday life at the Lazaret. One of them (figure 16) is titled simply *Martinican Creoles* (May 1941). It shows three women and three children posing before

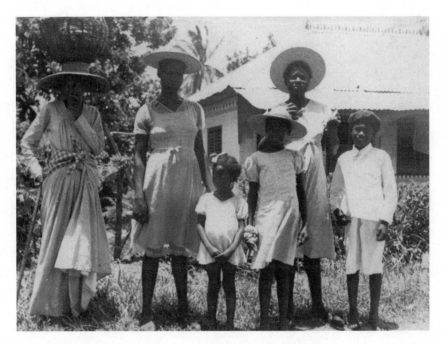

FIGURE 16. Photo by Antonin Pelc, which he captioned "Creoles, Martinique," May 1941. Photograph in the Antonin Pelc Archive, © National Gallery in Prague 2017.

what was probably one of the camp buildings. This may well have been one of the families tasked with feeding and tending to the inmates. In any event, contrary to Krull, who regarded locals with suspicion at best, Pelc's portraits of French West Indians, be they photographic or painted, suggest both empathy and a degree of fascination.

Another photo from the same month shows Divis, Pelc, Kopf, and two of their partners around a table on a veranda (figure 17). Mineral water, cigarettes, and rum can be discerned. A chicken has sneaked into the foreground. The building closely resembles the one depicted in Pelc's coeval drawing. The Czech group seems to be inward looking, no doubt a result of their relatively shaky French. The broad smile on at least one of the subjects again points to a sense of relief at having escaped the European inferno. The scene also appears to reflect quite decent detention conditions.

Meanwhile, Barth's testimony allows us to consider the camps from another standpoint, tipping the scale back in a bleaker direction. She describes the Lazaret's hygiene as deplorable: "The other serious lack was

FIGURE 17. Photo showing the Czech artists Alen Divis, Antonin Pelc, and Maxim Kopf and their partners at the Lazaret camp, May 1941. Photograph in the Antonin Pelc Archive, © National Gallery in Prague 2017.

latrines. There was no provision whatsoever for this."[31] Indeed, the 1905 plan for the Lazaret shows toilets located only on the extremity of the piers.[32] Barth proceeds to recount how her mother, Flake, "took a child's shovel along the beach every morning, doing burial service of human excrements, saying after all she had been a health official [in Berlin]."[33] As for Anna Seghers, she wrote from Martinique that her greatest fantasies involved sleeping under a sheet, using a toilet, having a tablecloth, and spending a night without the sound of screaming children.[34] Serge provided additional details: the camp had no lighting, no fresh water, and only straw mats for sleeping. Mineral water was sold for a franc a bottle, and medication was altogether unavailable. Serge described the food as "inedible." Consequently, refugees spent their meager remaining funds on purchasing tins of sardines and corned beef.[35] Breton, too, remembered having to buy sardine cans; yet what most marked him was the darkness of the Lazaret. Conditions were grim enough to make him miss the *Capitaine Paul Lemerle*.[36]

The harsh conditions in the camp were no tightly kept secret. Passing through Fort-de-France en route to Guiana, American journalist Nicol Smith was told by his hotelier that he was lucky "not to be in the big camp." This piqued Smith's curiosity, leading his interlocutor to elaborate, "The refugee camp [Lazaret] . . . is on the other side of the bay, a couple of kilometers beyond Fort-de-France. There are hundreds of refugees in it, and there are not enough beds to go around; indeed, there isn't even enough water." However, Smith seems to have been largely unmoved by the migrants' plight: his photographer even floated the notion that some of the refugees might have been spies.[37]

"A Concentration Camp in Martinique"

Krull's use of the term "concentration camp" to describe the Lazaret was no accident.[38] Serge famously characterized the *Paul Lemerle* itself as "an ersatz concentration camp of the sea," thereby casting serious doubts on its rescue value.[39] Although the term was certainly less charged than it would later become, it did serve to link the repressive practices of Vichy France and the Nazis.

Krull vividly described meeting with both the head of the gendarmerie in Martinique and Governor Yves Marie Nicol in person to complain of the conditions at the Lazaret. The former reportedly responded to her, "This should allow you to write articles about concentration camps in Martinique."[40] The glib retort was no doubt intended to relativize conditions at the Lazaret camp. Clearly, a war of words raged over the nature of this internment. In a March 21, 1941, dispatch, US vice-consul Boswell expressly specified to the State Department, "The camp at Lazaret is not a concentration camp but the most practicable place where persons in transit whose presence is not desired in Fort-de-France can be housed."[41] Nevertheless, the point remains that in the minds of the refugees, the experience of the Lazaret camp differed little from that of Les Milles before July 1942.

Barth also recalls that she and Serge complained to the authorities. They threatened to reveal to the world the harsh conditions that prevailed in the camp. The threat elicited a visit from Admiral Robert "in his resplendent white uniform." She suggested he visit "the kitchen" and the nonexistent latrines.[42] The overcrowded camps also housed wayward Czech troops,

FIGURE 18. Germaine Krull, photo showing a guard at the Lazaret camp, 1941.
Artist's rights: © Nachlass Germaine Krull; photo: © Museum Folkwang
Essen—ARTOTHEK

whose path we have crossed already. Nothing much seems to have come
from Admiral Robert's visit.

A few migrant testimonies mention the Martinican guards at the Lazaret. Krull photographed one of them arriving with a bucket, perhaps containing food (figure 18). Two scrawny chickens can be spotted near his
feet. Krull adds in her unpublished manuscript that several black families
lived at the Lazaret, where they raised pigs and chickens and served as camp
cooks. She suspected them of working for the secret police.[43] As for Serge,
he remembered discussing the course of the war with his black guards. According to the Belgian revolutionary, the guards summarily declared that
they would refuse to fight the Americans in the event of a US landing on
Martinique. Serge then fell back on a series of stereotypes to dismiss the
guards as "big athletic children."[44] Like Krull, who somehow imagined
Fort-de-France to resemble "a small Negro village," and like Vladek Spiegelman in Art Spiegelman's *Maus*, Serge too proves that surviving Nazi
persecution did not necessarily make one immune to racism directed at
blacks.[45] However, as we will see, some of the refugees, especially Breton,

Jacqueline Lamba, Seghers, Lam, and Helena Benitez, proved infinitely more open to Martinicans, forging lasting ties with them during their stays.

That the guards at the Lazaret were sympathetic to the cause of the democracies is noteworthy. For this reason, perhaps, security at the Lazaret was not very tight. On May 12, 1941, twenty-three foreign refugees interned at the Lazaret succeeded in breaking out. Having missed one boat, they contacted the owner of the speedboat *Florida,* one Gabriel Flambeau. Sensing an opportunity to make money, Flambeau charged the refugees on the lam five francs apiece to take them to Saint Lucia. However, the vessel was shabby, and certainly not equipped to take dozens of passengers. Water began infiltrating its hull shortly after it left shore; soon the engine was engulfed. As it sank off Trois-Îlets, the sentinel at the Pointe du Bout heard screams and alerted the head of the Lazaret camp. The crew and the Lazaret guards scrambled to save the refugees from drowning. Miraculously, they were all rescued. Besides the shock, the only lasting damage was the loss of one passenger's passport and money, which fell to the seabed as they trod water. Interestingly, Martinique's maritime services recommended against pressing charges against Flambeau. The report also made no mention of any punitive action taken against the refugees themselves. They presumably returned to the Lazaret.[46]

For all of these difficulties, there were some silver linings at the Lazaret and Balata camps. For one thing, security was decidedly lax at Balata, with very low barriers that could be easily hurdled.[47] Most importantly, the threat of Nazism was now more remote. Some even managed to find moments of enjoyment, hinted at in Pelc's drawing and photographs. Breton was in awe at Martinique's luxuriant vegetation, and at the shells he found along the beach near the Lazaret. He and Benitez also recount swimming in the bay of Pointe du Bout.[48]

Outside the Camps

Breton remembers the announcement made at the Lazaret that French nationals could go to Fort-de-France until five o'clock in the afternoon. However, Lieutenant Castaing proceeded to make an exception to his own rule when he added arbitrarily, "no, not Breton." No doubt his reputation as a Surrealist rebel preceded him. Breton did manage to have the decision rescinded some five days later.[49]

Vichy's naval police confronted Goldschmidt head on after he arranged to share a villa in Fort-de-France with several other passengers he had met aboard the *Carimaré*. "How dare you rent a place in town when you are Jewish and therefore not French," bellowed the hostile official. He then proceeded to place Goldschmidt in forced residence at a small hotel on the Morne-Rouge, warning him, "One more word and I'll toss you into the camp for stateless refugees"—no doubt the Lazaret.[50] Little wonder that Goldschmidt later recalled his month's stay in Martinique in 1941 as having been "inhospitable."[51]

Rémy, meanwhile, took the opportunity to prepare the next leg of his travel to South America. He planned on sailing to Argentina, and he had already secured a certificate of immigration from the Argentine Ministry of Agriculture. Now, on May 2, 1941, he visited Fort-de-France's city hall, where he obtained a certificate of upstanding moral conduct. He also found time that day to book an appointment with a doctor from whom he received a smallpox vaccination. Rémy kept busy: the following day, he visited the bishopric in Fort-de-France, where he obtained a certificate attesting that he belonged to the Catholic faith. No doubt the bishop realized that he was providing this certificate to a Jew. As for Rémy's motivations, he had probably been led to believe that such a document could not hurt when seeking entry to Argentina. Also on May 3, he visited Fort-de-France's court and obtained a certificate proving that he had never committed a felony. He was ready for departure to Argentina, where he would go on to serve the Free French cause.[52]

Rémy benefited from the relative freedom afforded to French nationals. However, even some of the refugees in Martinique's two camps obtained special permission to stay in town unchaperoned. In April 1941, under pressure from Vichy's Foreign Ministry, Admiral Charles Platon asked Admiral Robert to "soften" the detention conditions of two women, Mrs. Carrascal Llorca and Sitjes Carrascal, and the young boy Jaime Vachier Sitjes. All had arrived on the *Ipanema* and now awaited departure for Mexico. Even while urging clemency, Vichy's Foreign Ministry termed them "undesirables," no doubt survivors of the Republican side in Spain.[53] In any event, Admiral Robert's administration obeyed, and the group of Spaniards was lodged in a hotel of their own choosing, in Saint-Pierre, although still under a regime of "forced residence."[54]

Others obtained medical dispensation to leave the Lazaret. Occasionally, they drew the ire of local Vichy zealots. Smith relates an incident in which Jewish refugee guests at his hotel were dancing a waltz. Suddenly, a French officer erupted into the hall, brimming with rage. He exclaimed, "How dare you dance while France is in mourning [in the wake of the June 1940 defeat]! . . . How dare you make merry when you are the guest of an island colony of France that hides its grief behind closed walls?"[55] The refugees had inadvertently touched on both a mercurial temper and a sore point: Vichy had banned all public dances in its colonies, just as it had in mainland France.[56] The nation was officially in mourning.

Those on Official Business

Some travelers were fortunate to escape the harsh treatment and forced residence altogether. Such was the case of French anthropologist Paul-Emile Victor, famous for his polar explorations and his ethnographic work among the Inuit. Victor's parents were both Jewish; his father was born in Pilsen in 1877, his feminist and suffragette mother Maria Laura Baum in Vienna a year later. They had arrived in France in 1903, four years before Paul-Emile's birth near Geneva; thereupon, Paul-Emile's father contracted and Frenchified his name from Erich Heinrich Victor Steinschneider to Éric Victor.[57]

As France collapsed in 1940, Paul-Emile Victor was in Scandinavia, serving in an official capacity as a naval attaché, with the rank of first-class midshipman in the French Navy. He managed to return to France by a circuitous route. In the fall of 1940, he began preparing his departure for the United States, sending out feelers first to Bryn Mawr College, then to the Rockefeller Foundation. However, while other French functionaries, such as Lévi-Strauss and Goldschmidt, reached Martinique as suspects who had been squeezed out of their posts, Victor accomplished the incredible feat of striding into Fort-de-France on government business. In his bid to leave France, he successfully played his contacts at Vichy, receiving special support from his acquaintance, Education and Youth Minister Jacques Chevalier. He was thus able to depart on a paid mission to both Morocco and Martinique, where he was supposedly to continue his ethnographic work (a challenge, given that he studied the Inuit).[58]

Martinique was clearly not Victor's final destination. However, during his time on the island, he researched local pottery production in the town of Sainte-Anne, gave three lectures on the Inuit at Admiral Robert's request in January and February 1941, and agreed to organize scout movements and assist with educational reform. He was also involved in training teachers during a weeklong retreat, as well as in improving Martinique's sports facilities and programs. In his diary, he did mention with alarm how Anglophobia seemed the prime mover in local naval circles. Yet his biographer Thierry Fournier rightly points out that during this time Victor became complicit with parts of Vichy's ideological agenda:[59] Admiral Robert was busily reforming education in Martinique, replacing what he saw as a uselessly bookish culture with physical education and introducing religion into the curriculum.[60] Victor's daughter appears perplexed at her father's silence about Vichy rule and its consequences in Martinique: "Given his family history and his values, how can one explain his blindness? False naiveté? Excessive caution? Refusal to get involved? Silent complicity? Sense of opportunity?"[61]

Whatever the reason, it seems plain that Victor remained a pragmatist and was certainly no Vichy zealot. Indeed, he regularly visited the US consulate in Fort-de-France to obtain a visa for America. He wrote to his parents on March 3, 1941, that his visa application was bogged down by the fact that he was not a "poor migrant." He added, interestingly, "Sad but true: apparently, the process would go faster if I were Jewish."[62] One wonders how his parents reacted to this line, for they were both Jewish and presumably he had once identified as such himself. In any event, Victor must have impressed his American interlocutors, for unlike others, who elicited suspicions of all sorts, Boswell wrote of Victor that he was "satisfied that he is not connected with any organization devoted to the influencing or furthering in the United States the political activities . . . of any other government." Among his three referees, Victor listed the US naval attaché in Ankara, Turkey, as well as Richard Simon of the publishing house Simon and Schuster. As they had in mainland France, his professional contacts proved invaluable. In his application, Victor expressed his desire to conduct research in Washington and possibly "to participate in an archeological expedition to Alaska." On April 21, 1941, the State Department posed "no objection" to his receiving a Swiss quota emigration.[63] Victor would enroll in the US Air Force after reaching the United States.

Yet the point remains that while in Martinique, Victor was lodged simply but decently by the admiralty, and he was invited to hobnob with the very same naval officers who were tormenting Goldschmidt, Lévi-Strauss, Seghers, Breton, Lamba, Lam, Holzer, Serge, and the others. He even wrote to his parents of being "pampered."[64] It is also true that in Martinique, Victor was welcomed as a member of the naval fraternity, yet the lenient, even generous, treatment he experienced in Martinique stands in jarring contrast to that meted out to his academic peers.

While Victor reached Martinique as a member of the French Navy on secondment to Vichy's education minister, other French Jewish academics succeeded in transiting through Fort-de-France en route to America in quite different, although still official, capacities. Some of these capacities seem to have been pretexts conceived to shepherd Jewish scientists to safety. Thus, in January 1941, André Mayer, his physiologist wife, Jeanne (born Eugénie), and their son Jean reached Martinique as part of André Mayer's mission to the United States on behalf of the French Ministry of Public Health.[65]

Mayer was a gifted biochemist who had organized the Allied Chemical Warfare Service in the First World War. Then, in the wake of the Great War, he lobbied for the elimination of chemical weapons. He joined the prestigious Collège de France in 1922. By the 1930s, he had emerged as a major authority in the field of nutrition, as well as on hypothermia and in a host of other fields. In 1939, he served once more as chief scientist for the Allies on research into countering chemical weapons.[66]

After France fell, Mayer implored the French Foreign Ministry's Service des oeuvres for assistance in leaving Europe. On December 21, 1940, the sixty-five-year-old scientist wrote from Montpellier to Suzanne Borel of the Foreign Ministry's Service des oeuvres (Borel would soon join the Resistance): "I am once again throwing myself in your hands. You know why I have asked for your help."[67] Mayer had been fired from his post in accordance with Vichy's Jewish statute. Evidently, Borel and the Foreign Ministry successfully leaned on the Ministry of Public Health and Mayer was granted an official mission, tantamount to a ticket out of Europe.

While individuals at the French Foreign Ministry helped the Mayer family on one end, on the other side of the Atlantic the Rockefeller Foundation also assisted the Mayers in departing Marseille on the *Winnipeg* in January 1941. The foundation did so through Louis Rapkine and Henri

Laugier. Rapkine, a French Jewish scientist of Russian origin who trained at McGill University in Montréal, helped numerous Jewish French intellectuals reach the safety of America. Laugier operated in concert with him; he had served as the very first director of the now famous Centre national de recherche scientifique.[68]

Mayer would reach the US mainland via Puerto Rico. There, in March 1941, he gave a talk before a Gaullist organization, which drew the ire of the local French consul, loyal to Pétain, who complained accordingly to Vichy, grousing about a French public servant speaking before a dissident organization.[69] Mayer reached the United States later that month. He would spend the rest of the war in America, soon becoming a leading international adviser on questions of hunger and malnutrition. His son Jean Mayer would follow in his path, emerging in turn as a major expert in the field of nutrition.

Continued Persecution

While Victor and Mayer reached Martinique on official government business, and therefore enjoyed a degree of protection, refugees were still exposed to threats of all sorts. Indeed, the French colonial archives reveal that some refugees were singled out for special treatment of another kind. One especially mysterious case involved Germaine Flament (also known as Claude Carron), a twenty-nine-year-old orphaned refugee born in Istanbul of French parents. Flament arrived in Martinique from Marseille on the *Ipanema* in March 1941 hoping eventually to reach an uncle in the United States. The authorities initially refused to let her disembark, threatening to send her back to North Africa.

A postwar purge file describes how a plainclothes policeman named Louis Gérard (of the Sûreté navale et coloniale), who answered to Robert, Battet, and Castaing, gradually gained Flament's confidence. While other refugees were charged large sums for their internment in camps, the authorities paid for Flament to stay at the Hôtel de la Paix in Fort-de-France. However, she quickly discovered that her room was sandwiched between that of the US consul, Marcel Malige, and one of his vice-consuls. Upon realizing this, Flament smelled a rat and checked out, moving into the Hôtel de l'Europe. Gérard then tracked her down and began menacing her. The file alleges that Vichy's police exerted considerable pressure on Flament to spy on the Americans. The pressure took the form both of direct violence (the file alleges that Lieutenant Castaing beat her and vowed to shoot her) and of threats of deportation to the penal colony in French Guiana. Flament soon entered the circle of Rear Admiral Battet and his naval consorts and became an unwilling agent of the Sûreté navale et coloniale tasked with monitoring US consular activities.

On January 6, 1942, the unrelenting pressure finally drove Flament to Martinique's psychiatric ward, then to the asylum of Saint-Claude in Guadeloupe. After months of treatment, Flament's condition improved, thanks in part to medication provided by the US consulate. However, Flament experienced a relapse after being visited by a Vichy policeman. This especially "troubling" case of "police machination," to use the words of Martinique's purge commission in 1943, suggests that Vichy's security forces micromanaged surveillance and preyed on refugees they deemed vulnerable in the especially tense climate of 1941.[70]

Certainly, police had been given a very long leash. A January 1941 telegram from Vichy's Ministry of the Colonies to Martinique granted local officials "all latitude" in matters of surveillance, given the absence of a proper internment center in Martinique (apparently, the Lazaret, Balata, and other camps did not suffice).[71]

Vichy's police charged several other refugees with illegally entering the colony. Abraham Weisz and René Culot were arrested for traveling clandestinely on board the *Paul Lemerle* to Fort-de-France. One can assume from context that their papers were not in order, and that they did not hold any visas whatsoever. Both were subjected to *internement administratif* upon arrival, and they were sent first to Balata, in Martinique, before being transferred to the Fort Napoléon on Les Saintes (off the southern coast of Guadeloupe), where Gaullist sympathizers were held under conditions far harsher than those at the Lazaret camp.[72] Indeed, as more vessels arrived, police measures grew more draconian. On May 3, 1941, just before the cessation of shipping to the French Caribbean, Vichy's inspector Emile Devouton recommended that dependable white gendarmes from the metropole be relied on to ensure security around refugee camps. This measure was necessary, he contended, for "in the event of trouble, it was impossible to count on ... army units ... composed in large part of people from here."[73] To Devouton, at least, the refugees added to a sense of imminent danger. They clearly constituted a potential fifth column. This menace of subversion he read against another ominous backdrop: the fact that blacks outnumbered whites in French West Indies.

The Threat of Return and the Case
of Mario Montagnana

The greatest peril facing refugees was that of being sent back across the Atlantic. Fitzroy Baptiste has suggested that the enigmatic Comte de Cerezy was at least partly responsible for pressuring Admiral Robert into sending select Jewish refugees back.[74] In any event, in several instances, Vichy's authorities actually carried this out. Thus, Walter Ehrlich, from Pilsen in Czechoslovakia, reached Martinique from Morocco in October 1940, only to be sent back to Casablanca aboard the *Cuba* on October 24, 1940.[75] However, the *Cuba* was then intercepted by the British cruiser *Morton Bay*, which escorted it to Freetown in British West Africa.[76] Admiral Robert also occasionally adopted the less draconian practice of having refugees expelled to the Dutch half of the island of Saint Martin. Thus, in March 1941, he gave detailed instructions for the Lichtman family and for one Adolphe Sipos, having arrived aboard the *Winnipeg* a month previously, to be ushered to the Franco-Dutch border of Saint Martin, and expelled.[77]

A particularly harrowing story of aborted return to Europe occurred in 1941. On May 19, 1941, Vichy's Ministry of the Colonies cabled Fort-de-France. It explicitly requested that the Italian trade unionist Mario Montagnana, who was aboard the *Winnipeg* bound for Martinique, be sent back to Marseille as soon as he reached Fort-de-France.[78] Since the order rests in the archives within a pile of documents relating to armistice commission material, and given the context, it seems likely that the Italian Armistice Commission had demanded that this leading anti-Mussolini voice be blocked from escaping to the safety of the Western Hemisphere.

Montagnana was born in Turin in 1897 into a middle-class Jewish family. Some of his earliest political involvement can be traced to 1911–1912, when he opposed Italy's colonial venture in Libya. By 1913, he had joined a Socialist youth organization. He subsequently protested against Italy's intervention in the First World War. His revolutionary resolve grew firmer in the war's wake. In 1921, he represented the freshly created Italian Communist Party in Moscow on the occasion of the Third Communist International Congress. After Mussolini's 1922 seizure of power, Montagnana became a marked man, and he narrowly escaped summary execution. He fled to Paris on a false passport in 1926; that same year, he was sentenced to prison in absentia in Italy for his Communist activities.[79]

In Paris, Montagnana remained highly engaged, leading a national commission on foreign labor. In 1927, he was briefly expelled from France and wound up in Belgium, where he worked in a calculating-machine factory. He returned to France in 1929, before participating in the International World Congress of Labor Unions in Moscow the following year. In 1931, he was elected to the executive committee of the Italian Communist Party in exile. In 1937 he traveled to Spain to contribute to the struggle against Franco. By 1938, he directed the Paris-based antifascist newspaper *La voce degli italiani*. At the outbreak of the Second World War, he was interned first at Roland Garros tennis stadium, then at Le Vernet. Then, in 1941, he obtained a transfer to Les Milles, whence he hoped to emigrate. Initially, his wife, Anna Maria (née Favero), remained free, but by 1940 she was detained as well, first at the Vélodrome d'Hiver, then at the Rieucros camp.

Conditions in Le Vernet deteriorated further after France fell. Montagnana chronicled the precipitous decline in his rations, with bread allowances dropping from 450 to 240 grams a day. The only silver lining to the June 1940 armistices, wrote Montagnana wryly, was that France had not signed a "surrender on demand clause" with Italy as it had with Germany. Little did he know that a year later Mussolini's regime in all likelihood requested to have him brought back from Martinique to Europe.[80]

The League of American Writers intervened to help secure his and his wife's passage to Mexico. In September 1940, Montagnana was allowed to leave Le Vernet for Les Milles, where he began the arduous process of securing visas. By February 1941, Anna Maria had joined Mario in southern France, and by March 26, both were free in Marseille.[81]

There, the Montagnanas quickly zeroed in on several departure options, including the Lisbon and Martinique corridors. He sought advice on which ship to take from the camp commissioner at Les Milles. The latter warned him to board the first ship to Martinique: "You should leave the day after tomorrow or you will spend the rest of your life in the Vernet." Montagnana was livid at his brusque remark, but after the fact he conceded that, "in fact, we owe him our freedom since after that date we would not have left anymore"—a reference to the closing of the Martinique route. Montagnana added, "[The camp commissioner] wrote a note so that my departure would be facilitated in every office."[82] Armed with this letter, Mario and Anna Maria Montagnana then scrambled to secure a French exit visa, a Martinique transit visa, and the requisite permission for departure from the Italian Armistice Commission. The issuing of a ticket for the cargo ship was in theory contingent on all of these other documents, he specified. Despite the fact that their transit visas to New York were denied, the French prefecture renewed their exit visas, and the couple obtained authorization to travel to Martinique. HICEM subsidized the Montagnanas' voyage. However, they were still missing one key document. Indeed, they somehow managed to leave without securing the necessary document from the Italian Armistice Commission.[83]

Of course, the *Winnipeg*'s second wartime crossing did not go as expected. The ship never did reach Martinique. A Dutch war vessel intercepted it on May 26, 1941. The Martinique corridor had been permanently obstructed. As we will see later, the refugees on board the *Winnipeg*, including Mario Montagnana, eventually found their way to the safety of the Americas. The Montagnanas spent the rest of the war in Mexico. Mario Montagnana did not know it, but he had narrowly escaped being sent back to Europe from Martinique, on Vichy's orders and probably at Mussolini's request. One couple's joy was another one's sorrow. Indeed, for most refugees still languishing in southern France, the interception of the *Winnipeg* would prove a disaster, as it signaled the end of the most practical avenue of escape.

Dreams of North America and Fears of a Fifth Column

Martinique was by necessity a stopover for refugees seeking to reach North or South America. The vast majority of those who disembarked in the Antilles did indeed subsequently manage to depart for the United States, Brazil, Cuba, Mexico, Haiti, Puerto Rico, the Dominican Republic, or the neighboring island of Saint Lucia in relatively short order. Some refugees, such as Otto Borchardt, took matters into their own hands. Shortly after being transferred from the camp of Gurs to that of Les Milles, and two days before he was slated to sail to Martinique, on March 22, 1941, he wrote to the US consulate in Marseille asking officials there to transfer to the American consulate in Martinique the notice of his special visa for the

United States obtained through the International Relief Association in New York.[84] Borchardt considered Martinique one more hurdle en route to America.

Others, who evidently did not have visas for the United States, sought and received interesting tips on how to leave Martinique, much as refugees had relied on leads formal and informal in their quest to escape unoccupied France. Some may have had fake visas, others visas to countries such as Cuba or Mexico that were now dragging their heels, others still visas that expired while they were in the Lazaret or Balata camps waiting for ships or flights out of Martinique. Thus, in March 1941, a certain Mrs. Wallerstern, who was staying at the Central Hôtel in Fort-de-France, received a letter from Ciudad Trujillo. It explained that in the Dominican Republic there existed "a powerful organization dedicated to favoring the immigration of European Jews." The correspondent went on to specify that the organization was highly resourceful and had even managed to solve seemingly impossible cases.[85]

After arriving in Martinique, many refugees experienced an uncanny replay of the interminable waits they had endured in Marseille. They queued for long hours in the halls of an understaffed and rather makeshift US consulate. US consul Malige and his vice-consuls V. Harwood Blocker and Boswell set about scrupulously verifying refugee claims in Fort-de-France so as to formulate detailed reports on them for Washington. Malige was born in 1900 in Idaho to two French parents and spoke fluent French, so many interviews were conducted in that language.[86]

The legalism of the US consular team often seems wrongheaded in retrospect, although of course they represented an administration that was tightening immigration controls, and their margin of discretion was doubtless limited. In December 1940, Blocker wrote to the secretary of state to inform him that five Polish officers and noncommissioned officers had sought his permission to pass through the United States in transit, en route for Canada, where they wished to join free Polish forces to take up the fight once more to liberate their country from the Nazis.[87] Canada had already been at war since 1939, while the United States was still officially on the sidelines of the global conflict and would remain so until December 1941.

These demobilized men had managed to reach Martinique aboard the *Charles L. Dreyfus*. They were Air Commandant Stanislas Olzanik (also spelled Olszanick in some documents), Sublieutenant Chestav Einhorn, Sublieutenant Zygmunt Wolteger, Sublieutenant Roman Gurtler, and Chief Warrant Officer Stanislaw Deutsch. Olzanik had reached France after having waged a losing battle against the Luftwaffe in the skies over Poland in 1939. He had then fought Germany once more on the Western Front in France in May and June 1940, and he had taken his aircraft to Morocco as France surrendered. Einhorn had reached Toulouse in June 1940 and sought exit visas from Portugal, Spain, China, Panama, and Britain, a clear sign that he too wanted to leave now suddenly neutral France by any means possible to resume the fight. He had traversed Hungary, Yugoslavia, and Italy to reach France, then Morocco, and now Martinique.[88]

Blocker flatly refused the requests for transit to Canada, essentially on the basis that the men "are unknown locally and might or might not be fifth columnists." He acknowledged that "there is no evidence that these persons are in the pay of Germany" but reckoned that no evidence proved the contrary either. Here was a serious underestimation of the length to which these Polish patriots had gone to pursue the struggle when they could have surrendered on so many occasions. Blocker concluded his letter to Washington in a maddening display of circular logic: "It is said that those persons who went to St. Lucia did so because they were afraid of possible German influence in Martinique, whereas those who have remained here seem to have no fear of Germany or the present regime. This might indicate that [those still here] are German agents."[89] Such rumors spelled a terrible catch-twenty-two for refugees: the very fact that they were not able to leave was actually held against them, while if they tried to escape and were stopped by Vichy, they risked being sent to the penitentiaries of Les Saintes or Guiana.

By February 1941, Einhorn's brother, Julius, an attorney in New Jersey, initiated legal action to have his sibling admitted to the United States. Still, the US consulate in Martinique dragged its heels.[90] In April 1941, the US consulate reported that Einhorn, Gurtler, and Wolteger had reached Florida clandestinely after passing through Haiti and Cuba.[91] That same month, Olzanik sailed legally for New York from Fort-de-France aboard the *Guadeloupe*.[92]

By March 1941, the American authorities in Martinique had clearly conveyed to the State Department the procedures and consequences facing unwanted refugees in the French Caribbean: "[French] immigration authorities state that if [refugees at the Lazaret] do not find some means of proceeding to their destination within a month or six weeks after their arrival, they will be sent back to their port of departure, i.e. Marseille or Casablanca. Persons who do not have visas for a country other than Martinique are also sent to Lazaret."[93] The possibility of "repatriation" to Europe does not appear to have stirred American authorities. On the contrary, refugees who seemed to linger in Martinique soon became targeted as suspicious.

That month, Boswell added a new brick in the wall of conspiracy theories that was being erected at the US consulate in Martinique. He wrote to the State Department of ships having brought "refugees from Marseille and Casablanca, of which the majority are French intermingled with Czechoslovaks, Belgians, Poles and Germans." He described "constant rumors that while these German refugees hold themselves out to be bona fide refugees, there are among them a number of Nazi agents who are using Martinique as a jumping-off point for travel to various American republics." He added that he had tried to verify these rumors, unsuccessfully, but concluded in his letter to Washington, "the fact that [the rumors] are so persistent leads me to believe that there may be some basis for them."[94] Again, it seems that German-speaking refugees in particular were subject to a blanket of suspicion that proved impossible to shed.

By July 1941, even Malige was at wits' end, having followed every suspicious lead in vain. An exasperated Malige concluded, "Germans here? We are amused by such stories—except when we have to devote overtime to gathering actual proof that they are wrong."[95]

What is more, even Malige and his colleagues realized in some instances that US regulations were nothing short of Kafkaesque. On May 20, 1941, he drew the State Department's attention to the fact that "this office is becoming burdened with refugee callers delayed here because of outgoing travel facilities." He asked for automatic renewals in instances in which immigration visas expired for those still waiting in Martinique.[96] The matter went to court in the case of one migrant who reached Martinique from Marseille aboard the *Paul Lemerle* with a "nonpreference German quota visa issued at Marseille, January 16, 1941." The visa was still valid for three weeks after the passenger reached Fort-de-France, but no ship or plane left for America during that time period. He finally reached New York aboard the *Duc d'Aumale* and won his legal case on appeal, gaining permanent residence.[97]

Death on the Island

The great majority of refugees found their way to the United States, Cuba, Saint Lucia, the Dominican Republic, Canada, Mexico, or Haiti. However, a handful did not succeed in leaving, caught between American suspicion of spies and the general indifference of many nations in the Western Hemisphere toward stateless refugees, especially former Germans.

In June 1941, upon reaching the Dominican Republic, Seghers reminisced about German exiles with whom she had rubbed shoulders in Martinique. She wrote, "Breuer and Kersten greeted us at the pier in Pointe du Bout [the Lazaret camp]. Kersten has been stuck there for six months because he is in the 'western hemisphere' and therefore no longer in danger in the eyes of the Americans. The poor chap is of course totally broken."[98] Seghers was referring to German academic Kurt Kersten and his friend in misfortune, Jewish Socialist Robert Breuer.[99]

Kersten was born into a Protestant family in Kassel in 1891. He earned his doctorate in history at the age of twenty-two and grew into a distinguished historian who wrote extensively on Peter the Great, Otto von Bismarck, and the German Revolution of 1848 (his book on the revolution was banned first by the Nazis, then later by the German Democratic Republic). He also translated the Goncourt brothers into German. Outside the ivory tower, he was decorated several times over the course of the First World War but emerged from the conflict a convinced pacifist. After Hitler's election to power, he fled first to Zurich and then to Prague. He later found his way to Paris, where he remained a fervent anti-Nazi. The Nazis denaturalized him in April 1937.[100]

Breuer's real name was Lucien Friedlander. Trained in theology, he was an influential early member of the Social Democratic Party of Germany. Also an avid art critic, Breuer emerged as an important anti-Nazi voice. He immigrated to France in 1933, where he soon became an active supporter of the French Popular Front. Indeed, it was through the contacts of French Socialist former prime minister Léon Blum and German Socialist Rudolf Breitscheid that Breuer found his way first to Casablanca, then to Martinique aboard the *Charles Dreyfus* in October 1940. This was the first commercial ship bound to arrive in Martinique since the fall of France, and Kersten and Breuer would watch one vessel after another reach the isle, only to see its refugees depart for New York, Havana, Ciudad Trujillo, or Mexico while they stayed agonizingly put.[101]

Kersten's ominously titled manuscript "Death on the Island" picks up the story from here. The two men languish for months at the Lazaret, and they are told by American authorities that because Martinique is not part of the "danger zone," they cannot be received as refugees in America. Kersten and Breuer find themselves in a very delicate position, as German speakers surrounded by French West Indians, Czechs, Jews, and others all intensely distrustful of Germany. At this time, the American press is issuing fantastical reports of Nazis roaming the island. The two German dissidents are engulfed in clouds of suspicion. Some even imagine them to be "the future Gauleiters of Martinique," sent by Hitler to covertly control the island. Even their Martinican bartender friend conveys rumors that the *Winnipeg* has brought a "German commando" to Martinique. Kersten resigns himself to the fact that the two men "will be seen as spies everywhere."[102]

Kersten and Breuer contemplate escaping to Saint Lucia several times, but the hope for exit papers rekindles periodically, keeping them on location. They are later transferred to the camp at Balata (Breuer on May 21, 1941), where they mingle with other refugees and local West Indian dissidents. They also read, socialize, and translate texts.[103]

As the years pass, Breuer's health grows more fragile. He is afflicted with fevers, likely malaria. At the time, French colonies face a significant shortage in quinine, a penury that likely hastens his demise. Breuer passes away in Fort-de-France's hospital on April 30, 1943, mere months before the island switches over to de Gaulle's Fighting French.[104]

Kersten tells of supporting the July 1943 anti-Vichy insurrection in Martinique, led by Commandant Henri Tourtet out of Balata, precisely the place where Kersten is interned. He rubs shoulders with young, mostly local, soldiers who are pining to fight the Nazis and are furious at Vichy's navy for having kept the island in the Axis orbit for three long years. Although Kersten does not say as much, the revolt of July 1943 that ended with Martinique and Guadeloupe's siding with de Gaulle was as much a struggle between factions of the French navy and army in Martinique as it was an ideological conflict. Kersten's relation of the events is worth quoting. He intensely associates with Commandant Tourtet's Balata unit against Vichy's naval forces: "*Our* company was ready to defend itself. We were at

war. Watches and patrols were checking the roads, houses in the neigh-
bourhood were barred, firing windows created, other companies joined us
and the population smuggled food to us. And then the troops solemnly declared themselves in 'dissidence.' Over the gate the tricolor flag with the
cross of Lorraine was raised."[105] At last, it seemed, Kersten had achieved
insider status. However, his close friend was dead, and the American continent no closer in reach. He was finally allowed to immigrate to the United
States only in 1946.

Unbeknownst to Kersten and Breuer, US consul Malige had taken pity on
them, although to no great effect. The American authorities in Martinique
repeatedly pestered the State Department about the pair. In 1941, much correspondence dealt with whether the two men would become a "public
charge" in America.[106] By January 1942, Malige explained to the State Department that local Vichy authorities had actually shown patience, and that
it was high time for the United States to authorize the entry of the refugees
he listed, lest that patience run out. As he wrote on January 28, 1942,

> De Kuppersal, Alfred Austrian born at Vienna on 14 July 1910; de Kup-
> persal, Mrs. Claire, Hungarian, born in Budapest, Hungary, on 4
> July 1922; Friedlander, Lucien; German (Saar, born in Pezeki, Germany,
> 28 June 1878); Jahr, Wolf, Belgian, born in Krakow, Poland on 6
> October 1891; Jahr, Mrs Rachel, Belgian, born in Antwerp, 28 De-
> cember 1892 (and 2 children); Kersten, Kurt, German born in Wehlheiden,
> Germany, 19 April 1891. During the sixteen months these persons have
> been in Martinique, the local authorities have acted sympathetically on
> their plea that they face reprisals if returned to Europe. The authorities
> have become more and more skeptical about American visas ever being
> accorded, and now have requested a statement from this Consulate as to
> the prospects for a visa in each case, in order that they may decide defi-
> nitely as to the persons to be deported to Europe. Since the [US] Con-
> sulate is constantly being approached regarding the matter both by the
> authorities and the aliens, the latter more than ever in view of the threat
> to their welfare, receipt of the Department's reply as soon as possible
> would be appreciated.[107]

Malige was not bluffing when he suggested that the refugees might be sent
back. He had received a copy of a January 5, 1942, letter from Frigate Captain Henry Pelliet to Admiral Robert. The letter indicated that the argument that the Germans would commit reprisals against these refugees

should they be sent back to Marseille was losing credibility, given how un-receptive Washington had proved to admitting them.[108] Evidently, refugees had left the ominous limbo of Marseille for the only slightly less threat-ening limbo of Fort-de-France.

Local Complicities

Unsurprisingly, the population of the French Caribbean was not unani-mous in how it reacted to the influx of refugees. Some bemoaned the im-position on islands already suffering from shortages. Some associated the German refugees with Nazis and responded curtly or with outright hos-tility. Kersten relates, for example, how he approached a fisherman to buy some of his catch and was told abruptly, "I don't sell fish to the whites, and especially not to Germans."[109] However, many others clearly sympathized with the new arrivals, be it on political or humanitarian grounds; still others actively came to their aid.

In 1941, Martinique was bursting at the seams with refugees. "Marti-nique was never intended by the good lord to have half the world unloaded at its doorstep," griped a Fort-de-France hotel owner in American jour-nalist Smith's wartime account titled *Black Martinique, Red Guiana*.[110] Indeed, the journalist for *Cosmopolitan* was told that refugees occupied virtually every single hotel room on the island, leaving none for him. And, added his interlocutor, those refuges were the fortunate ones, for they had been dispensed from the Lazaret and Balata camps on health or other grounds.

Solidarity soon blossomed between some French West Indians and some refugees. Kersten recounts that he and Breuer befriended a West Indian family near the Lazaret. The father was a barman. Curiously, the only member of the family Kersten ever names is the daughter Clothilde. The two Germans spent endless hours drinking and fraternizing with the bar-tender.[111] Meanwhile, Barth also recalls the "young men" interned at the Lazaret "lov[ing] to go to a little place outside the camp where you could drink rum for very little money."[112] This account meshes perfectly with Kersten's testimony, minus the human connection.

Kersten also tells how he crossed paths with another Martiniquais man who had been posted as part of the French occupying force in the Ruhr in the wake of the First World War. Kersten relates that the man claimed to have had cordial relations with German civilians in the Ruhr, the polar opposite of what Hitler would later assert in his endless rants against the purported French racial humiliation imposed on Germany in the Ruhr—that is, the postwar occupation of part of Germany by French colonial troops, known in German as the "black shame."[113]

French West Indians who fraternized with refugees between 1940 and 1943 ran serious risks on this bastion of Pétainism. In June 1941, the gendarmerie investigated a certain Berthe Rivety, who was accused of harboring ties with both detained Czech troops and, perhaps more damningly, the refugees of the Lazaret camp who "frequently came to this bar." Ultimately, the investigation concluded that her job—serving in a local grocery that doubled as a bar called Au Rendez-Vous des Pétroliers at L'Anse Mitan (right by the Pointe du Bout, where the Lazaret was located)—more than any ideological convictions, probably accounted for her suspicious company.[114] This may well have been the same family described by Kersten.

Vichy's gendarmerie followed two similar cases with equal attention. It accused Jean Joseph, a resident of Balata, of complicity with the Keszler family interned at the Balata camp. The latter had arrived in Martinique on board the *Carimaré*, before leaving for the United States on May 21, 1941, on the *Duc d'Aumale*. Metro-Goldwyn-Mayer Studios had apparently agreed to hire Mr. Keszler in Hollywood. Although Joseph was charged with having aided the Keszlers and arranged for their removal from the camp, he was nevertheless cleared of wrongdoing. Conversely, Madame des Etages, whose husband was already in Vichy custody for aiding Gaullists to escape to neighboring British islands, was roundly rebuked for befriending Mrs. Kolb, "a Jew of Swiss nationality, in transit waiting to leave for the Dominican Republic, and awaiting the departure of the next boat."[115]

Vichy officials were evidently preoccupied by the links that were being established between refugees and Martinicans. By April 1941, Vichy's inspector in Martinique, Devouton, had learned through anonymous sources that "a certain number of migrants, especially Jewish ones, are seeking to fraternize with the local colored population by linking their fate with that of blacks, and contending that they are both victims of Germany's racial policies."[116] Here was a powerful avowal that the persecuted refugees had found common cause with Martinicans. It no doubt also reinforced a dual victimization that was already fairly common knowledge. A schoolteacher in late 1930s Martinique had once lectured Fanon, "When you hear people speaking ill of the Jews, keep your ears pricked, they're talking about you."[117]

"La dissidence," as the resistance movement to Vichy in the French Caribbean was known, was as keen as Vichy authorities to ascertain the origin and identity of the boatloads of refugees streaming into Fort-de-France. In October 1940, Free French governor Félix Eboué's Martinique contact Pujol, a leading figure in directing the flow of dissidents to Saint Lucia, noted in his diary, "Word spreads of a boat coming from France; we must check that there are no Germans on board." Upon inspection, Pujol added, "The boat is the *Charles Dreyfus*. The passengers are Jews and de-militarized Czechoslovak soldiers—who, with the help of officers in the army, of Maurice des Etages, and of de Goupi, the head of the veterans' league, as well as fishermen from St. Lucia, were spirited across to St. Lucia and from there on to England."[118]

One of the greatest complicities of all was intellectual, and it involved Aimé and Suzanne Césaire and the Surrealists on board the vessels from Martinique. They took advantage of the little room for maneuvering afforded to them—even the day passes from the Lazaret—to forge deep ties.

Intrigue and Intelligence

Considerable intrigue surrounded some of the passages from Marseille to Martinique: Vichy officials endlessly denied rumors that Gestapo or other German agents found their way to Fort-de-France among the mass of migrants. We will see that US concerns over these suspicions and false rumors ultimately contributed to closing the Marseille-to-Martinique line in late May 1941.

That said, some files do present evidence of espionage, subterfuge, or machinations, nearly all of it for the Allies, ironically. Some refugees took part in high-level efforts to swing the island over to the Allied side. Mario Leri was one such figure. Born in Venice to a Jewish family in 1894, he served in the First World War and was twice wounded during the conflict. In 1918, he took over his parents' antiques business. Between the wars, rumors swirled that he operated for the French secret service. In any event, his hatred of Mussolini's regime appears genuine. It is unclear on which ship Leri reached Martinique from Marseille, but it is believed he sailed after receiving a *sauf-conduit* from the French authorities.[119]

By April 1943, Leri had found refuge in the Dominican Republic. There, he tried to liaise with an American delegation. Having previously established connections with Vichy officials in Martinique, he was persuaded he could work hand in hand with the United States to help convince Admiral Robert to switch sides. His approach was certainly original. He believed he could prove to Robert that he was being duped, and that "his advisors were just politicians." Leri believed Robert to be upright but misguided. Ultimately, American intelligence deemed Leri's story "insufficient," adding that "he is the mystery man of Martinique. In Martinique, everyone seems to know him, but no one really seems to know him intimately."[120] The efforts of this mysterious character right out of a Graham Greene novel seem to have been in vain.

Among those aboard the ships to Martinique were members of France's intelligence services who steadfastly refused to bow to Vichy and the Third Reich. Born in 1899, first trained as a lawyer, René Hauth, whom we have already encountered, emerged as a leading journalist in the 1920s, working briefly for newspapers in Madrid and Prague. He then established himself with the *Dernières nouvelles d'Alsace* in 1930s but also served as correspondent for *Le Temps* and Reuters. At some point before 1939, he joined the French counterespionage services and was sent in that capacity to Syria and the Balkans. He was in Zagreb when France fell. From there he headed to Belgrade in August 1940, and then wound his way back to Lyon.[121] There was no internal, organized resistance to speak of in August 1940. In Lyon he received a phone call from Marseille announcing the departure of a ship to Martinique, whence he might be able to reach New York. Hauth scrambled to put his affairs in order. He faced multiple administrative hurdles: obtaining French exit papers, admission to the colonies, and the right to depart with substantial funds (a sign that he was leaving for some time); assembling his belongings; and finally securing a spot on board. He wrote to his cousins of needing a "tour de force" in each of these "specialties." Exhausted by this administrative obstacle course, he sighed with relief as he boarded at having obtaining "all of the viatica of all administrations." He set sail on the *Wyoming* on February 6, 1941.[122]

As a French national, Hauth was allowed to check into the Hôtel de la Paix upon arriving in Martinique on February 25, 1941. He soon transferred to another establishment, the small Lido hotel in nearby Schoelcher. In early March 1941, he presented himself to the American consulate in Martinique, seeking entry to the United States. The US National Archives show that in March 1941 the State Department asked the US consul to Martinique, Malige, to provide additional information pertaining to Hauth's "political views" and the "nature of his past activities."[123] The fact that he spoke fluent German and hailed from Alsace, a region then annexed by the Nazis, may have rendered him suspicious to American authorities in and of itself. As Hauth noted in a letter to his wife, US officials were doing due diligence to ensure that he was not "a fifth columnist."[124] Of course, the occupation of his native Alsace by the Nazis was one of the very reasons for his desire to support the Allied cause from America.

Hauth managed to prevail, convincing the US authorities of his patriotism. He reached New York from Martinique, via Haiti and Puerto Rico. By 1943, he had become secretary general of the France-Amérique Gaullist organization in the United States. A year later, he headed the Agence France Presse services in Washington.[125] While in the United States, he also worked on French adaptations of Hollywood films. Hauth would die aboard the Lockheed Constellation, which crashed off the Azores in October 1949, also killing French boxer Marcel Cerdan. A recent novel by Adrien Bosc on the Lockheed crash depicts Hauth as having worked for the US Secret Service during the war; while most of the book is rooted in historical fact, this particular detail appears to have been concocted or embellished.[126]

Meanwhile, many refugees who were denied entry to the United States, or who preferred other options, joined West Indian dissidents and deserting Vichy naval personnel on the British islands of Saint Lucia and Dominica. These migrants often traveled under assumed identities, making it nearly impossible to pinpoint who they were. For example, in 1941 Governor Nicol contacted the Ministry of the Colonies at Vichy concerning a certain Charles Smudex. This individual, who also went by the surname Doukek, had arrived in Fort-de-France aboard the *Charles L. Dreyfus*. On November 28, 1940, he departed "clandestinely" from Martinique for an unnamed neighboring British island, without leaving any trail of his origins or intentions.[127]

Czech servicemen stranded in Martinique in 1941 also managed to leave for Dominica and Saint Lucia. After the Germans seized Czechoslovakia,

Jan Zemek began an epic quest to continue the struggle against Nazi Germany. Overcoming numerous setbacks, including months spent in a Hungarian jail, he crossed the Balkans to Syria, and from there reached Agde in southern France. He served as a telephone liaison agent in the French ranks during the Battle of France. In the wake of the armistice, he set off for Casablanca in August 1940, and from there boarded a ship to Martinique. Along with several of his countrymen, he then decamped to Dominica. From there, the British authorities sent him to Britain, where he volunteered to join a Czech unit. He was parachuted into his homeland in 1941 to conduct covert operations, one of them linked to operation Anthropoid, the assassination of Reinhard Heydrich.[128] Martinique was fast emerging as a back door through which partisans were returning to the front of this global war, albeit by a very convoluted path.

Among the many migrants to arrive in Martinique then promptly leave for British islands was the more enigmatic Walter Von Leubuscher. An Austrian national born in Marburg (modern-day Maribor in Slovenia), he had left for France in 1938 a self-professed "political refugee."[129] He had in fact been a former Austrian Nazi, even apparently an SS squad leader (*Oberscharführer*) in Vienna at a time when Austria was torn by civil strife. However, by 1937, Leubuscher switched sides, renounced Nazism, and was now hunted down by the Nazis as a traitor.[130] Although an accomplished pilot, he served in the French infantry during the Battle of France in 1940 (perhaps a sign he was not fully trusted). After the armistice, he attempted in vain to cross the Pyrenees under the pseudonym Pierre Duval. From Marseille he managed to find his way to Morocco, and from there to Martinique aboard the *Charles L. Dreyfus*. He then escaped Martinique by crossing the Saint Lucia channel. In Castries, on February 3, 1941, he signed a declaration stating that he wished to join the British Royal Air Force. Barring that, he was willing to serve in the Free French Air Force.[131] His name appears in Frenchified form (de Leubuscher) in Henri Ecochard's list of Free French members, so he must have entered de Gaulle's ranks.[132]

Purgatory

It is against this backdrop of refugees pouring across the channels separating French and British isles in the Caribbean that we need to understand the fear of spies that reached a fever pitch in 1941. But what are we to make of the Martinique stopover itself? As with the departure from Marseille, it proves difficult to place a label on the waiting period so many refugees experienced in Martinique. Many were mercilessly tormented by Vichy's naval police. A few managed to eke out a more dignified living. Some were sent back across the Atlantic, and many more escaped to Dominica and Saint Lucia.

One thing is clear: Vichy's nightmare of a complicity forming between refugees and dissident West Indians came true. An ambivalent haven akin to a purgatory for many of the migrants, the Martinique refugee conduit would ultimately elicit remarkable encounters between a handful of travelers on the one hand and leading Martinican thinkers on the other.

CHAPTER SEVEN

Surrealism Meets Negritude

THE ENCOUNTER BETWEEN A GROUP OF Martinican intellectuals and select refugees from Marseille bore marvelous fruit. The first connection was purely fortuitous. André Breton despaired as he perused the thinning shelves of "insanely disparate" books in one of the Martinique's bookstores. The island's forced isolation had taken its toll on this cultural front, as well as on the local diet. Fittingly perhaps, it was not in a bookstore at all but in a haberdashery that a local journal caught the Surrealist's eye. He had entered the shop to find a ribbon for his daughter Aube; instead he stumbled on a remarkable intellectual surprise. The inaugural issue of the journal *Tropiques* that he discovered had just been printed in April 1941. Breton recounts that his initial expectations were low: the "police reaction" in Martinique alone commanded skepticism. However, as he cracked open the journal, epiphany struck. "All of the grinding shadows were torn, and broke apart; all the lies, all of the derisions fell into tatters." He contrasted the journal with recent publications in France, which in his opinion all bore the hallmark of "masochism" toward the Third Republic, if not "servility" toward the occupier. As Alvan A. Ikoku has suggested, the idealized "South" that emerged in Breton's writings served as the antithesis of an oppressive North embodied by Philippe Pétain and Vichy.[1]

The shopkeeper turned out to be none other than René Ménil's sister. The Martinican philosopher René Ménil was the cofounder of the journal *Tropiques* and had already rubbed shoulders with Surrealists in 1930s Paris. Through the Ménils, Breton was soon introduced to the team behind *Tropiques,* starting with Aimé and Suzanne Césaire. Aimé Césaire had also suffered from the island's isolation, noting that Martinican intellectuals virtually pounced on newcomers. Both sides, it seemed, had hoped for just such a meeting of minds.[2]

Like any encounter narrative, this one followed a set of conventions, even morphing into a foundation myth. Hence, as Jean-Claude Blachère has remarked, the story was woven around Aube's ribbon and around Ménil's sister as a kind of fairylike go-between.[3] It hinged at least partly on the importance that Surrealists attributed to fate and revelation. Yet, bearing all of this in mind, the story, its silences, and the cultural production engendered by the confluence of Surrealism and Negritude all prove especially rich and evocative. The exchanges that resulted would generate profound and fecund reflections on questions of identity, race, authenticity, and rediscovery.

Participants recall that during the weeks that followed the moment of encounter, Breton, Jacqueline Lamba, Wifredo Lam, Aimé Césaire, and Helena Holzer (later Benitez) spent long hours conversing in a local Fort-de-France bar. Benitez remembers that she and Lam met with Césaire at a café in Fort-de-France. Some days later, the Césaires led the group on a hike through the lush forest of Absalon, north of Fort-de-France. According to Benitez, this was the first introduction to the rainforest for her and Lam.[4] As we will see, Martinique's lush nature would profoundly impact the Cuban painter. If the first epiphany had involved opening *Tropiques,* then Absalon constituted the second. Soon, these different intellectuals reworked the Absalon motif into an "experimental forest."[5] In their "Creole dialogue," André Masson and Breton evoked the wonder of Absalon's creepers and vines, the rainforest's lushness, its "precipices," its "bamboos enveloped in smoking vapors" of tropical humidity.[6] In fact, the verdant valley remained at the heart of correspondence between the Césaires and Breton and Lamba even after the latter two left the island for New York. Thus, in October 1941 Breton requested snapshots of the valley they had visited together; Suzanne Césaire responded that photographers were unfortunately short of photo paper. Then, in April 1942, Aimé Césaire wrote to Breton, "We see the admirable Absalon valley only with you and through you: it is one of the few parts of this land that is still bearable to me physically."[7]

Before the band dispersed, hikes and animated discussions in cafés segued to poetry readings. Aimé and Suzanne Césaire reconvened the entire group for a reading of one of Césaire's poems in progress. Soon the

Massons joined the team, including on the hikes in Absalon valley.[8] The group also had ample time to stroll about and converse—at least for those who did not have to return to the Lazaret for evening roll call (as did Lam and Benitez, who were foreign refugees).

There was, however, an asymmetry in leisure time. While the visitors were officially banned from working, the team in Fort-de-France was busy with classes and cultural projects. Aimé Césaire was no average teacher. He was born in 1913 in Martinique, the son of a tax collector and a seamstress. A brilliant student, he won entrance to Louis-le-Grand in Paris in 1931, where he first met Senegalese intellectual Léopold Sédar Senghor. Three years later, he cofounded the black militant review *L'Étudiant noir,* in which he and his colleagues celebrated the concept of blackness or Negritude. In 1935, he entered the prestigious École normale supérieure in Paris. In 1937, he wed Suzanne Roussi, the daughter of a Martiniquais female schoolteacher. Two years later he published his influential *Cahier d'un retour au pays natal,* a call to arms couched in Surrealist terms, and one of the founding texts of the Negritude movement. In December 1939, the couple returned to Martinique, where Suzanne succeeded in landing a spot in another Fort-de-France school, while Aimé took up his post at the Lycée Schoelcher.

This brings us back to Aimé Césaire the young teacher, in his first post at Fort-de-France's finest educational establishment as the Vichy regime took hold. Edouard Glissant, who was thirteen at the time, remembers the senior classes in his school convening with Breton in 1941. Césaire had taught Surrealism in class, and meeting Breton, the so-called Pope of Surrealism, in person must have marked the finest experience of show-and-tell that his students would experience. Breton was a master at shocking, grabbing attention, and shattering received wisdom. Although too young to have been in Césaire's class, Glissant remembers tagging along and listening in awe to the impromptu class with the Surrealist, while seated on a bench of the Savane Park.[9]

Of the refugees, why was it predominantly Breton, Lamba, and Masson, as well as the Cuban painter Lam and his spouse, Holzer, who liaised with local Caribbean intellectuals? Why did the Spanish Republican and German Jewish refugees seemingly fail to forge the same ties? Language may have played a role, although Lam's French was shaky at best, which somewhat undermines the linguistic hypothesis (Lam's French-language correspondence to Breton does make use of the pluperfect subjunctive—a sure sign of proficiency—but Lam also specifies that his French prose has been polished by Holzer).[10] A more probable answer has to do with detention conditions. After a few days of internment at the Lazaret, Breton, Lamba, and their daughter had been allowed to leave. Admittedly, Lam and Holzer were still inmates, but they took advantage of their day releases to stroll and converse with the Césaires. One evening, they missed curfew and spent the evening at the Césaires'; the next morning, a furious Lazaret camp manager threatened to report them.[11] In short, because they were detained outside Fort-de-France, German and Spanish refugees simply had fewer opportunities to connect with local intellectuals.

In addition, even when they took advantage of day passes to leave their camp, refugees tended to lie low. After all, many of the foreign migrants were threatened with deportation or "return" to Morocco or even to France. Even French nationals found themselves on dangerous ground. A gendarmerie captain had warned Breton, "Remember, there is nobody for you to see here. Especially avoid the colored element. They are big children. What you tell them is bound to be misunderstood. Write all the books you want after you have left."[12] Breton was then told that he was being placed under "discreet surveillance." In other words, conditions were hardly propitious for building networks. And so the Lycée Schoelcher never received the visiting all-star team it might have: Bertrand Goldschmidt in chemistry and physics, André Mayer in the natural sciences, Minna Flake in medicine, Claude Lévi-Strauss in anthropology, Lam in art, Kurt Kersten in history, and Anna Seghers in German literature.

Contingency played an important role as well. Thus, despite spending much longer on the island, Kersten never crossed paths with Aimé and Suzanne Césaire, even though he often managed to leave the camp. He even frequented the Bibliothèque Schoelcher, where, in theory, odds favored meeting local scholars. His description of the library encapsulates the German historian's own preset ideas and trepidation: at first he felt "alien" when he entered the grand building, because he was the only white reader that day. But he soon warmed to the place. He was particularly delighted at being able to peruse the shelves himself, a luxury North American researchers take for granted but that many Europeans will still recognize as a privilege to this day. The ethereal bubble burst when he left the library and was insulted by local children in Creole.[13] Being a German speaker in wartime Martinique came with baggage of its own.

In some instances, the impact was delayed. Although she complained about internment conditions in Martinique while she was there in 1941, three years later in Mexico, Seghers waxed poetic about the island in a letter to Kersten, who was still stranded outside Fort-de-France. She wrote that she could well imagine having stayed in Martinique, and she commissioned an article from Kersten on the June 1943 Balata revolt that marked the end of Vichy. She was especially keen to learn of its impact "on the black population." Finally, she expressed hope that she might one day return for a lengthier stay in the French West Indies, which she compared to the city-states of Renaissance Italy in their heyday.[14] A kind of time lag seems to have marked Seghers' fascination with Martinique. Decades later she would produce a literary work devoted to slavery and slave revolts in the French Caribbean.[15]

Language, lags, lodgings, locations, and luck are not the only factors that explain why some refugees failed to connect with local artists and intellectuals. We have seen that Victor Serge's, Germaine Krull's, and to some extent Kersten's closed-mindedness and racial hierarchies prevented deep engagement with Martinicans. They probably also precluded the kind of postulate that Breton formulated: that Aimé Césaire was a poet of the highest order, and *Tropiques* a publication more daring and original than anything produced in mainland France at the time. In other words, questions of sensitivity and openness conditioned who succeeded in forging meaningful ties in the Caribbean and who did not.

Tropiques

Enough of missed opportunities when so many exchanges actually transpired. Aimé Césaire deemed his encounter with Breton of the utmost importance, comparing its significance to his rendezvous with Senghor a decade earlier in a meeting of minds that helped define Negritude.[16] Similarly, a beaming Suzanne Césaire explained to Breton and Jacqueline Lamba that "their wonderful encounter" had marked a "key moment in their lives."[17] As Blachère has observed, "the encounter was magical" precisely "because it was improbable."[18]

It is not hard to conceive that Surrealism, steeped as it was in irreverence and revolt, constituted an ideal weapon with which to combat Vichy's authoritarianism and racism. One source has termed the movement "a revolutionary individualism in which thought is all powerful, in which thinking is to be transformed, and then in turn the lives of men."[19] The encounter between this current and Negritude, which celebrated blackness and African roots, generated considerable energy and attention. And it also reaped rich rewards over the long term. Indeed, one could argue that the cocktail fared better than Surrealism did on its own, at least in achieving concrete political results (although the case can of course be made that Surrealism influenced everything from existentialism to the philosophy of the absurd).[20]

As Albert James Arnold has suggested, it was thanks to Surrealist networks that Aimé Césaire was propelled into the limelight after the war.[21] The benefit worked both ways: as Ikoku indicates, Breton "co-opted" and "appropriated" Césaire's work, in particular his seminal *Cahier d'un retour au pays natal*.[22] Indeed, the ties between these intellectuals proved mutually beneficial, with the Césaires winning influential champions and an unexpected platform and Breton finding a new face for his weakened and divided movement (weakened in part by his departure from Marseille, which some of his comrades considered desertion).[23] In no way were allegiances unconditional, however. For instance, *Tropiques* featured several tributes to Breton's former confidant and now sworn enemy Paul Eluard, who had been added to the list of "traitors" to the movement that included Louis Aragon. These Surrealist rifts had many causes, but their root had to do with Aragon's toeing Moscow's line after 1929, and Breton's dissenting from it.

Thus, while Negritude has been tied to *L'étudiant noir,* the remarkable synergy between a handful of refugees and an equally tight-knit cluster of Antillean intellectuals was enshrined most prominently and enduringly in the pages of *Tropiques.* The journal's very existence, let alone its survival under Vichy, remains something of an enigma, as we are about to see. There can be no doubt that dialogue with Breton and Lam fueled the creative engines of the *Tropiques* team, comprising Ménil, Suzanne and Aimé Césaire, and Aimé Césaire's brother-in-law, Aristide Maugée, a committed anticolonialist who would go on to become mayor of Gros-Morne after the war. The synergy had as its core the profound friendship that blossomed between local thinkers and writers and select travelers from Marseille.[24]

The form and content of the articles in *Tropiques* explicitly referenced Surrealism, and several pieces were devoted to Breton and his movement, while two dealt specifically with the work of Lam. This homage to Surrealism required courage, at a time when the movement's antifascist and revolutionary leanings were well established, and Vichy's navy considered Breton persona non grata. Of course, Surrealism was but one influence among many. The journal also featured a deep engagement with Afro-American literature and Cuban and Haitian themes, not to mention Martinican rediscovery. Aimé Césaire considered *Tropiques* first and foremost a Martinican exercise in "recentering."[25]

To achieve this recentering, Césaire turned to Surrealism, this unexpected new "windfall," as one component of his larger toolkit.[26] It was Surrealism's promise of breaking with conventions and starting anew that opened an especially auspicious path. As he explained in 2002 to an interviewer asking him about his wartime encounter with the Surrealists, "I said to myself: let's throw away everything conventional, this salon French, the Martinican imitations of French literature. . . . Let's toss all that out! Dig into yourself! Go on, dig deeper and deeper! And when you have dug enough, you'll find something. You'll find the foundational black."[27] This desire to "recover an authentic self," to borrow J. Michael Dash's phrase, had already been articulated in Césaire's epic poem *Cahier d'un retour au pays natal*.[28] But in *Tropiques,* Césaire went further still. Only by shattering conventional frameworks could black be made beautiful. In this sense, Surrealism provided the ax with which to destroy existing paradigms, while Negritude presented the mold for a brighter future.

Notwithstanding all of these influences and agendas, and despite the undeniable impact of his journal, Césaire cautioned many years later that "one cannot set too high a bar for *Tropiques*. The journal was born at a particularly thankless time in very dangerous circumstances." Before turning to the question of danger, let us focus first on the material difficulties of the day. Like any startup periodical, it faced multiple challenges, exacerbated in this case by the particular context of wartime Martinique. First of all, the editors needed to find writers willing to participate in the venture. Césaire explained that he called on his teaching colleagues at his Lycée Schoelcher for contributions. Hence the first issues' "professorial and rather eclectic feel." However, the small circle of authors was not strictly limited to teachers and Surrealists. For instance, the Césaires called on Henri Stehlé to explore the island's flora. As we have seen, Stehlé worked for the colony's agricultural service and shared little of *Tropiques'* agenda or project. But he brought know-how that the others lacked on matters of flora.[29]

Second, the project faced daunting economic challenges. Césaire and his colleagues funded the journal themselves, out of pocket. A third problem involved the shortage of paper and books for what was ostensibly a cultural review. Césaire insists that if *Tropiques* featured shortcomings, it was quite simply "because there were no books" in Martinique. By way of example, he cites the complete absence of a novel by Stéphane Malarmé in any of the island's libraries. As for the famous Schoelcher Library, he called it "a little colonial holding" without so much as the complete publications of Charles Baudelaire.[30] An archival clipping listing the libraries on Martinique in 1945 confirms Césaire's point: it enumerates ten libraries in all, counting the presumably modest holdings of the officers' mess, of the commercial school alumni association, and of the technical school. Another document lists the island's nine bookstores in 1945, all of them in Fort-de-France; interestingly, four of the nine were owned by women.[31] However, this does not necessarily reflect the situation in 1941. By 1945, Fort-de-France had undergone something of a cultural renaissance and had reconnected with francophone book circuits. A report from August 1944 underscored that the Bibliothèque Schoelcher had just received a considerable boost to collections that until recently had remained completely frozen since the defeat of 1940. Indeed, it now suddenly "obtained just about everything that has been written in French these past few years in the United States and Canada."[32] The blockade had been lifted, and although connections with France had not yet resumed, those with Québec certainly had.[33]

The greatest challenge of all involved the threat of Vichy censorship. Some scholars see in *Tropiques* a daring flouting of Vichy's draconian press laws by a new generation of thinkers and artists. In this view, the *Tropiques* team sought to sing the praises of Caribbeanness and blackness while simultaneously launching "veiled attacks" on Vichy, and even on colonialism itself, through "dissimulation" and "subversion."[34] Ménil has disclosed, "As we wrote our articles, we had to find just the right dosage of opposition to Vichy's doctrines . . . without however, provoking the censors to ban the publication."[35] He adds, "The students . . . who were virtually the only readers of *Tropiques* during the forties . . . knew that it was necessary to 'read between the lines,' fill in the blanks and the silences, and interpret the symbols, ellipses and antiphrasis."[36] In other words, *Tropiques* was at least partly drafted in code, in a manner truly intelligible only to a small circle of Martinicans. In many ways, these arguments are reminiscent of Jean-Paul Sartre's contested claim that his 1943 play *The Flies* had slipped past German censors while issuing a resistance message that was understood as such by French audiences only.[37]

There is evidence to support the "coded language" theory: Vichy officials in the Caribbean famously did censor *Tropiques,* banning the journal altogether in May 1943, during the twilight of Vichy's rule on the island. This was quite simply because circumstances had taken the team past the "coded" phase. Indeed, Aimé Césaire explains that the authors of the journal became "emboldened" between 1941 and 1943. While early issues had been devoted almost entirely to fairly abstract poetry, later ones focused on everything from ethnology to botany, folklore, art, and history, thereby skirting perilously closer to identity politics.[38]

Although some of the censorship files of Vichy's navy in the Caribbean were destroyed in 1943,[39] there can be little doubt that *Tropiques* raised eyebrows under Vichy even before drawing its ire. By April 10, 1942, Césaire was writing to Breton that "hostility towards *Tropiques* was now openly declared." Fifteen months later, in the wake of Vichy's defeat in the Caribbean, Césaire elaborated that *Tropiques* had been "censored" under Admiral Georges Robert, adding that it had also been "mutilated twenty times over," before finally being banned outright. It is not entirely clear what Césaire meant by "mutilated."[40] Perhaps the regime had begun to threaten to withhold publication or tried to shape its tone. No archival evidence has survived to support this hypothesis. In point of fact, Vichy banned only one issue of *Tropiques,* and the break came as the naval regime was beginning to capsize in May 1943.

Thus, while the subversive model certainly makes sense, *Tropiques* also cannot be understood independently from the Vichy French context. Indeed, beyond merely being authorized or tolerated, the journal was even printed on the same press as *Le Courrier des Antilles* and thus bore a measure of government approval.[41] Daniel Maximin explains that it was Suzanne Césaire herself who regularly presented tables of contents and even whole articles for approval to the naval censor.[42]

A step backward is required here to consider the small world of publishing in Martinique under Vichy. While *Tropiques* continued to appear, the regime proved very thorough in its censorship of other reviews and newspapers, cutting out large swaths of many of them, even those sympathetic to its cause.[43] And, in addition to removing columns, Vichy inserted many more, not merely in the regime's local mouthpiece, the *Bulletin hebdomadaire*. A file in Martinique's archives shows check marks in columns across a list of newspapers, noting which articles had clearly been fed to them by the authorities. An informal system of rotations ensured that the placed pieces saturated different newspapers on different days so as to avoid the appearance of craven conformity. On September 18, 1941, Lieutenant Pierre Bayle even contacted local newspaper directors to explain that the authorities would pay for the articles they "inserted." He then outlined how this operation would take place.[44] Although *Tropiques* was not on the list (only newspapers were, not journals), this does raise the question of how much leeway the journal could enjoy. In short, the least one can say is that local Vichy authorities paid unusually close attention to the press, shaping it in a variety of ways.

Let us briefly assume that Vichy's local information services granted *Tropiques* greater leeway than they did other print media, asking only to review in advance the material Suzanne Césaire brought to Lieutenant Bayle. Why would the authorities have tolerated such an exception? Why allow *Tropiques* to appear at all? If Vichy authorities were initially deceived into permitting the publication and continuation of *Tropiques,* then they were duped by its promise of cultural authenticity. In a 1994 interview, Aimé Césaire spoke of an "obsession with identity" that consumed *Tropiques.* He added that, fortunately, Vichy's censors could not grasp the complexity of his prose and only understood it when it was "too late."[45] In this version of events, the Césaires and their team, in tandem with the Surrealist refugees, had managed to outwit Vichy officials.

Some proof does support this notion, starting with the famous May 10, 1943, letter from Vichy lieutenant Bayle announcing the journal's suspension. He candidly explained that he had previously seen in *Tropiques* the expression of proud regionalism and folklore. He had been sympathetic to the cause. He had hoped that the Césaires would be to Martinique what Frédéric Mistral had been to Provence: exponents of nostalgia and bards of local flavors, expressions, and customs. Now he realized, however, that the review was actually "revolutionary, racial and sectarian."[46] He came close to using the word "nationalistic." In other words, Bayle flatly admitted he had been fooled.

Aimé Césaire obviously knew that one could play with concepts of identity, even ironically, shifting from "regionalism" to "nationalism." One of his most influential mentors in Martinique in the 1930s was his history teacher, a Norman by the name of Eugène Revert. Revert apparently enjoyed deliberately exaggerating regional Norman accents and stereotypes. Césaire describes this history teacher as "playing the Norman farmer." At this time, of course, the Ministry of the Colonies in Paris referred to Martinique, like Normandy or Provence, as a "petite patrie" whose cult was compatible with that of the "grande patrie," which is to say France.[47] Césaire would therefore have fully understood the interplay between imperial and local identities, and the margin of maneuver available to him to promote Martiniqueness.

Several articles in *Tropiques* support the notion that the censors were fooled by dual meanings, veiled attacks, and stealth. Subtle and less subtle barbs targeted Vichy soft spots. Consider the pointed aside that Suzanne Césaire offers in an April 1942 article, "A Civilization's Discontent." She describes "chronic undernourishment" on Martinique in the time of slavery, before adding, "something that remains a current reality."[48] The mark was cleverly chosen, for, as we have seen, even Vichy's governor Yves Marie Nicol readily acknowledged that food shortages had become chronic in Martinique. There was no denying the obvious.

Similarly, in the February 1943 issue of *Tropiques,* Ménil sketched the portrait of a pathological fictional "dictator." Said dictator harangued twenty million listeners from his balcony while using the latest technologies, including giant projectors that shot the image of four-leaf clovers into the sky. He called on his people to become "the conquistadors of the modern age." The dictator relied on "psychological engineers" to better whip up the frenzy of a "hypnotized" crowd. Little more than a mental nudge was needed to conjure up Joseph Goebbels, Leni Riefenstahl, Adolf Hitler, and Benito Mussolini, and to substitute clovers for swastikas.[49] And yet, once more, Vichy's censors could hardly take offense: Ménil's dictator was no paternalist octogenarian like Pétain. Rather, he was a blustering, theatrical, and devious master of psychological persuasion. While Vichy's leader was sacrosanct to the local naval censors, the same could not be said for the leaders of Italy and Germany.

The dictator example constituted a theme that was out of bounds. Had Vichy's local henchmen groused, they might have been perceived as protesting too much. However, covert meanings in *Tropiques* can also be discerned in Ménil and Aimé Césaire's "An Introduction to Martinican Folklore" in the January 1942 installment. The piece begins in a remote "once upon a time," a chronology that invites analogies. And indeed, the tone is set right away: "The whole population is hungry." Any Martinican would have made the connection to the present when reading of "an obsession with empty bellies." The remote time is once more that of slavery. The authors describe how it ushered in not only "hunger" but also a "cycle of fear": "The master and companion of slavery: the whip and denunciation." Denunciations were running rampant in Vichy-controlled Martinique. In Ménil and Césaire's penultimate paragraph, hunger, fear, and defeat were linked. Here was a sufficiently subtle, yet eminently clear, conjuring of the local past to condemn Vichy oppression in the present.[50]

Perhaps Vichy's censors were not so much duped as intimidated. Guadeloupean poet and novelist Maximin puts forward this intriguing notion in his novel *L'Isolé soleil*, set in the French Caribbean under Vichy. He observes that Vichy officials knew that some of the teachers at the Lycée Schoelcher were Communists; Vichy's naval police also understood how hostile Aimé Césaire and Ménil were to their regime. And yet, as Maximin suggests, all parties seemed to implicitly recognize that demographic power relations were not in the censors' favor. Under the circumstances, Vichy's henchmen decided "to tolerate that [the high school] continue to manufacture Surrealist graduates ... while biding their time for the dangerous broth of Fort-de-France culture to fizzle out, with the end of the Allied blockade, allowing it to disperse to the far-away Sorbonne."[51]

There is, however, one more reading of *Tropiques* that suggests points of convergence between censors and those submitting their publication to censorship. Here the duping falls to the side, and what the French call the *second degré* (second layer of interpretation) retreats before the first, more literal, meaning. In this interpretation, Lieutenant Bayle was fooled not so much by *Tropiques* as by Vichy's own unconditional promotion of authenticity, of "regionalism," and of nostalgia for a remote, purer past, which backfired before his eyes. Consider for instance Vichy's youth minister Georges Lamirand's instructions that were dispatched to all colonial governors from Hanoi to Dakar and Martinique in March 1941, in anticipation of Joan of Arc Day festivities:

> 1) Evoke and invoke Joan of Arc, the incarnation of the will to live
> French, of total devotion, of faith and heroism. . . . 2) Call on . . . the glo
> ries and history of the region where you are posted, its great men and its
> great women. 3) Conjure up legends, traditions, regional qualities and
> folklore—songs, dances etc. 4) Draw a lesson by providing contemporary
> examples.[52]

In other words, Bayle was fully cognizant of, and had participated in,
Vichy's effort to celebrate local pasts, to promote folklore, traditional
dances, music, and even national heroes and heroines of Joan of Arc's ilk.
Until May 1943, he seems to have considered *Tropiques'* agenda to have
been compatible with this spirit. He doubtless rejected Surrealism—the
sledgehammer with which the Césaires wished to crush conventions—but
he appears to have seen promise in the nostalgic and "authentic" identity
that the Césaires wished to build out of the rubble. Beyond the Caribbean,
this surprising convergence also occurred in other French colonies under
Vichy rule, in West Africa and Indochina, most notably. Harry Gamble's
work suggests that many African intellectuals, such as Senegalese educator
and politician Mamadou Dia, shared Vichy's desire for racialized "cultural
authenticity" and channeled it toward nationalism.[53]

In *Tropiques'* inaugural 1941 issue, Ménil evoked culture, identity, and
mimicry in terms that certainly would have pleased Bayle. Ménil spelled out
that culture was "untransmissible" and "not detachable." He wrote that
heretofore Martinicans had merely "read the cultures of others." They had
been reduced to "mechanized" copiers, "reciting words that others have invented." Now, however, he claimed, "the wind is turning." Gone were the
inauthentic "pastiches" of yesterday.[54] In other words, to true France there
existed a Martinican equivalent of which islanders should be proud: a
true Martinique.[55] Rarely has a more impassioned plea been formulated for
authenticity and immutable essence.

Much the same tone pervades Suzanne Césaire's April 1942 essay in
Tropiques entitled "A Civilization's Decline." In it, Césaire overturns stereotypes of French West Indians and chronicles the horrors of slavery. In
so doing, she elaborates a new, positive vision. She repudiates the doctrine
of assimilation and lambastes the notion that "liberation equals assimila-

tion." By the same token Césaire also identifies alienation as the prime problem facing Martinique. Anticipating Frantz Fanon, she writes of the Martiniquais' need to "recognize his true character," and she decries the islanders' current identity as constituting nothing less than "collective self-deceit." She concludes, "This earth, our earth, can only be what we want it to be."[56] Again, one can imagine Vichy's censors nodding their heads, sensing echoes of Marshal Pétain's cult of authenticity and obsession with the soil.

Beyond the coded language, duping, intimidation, and convergence hypotheses, another theory might explain how *Tropiques* continued to be published between 1941 and 1943: the protection theory. In 2010, Aimé Césaire's biographer Romuald Fonkoua hatched an idea as compelling as it was explosive to explain how and why *Tropiques* got by Vichy's usually zealous censors. It revolved around Georges Pelorson. Pelorson, a fellow graduate of the École normale supérieure, had helped publish Césaire's famous *Cahier d'un retour au pays natal* in his eclectic journal *Volontés* in 1939. The two exchanged correspondence to revise and publish the text. Césaire's École normale supérieure professor Pierre Petitbon had served as an intermediary between the two men, although Pelorson also knew Césaire's close friend Senghor. Indeed, *Volontés* relied on École normale supérieure networks and had the flavor of the famous rue d'Ulm school.[57]

So far, so good. However, after the fall of France in 1940, Pelorson emerged as a staunch collaborationist who served as head of youth propaganda services in the occupied zone. Fonkoua argues that this high-level Vichy connection better accounts for *Tropiques'* apparent immunity from the censors than does Césaire's vague notion that Vichy's officials in Martinique had been outmaneuvered. The theory is intriguing and plausible, yet Fonkoua's footnotes never offer definitive evidence to support it.[58] Under the circumstances, it might be most useful to think of *Tropiques* as having been "covered" or protected from Vichy's normally tenacious sailor-censors by several broadly defined and compatible elements: the journal's essentialist bent, its carefully calibrated prose, and the ties of one of its founders to a leading mind at Vichy. These ties would presumably have drawn attention because of where the famous *Cahier d'un retour au pays natal* was published and by whom.

In point of fact, Pelorson became an extremist even by Vichy standards. In fairness to Césaire, few signs presaged this turn of events in 1939. While a student at Louis-le-Grand, Pelorson had rubbed shoulders with figures as politically varied as playwright Samuel Beckett, philosopher Simone Weil, and Fascist writers Maurice Bardèche and Robert Brasillach.[59] As a totally bilingual (French-English) poet and translator who directed a bilingual school in Neuilly, little seemed to predispose Pelorson for Vichy. And yet, as Vincent Giroud has shown, already in the late 1930s, in the periodical *Volontés,* Pelorson anticipated elements of Pétain's ideology, especially the notion of a return to authenticity and to the earth. As France fell, Pelorson began to share or at least violently express the same Anglophobic sentiments that his Irish wife had long harbored. As he took up his post of lead youth propagandist for Vichy in occupied France, he channeled his regime's hatred for Charles de Gaulle's Free French, whom he portrayed as London's mercenaries. His desire to centralize Vichy youth programs has led some to see him as an imitator of the Hitler Youth movement in France. What is certain is that Vichy moderates soon grew suspicious of him, with good reason: he turned on Minister of Youth Lamirand for his alleged timidity and his "clerico-reactionary" views, which implied an insufficiently racist approach. Pelorson bitterly complained that some famous youth centers, such as Uriage, had failed to undertake anti-Semitic purges. He steadfastly supported Fascist youth organizations that Lamirand would not. Pelorson's backers included enthusiastic collaborationists such as Abel Bonnard and Information Minister Paul Marion. After the war, Pelorson lay low, then reinvented himself into Georges Belmont. Under that nom de plume he became the leading translator of Henry Miller into French, as well as a prolific writer.[60]

Reflections of a "Foul and Slimy Era"

The Pelorson connection hints at surprising and pragmatic points of commonality and ambiguity in matters of identity politics. It also suggests the importance of networks and strategies deployed to publish *Tropiques.* However, if proof of Césaire's utter rejection of Vichy were needed, it comes from another part of Césaire's oeuvre from the same era.

Alex Gil has delved deeply into one of Césaire's lesser-known works, entitled *Et les chiens se taisaient* (And the dogs fell silent). Gil convincingly demonstrates that Césaire began the first version of the historical play, or "dramatic oratorio,"[61] in 1941 and concluded the draft in 1943.[62] This first typescript, which Gil dug up in a library at Saint-Dié in the Vosges in 2008, scarcely resembles the 1956 publication under the same title. The Saint-Dié version revolves entirely around the course of the Haitian Revolution (1791–1804). As John Patrick Walsh has demonstrated, Césaire made considerable use of the local Caribbean past, especially of Haitian revolutionary Toussaint Louverture, to further his political claims, most notably in the delicate balance he was constantly calibrating with respect to relations between metropole and colony.[63]

Gil makes the case that in this secret manuscript Césaire could say things that he could not in *Tropiques*.[64] Indeed, the typescript is pregnant with allusions to the years 1941–1943. Much as Admiral Robert positioned his warships as chess pieces to keep Martinique in check, so did "Arachnidan Europe move its digits and its ships" to crush Louverture's revolutionary experiment.[65] Further on, Haitians fearful of retaliation by whites call for the murder of the great revolutionary Louverture; little imagination is needed to see local supporters of Admiral Robert in them.[66] Louverture calls these frightened collaborationists "cod souls." The repeated cries of "death to whites"[67] that dot the typescript would also have been unimaginable in the pages of *Tropiques*. On this score, incidentally, Césaire's political play did run afoul of history. As Laurent Dubois has argued, racial categories have too long been used to explain ideological positioning during the Haitian Revolution: in reality, Louverture shared more in common with many of his French enemies than he did with most former slaves and free people of color. As Dubois demonstrates, "there was quite a bit of diversity on both sides" of the Haitian Revolution, which should in no case be reduced to a "race war."[68]

Yet binaries are precisely what drive the original *Et les chiens se taisaient*. Further into Césaire's manuscript, at an assembly of planters, dignitaries harangue one another. One yells, "You know what awaits a traitor," to which his interlocutor responds, "You know what awaits those who support tyranny."[69] Again, Vichy's local accomplices in the Caribbean seem targeted. As for the colonizers, one of them in Césaire's draft of the play seems convinced of the impossibility that slaves could ever successfully revolt. He dubs the Antilles a "very gentle land."[70] Here the paternalism of twentieth-century governors and békés echoes across the centuries. The French attempt to crush Louverture's revolutionary experiment provides an opportunity for Césaire to evoke plans to reinstate slavery. He implies that the French reconquest, like Vichy rule, marked a dropping of the masks, the advent of unabashed racism. What the "whites" brought in both instances was "degradation and servitude with no hope."[71]

More generally, the backdrop of turncoats, spies, and slavery seems to have been deliberately chosen as a highly pertinent canvas between 1941 and 1943. Here is how Césaire accounted for the framing of *Et les chiens se taisaient* in an April 4, 1944, letter to Breton: "Born under Vichy, born against Vichy, at the zenith of white racism and clericalism, at the highest point of black resignation, the manuscript certainly bears some of the disagreeable markers of the circumstances under which it was composed."[72] Why this change of heart in 1944? Césaire was no doubt commencing his ideological transition toward supporting Martinique's full absorption into what would become the postwar French republic, the famous departmentalization process that he would champion in 1946.

No doubt these lines also served to formulate an explanation for the binaries and the cries of "death to whites" that dotted the first manuscript of *Et les chiens se taisaient*. Césaire now recast these cries as excusable lapses, committed as part of an overreaction to Vichy oppression. In turn, this overreaction could only be understood in the context of Vichy. In August 1944, he would write to Breton of the hardening of Vichy rule between Breton's departure to New York in July 1941 and the fall of Vichy in Martinique two years later: "Police surveillance, denunciation, racism. From an intellectual standpoint, obscurantism; censorship of the press. . . . Generally speaking, scientific isolation, darkness and night. Overall, a foul and slimy era."[73]

Tropiques after Vichy

The fate of *Tropiques* after the fall of Vichy in Martinique further illuminates its legacies, as well as its contradictions. In the very month of Césaire's letter to Breton—August 1944—Fighting French lieutenant André Kaminker submitted a report to the governor of Martinique Georges-Louis Ponton on the island's press since the end of Vichy's control of the island a year prior. Kaminker was the father of French actress Simone Signoret. A remarkably gifted interpreter who joined de Gaulle's Free French in London in 1940, Kaminker's Jewish origins hailed back to the region that was once Poland and has since become Ukraine. By 1944, he directed Martinique's information services, an administrative position that placed him at the

helm of both radio and the written press. Kaminker was not sheltered from
anti-Semitic attacks even in post-Vichy Martinique. For instance, an anonymous letter from "protesting radio listeners" demanded to know why Kaminker would have used the nom de guerre André Sablons. The listeners
asked for him to be "unmasked" and to quit playing a "double game."[74]
They all but implied that Kaminker was not really French or that he represented what Vichy termed "anti-France."

Kaminker's August 1944 report surveyed the plethora of newspapers
and periodicals published in Martinique after the fall of Vichy on the island. The section on *Tropiques* dwelled on Aimé Césaire's obvious peda-
gogical qualities and his current success as an orator and academic visiting
Haiti. However, the lieutenant's political critique of *Tropiques* pulled no
punches. Césaire demonstrated "evident black racism," contended Kaminker, who believed that Césaire's recentering project might lead him
down the slippery slope of "separatism." However, Kaminker suggested
that Césaire's visit of Haiti, and in particular his juxtaposition of Haiti's
"social conditions" with those of Martinique, were leading him to recon-
sider demands for outright independence.[75] Kaminker seems to have missed
the point about Césaire's presence in Haiti. Indeed, in 1941, that country
had established a national ethnology bureau and was engaged in a process of rediscovering local folklore and religion that closely mirrored the
Tropiques' transformation in Martinique in both its chronology and its
contours. Between 1941 and 1944, ethnographers Jacques Roumain and
Alfred Métraux operated through this new bureau they had helped create,
relying on local Haitian informants for insight into the practice of vodou
(their undertaking challenged not so much the state, as *Tropiques* had in
Martinique, as the Catholic Church's hostility to vodou).[76]

Also noteworthy is Kaminker's observation that in 1944 his information services had censored *Tropiques* once again. He indicates that he
banned Césaire from publishing an "indecently violent" attack on the
bishop of Martinique Henri Varin de la Brunelière, following a heated exchange between the two men. Kaminker adds that the initial clash between
Césaire and the bishop had taken place in the wake of a talk by René
Etiemble, and that the bishop fired the first rhetorical shot. This represented
an act of "remarkable clumsiness" on the prelate's part, observed Kaminker,
given recent efforts by some members of the church to embrace the Free
French cause and repudiate Vichy.[77] So why have Césaire censored?

Extant sources do not reveal precisely which part of Césaire's response to Bishop Varin de la Brunelière was excised, but a version of Césaire's open letter to the bishop did appear in the May 1944 issue of *Tropiques*. In it, Césaire donned the mantle of French secularism to ridicule the bishop's claim that the republic's values of liberty, equality, and fraternity were also those of Christianity. He bristled at Varin de la Brunelière's suggestion that Christianity and abolitionism formed a common cause, and he invoked the "atheist" Victor Schoelcher to prove his point. He concluded dramatically, "Monsignor, leave our dead alone." Césaire then shifted to the much more recent past, invoking the Vatican's concordat with Mussolini that was signed as his troops committed war crimes in northeast Africa (the Lateran accords actually happened first). Finally there was a brief allusion to clergy "having thrown itself into the arms of Philippe Pétain," a passage perhaps shortened by Kaminker's office.[78]

Etiemble, whose presentation Kaminker cites as having sparked the conflict between Césaire and the bishop, had visited Martinique on an official five-week mission in 1944, dispatched by de Gaulle's Fighting French. He produced a rich report at the end of his stay. A graduate of the École normale supérieure, Etiemble emerged as one of France's leading China specialists but also as a literary critic of Arthur Rimbaud, Marcel Proust, and Jean Paulhan, among others. In his report, Etiemble explains that he made a point of meeting all parties in post-Vichy Martinique, both black and white, even those nostalgic for the previous regime. Etiemble's report on his visit bears all of the hallmarks of deep pessimism and reveals only a handful of bright spots. Corrupt politicians from the 1930s now felt vindicated and were reelected. Many of them were in the pay of the rum magnates, he contended. Give Aimé Césaire ten years, and he too will have been bought off, claimed one of Etiemble's interlocutors. Some people even missed the days when "propaganda was produced well," starting with the Vichy regime's *Bulletin hebdomadaire*. To many the change of regime had ushered in "the restoration of the middlers and the sellouts."[79]

Etiemble recalls giving a presentation in Fort-de-France on how Vichy constituted the very antithesis of French values. The piece invoked Blaise Pascal, Michel de Montaigne, and Voltaire, as well as leading voices for colonial reform in France including André Gide, Denise Moran, and Andrée Viollis.[80] It would subsequently appear in the May 1944 issue of *Tropiques*. In his report, Etiemble underscores the mixed reactions to his presentation: during the question period, audience members observed that French officials who seemed immune to racism back home acquired the condition overseas, after rubbing shoulders with wealthy Martinican Creoles.[81] This phenomenon, of racism's being more pronounced in the colonies than in the metropole, was certainly not new, and it represented a throwback to the time when Parisian abolitionists butted heads with the colonial lobby in Martinique.[82] It had endured thereafter as a kind of shorthand, with France standing for freedom, while colonists in Martinique embodied enduring racism.[83] In any event, it may well have been this sensitive topic that caused the bishop to clash with Aimé Césaire.

Etiemble reached radically different conclusions from Kaminker's concerning Césaire. Indeed, Césaire represents one of the few rays of hope in Etiemble's report. According to Etiemble, the apostle of Negritude shared General de Gaulle's ideals. He was, moreover, gaining in popularity: while the very first runs had been ridiculously small (on the scale of an in-house school publication), a thousand copies of the next issue of *Tropiques* were about to be printed. Meanwhile, Césaire's presentations were attended by "four thousand people," and his classes at the *lycée* drew audiences "from around the world." As for Césaire's politics, Etiemble saw him "rehabilitating" blackness after Vichy had denigrated it. In this view, the renascent republic after 1945 was to be color blind, even as it recognized blackness. Etiemble predicted that "Césaire will soon be one of the great forces, if not the great force, of the Antilles. And he is profoundly attached to France."[84]

Wifredo Lam

While the Césaires stood at the core of the exchanges with arriving refugees, Sino-Afro-Cuban painter Lam, who traveled from Marseille to Martinique with Breton, Serge, and Seghers, also occupied a central role. Lam has recently emerged from the shadow of one of his mentors, Pablo Picasso, to be considered on his own terms as a master of modernism whose work was infused with African and Caribbean meanings and forms. Lam left his native Cuba for Spain in 1923 to further his artistic career. In Europe, he rebounded from multiple tragedies, most notably the death of his first wife and son from tuberculosis. He served the Republican cause during the Spanish Civil War, both in actual combat and by creating a propaganda poster and crafting munitions. Artistically, Lam's work in the 1920s bore the influence of the Madrid school, as well as of Henri Matisse. After 1936, Picasso exercised a powerful attraction over Lam.[85]

Despite their relative brevity—some forty days in Martinique—the escape to Martinique and the sojourn there profoundly impacted the painter.[86] For one thing, his encounter with the *Tropiques* team proved seminal. The journal published the first-ever sustained and enthusiastic article on Lam's work in February 1943, after the painter had left the island. Scholars have attributed the essay to gallery owner and friend of Picasso's Pierre Loeb (it is signed only "Pierre"). In it, Loeb recalls the art world of the 1930s. He reveals an interesting anecdote, and an ironic engagement with questions of identity and authenticity. As Loeb marveled at Lam's paintings in a Parisian gallery, he muttered to Picasso, "He is influenced by Negro painters." To which Picasso responded curtly, "He has the right to be, he is a Negro!" Loeb added his own enthusiastic appreciation of Lam's art: "I had been waiting for your art. . . . For a long time [I too] lived surrounded by Bantu sculptures, by decorated skulls, by Côte d'Ivoire masks, by New Hebrides tree ferns, by Papuan canoes, by desolate Easter Island fetishes." The piece concluded by calling Lam Aimé Césaire's "brother."[87] The Martinique route had produced a dissident fraternity.

Lam and Césaire specialists agree that the Cuban painter was particularly captivated by Césaire's *Cahier d'un retour au pays natal,* as was Césaire with Lam's plethoric Afro-Caribbean allegories and references. Lou Laurin-Lam (Lam's Swedish third wife, after Benitez) has pointed out that the two men found much common ground in 1941. Aesthetically, both rejected the exotic art of Cuban artists who liked to depict "docile" black sugar harvesters.[88] In Lam, Césaire saw a proponent of "poetic *maronnage*" and a guiding beacon of freedom for the Caribbean.[89] The relationship between Lam and Césaire evolved from political and artistic complicity to deep friendship: in May 1941, Césaire autographed an offprint of his *Cahier d'un retour au pays natal* for Lam as a token of his "friendship and admiration," as well as their common "hopes and fervor."[90]

In January 1945, *Tropiques* once more took up Lam's work. This time Pierre Mabille penned the article. Dr. Mabille, a close friend of Breton's and of Picasso's, had escaped France to Guadeloupe, where he practiced medicine in 1941, before decamping from Guadeloupe to serve as a Free French cultural attaché in Haiti. The 1945 piece makes two especially revealing points. First, Mabille makes the case that Lam discovered African sculptures and masks for the first time in Madrid after his arrival in the Spanish capital from Cuba in 1923: it was "through the intermediary of ethnologists" that this future student of Picasso came to contemplate Afro-Caribbean identity. Mabille adds, insightfully, that before being placed under museum glass, these objects had been uprooted from their original location and meanings, not to mention torn from their owners.[91]

Second, in his concluding paragraph, Mabille daringly expounds on what he sees as two polar opposites: Lam's masterpiece *The Jungle* on the one hand, and Hitler's Reich chancellery balcony on the other. He writes, "For my part, I see a total opposition between this jungle where life explodes on all sides, free, dangerous, gushing from the most luxuriant vegetation, ready for any combination, any transmutation, any possession, and that other sinister jungle where a Führer, perched on a pedestal, awaits the departure, along the neo-classical promenades of Berlin, of mechanized cohorts prepared, after destroying every living thing, for annihilation in their turn in the rigorous parallelism of endless cemeteries."[92] The comparison between a magical canvas and a regime that claimed to make, and had the audacity to define what constituted art may seem jarring. So too is the juxtaposition of the two settings. Yet to Mabille, the contrast was pertinent: Lam's *Jungle* celebrated fusion, exuberance, and creation, in stark contrast to Nazi order and violence. Given that *The Jungle* was at least partly conceived in Martinique in 1941, Mabille may have simply been removing an ideological middleman. In this kind of shortcut dear to the Surrealists, Lam's painting was nothing less than the antithesis of the regime that interned him at the Lazaret. The missing pieces to this analogy involved the many anti-Nazi dissidents with whom Lam had broken bread at the Lazaret: Seghers, Flake, and the others.

This brings us to the question of inspirations for *The Jungle*. Art historians have emphasized the work's dialogue with Picasso's *Demoiselles d'Avignon* and its departure from Lam's previous work. From my standpoint, it was the break with Europe in 1941 and Lam's first return to the Caribbean since 1923 that bore the most immediate impact on this new and highly distinctive period of Lam's work, emblematized by the magnificent painting. Indeed, an ensemble of Lam paintings undertaken in 1942 preceded and anticipated the larger *Jungle* canvas: these include *Goddess with Foliage* and *Person with Scissors*.[93] All of these paintings were likely shaped to some degree by the hikes in the valley of Absalon with the

Césaires, Lamba, Breton, and Masson. Julia P. Herzberg has insisted on the influence of Breton over Lam, in particular the "liberating" quality that Surrealism offered the Cuban painter, which led him to adopt more abstract and "subversive" representations of nature.[94]

Indeed, the 1941 hike to witness the natural wonders of the valley of Absalon seems to have particularly marked Lam and directly influenced *The Jungle*. It seems likely that several such hikes were undertaken, since at least one of them took place under the driving rain.[95] However, with Lam having failed to write about the episodes himself, one has to rely on other testimonies. His then-spouse Holzer has explained, "During this outing [to Absalon], Wifredo and I came to appreciate for the first time the structure and character of a virgin forest—the jungle. Trees with enormous leaves . . . palm trees of many different types, including the Voyager palm with its fan wide open; ferns grown to tall, thin, elegant trees; orchids, lianas, the gigantic leave of the yautia plant abounded. All were vibrant with color, striving for light and shimmering in countless shades of green where the sun penetrated the canopy of foliage."[96] Ménil has similarly suggested that *The Jungle* was conceived in the immediate wake of the Absalon stroll.[97] In a letter to Pierre Masson, Breton described "a green labyrinth."[98] Lowery Stokes Sims depicts the vegetation in Lam's painting as "uncultivated, wild and impassable,"[99] an apt description of the Absalon lushness.

It is possible, of course, to overstate the importance of Lam's roughly forty-day stay in Martinique, especially if one considers it strictly through a local lens. Despite his friendship with the Césaires, Lam seems not to have met French West Indian visual artists. In contrast, French painter René Hibran, who arrived aboard one of the ships to Martinique in 1941 and remained there, would have a more lasting impact on a new generation of Martinican painters.[100]

As for the impact of Absalon on *The Jungle,* one certainly registers a lag between the hike in 1941 and the painting's completion in 1943. Practical considerations partially account for this. Lam and Holzer were impoverished by the time they reached the Dominican Republic, their first destination after Martinique. They had not been gainfully employed since their departure from France, and even in Marseille, they had relied on the support of others. In the Dominican Republic, they faced eviction from a hotel whose bill they could not pay. Even after reaching his native Cuba in August 1941, Lam complained that conditions precluded him from painting.

His family was destitute. He took stock of a general scarcity of art supplies and declared it "impossible" to purchase any in Cuba.[101] What is more, Cuba did not exactly enthrall Lam in 1941. It certainly did not generate inspiration. He flatly depicted the island as "morally putrefied and corrupt" and "intellectually and artistically nil."[102] All of this suggests the lingering influence of Martinique and even Marseille over a more recent Cuban inspiration.

Indeed, beyond Absalon, it was Lam's entire experience of exodus that shaped the *Jungle* project. Thus, in a September 3, 1942, letter, Lam acknowledged his debt to fellow Villa Air-Bel resident and *Paul Lemerle* passenger Breton. Lam wrote of having composed smaller works with an eye to setting the characters in relation with one another in a gigantic painting (this was certainly *The Jungle*). Of the "shape experiments" that he was thus planning to place in dialogue, he wrote, "I have pursued [them] much more intensely following the encounter with you [Breton] since Marseille."[103] Last but not least, in April 1943, as he was completing *The Jungle,* Lam noted the importance of the lush "tropics" to this project, undoubtedly a dual reference to the journal published in Martinique by the Césaires and to the forest of Absalon, which Holzer herself termed a jungle.[104] At this very time Lam was also busy illustrating the Spanish translation of Césaire's *Cahier d'un retour au pays natal,* in which he "enact[ed] his own discovery of Césaire," reminiscent of Breton's.[105]

The hypothesis of Martinique's impact on *The Jungle* does need to be tempered somewhat. By September 1942, Lam had evidently found acceptable art supplies and wrote to Breton of painting "like a man possessed."[106] In December 1942, he moved from central Havana to more verdant Marianao. There he recounted to Breton in April 1943, "Nature here is always new to me. I am painting in green tones because we now live far from Havana in a house surrounded by a garden and trees."[107] *The Jungle* thus bears the mark of Marianao as well, and it can be read as a distillation of artistic experiences and experiments the painter had undergone since 1940.

André Masson

André Masson, too, lies at the heart of this vibrant artistic dialogue. His remarkable illustrations to Breton's *Martinique, charmeuse de serpents* similarly dwell on the density and luxuriousness of Absalon's forest, showing jagged balisier (red or yellow *palulu*) flowers and thick tree ferns. Masson is a fascinating figure, deeply marked by the Great War in which he fought, as well as by a host of other influences—including Chinese ones after visiting the Boston Museum of Fine Art in 1942. His Surrealist trajectory is also characterized by singularity: unlike many others in that so-called school, he was not a product of Dada, and he repeatedly broke with Breton, both before and after his Martinique stay. In that sense, for all of the dangers the refugees faced, the Martinique moment was something of a calm in the middle of a storm.[108]

Of these various influences, the ones Masson absorbed in Martinique have long remained underappreciated. The catalog of a 2016 exhibit in Marseille, celebrating Masson's rescue by Varian Fry, finally recognized Masson's stay to have constituted an artistically "foundational" experience. In addition to the Absalon hike, it cites long conversations at Martinique's rum bars, reminiscent of those described by Kersten. But mostly, the exhibit's catalog considers the ways in which Masson eroticized the isle and appropriated its folklore, even its autochthonous past.[109]

This last point is especially noteworthy. Breton, Masson, and Lam all seem to have sought out autochthonous Arawak and Carib influences, legacies, and forms in Martinique and elsewhere. There is admittedly no epistolary trace of the group having visited some of the pre-Columbian petroglyphs on Martinique or Guadeloupe. But certainly Breton, Masson, and Lam's companion Mabille marveled at the museum of pre-Columbian art he visited in Ciudad Trujillo, after reaching the Dominican capital in 1941 from Martinique and Guadeloupe. He added, for Breton's benefit, "There can be no doubt that Surrealism is the only artistic expression in profound accord with the entire Central American region."[110]

In addition to reflecting some indigenous influences, much of Masson's production in and about Martinique incorporates local fauna and flora, mixing them with human figures and landscapes in a manner reminiscent of, and often prefiguring, Lam's. His 1941 sketch *Paysage Martinique* features Martinique's *mornes* (hills) and other natural relief in the shape of limbs and torsos (figure 19). The anthropomorphized and contorted island seems to heave and jerk, starting with its volcano. Here too we may be experiencing aftershocks from Césaire's *Cahier d'un retour au pays natal*, which had likewise featured seismic and volcanic references.[111]

FIGURE 19. André Masson, *Paysage Martinique*, 1941. Private collection.
© Estate of André Masson/SODRAC (2017).

Masson's 1941 drawing *Le balisier* blends the strikingly red flower with a female nude whose hair is knotted in the style embraced by many Creole women of the time. This intertwining of female and natural forms is even more striking in Masson's 1941 drawing entitled simply *Martinique* (figure 20). It presents a female figure bearing a similar Creole hairstyle who is straddling, emerging from, or actually ensconced in the dense foliage. Several balisier flowers can be discerned, the largest to the figure's left. Her contours have become one with the Absalon forest.

Masson's 1941 multiple *Crabe de terre* (land crab) sketches, which anticipate a painting by the same title, focus on one of the more captivating of Martinique's creatures, its colossal land crabs. The drawing shown in figure 21 seems to integrate bird and snake forms into the imposing crustacean, seen here from the front. Again, Martinique's abundance and fecundity, indeed, its perceived tropical disproportionality, appear to be embodied in the giant creature.

FIGURE 20. André Masson, *Martinique*, 1941. Private collection. © Estate of André Masson/SODRAC (2017).

FIGURE 21. André Masson, *Crabe de terre*, 1941. Private collection. © Estate of André Masson/SODRAC (2017).

Another of Masson's Martinique 1941 drawings is titled simply *The Jungle,* two years before Lam used the same name for his tableau. And a gouache held at the Peggy Guggenheim Museum in Venice, completed in 1942 but likely inspired by Martinique's nature, is titled *Bird Fascinated by a Snake.* As these titles suggest once again, in Masson's hands, Martinique becomes entrancing, an experience for the senses, an eroticized source of fascination, fecundity, and difference.

Shared Motifs and Exile Tropes

The synergies between Lam, Masson, Breton, and the Césaires clearly resulted from encounters and dialogue. Not all connections proved so fruitful, however. In November 1941, a perturbed Lam wrote Breton. He indicated that he had received word of Serge through his son Wlady. The Serges and Lam had rubbed shoulders at the Lazaret and in Marseille, of course. Victor Serge's poetry volume was now due to appear in Spanish in Mexico, and Victor Serge had asked whether Lam might be kind enough to sketch a cover for the book. Lam was reluctant. "You know my opinion of his two or three poems on Martinique," he wrote, before asking Breton, "Do you think I should accept his request? What do you advise me to do?"[112] Evidently, Lam was not enamored with Serge's literary production.

Perhaps more interesting than failed collaborative projects are the amazing continuities of forms and motifs even in cases with no cross-fertilization. Indeed, it would seem that even refugees interned at the Lazaret and Balata who never mingled with the Césaires, and may not have strolled in the valley of Absalon, deployed similar tropes. A drawing that Czech artist Antonin Pelc executed in Martinique in May 1941 (figure 22) features lush botanic intertwining and a female figure, in some ways reminiscent of the pieces Masson drew at this same time.

In another medium, Walter Mehring's poem "Love Song à la Martinique" anthropomorphizes and eroticizes the island in a manner similar to Masson's *Antille* and *Martinique*: "Lovely Martinique refresh me, keep desire a-tingle, while I drive tensely into your enclosing jungle." Were the poem not originally written in German, it could easily have been penned by Breton or Masson. Like the French Surrealists, who were obsessed with Le Douanier Rousseau's painting, Mehring features snakes in his text. And, like them, Mehring is captivated by the diminutive *colibri*, or hummingbird:

> Why [do] serpents twine and hiss within your primal greeneries?
> The tangled thickets pulse; while hummingbirds appease
> Their thirst upon the pearly drops . . .

> Von welcher Sehnsucht tropfen diese Tränen?
> Aus Deinem Urwald züngeln Ringelnattern
> Dein Dickicht atmet—Kolibris im Flattern
> Nippen den Perlenchweiß von Deiner Haut . . . [113]

FIGURE 22. Drawing by Antonin Pelc, Martinique, May 1941. Rights
© National Gallery in Prague 2017.

Such convergences suggest a shared European wonder at Martinique's prodigious nature. In this instance, however, the shared wonder is the result
not of dialogue but of common avant-garde values, training, and mind-sets,
all instrumental in shaping these Caribbean experiences. It is as if they had
shared a script about the Caribbean even before setting foot there.

Mehring's poem closes with the island's Vichy governor catching the poet in bed with Martinique:

> Ah, if your Governor
> Would find me here abed with you, how he would roar
> His disapproval, and then chain me up in documents.
> Because I had mounted you without a consul's writ,
> Faced by this bawdy international mess, the inkwell-gents
> Wouldn't know what to do with it . . .
> Dear Sweet Martinique, five nights we slept and played our
>   boudoir tricks,
> Within the Brothel of High Politics.
>
> Fänd mich Dein Gouverneur in Deinen Betten
> Er legte mich auf frischer Tat in Ketten
> Weil ich ganz ohne Ausweis bei Dir bin . . .
> Vor Tintenfässern kuppeln Diplomaten und verhandeln
> Mit welcher Großmacht sie Dich künftighin verbandeln
> Fünf Nächte schlief ich, süße Martinique,
> Im dem Bordell "Sur Hohen Politik." [114]

Here, Martinique is eroticized once more, as it is by Masson and Breton. But mostly, the verses reveal the exuberant creativity of the Lazaret group, shackled by Vichy's henchmen while entangled in an "international mess." The latter is an allusion to the vexing question of where the refugees would go next. That particular thread runs through the entire poem. In Austrian German (Vienna was Mehring's last German-language home), as in French and originally Provençal, *bordell* or *bordel*, meaning "brothel," also conveyed "a mess." [115] It therefore became a metaphor for the condition of being stranded and awaiting departure first in Marseille, then in Martinique, for an unknown destination. Meanwhile, the Kafkaesque practices of the "inkwell-gents" echoed those Mehring had faced since leaving Germany. Indeed, in an earlier, June 1939 verse penned in Nice, Mehring had written,

> I fled the foul dictatorship of Death
> and I escaped. For love, no less than hate
> Had stamped my visa at each border gate.
>
> Die Diktatur des Todes drohn . . .
> Noch leb ich—Liebe so wie Hass
> Verlängern mir den Leben-Pass. [116]

In short, the mere reminder of Vichy paperwork and bureaucracy had rudely interrupted Mehring's amorous interlude with Martinique.

Assessing Impacts

Mehring's verses on the island's regime remind us that the intermixing of Surrealism and Negritude in 1941 Martinique took place against an authoritarian backdrop, with some of its protagonists on day leave, others imprisoned, others under close watch, and still others under the threat of expulsion back to France or North Africa. Under the circumstances, the *Tropiques* team sometimes played a dissident melody, and at other times a riff that easily could be confused with a Vichy refrain. Out of this complex background, a flattened postwar narrative emerged after 1943.

In October 1943, Suzanne Césaire boldly suggested that the potent connection resulting from the encounter between the Césaires and Breton had held high the torch of freedom under Vichy. She argued, "Not for a moment during the hard years of Vichy domination did the image of freedom completely fade here, and Surrealism was responsible for that."[117] Glissant has gone so far as to suggest that the encounter with Surrealists marked a decisive turn that took the French Caribbean down a separate path from that of the Anglophone Caribbean.[118]

Both claims can be contested, of course. Surrealists and Negritude thinkers held no monopoly over resistance: certainly, dissidents who left for Dominica and Saint Lucia to fight in Free French uniform hold an equal, if not a greater, right to the claim. Yet there is no denying either the richness or the ambiguity of the wartime years in Martinique from a cultural standpoint. Lam, Breton, Masson, and Césaire profoundly influenced one another's work. In so doing, they opened new horizons and built a stepping-stone of postwar liberation ideology.

The dialogue with Mabille, Breton, and others would continue in New York, Haiti, and beyond. While they forged ahead on their travels, however, the window of opportunity that had allowed them to voyage to Martinique in the first place was cut tragically short at the end of May 1941.

CHAPTER EIGHT

The Window Closes

N APRIL 1941, a Reuters cable purported that a Nazi delegation some ninety members strong, including Gestapo agents, had reached Martinique. Word quickly spread across the Caribbean through the Cuban press.[1] False rumors of this type were legion. One of the most common involved the notion that wolves were hiding in sheep's clothing, in other words, that Nazi agents lurked aboard the cargo ships bound for Fort-de-France.[2] Such unsubstantiated claims spread even in mainstream publications. An especially egregious example can be found in the September 15, 1941, issue of *Life* magazine, which trumpeted, "Today Martinique's ... chief export is a pro-Nazi propaganda bulletin. ... Its chief imports are German Gestapo agents masquerading as refugees from France."[3] The so-called news was already stale, since the Martinique refugee corridor had been suspended on May 26, 1941. Not only was *Life*'s chronology off the mark, but its assertions were baseless as well—at least the second part of them. And yet the cumulative damage of such false rumors was already done, and it was considerable.

Recurring US and UK concerns over a fifth column played themselves out in different ways, including by ricochet. Indeed, Vichy sensitivity to American fears that Nazi spies might have been on board the vessels bound for Fort-de-France weighed heavily. After all, Vichy's officials in the Caribbean found themselves in a delicate position, at the mercy of blockades and possible preemptive strikes. This fraught dynamic is borne out by a host of sources. As early as December 1940, with the arrival of the *Charles L. Dreyfus* in Fort-de-France, US authorities in the French Caribbean described the forty "Czechoslovaks, Austrians, Germans, and Poles" on board as follows: "They are unknown locally and may or may not be fifth columnists."[4] In other words, US consul Marcel Malige had consulted French officials about the identity of each of the forty migrants. By May 1941, Malige was urging Admiral Georges Robert to exercise caution to ensure that so-called undesirables did not make their way into the "Western Hemisphere."[5] Because Robert was negotiating with the United States for his own survival while he simultaneously continued to rely on Vichy for his legitimacy, the refugee question constituted a thorn in both of his sides.

American pressure proved unrelenting. Already in October 1940, Vichy's naval captain Louis Benech exhorted the navy to allay American worries. US authorities expressed concern that any ship fuel brought to the Caribbean might end up serving to refuel German submarines. Benech added that the United States was keeping close tabs on Vichy vessels and already had drawn up plans to "requisition" the *Winnipeg* and the *Wyoming*. In order to maintain Vichy's "freedom of action" in the Caribbean, he recommended exercising "great caution" in order not to elicit US suspicions.[6]

While the boats gave rise to suspicion, the passengers fueled outright paranoia. This had partly to do with American internal politics. Assistant Secretary of State Breckenridge Long was among those who imagined covert Nazi infiltration behind every relief effort to save European Jews. He insisted that Adolf Hitler's regime was threatening to execute the family members of refugees who refused to serve as spies. Even President Franklin D. Roosevelt echoed the claim.[7]

On May 10, 1941, ceding to American concerns over arriving passengers with German-sounding names, Admiral Robert agreed to share all passenger manifests of incoming ships.[8] Then, on May 12, Vichy's colonial ministry cabled Fort-de-France, in answer to its May 7 telegram concerning the US position. Vichy then announced that "all necessary steps had been taken in order to achieve a close filtering of migrants transiting through the French Caribbean."[9] In this sense, US pressure was causing the Martinique route to unravel even before the Dutch boarded two cargo ships at the end of May and beginning of June 1941.

Still, refugees were already en route, and they had to be dealt with. On May 17, 1941, Admiral Robert took steps to admit arriving passengers

from the *Mont Viso* and the *Winnipeg*, in the knowledge that they would
not be allowed to leave for the United States. The *Arica* had already reached
Fort-de-France on May 10 with many refugees on board. Given the overcrowding of the Lazaret, new incoming passengers were to be "housed" at
Balata.[10]

Ultimately, international tensions doomed the French Caribbean route.
We have seen that Vichy's Atlantic corridor was under threat for some time.
Already in November 1940, the Vichy government notified the Germans
that the British had seized a liner under the French flag, the *Cuba*, sailing
from Fort-de-France to Casablanca, with some 1,200 passengers on
board.[11] By late March 1941, Vichy's Ministry of the Colonies was clearly
concerned about the safety of the French Caribbean shipping lane. It even
briefly banned the families of administrative and military officials from
boarding such ships, because of the growing likelihood of British or US intervention on the high seas.[12]

The restriction in question affected prospective refugees as well, espe-
cially Jewish French nationals seeking the safety of the Americas. Famed
French historian Marc Bloch had tried to leave with his family for the
United States via Martinique in 1941. Already in February of that year, the
New School of Social Research's president Alvin Johnson had recom-
mended the Martinique route as the best option for Bloch and his family
to gain safe passage to New York.[13] By March, Bloch had contacted the
Service des oeuvres of the French Foreign Ministry, the same conduit that
André Mayer and his family had successfully used. On April 2, 1941, the
Service des oeuvres in turn reached out to the Colonial Ministry via Admiral Darlan, explaining that Marc Bloch was undertaking a research mission on behalf of the Ministry of Education, and listing the family members
Bloch wished to bring with him. On April 11, Captain Michel Marie Edouard Caron responded on behalf of Colonial Minister Charles Platon.
Because the historian was on official government business, the colonial
ministry would certainly grant passage for Bloch but not for any accompanying family members, due to new and "strict orders from the admiralty" on
family members taking the Martinique route. Perhaps, Caron hinted, these
restrictions might eventually be lifted, in which case he would gladly allow
the historian's loved ones to travel with him.[14]

Bloch resolved not to leave when he realized that he would have to do
so alone. In July 1941, he confided with muted regret to a friend, "No

doubt we could have gone to Martinique before April and waited there . . . to obtain quota-visas which I was told are easier to obtain [in Martinique]." However, he added, this scheme would have involved leaving his mother behind in Fort-de-France, waiting for the necessary documents.[15] Bloch would stay put in mainland France instead. He joined the Resistance after the Germans invaded the southern zone in 1942. He hid out in Caluire, the same district of Lyon where the Germans arrested resistance coordinator Jean Moulin at a doctor's office in June 1943.[16] The Nazis arrested the fifty-seven-year-old historian in March 1944 and executed him three months later, alongside twenty-nine other resisters.

In July 1941, Bloch and his family had been left to wonder what might have been. In point of fact, in a matter of weeks after Caron sent the fateful message about his accompanying family members, the entire Martinique corridor unraveled. The final act began on April 27, 1941, when the Dutch intelligence services in Curacao relayed word that twenty-five Nazi agents might be bound for the French Caribbean.[17]

Dutch naval authorities, as well as officials in the Dutch Caribbean loyal to the Dutch government in exile at Stratton House in London, would play a significant role in the final act of the Martinique corridor. It is worth mentioning, parenthetically, that German Jews who had sought refuge in the Dutch West Indies received harsh treatment. They were labeled enemy nationals, treated with suspicion, and interned as of July 1940 in conditions not dissimilar to those refugees experienced in Martinique.[18]

Still, the main impetus came from Washington and London. On May 17, 1941, Vichy's admiral Robert described "a new American attitude" that restricted any French ships from docking in the United States. Robert added that US authorities were even reconsidering previously issued visas. In light of this US crackdown, Robert insisted that "massive shipments of refugees [from France] must be suspended."[19] Then, on May 21, acceding to Robert's demand, Vichy ceased delivering transit visas through Martinique altogether, essentially condemning the Martinique route only four days before the *Winnipeg* was intercepted.[20] Doors were being slammed shut on all sides.

The May 26 interception of the *Winnipeg* and the June 1 commandeering of the *Arica* by the same Dutch warship lie at the heart of this chain of events and clearly mark the point of no return. The *Winnipeg* was approaching Martinique crammed with refugees when it was boarded, while the *Arica* was leaving Fort-de-France loaded with rum and sugar, having already deposited its refugees.[21] Henceforth, all maritime, commercial, and even surface postal links between the French Caribbean and the metropole were severed (although limited shipping would soon resume to and from North Africa).[22] In other words, the Marseille–Fort-de-France route ceased to exist, and, with it, the exodus of refugees to the French Caribbean.

Certainly, Vichy's Colonial Ministry and naval officials share a part of the blame for the Fort-de-France route's undoing. We have seen how officials in the French Caribbean constantly complained to their superiors at Vichy, bemoaning the "dumping" of refugees on Martinique. Among the dozens of these alarming reports from leading authorities in the Antilles, one stands out in particular. It was penned by Vichy's inspector to the colonies, Emile Devouton, a critical figure whose word weighed mightily in the halls of Vichy's Colonial Ministry. In his April 11, 1941, report to the minister of the colonies, Devouton observed,

> The influx to the French Antilles of numerous migrants, the majority of them foreigners, represents an undeniable danger. Admiral [Robert] has ordered that the governors take measures to ensure that these foreigners not extend their stay (expulsion of those who do not obtain entry visas in countries of the Western Hemisphere, house arrest for migrants deemed suspicious, surveillance of others). In order to reduce the length of their stay as much as possible, it is important that in future, migrants leaving Europe for the French Antilles do so only once they have received the visa necessary to enter a foreign country.[23]

Devouton thereby took aim at the loophole that had made the Martinique route possible: its status as a French territory in the Americas, which meant that it did not require an additional entry visa.

On balance, then, explanations as to why the Peyrouton plan unraveled in late May 1941 are multifold. They include American hypersensitivity to a possible fifth column, colonial Pétainists' opposition to refugee arrivals at least partly connected to this US sensitivity, Anglo-American concerns over the earnestness of Vichy's purported neutrality, as well as an ongoing British desire to bring about regime change in Martinique through a more effective blockade. Between unrelenting US pressure on Vichy to identify all refugees and to come clean on alleged shady traffic, Vichy's resulting

May 21 telegram suspending the refugee flow, and the Dutch interception of the *Winnipeg* at two o'clock in the morning on May 26, it is hard to ascribe a single responsibility for the closure of the maritime route.

Other pragmatic considerations came into play. As mixed cargoes, the *Winnipeg* and *Arica* were captured in part to compensate for a very basic but serious British need for freighters. Not only did the United Kingdom require cargo ships, but it also sought to keep so-called neutral ones out of enemy hands. As the Foreign Office indicated to Washington on June 1, 1941: "every French ship seized is one less for the Axis."[24] Trade, too, proved a major motivation for intercepting the ship. After it was boarded, London immediately claimed that the vermouth and Vichy water bottles in its hold constituted "prima facie" evidence for "condemnation on enemy export grounds."[25] In other words, this episode should also be seen as part of a global sea war over shipping.

One additional factor should be considered. On May 15, 1941, Vichy relayed new instructions from the German Armistice Committee. The commission sought more strictly to control passengers, to ensure that so-called enemies of the Third Reich not be allowed to leave and join the fight against the Axis. The Germans too were worried about who was boarding these ships. The measure was extended to French civilians between the ages of eighteen and fifty, who should henceforth be vetted to avoid the exit of "camouflaged combatants."[26] This was the net that French scientist Bertrand Goldschmidt had so narrowly escaped, although he did not realize that it had actually been cast from Berlin.

The screws on the Martinique route were being tightened in every possible direction, from Washington, Berlin, Vichy, and London. The precariousness of the shipping lane in many ways mirrored that of Vichy-controlled Martinique itself. It is difficult to reconstitute today the tensions at work around this Vichy enclave in 1940–1941. The very fact that French ships were not being sunk en route to Martinique constituted sufficient grounds to arouse Anglo-American suspicions.

When reports surfaced of a German sailor appearing in Martinique months later, in February 1942—in reality, a U-boat officer whose leg had been blown off by an explosion on his submarine's deck gun, and whose shipmates dropped him off on an emergency stopover in Martinique— American fear gave way to hysteria.[27] In point of fact, we know from the U-boat's log that its captain, Lieutenant Werner Hartenstein, had been unsure as to what kind of welcome he would receive in Martinique, even for this brief medical stopover. Indeed, he did not even possess coastal maps of Martinique, which suggests that his vessel had never previously ventured into its waters.[28] In other words, American theories that German submarines regularly refueled in Martinique, or were somehow guided by Vichy radio, were in all likelihood incorrect. From 1941 to 1942, US attention seemed riveted on a largely overstated Caribbean threat. Martinique in 1941–1942 foreshadowed the same sorts of fears of enemy proximity that Fidel Castro's Cuba would during the Cold War.

Besides these tensions, one must consider the American reluctance to admit refugees into the United States—one chronicled extensively by David Wyman, Richard Breitman, Alan Kraut, and Henry Feingold.[29] This American stance produced a ripple effect that reached Martinique time and again, serving as an excuse to refuse refugees and no doubt genuinely convincing Vichy governors to maintain a low profile on issues that could be mistaken for refugee smuggling or even espionage.

As Varian Fry sadly recorded, the US position on refugees hardened considerably over the course of 1941. The blocking of the Martinique route represented only one step in this vaster process. In the immediate wake of the May 1941 boarding of the *Winnipeg*, correspondence between the State Department and the US consulate in Martinique reveals a further hardening of the American position. A June 5, 1941, telegram from the secretary of state explained, "In view of the known practices of foreign Agents of Germany, Italy and Russia of bringing pressure to bear on persons in the United States . . . who have close relatives still living in territory controlled by such countries, to work as their Agents here under threats of harm to such relatives if met with refusal, the Department considers that both Immigration and nonimmigrant visas should be withheld from all aliens having close relatives still residing in territories controlled by such countries if it is believed such applicants may be induced through such threats to act as Agents."[30] The State Department now warned that even bona fide refugees might be little more than pawns controlled by Rome, Berlin, or Moscow. Seeking out and uncovering duplicity was no longer good enough when even the earnest constituted the threat of a fifth column.

On the Vichy French side, these American reactions need to be placed in the context of several decades of fears circulating in the French Caribbean, according to which the United States might seek to annex the French Caribbean outright (the idea was not so farfetched, as the United States had recently occupied Haiti). Already, between the wars, rumors had circulated across the Caribbean that Martinique and Guadeloupe might be bartered in exchange for reduced debt repayment from the First World War. By 1941, unbeknownst to Vichy authorities, a resistance movement in Guadeloupe had even called on American intervention, with a view to establishing a future US protectorate over the islands.[31] In other words, Vichy French anxieties over US intentions were themselves built on successive layers of tensions with the Monroe Doctrine. The boarding of the *Winnipeg* was thus the final act of a much longer drama.

Interception at Sea

For all of this tectonic buildup and for all of the aftershocks it generated, the single most important factor in the Martinique route's demise involved the boarding of the *Winnipeg*. The spectacular interception of the *Winnipeg* occurred in the dead of night. The hundred-meter-long Dutch sloop *Van Kinsbergen* had been patrolling the waters between Dominica and Martinique since May 23, 1941. The sloop was particularly well suited to destroying submarines, but it also regularly investigated other ships over the course of its patrols.[32] Just past midnight, in the early hours of May 26, it spotted the French cargo, formally identified it, and proceeded to flash luminous warning signals at it. The *Van Kinsbergen*'s log shows that the *Winnipeg* initially ignored the signals but was finally cowed by a warning shot across its bow. Dutch sailors then dashed to the French freighter aboard two speedboats. Once on board, they ordered it to follow them to Trinidad. The *Winnipeg*'s captain grudgingly obeyed. However, as day broke, a French aircraft reached the two vessels, probably alerted by radio before the *Winnipeg* was boarded. Between seven o'clock and nine forty-five in the morning on May 27, the plane hovered above the *Van Kinsbergen* as it escorted the *Winnipeg* to Trinidad, no doubt causing grave concern among the refugees. An incident could easily have occurred; Dutch records show that the *Van Kinsbergen* had trained its guns on the Vichy French aircraft.[33]

Pro-Vichy passenger Raymond Sallé's testimony adds several noteworthy elements. Sallé specifies that four ships in total had cornered the

Winnipeg, rendering escape impossible. Next, he specifies that some fifty to sixty Dutchmen raced toward the *Winnipeg* aboard their shuttlecrafts, then climbed aboard the ship with weapons drawn. Thereupon they forcibly escorted the mixed cargo to the British colony of Trinidad, on suspicion that Nazi agents might be on board. Sallé adds that wild rumors abounded, the most plausible being that the French crew and soldiers on board included pro-German sympathizers, the least likely being that actual Nazis were on the ship. Other rumors swirled according to which some passengers had heaved compromising documents overboard just as the Dutch were boarding the *Winnipeg.*[34]

On June 6, the UK admiralty's weekly intelligence report observed that the *Winnipeg* had "over two hundred Germans on board" at the time of its interception.[35] This secret report lay below the surface, so to speak; above it, a furious "information" battle was under way. In a remarkably understated note, Vichy cabled its embassy in Havana on June 3 that it "would be useful" to "underscore" that the refugees the English-language press was depicting as Nazis were in large part Jewish.[36] As it turned out, according to French sources, the *Winnipeg* had on board 155 German nationals, 17 Germans stripped of their citizenship, another 53 "stateless" people connected with Germany in some way, and a further 23 "coming from Germany" (British sources, less attentive to passports and denaturalization, cite the conflicting figure of 210 Germans). In other words, these were both German Jews and German gentiles stripped of their citizenship for political reasons by the Third Reich. They were sworn enemies of Hitler's regime.[37] Surely after several days of interrogation, British officials must have come to realize this as well. According to the *Washington Post,* upon arriving in the United States, some of the refugees "vehemently contradicted that several hundred German-born refugees were being held by British officials in Trinidad as Nazi agents." The report added, "They intimated the British would have far more reason to suspect the pro-German French officers, crew and at least fifty French army officers and soldiers most of whom openly said they were pro-Nazi."[38] And yet, the Dutch appear to have acted on intelligence about Germans on board, not because of Vichy loyalists engaged in collaboration with Germany. Furthermore, the vetting procedures in Trinidad evidently focused on unmasking Nazis on board. How did the Americans and the British, not to mention the Dutch, get things so terribly wrong?

The answer is twofold, and it hinges on two elements: the steadfast Vichy loyalism of many in Martinique on the one hand, and the role of rumor on the other. That Vichy ruled Martinique, at a time when Vichy's leaders in France sought and advocated for greater collaboration with Hitler, stoked such hearsay in and of itself. That so many travelers were also fiercely loyal to Marshal Philippe Pétain (even some of the ones of Jewish ancestry, such as Sarah Bernhardt's granddaughter Lysiane Bernhardt)[39] no doubt also heightened Dutch, American, and British suspicions. This point in turn fueled *bobards,* or false rumors, and conspiracy theories that imagined German spies at work everywhere. The rumors themselves should be situated within a highly tense maritime atmosphere, at a time when Germany was not only triumphant on the battlefields but also seemed to be gaining the upper hand in the Battle of the Atlantic.

Here again, the testimony of *Winnipeg* passenger Sallé sheds light on the edgy mood that surrounded the boarding of the *Winnipeg* and endured over the weeks of tension that followed. Sallé mentions that the British authorities searched the boat carefully for "military material," perhaps some German equipment or method of communicating with U-boats.[40] More revealingly, Sallé discerned, correctly in this case, "an intense Anglo-Saxon fear for whatever falls under the rubric of a fifth column." He cited a revealing incident during which French youngsters taken off the *Winnipeg* and stranded in a camp in Trinidad tried to amuse themselves by singing the popular French campfire song known as the "Chant des Montagnards," only to see a British officer misinterpret the verse "Halte-là" to mean "Heil Hitler."[41]

In the days that followed the seizure of the *Winnipeg,* British officials, in particular two young bilingual women, interrogated each of its passengers. French nationals were asked if they would join General Charles de Gaulle's Free French. Few seem to have accepted the offer. Military and civilian personnel were separated into two different camps. Civilian passengers from the *Arica* soon joined those of the *Winnipeg* in a camp outside Port-of-Spain. Non-French refugees were interrogated separately. German refugee Yolla Niclas-Sachs remembers that the British "did not treat [the refugees] as enemies but as human beings." She was pleasantly surprised by the cleanliness of the barracks in which she was detained, which must have stood in stark contrast to accommodations both at Gurs and even aboard the *Winnipeg.* Still, for some refugees, prevailing conditions in the

Trinidadian camp, including barbed wire, must have called to mind detention in France.[42]

While German refugees were for the most part relieved at being in British hands, the same cannot be said of the French travelers aboard the *Winnipeg*. At least three French passengers, including Sallé, subsequently complained that their portraits of Marshal Pétain were seized and never returned.[43] Another passenger, Henri Manez, reported that the British confiscated his copy of the German propaganda magazine *Signal*.[44] More seriously, the entire ordeal led one passenger to plunge into a state of mental illness. US authorities tried to broker a deal to have the patient rapidly released and sent to Martinique.[45]

By September 1941, unable to convince the crews of the *Winnipeg* and the *Arica* to switch over to their cause, the British expropriated the two ships and equipped them with British crews.[46] The Battle of the Atlantic had not yet turned in the favor of the British, and times were desperate.

From the standpoint of the refugee flow, the *Winnipeg*'s capture sent ripples across the Atlantic. Refugee organizations scrambled to see whether the vital Martinique route could be salvaged at all. On May 26, the very day of the *Winnipeg*'s interception, the Joint Distribution Committee (JDC) office in Lisbon telegraphed its headquarters in New York, "Herbert feels all Martinique transit visas finished but groups still making efforts to keep subject alive."[47] All the efforts in the world, however, could not reverse the new state of affairs. Some refugee ships were left in limbo, like the *Mont Viso* and the *Wyoming*, held in Casablanca just as they were about to leave for Martinique with a combined 676 foreign migrants (not counting French travelers) on board.[48] HICEM intervened to assist many of them.[49] Pianists Erich Itor and Frida Kahn were among the *Mont Viso* travelers who eventually found their way to New York from Casablanca.

The *Alsina*'s Odyssey

The *Alsina* constitutes a separate case, as its ordeal began even before the boarding of the *Winnipeg*. Initially bound for Buenos Aires from Marseille, crammed with some six hundred refugees, the *Alsina* was redirected to Dakar, then to Martinique. Finally, it was rerouted back to Casablanca because of a British refusal to allow the ship to continue to South America. Even if the British could have been persuaded otherwise, the *Alsina* now faced an across-the-board refusal to receive it in Latin America. No doubt some South American nations feared the influence of leading Spanish Republicans on board. Among the many Spanish refugees on the *Alsina* was Niceto Alcalá-Zamora, the former prime minister and president of the Spanish Republican government.

Interminable negotiations consumed the months of April through June 1941 as Vichy scrambled to find a new destination for the ship. Vichy's Foreign Ministry tried in vain to have the boat stop in either Haiti or the Dominican Republic.[50] Nongovernment actors also tried to intervene. Already on April 1 and again on April 23, 1941, meetings were called at the Emergency Rescue Committee's New York office to try to find a "practical plan for the evacuation of the refugees aboard the *Alsina*."[51]

Meanwhile, at Vichy no simple resolution was in sight. On May 6, 1941, Admiral Platon explained to Admiral François Darlan that he had blocked the voyagers from staying permanently in Dakar and wished to prevent the ship from reaching Martinique. Platon stated bluntly, "The same reasons that drive you to want to distance these people from mainland France dictate that I not allow them into territories under my authority [that is, the colonies]."[52] Platon recommended that the passengers be directed to Brazil instead of Martinique. Once again, the exodus was being read as an expulsion. The Ministry of the Colonies made it clear that it did not see why "undesirables" should be any more welcome in French colonies than at home.

Darlan evidently did not accept this line of reasoning, because four days later, Vichy's admiralty advised Martinique that the passengers of the *Alsina,* including many "Spanish and Jewish refugees," would soon arrive in Fort-de-France, and that relatively few of them would find asylum in the continental Americas. Martinique would therefore end up with "the inevitable detritus left over after the filtration process."[53] Refugees were once again metaphorically reduced to scum.

Meanwhile, the United States would not bend its position. On May 8, 1941, Vichy's ambassador reported that Washington demanded to know where the refugees would go after Martinique.[54] Again, pressure was exerted on Vichy's Ministry of the Colonies. On May 16, Platon responded curtly that Admiral Robert in Martinique was concerned that he would be dragged into case-by-case haggling with the United States, which would lead to "a number of [the *Alsina*'s] Spanish and Jewish refugees having to stay in the French Antilles." Platon therefore recommended that any *Alsina* passengers refused by the United States, Brazil, or the Dominican Republic should be redirected to Morocco or Algeria.[55]

In this context, and in the wake of the *Winnipeg* incident, Vichy's admiralty resolved not to allow the *Alsina* to land in Martinique after all.[56] The *Alsina* was therefore redirected back to Dakar, where it had already docked before for some considerable time. The showdown between the Ministry of the Colonies and the Ministry of the Interior continued, and it bounced the *Alsina* to and fro. The wayward ship's voyage was fast turning into a nightmare.

The Argentine press evoked a voyage worthy of Daniel Defoe, Jonathan Swift, Jules Verne, or Voltaire.[57] Families grew on board: on May 10, 1940, Anita Ninon Sperling (née Dekock) was born during a stopover in Dakar over the course of this epic voyage. The saga was inscribed in her very identity. As a middle name, she received the first name of a fellow passenger. Another Belgian traveler, Suzanne Bernheim, coordinated the gift of a crib for the newborn, complete with clothes and sheets, provided by the Belgian Mrs. Gherson and the French Mrs. Lévy. Anita Sperling remembers being told that the clothes had been confected from passengers' own sweaters, reknitted for the occasion. She adds that the crew also "liberated" sheets to be used as diapers.[58]

Faced with the refusal of authorities in Algeria and Morocco to admit the refugees, by May 30 Vichy's Foreign Ministry seriously considered bringing the *Alsina* and the *Wyoming* back to Marseille. In this sense, an outcome similar to that of the *St. Louis* was only narrowly averted. In 1939, the *St. Louis* had to return to Europe with nearly a thousand Jewish refugees after the United States, Cuba, and Canada refused it entry.[59] Upon reflection, however, Vichy's Foreign Ministry decided to exhaust all options for the *Alsina* and its passengers. It did so, it professed, so that no nation could subsequently "reproach [the French government] for not having exhausted all possible options to evacuate the refugees in question to the New World."[60] This would seem to prove Vichy's early commitment to emigration. In any event, coming at the height of what had become an international crisis that was beginning to elicit media attention, this eagerness to avoid blame for the ultimate fate of the refugees seems striking indeed.

By June 4, Vichy cabled Rabat as a last resort. This time the arguments presented were not humanitarian but rather hinged on the question of excess foreign mouths to feed in France. Given that the "return to France of the people on board would seriously complicate the problems faced by the metropole," Vichy's Foreign Ministry saw no option but to keep the refugees in "military camps" near Casablanca. The *Alsina* was due to arrive in the Moroccan port city on June 9.[61] Charles Noguès, Vichy's representative in Morocco, grudgingly complied, agreeing to receive the passengers of both the *Wyoming* and the *Alsina*. But he complained that the influx would only worsen the protectorate's humanitarian crisis. Some 4,500 refugees were already crammed in Moroccan camps, and another 10,000 "foreigners and Jews" eked out a precarious existence outside the camps. In a revealing note, Noguès deemed that the arrival of the two vessels would compromise French prestige, because France seemed unable to "counter the maneuvers of the Jews." He expressed hope that the refugees would soon be sent to faraway shores, to the Americas or "other French colonies."[62]

Ultimately, refugees found different routes to freedom. In June 1941, Fry intervened once more to aid the roughly one hundred refugees he had helped place aboard the *Wyoming* and *Mont Viso* in the first place. Despite all of the hurdles involved, he still hoped to have them reach Martinique, perhaps on "one last boat," and from there the United States. He realized this was a long shot, but he also knew of the even greater limitations of the Spanish and Portuguese conduits, both of which had closed.[63] Responding to the same hope, which by now had swelled into a rumor, the JDC reported on June 24, 1941, that the stranded refugees in Morocco might be picked up by a ship leaving from Marseille, ultimately bound for Martinique.[64] None of this came to pass, as the Martinique refugee channel was now doomed.

On June 6, 1941, an Argentine Jewish organization reported that "negotiations about sending the boat to Buenos Aires have been discontinued." It specified that many of the *Alsina*'s passengers were being transferred to Portuguese Guinea (present-day Guinea-Bissau). Indeed, a telegram from the JDC in Lisbon issued three days earlier confirmed that *Alsina* passengers were being "removed to Portuguese Guinea whence they can embark various places including Lisbon."[65] Neutral Portugal appears to have agreed to an informal triangular agreement with Vichy France and the United States. In the end, a bevy of migrants—202, to be precise—were finally brought to New York after an epic Atlantic journey.[66] The JDC issued a statement on August 6, 1940, announcing that "two hundred refugees from Nazism . . . will arrive aboard the *SS Guinée* which docks this morning at Pier 8, Staten Island."[67] In addition to *Alsina* passengers, the announcement referred to refugees "aboard the steamers *Wyoming* and *Mont Viso*, which sailed from Marseille for Martinique and were turned back to Africa due to international tension." Other ships would carry more refugees from the *Alsina, Wyoming,* and *Mont Viso.* Sperling reached New York in September 1941 aboard the Portuguese ship the *Serpa Pinto.*[68]

The Lane Partly Resumes—without Refugees

After a two-month hiatus that began with the boarding of the *Winnipeg,* the United States permitted shipping to resume between North Africa and the Caribbean, but not the metropole, thereby dooming the direct Marseille-to-Martinique route. The Casablanca-to-Martinique leg was reestablished on September 30, 1941, with the caveat that the British could inspect the passenger lists.[69] This meant, effectively, that it had become much harder for migrants to reach Martinique even from Morocco, where many refugees still languished.[70]

A few migrants stranded in Morocco did manage to find their way through the mesh of controls after the September resumption of the maritime route. On October 21, 1941, Admiral Robert complained to Vichy of a Polish Jew by the name of Hermann Langnas and a Czech Jew named Marie Gerschon, both of whom who had just reached Martinique from Casablanca aboard the *Mont Viso.* Robert thundered, "Such passengers, arriving without my having received previous notice, can only give unnecessary rise to Anglo-Saxon suspicions, and do damage to maritime routes."[71]

Langnas and Gerschon were exceptions who confirmed the rule: starting in September 1941 the vast majority of would-be migrants were halted in their tracks and forced to remain in limbo in Casablanca. In December 1941, for instance, Vichy's Foreign Ministry learned via Washington that the United Kingdom had blocked a certain François Perron from reaching New York from Casablanca via Martinique, and a certain Mrs. Ozanne from reaching Venezuela from Morocco through Fort-de-France. The letter specified that henceforth only passengers with a final destination of Martinique or Guadeloupe would be allowed to embark in Morocco.[72]

The December 1941 entry of the United States in the war further heightened tensions around Martinique. However, the island had ceased to constitute a meaningful exit corridor by that point. The Martinique conduit
had been crushed by international tensions in May 1941. The wayward
Martinique-bound passengers of the *Winnipeg, Wyoming, Mont Viso,* and
Alsina at least managed to find their way to safe shores after endless negotiations and countless ports of call. Many others stranded in Marseille,
some of them with tickets in hand for the French Caribbean, were left with
few remaining options save for Morocco by ship or Spain or Switzerland
overland. Alternatively, they could try to seek cover in France itself.

Existing scholarship on the United States and the question of wartime
refugees has dwelled on Washington's refusal to provide shipping for rescue
plans in 1942 and 1943. Refugees were simply not deemed a top concern
at that time: transport of troops, materiel, and the wounded took priority.[73]
However, my findings suggest that US influence on the shipping question
was already determinant and devastating in 1941. After all, "the best
avenue of escape," as Fry had termed the Martinique route, had not relied
on a single US, British, or Canadian ship. It could not for an instant have
been seen as diverting from the war effort. If anything, it had brought many
a fighter to the Free French, and some to British ranks, thanks to volunteers from different countries who found their way from Marseille to Dominica and Saint Lucia via Martinique. The route was cut short largely
because of misgivings over a putative, and completely overblown, threat to
American and British interests. As for the intercepted cargo ships that had
previously served as improvised refugee transport vessels, the British and
Americans swiftly seized them for military purposes.

Epilogue

FOR MOST OF the migrants bound for Martinique in 1940 and 1941, exile had become a matter of course. Humanitarian organizations rightly spoke of "reemigration." Some German dissidents who eventually took the boats to Martinique, such as painter Carl Heidenreich, had first fought Francisco Franco and his German advisers in Spain before retreating to southern France.[1] Other refugees, such as Lothar Popp, had left Germany for countries that the Nazis would subsequently invade between 1938 and 1940, be it Austria, Czechoslovakia, Poland, or Belgium, only to depart again, this time for Paris. In June 1940, they packed up once more, keeping one step ahead of the Wehrmacht if they could. Many reached the unoccupied zone, in what Germaine Krull called the "final escape."[2] They congregated in Marseille, where they tried by every means possible to cross the seas to safety.

Along the way, some had acquired French citizenship, placed their children in the republic's schools, and given them French names. Erich Itor and Frida Kahn wrote to each other in French from Les Milles to Marseille and back, perhaps as an act of transparency, knowing that their correspondence was being read anyway, or perhaps as a political rejection of Erich's native German tongue.[3] If they were not already so at the time of their departure, by now many of these migrants had become polyglot and cosmopolitan. They may have been denaturalized by Nazi Germany, yet in many ways they had emerged as global citizens.

This is not to suggest that exile was easy. To many in the 1930s, each new expatriation constituted an agonizing, drawn-out rearguard action against the ultimate foe. It was also a matter of survival. Even though the German army had not yet crossed into the unoccupied zone, most refugees felt considerable weight on their shoulders already before the Nazis stormed southern France in November 1942.

The community of exiles bound for Martinique was profoundly connected, although admittedly not unified or homogenous. After the war, some, such as Anna Seghers and Antonin Pelc, would end up on the communist side of the iron curtain. And yet a bond evidently transcended the individual ships that refugees took to safety. For example, in January 1945, former *Wyoming* passenger René Hauth contacted former *Charles L. Dreyfus* passenger Kurt Kersten, asking to publish his latest manuscript.[4] In a sense, the ties even preceded the Martinique odyssey. In the 1930s, for instance, Fred Stein had photographed both Walter Mehring and Seghers. Each member of the trio, subjects and photographer alike, would take a different vessel from Marseille to Fort-de-France in 1941.[5] This was, it bears repeating, an elite coterie of dissident women, men, and children fortunate enough to escape.

Many would never entirely get over the multiple exiles and uprootings they experienced. In Mexico, where she construed a traffic accident as a possible plot to murder her, Seghers grew intensely nostalgic not only over her lost Germany but also about her time in Martinique.[6] In truth, the saga deeply marked everyone who experienced it.

This was certainly the case of Renée Barth, Dr. Minna Flake's daughter, who sailed with her to Martinique. In 1976, as she turned sixty and left New York for Connecticut, Renée Barth confessed to the family's wartime benefactor Walter Friedlander that she still felt "a professional *déclassée* and *déracinée*."[7] Friedlander, meanwhile, wrote her assiduously, one time asking her for the address of Barth's fellow Martinique passenger and exile Dyno Löwenstein.[8]

Over the decades, the condition of exile also colored Barth's relationship with her youngest daughter, Barbara. In 1969, at the height of hippy counterculture, Renée wrote in despair to Friedlander that Barbara was living in a "kind of commune" in San Francisco.[9] She asked if the Berkeley professor could intervene "with a light touch," given that neither Barbara nor her companion could keep a job and Renée suspected them of doing drugs. Renée was clearly consumed with parental angst. She also lucidly registered a generation gap. However, in 1972, her tone changed utterly.

She beamed in a letter to Friedlander that Barbara's life had turned around. This she attributed in no small part to her daughter's new companion, whom she described as follows: "He is older than she; left Germany at age 13 to go to Shanghai; his mother was Jewish and didn't survive . . . he came to the US in 1949."[10] According to Renée, her daughter had finally found a soul mate in a fellow "refugee kid."[11] In an America she scarcely recognized, between the Nixon presidency and the Vietnam War, which she both rejected, and hippies whom she did not understand, exile and uprootedness had become the strongest bonds of all. Paradoxically, displacement appeared to provide an anchoring and stabilizing force of its own. Or at least it seemed to offer a shared value.

In other words, the lasting ties forged over the course of the Martinique exodus endured, and they bore fruit of their own. Nowhere was this clearer than in the Caribbean. In 1945 and 1946, André Breton once more sojourned in the region, in a tour undertaken thanks to the assistance of Pierre Mabille and Claude Lévi-Strauss, among others.[12] Breton gave a seminal talk in Haiti in December 1945 that was reproduced in the youth newspaper *La Ruche*, on January 1, 1946.

The wide-ranging speech has sometimes been seen as anticipating and even precipitating the Haitian Revolution of 1946.[13] And yet, a close reading suggests it was as backward looking as it was forward looking. Before a crowded room at the Savoy-Club in Port-au-Prince, in his return to the region, Breton formulated a confession. He had felt "apprehension" in 1941 Martinique at the thought of "introducing a plant like Surrealism" to the Caribbean, he averred. Indeed, he noted that although Surrealism aspired to universalism, nothing initially guaranteed that it would thrive "in other climes"—that is, beyond Europe. Here Breton appropriated nineteenth-century theories of acclimatization to signal the possible limits of universalism. In the process, he also ascribed himself the role of gardener, or, better still, horticultural experimentalist. Put another way, Breton saw himself as Surrealism's global carrier.

Breton proceeded to suggest that Haitians were inherently predisposed to Surrealism, as supposedly evidenced by their practice of vodou. He added that the movement, in turn, was especially welcoming to people of color. Then came the pièce de résistance: "Throughout the war that has just ended, the greatest impulsions towards new paths in Surrealism were provided by two of my great friends 'of color': Aimé Césaire in poetry, and

Wifredo Lam in art. And it is thanks to them that I find myself in your midst, and not on some other part of the globe."[14] Breton's trajectory of exile had, in his eyes, provided a salutary turn for Surrealism by revealing the Caribbean's greatest talents. Given Surrealism's predilection for chance encounters, Breton would no doubt accept a historian's opinion that contingency had played a greater role in forging this improbable, yet fecund, set of confluences. National liberation struggles, *tier-mondisme,* and advocates of pan-Africanism and pan-Caribbeanness would all sprout roots in the fertile ground of the 1941 Martinique encounter.

ABBREVIATIONS

ADBDR   Archives départementales des Bouches-du-Rhône, Marseille, France*

ADG   Archives départementales de la Guadeloupe, Gourbeyre, Guadeloupe, France

ADM   Archives de la Martinique, Fort-de-France, Martinique, France

ADN   Archives diplomatiques, Nantes, France

ANF   Archives nationales (contemporary section), Pierrefitte, France

ANOM   Archives nationales d'outre-mer, Aix-en-Provence, France

BJD   Bibliothèque littéraire Jacques Doucet, Paris, France

BLY   Beinecke Library and Archives, Yale University, New Haven, Connecticut, USA

CCP   Center for Creative Photography, Archives, Tucson, Arizona, USA

CDJC   Centre de documentation juive contemporaine archives, Paris, France**

CICR   Red Cross Archives, Geneva, Switzerland

CRB   Butler Rare Books Library and Archives, Columbia University, New York, New York, USA

DEA   Deutsche Nationalbibliothek, Deutsches Exilarchiv, Frankfurt am Main, Germany

FCDG   Fondation Charles de Gaulle Archives, Paris, France

FL   French Lines (Compagnie générale transatlantique) Archives, Le Havre, France

---

* The judicial files at the ADBDR were held in Aix-en-Provence when I consulted them in 2015. They are scheduled to move to Marseille to join the main ADBDR collections in 2018.

** The CDJC collections are now part of the Mémorial de la Shoah Archives in Paris.

GJECA	German Jewish Intellectual Émigré Collection, Albany, New York, USA
LBI	Leo Baeck Institute, New York, New York, USA (online holdings)
MAE	Ministère des Affaires Etrangères Archives, La Courneuve, France
MF	Museum Folkwang, Essen, Germany
NAN	Nationaal Archief, Den Haag, Netherlands
NAUK	National Archives of the United Kingdom, Kew, England
NGC	National Gallery of Canada, Library and Archives, Ottawa, Canada
NGP	Archives of the National Gallery, Prague, Czech Republic
NYPLA	Archives of the New York Public Library, New York, New York, USA
SHDG	Service historique de la Défense archives (Gendarmerie), Vincennes, France
SHMB	Service historique de la Défense archives (Marine), Brest, France.
SHMT	Service historique de la Défense archives (Marine), Toulon, France
SHMV	Service historique de la Défense archives (Marine), Vincennes, France
UGASC	University of Glasgow Archives and Special Collections, Glasgow, Scotland, UK
USHM	United States Holocaust Memorial Archives, Washington, DC, USA
USNA	US National Archives, College Park, Maryland, USA

NOTES

Introduction

1. Tela Zasloff, *A Rescuer's Story: Pastor Pierre-Charles Toureille in Vichy France* (Madison: University of Wisconsin Press, 2003).

2. CICR, BG 17/05, 97, Geneva, July 17, 1941. Unless otherwise noted, translations are my own.

3. On Varian Fry's ERC, see Andy Marino, *American Pimpernel: The Story of Varian Fry* (London: Hutchinson, 1999), as well as Pierre Sauvage's forthcoming documentary film.

4. Noah Isenberg, *We'll Always Have Casablanca* (New York: W. W. Norton, 2017), 43, 143–145.

5. See Sanjay Subrahmanyam, *From Tagus to the Ganges: Explorations in Connected History* (Oxford: Oxford University Press, 2012).

6. Victor Serge, *Carnets, 1936–1947* (Paris: Agone, 2012), 75.

7. Aimé Césaire, *Discourse on Colonialism* (New York: Monthly Review Press, 2000), 36.

8. Michael Rothberg, *Multidirectional Memory: Remembering the Holocaust in the Age of Decolonization* (Stanford, CA: Stanford University Press, 2009), 72.

9. See, for instance, Philippe Joutard, Jacques Poujol, and Patrick Cabanel, eds., *Cévennes, terre de refuge, 1940–1944* (Montpellier, France: Presses du Languedoc, 1987); Philip Hallie, *Lest Innocent Blood Be Shed* (New York: Harper, 1994); Jacques Sémelin, *Persécutions et entraide en France occupée* (Paris: Les Arènes, 2013); Jacques Sémelin, Claire Andrieu, and Sarah Gensburger, *La Résistance aux génocides: De la pluralité des actes de sauvetage* (Paris: Presses de Sciences Po, 2008); and Vicki Caron, ed., "The Rescue of Jews in France and Its Empire during World War II," special issue, *French Politics, Culture and Society* 30, no. 2 (Summer 2012).

10. On the Dominican Republic, see Allen Wells, *Tropical Zion: General Trujillo, FDR and the Jews of Sosua* (Durham, NC: Duke University Press, 2009);

Marion A. Kaplan, *Dominican Haven: The Jewish Refugee Settlement in Sosua, 1940–1945* (New York: Museum of Jewish Heritage, 2008); and Suzanne Gigliotti, "Acapulco in the Atlantic: Revisiting Sosúa, a Jewish Refugee Colony in the Caribbean," *Immigrants and Minorities* 24 (2006): 22–50. On Shanghai, see Gao Bei, *Shanghai Sanctuary: Chinese and Japanese Policy toward European Refugees during World War II* (Oxford: Oxford University Press, 2013).

11. Nancy L. Green, "The Politics of Exit: Reversing the Immigration Paradigm," *Journal of Modern History* 77, no. 2 (June 2005): 265, 268.

1. Undesirables

1. Denis Peschanski, *La France des camps* (Paris: Gallimard, 2002), 31.

2. Ibid., 72.

3. Ibid., 33–34, 73; Vicki Caron, *Uneasy Asylum: France and the Jewish Refugee Crisis, 1933–1942* (Stanford, CA: Stanford University Press, 1999), 2, 327.

4. Laurent Joly, *Vichy dans la "Solution finale," 1941–1944* (Paris: Grasset, 2006), 58–59.

5. Timothy P. Maga, "Closing the Door: The French Government and Refugee Policy, 1933–1939," *French Historical Studies* 12, no. 3 (Spring 1982): 424–442. On French efforts to keep tabs on these immigrant communities, see Mary Lewis, *The Boundaries of the Republic: Migrant Rights and the Limits of Universalism in France, 1918–1940* (Stanford, CA: Stanford University Press, 2007), and Clifford Rosenberg, *Policing Paris: The Origins of Modern Immigration Control between the Wars* (Ithaca, NY: Cornell University Press, 2006).

6. Michael Marrus and Robert Paxton, *Vichy France and the Jews* (New York: Schocken Books, 1983), 167.

7. Peschanski, *La France des camps,* 229.

8. Ibid., 194–196; Caron, *Uneasy Asylum,* 3, 321–325; Adam Rayski, *Le choix des juifs sous Vichy* (Paris: La Découverte, 1992), 120; Michael Marrus, "Vichy before Vichy: Antisemitic Currents in France during the 1930s," *Wiener Library Bulletin* 33, no. 51/52 (1980): 13–19; Gérard Noiriel, *Les origines républicaines de Vichy* (Paris: Fayard, 2013).

9. Caron, *Uneasy Asylum,* 325.

10. For the total before November 1942, see Peschanski, *La France des camps,* 159. On heel dragging, see Daniel Bénédite, *La filière marseillaise: Un chemin vers la liberté sous l'occupation* (Paris: Clancier Guénaud, 1984), 158.

11. Peschanski, *La France des camps,* 208–212.

12. Anne Grynberg, "Les camps du sud de la France: De l'internement à la déportation," *Annales, economies, sociétés, civilisations* 48, no. 3 (1993): 557. On this law, see Marrus and Paxton, *Vichy France and the Jews,* 4, 167.

13. The question of responsibility for the 1940 defeat has a long history of its own. See, most notably, Marc Bloch, *Strange Defeat* (New York: W. W. Norton, 1999); John Cairns, "Great Britain and the Fall of France: A Study in Allied Disunity," *Journal of Modern History* 27, no. 4 (December 1955): 365–409; Joel Blatt, ed., *The French Defeat of 1940: Reassessments* (New York: Berghahn,

1997); Julian Jackson, *The Fall of France: The Nazi Invasion of 1940* (Oxford: Oxford University Press, 2003); and Philip Nord, *France, 1940: Defending the Republic* (New Haven, CT: Yale University Press, 2015).

14. Robert Paxton, *Vichy France, Old Guard and New Order* (New York: Columbia University Press, 1982), 4, 22, 147, 171.

15. Quoted in Laurent Joly, *Xavier Vallat* (Paris: Grasset, 2001), 217.

16. Caron, *Uneasy Asylum,* 333.

17. ADBDR, 76 W 188, Vichy Ministry of Interior to the Prefect of the Bouches-du-Rhône, November 20, 1940.

18. Peschanksi, *La France des camps,* 221.

19. Robert Mencherini, ed., *Provence-Auschwitz: De l'internement des étrangers à la déportation des juifs* (Aix-en-Provence: Presses Universitaires de Provence, 2008), 16–29; Donna Ryan, *The Holocaust and the Jews of Marseille* (Urbana: University of Illinois Press, 1996), 95–96.

20. CICR, BG 17/05, 96, September 6, 1940.

21. Quoted in Peschanski, *La France des camps,* 154.

22. CICR, BG 17/05, 96, anonymous September 6, 1940 report on Saint-Cyprien.

23. Marrus and Paxton, *Vichy France and the Jews,* 174–175.

24. CICR, OCMS D122, "Note to the Attention of the Joint Relief Commission of the International Red Cross," March 10, 1942; September 24, 1940, Red Cross report, in *Recueil de documents des archives du Comité international de la Croix Rouge sur le sort des juifs de France internés et déportés, 1939–1945,* ed. Serge Klarsfeld (Paris: Beate Klarsfled Foundation, 1999), 1:73.

25. Dr. Eugen Netter, quoted in Claude Laharie, "Déportation et internement au camp de Gurs de 6538 juifs allemands originaires du pays de Bade et du Palatinat," in *Les camps du sud-ouest de la France, 1939–1944,* ed. Monique Lise-Cohen and Eric Malo (Toulouse: Privat, 1994), 109.

26. Ryan, *Holocaust,* 96, 100–102.

27. Ibid., 102; Robert Mencherini et al., *Mémoire du camp des Milles, 1939–1942* (Marseille: Le Bec en l'Air, 2013), 27–28.

28. On art at Les Milles, see Fondation du Camp des Milles, *Bellmer, Ernst, Springer, Wols au camp des Milles* (Paris: Flammarion, 2013), and Pnina Rosenberg, *L'art des indésirables: L'art dans les camps d'internement français, 1939–1944* (Paris: L'Harmattan, 2003).

29. On the attribution of the painting to Bodek and for Bodek's biography, see Mencherini et al., *Mémoire du camp des Milles,* 46–50. The interpretation of the mural presented here is my own.

30. Marrus and Paxton, *Vichy France and the Jews,* 219, 233.

31. Grynberg, "Les camps," 559; Adam Rayski, *Le choix des juifs,* 122.

32. Serge Klarsfeld, *Vichy-Auschwitz: La "Solution Finale" de la question juive en France* (Paris: Fayard, 2001), 147.

33. Marrus and Paxton, *Vichy France and the Jews,* 248, 257; Grynberg, "Les camps," 559.

34. Renée Poznanski, *Les juifs en France pendant la seconde guerre mondiale* (Paris: Hachette, 1997), 334; Robert Paxton and Michael Marrus, *Vichy et les*

juifs (Paris: Calmann-Lévy, 2015), 327 (note that this passage is new to the updated 2015 French edition).

35. Serge Klarsfeld, "La livraison par Vichy des juifs de la zone libre dans les plans SS de déportation des juifs de France," in Lise-Cohen and Malo, *Les camps du sud-ouest,* 133, 139.

36. CICR, OCMS D122, Dr. René Zimer, Geneva, November 10, 1942.

37. CICR, OCMS D120, "Statistique des étrangers hébergés ou internes," September 1941.

38. Mary Jayne Gold, *Marseille année 40* (Paris: Phébus, 2001), 265–273; Pierre Sauvage, *And Crown Thy Good: Varian Fry in Marseille,* excerpts from the film in progress, Columbia University, March 24, 2011.

39. Poznanksi, *Les juifs en France,* 265; Joly, *Vichy dans la "Solution finale,"* 189.

40. CCICR, BG 17/05, 94, Correspondence between Suzanne Ferrière of the Red Cross in Geneva and Marcelle Trillat of the Service social d'aide aux émigrants, Lyon. Ferrière to Trillat, July 30, 1942; response from Trillat to Ferrière, August 10, 1942.

41. LBI, Yolla Niclas-Sachs, "Looking Back from New Horizons," unpublished memoir, 1974, 20–21.

42. ADBDR, 76 W 111, telephone note from Miss Favale, Marseille, December 25, 1940.

43. Ryan, *Holocaust,* 105. See also Lion Feuchtwanger, *The Devil in France: My Encounter with Him in the Summer of 1940* (New York: Viking, 1941), 193–220 ("invitation" on 217).

44. In another connection with the French Caribbean, in May 1942 gifted Guianese lawyer and former deputy and undersecretary to the colonies Gaston Monnerville defended a Jewish woman in Aix-en-Provence and won. He challenged the prosecutor's contention that the onus rested on her having to prove that she was not Jewish by virtue of Vichy's statutes. See Olivier Wieviorka, *Orphans of the Republic: The Nation's Legislators in Vichy France* (Cambridge, MA: Harvard University Press, 2009), 226.

45. ANF, 41AJ 321, "Prison des Présentines, état des ressortissants allemands" March 26, 1942; ADBDR, 1490 W 217 (Justice files, formerly held in Aix-en-Provence), list of trials, September 3, 1941; the verdict and explanation for it appears in ADBDR, 109 W 6 (Justice files, formerly held in Aix-en-Provence), case 1604.

46. Serge Klarsfeld, *Le mémorial de la déportation des juifs de France* (Paris: Centre de Documentation Juive Contemporaine, 1978), list for convoy 75 (May 30, 1944), n.p.

47. ADBDR, 1490 W 217 (Justice files, formerly held in Aix-en-Provence), list of trials at Aix-en-Provence. On the frenetic crackdown on abortion, immigrants, and Jews in the courts of a nearby *département,* see Riadh Ben Khalifa, *Délinquance en temps de crise: L'ordinaire exceptionnel devant la justice correctionnelle des Alpes-Maritimes, 1938–1944* (Paris: Honoré Champion, 2015).

48. Walter Mehring, *No Road Back* (New York: Samuel Curl, 1944), 59.

49. Walter Mehring, *The Lost Library: Autobiography of a Culture* (Indianapolis: Bobbs-Merrill, 1950), 265.

50. GJECA, ERC Archives, box 2, folder 3, Fry to Mehring, September 7, 1940.

51. Varian Fry, *Surrender on Demand* (Boulder, CO: Johnson Books, 1997), 49; Gold, *Marseille année 1940*, 219–220.

52. Words written in English in an otherwise French letter.

53. USHM, ERC Archives, Frank File.

54. Bénédite, *La filière marseillaise*, 133

55. USHM, Pyrénées orientales departemental archives, RG43.036. On the problems of trying to bring relatives from Europe to the United States at this time, see Michael Winerip, "Dear Cousin Julius, We Trust on Our God and on You," *New York Times Magazine,* April 27, 1997; and Debórah Dwork and Robert Jan Van Pelt, *Flight from the Reich: Refugee Jews, 1933–1946* (New York: W. W. Norton, 2009), 141–146.

56. Peschanski provides the figure of 7,700. Laharie lists 6,538 from Baden and 1,125 from Palatine and Saarland. Peschanski, *La France des camps,* 227. Claude Laharie, "Déportation et internement au camp de Gurs de 6538 juifs allemands originaires du pays de Bade et du Palatinat," in Monique Lise-Cohen and Eric Malo, eds., *Les camps du sud-ouest de la France, 1939–1944* (Toulouse: Privat, 1994). On the extension of the Alsace-Lorraine clause, see Grynberg, "Les camps," 563. David Cesarini argues that they were also responding to rumors that Vichy would arrange to send them to Madagascar. David Cesarini, *Final Solution: The Fate of the Jews, 1933–1949* (New York: St. Martin's, 2016), 301.

57. USHM, Pyrénées orientales departemental archives, RG43.036. For the family history, see Wolfgang Strauss, "Max Strauss," 2004, http://gedenkbuch.informedia.de/index.php/PID/12/name/4297/suche/S.html (consulted in November 2015). On the OSE, see Poznanski, *Les juifs en France*, 231–233.

58. USHM, Pyrénées orientales departemental archives, RG43.036.

59. MF, Germaine Krull Archives, "Camp de concentration à la Martinique," unpublished manuscript.

60. USHM, Pyrénées orientales departemental archives, RG43.036.

61. Peschanski, *La France des camps,* 210.

62. USHM, Pyrénées orientales departemental archives, RG43.036.

63. Caron, *Uneasy Asylum,* 336.

64. Jean-Michel Palmier, *Weimar en Exil* (Paris: Payot, 1988), 2:131.

65. CICR, BG 17/05, 97, "Réfugiés en France non-occupée," December 18, 1941.

66. Ulrike Voswinckel and Frank Beringer, *Exils méditerranéens: Écrivains allemands dans le sud de la France, 1933–1941* (Paris: Le Seuil, 2009), 262.

67. Margot Peigne, "De l'Algérie au Mexique: L'organisation des demandes d'asile des exilés espagnols," in *Sables d'exil: Les républicains espagnols dans les camps d'internement au Maghreb, 1939–1945,* ed. Andrée Bachoud and Bernard Sicot (Perpignan, France: Mare Nostrum, 2009), 126.

68. Robert Mencherini, ed., *Étrangers antifascistes à Marseille, 1940–1944: Homage au Consul du Mexique Gilberto Bosques* (Marseille: Gaussen, 2014), 35–39, 99–119; Peschanski, *La France des camps*, 221–222.

69. Bénédite, *La filière marseillaise*, 158. Ryan places the optimal window for emigration from Marseille between October 1940 and the summer of 1941. See Ryan, *Holocaust*, 98.

70. Klarsfeld, *Recueil de documents*, vol. 1, Cramer visit to the camps of the unoccupied zone, January 8, 1941.

71. CICR, BG 17/05, 97, "Réfugiés en France non-occupée," December 18, 1941. On Nazi concerns that Spanish Republicans would join the allies, see Peschanski, *La France des camps*, 222. On the Russell Act, see Marrus and Paxton, *Vichy France and the Jews*, 114. On the rule about relatives in zones under German control, and the dual investigation policy, see Richard Breitman and Alan Kraut, *American Refugee Policy and European Jewry, 1933–1945* (Bloomington: Indiana University Press, 1987), 135–136.

72. ADBDR, 255J5, Fry to Bénédite, November 25, 1941.

73. ADBDR, 255J6, Bénédite to Fry, August 23, 1942, 3.

74. Dwork and Van Pelt, *Flight from the Reich*, 191. Note that language discrepancies could appear within a single project. Thus, Nazi schemes to drive Jews away from so-called Greater Germany in 1940 were variously termed "forced emigration," "evacuation," and "deportation." See Götz Aly, *"Final Solution": Nazi Population Policy and the Murder of European Jews* (London: Arnold, 1999), 124.

75. Christopher Browning, *Nazi Policy, Jewish Workers, German Killers* (Cambridge: Cambridge University Press, 2000), 39–40.

76. Cesarini, *Final Solution*, 594.

77. Mark Polizzotti, *Revolution of the Mind: The Life of André Breton* (New York: Farrar, Straus and Giroux, 1995), 475; Rosemary Sullivan, *Villa Air-Bel: World War II, Escape and a House in Marseille* (New York: Harper Collins, 2006), 255.

78. On these perils and others, see Jean-Michel Guiraud, *La vie intellectuelle et artistique à Marseille à l'époque de Vichy et sous l'occupation, 1940–1944* (Gémenos, France: Editions Jeanne Laffitte, 1998), 115.

79. ADBDR, 76 W 188, Vichy Ministry of Interior to the Prefect of the Bouches-du-Rhône, November 20, 1940.

80. ADBDR, 76 W 111, Marseille police, December 12, 1941.

81. Voswinckel and Beringer, *Exils méditerranéens*, 115.

82. Neumann diary, in ibid., 281, 283.

83. ADBDR, 76 W 188, additif à la liste des étrangers auxquels doit être refusé le visa de sortie, April 9, 1941.

84. USHM, American Friends Service Committee Records Relating to Humanitarian Work in France, section 8, Marseille office, subseries correspondence, box 54, folder 61.

85. USHM, American Friends Service Committee Records Relating to Humanitarian Work in France, section 8, Marseille office, subseries reports, box 60, folder 55l, summary of activities for 1941, pp. 2–3.

86. Mehring, *No Road Back,* 65.

87. Victor Serge, *Mémoires d'un révolutionnaire, 1901–1941* (Paris: Le Seuil, 1978), 384.

88. Anna Seghers, *Transit* (New York: New York Review of Books, 2013), 153.

89. Ryan, *Holocaust,* 81. On the policing over this mosaic, and the control of immigrants in Marseille, see Lewis, *Boundaries of the Republic.*

90. Seghers, *Transit,* 233–234.

91. Neumann diary, in Voswinckel and Beringer, *Exils méditerranéens,* 287. Wolff had been the first publisher of Franz Kafka. Thanks to Fry's ERC, he found his way to New York via Spain and Portugal in 1941.

92. Serge, *Mémoires d'un révolutionnaire,* 389. The expression was quite common and was used in German—"der Kampf um das amerikanische Visum"— by other refugees, including one Weinberger, an Austrian refugee in France. Wiener Library, *Testaments to the Holocaust,* series 1, section 2, reel 60 (index number P III 1 No. 486, France), EW 11, 11432–11511.

93. BLY, GEN MSS 238, box 1 folder 10, correspondence under C, undated letter from Chevalier.

94. ADBDR, 76 W 184, "Rapports quotidiens du commissariat central," entry for March 31, 1941. Rewald's presence on the *Carimaré* is revealed in USNA, RG 84, box 3, passenger manifest for the *Carimaré*'s passengers continuing to the United States.

95. ADBDR, 76 W 184, "Rapports quotidiens du commissariat central," entry for August 6, 1940. Henriot would go on to wage war on the resistance; he would also emerge as a violent anti-Semite.

96. Fry, *Surrender on Demand,* 19, 33; Gold, *Marseille année 1940,* 207; Guiraud, *La vie intellectuelle et artistique,* 117.

97. GJECA, ERC Archives, box 2, folder 3, "Note concernant ce qui a été fait par le Centre Américain de Secours en faveur de Walter Mehring," March 25, 1941. Andy Marino claims that it was the Italian Armistice Commission. Marino, *American Pimpernel: The Story of Varian Fry* (London: Hutchinson, 1999), 262.

98. ANF, 38AJ61, Vichy, "Inspection générale de la police administrative," May 6, 1941.

99. ANF, 38AJ61, Vichy, "Renseignements généraux," October 28, 1941. On this about-face by Cuba, see Poznanski, *Les juifs en France,* 210.

100. ANF, 38AJ61, "Renseignements (contrôle technique)," November 30, 1941.

101. Renée Dray-Bensousan, *Les juifs à Marseille, 1940–1944* (Paris: Les Belles Lettres, 2004), 176–177; Marrus and Paxton, *Vichy France and the Jews,* 162–163.

102. Marrus and Paxton, *Vichy France and the Jews,* 310.

103. Jean-Louis Crémieux-Brilhac, *L'étrange victoire* (Paris: Gallimard, 2016), 128.

104. Jean Malaquais, *Journal du Métèque* (Paris: Phébus, 1997), 11, 311.

105. Ibid., 250.

106. Ibid., 242, 245.

107. Neumann diary, in Voswinckel and Beringer, *Exils méditerranéens*, 283.
108. Malaquais, *Journal du Métèque*, 288, 322.
109. Geneviève Nakach, *Malaquais rebelle* (Paris: Cherche Midi, 2011), 155.
110. Malaquais, *Journal du Métèque*, 269, 280, 319.
111. These last details are provided by Malaquais biographer Geneviève Nakash, who was able to confirm the rescue attempt at Les Milles by interviewing the wife of Malaquais' friend Marc Chirik, who recounted Malaquais' "extraordinary courage." Nakach, *Malaquais rebelle,* 159.
112. Serge, *Mémoires d'un révolutionnaire,* 388.
113. Jean Malaquais, *Planète sans visa* (Paris: Phébus, 1999), 74.
114. Malaquais, *Journal du Métèque,* 247, 271, 274, 278, 286, 313, 314, 324. In a recent testimony, Laura Bosques recalls Yurkevich drawing the portrait of her young brother. See Mencherini, *Étrangers antifascistes à Marseille,* 123.
115. Malaquais, *Journal du Métèque,* 322, 324, 327, 329.
116. Galina Yurkevitch diary (kindly forwarded by Elisabeth Malaquais), entry for September 20, 1942.
117. Malaquais, *Journal du Métèque,* 333.
118. Marrus and Paxton, *Vichy France and the Jews,* 247–248.
119. Ryan, *Holocaust,* 126.
120. Jean-Pierre Azéma and Olivier Wieviorka, *Vichy, 1940–1944* (Paris: Perrin, 2000), 226.
121. Galina Yurkevitch diary, entry for November 25, 1942.

2. Opening the Martinique Corridor

1. Claude Lévi-Strauss, *Tristes tropiques* (Paris: Plon, 1955), 17–18.
2. Claude Lévi-Strauss, letter to the author, September 9, 1997.
3. Ruth Davidoff, *Volaron las palomas* (Mexico City: El Tucan de Virginia, 2007); Misha Davidoff, "Where Europe Comes to an End," *Límulus,* last accessed August 31, 2017, http://limulus.mx/donde-europa-llega-a-su-fin/?lang=en.
4. Varian Fry, *Surrender on Demand* (Boulder, CO: Johnson Books, 1997), 187.
5. CRB, Varian Fry Papers, box 8, ERC telegram, Frank Kingdon to Cornelia Van Auken Chapin, May 18, 1941 (emphasis mine).
6. Marc Olivier Baruch, *Servir l'Etat français: L'administration en France de 1940 à 1944* (Paris: Fayard, 1997), 226.
7. Cynthia Bisson, "Peyrouton," in *Historical Dictionary of World War II France,* ed. Bertram Gordon (Westport, CT: Greenwood, 1998), 281–282; Marcel Peyrouton, *Du service public à la prison commune* (Paris: Plon, 1950).
8. Vicki Caron, *Uneasy Asylum: France and the Jewish Refugee Crisis, 1933–1942* (Stanford, CA: Stanford University Press, 1999), 336.
9. ANOM, 1Affpol 768, Peyrouton to the Minister of the Colonies, November 29, 1940.
10. ANOM, 1Affpol 768, Platon to the Governor of Martinique. A copy can be found in ANOM, 1TEL 701.

11. ANOM, FM, 1TEL 688, Bressoles to Vichy, October 23, 1940.

12. For the territorialists, see Gur Alroey, *Zionism without Zion: The Jewish Territorial Organization and Its Conflict with the Zionist Organization* (Detroit: Wayne State University Press, 2016). For their rooting their ideas in the writings of Herzl, see ibid., 123. Adam Rovner has also tackled territorialism in *In the Shadow of Zion: Promised Lands before Israel* (New York: New York University Press, 2014), 222–223. On Guiana, see Caron, *Uneasy Asylum,* 222–223, as well as Laurent Joly, *Vichy dans la "Solution finale," 1941–1944* (Paris: Grasset, 2006), 62. On Guinea, see David Jessula, "Un projet d'établissement d'Israélites en 1939 en Guinée française," *Notes africaines* 156 (October 1977): 97–100. On the 1912 Angolan scheme, see Joao Medina and Joel Barromi, "The Jewish Colonization Project in Angola," *Studies in Zionism* 12, no. 1 (1991): 1–16.

13. Eric Jennings, "Writing Madagascar Back into the Madagascar Plan," *Holocaust and Genocide Studies* 21, no. 2 (Fall 2007): 187–217, updated and further developed in Eric Jennings, *Perspectives on French Colonial Madagascar* (New York: Palgrave, 2017), chapter 6; Caron, *Uneasy Asylum,* 146–55; Joly, *Vichy dans la "Solution finale,"* 274; Magnus Brechtken, *Madagaskar für die Juden: Antisemitische Idee und politische Praxis* (Munich: Studien zur Zeitgeschichte, 1997), 97–109; Leni Yahil, "Madagascar: Phantom of a Solution for the Jewish Question," in *Jews and Non-Jews in Eastern Europe, 1918–1945,* ed. George Mosse and Bela Vago (New Brunswick, NJ: Transaction Books, 1974), 315–334; Michael Marrus, *The Unwanted: European Refugees in the Twentieth Century* (New York: Oxford University Press, 1985), 186–187; Michael Marrus and Robert Paxton, *Vichy France and the Jews* (New York: Schocken Books, 1983), 60–62; Christopher Browning, *Nazi Policy, Jewish Workers, German Killers* (Cambridge: Cambridge University Press, 2000), 15–17 (quotation on 17); Christopher Browning, *The Path to Genocide* (Cambridge: Cambridge University Press, 1992), 18–33; Rovner, *In the Shadow of Zion,* 143; Christian Guerlach, *The Extermination of the European Jews* (Cambridge: Cambridge University Press, 2016), 61.

14. Pablo Neruda, *Memoirs* (New York: Farrar, Straus and Giroux, 1977), 145–148; Julio Gálvez Barraza, *Winnipeg: Testimonios de un exilio* (Sevilla: Biblioteca del eixilio, 2014); "La traversée de l'espoir," television documentary by Olivier Guiton (co-producers On Line productions, Point du Jour, PCT, la Cinquième).

15. ANOM, 1Affpol 768, Minister of the Interior to Minister of the Colonies, November 29, 1940.

16. Robert Aron describes Platon as follows: "This ex-Professor from the Ecole supérieure de la Marine, an austere Protestant, believed that the salvation of France lay in total collaboration with the Reich." Robert Aron, *The Vichy Regime* (New York: Putnam, 1958), 129.

17. Caron, *Uneasy Asylum,* 333, 335; Susan Zuccotti, *The Holocaust, the French, and the Jews* (New York: Basic Books, 1993), 67.

18. Marrus and Paxton, *Vichy France and the Jews,* 247.

19. Eric Jennings, *Vichy in the Tropics: Pétain's National Revolution in Madagascar, Guadeloupe and Indochina* (Stanford, CA: Stanford University Press,

2001), 20–22, 44–46; Eric Jennings and Sébastien Verney, "Vichy aux colonies: L'exportation des statuts des juifs dans l'empire," *Archives juives* 41 (Spring 2008): 108–119.

20. Marrus and Paxton, *Vichy France and the Jews,* 163.

21. ANOM, 1Affpol 768, Platon to Fort-de-France, February 1, 1941, and, in the same file, note from Du Porzic, and record of an 11:15 a.m., January 31, 1941, phone call between the Ministry of the Colonies and the Marseille police chief. On Du Porzic's zealous anti-Semitism, see Simon Kitson, *Police and Politics in Marseille, 1936–1946* (Leiden: Brill, 2014), 109.

22. ANOM, 1TEL 688, Bressoles to Vichy, October 23, 1940.

23. ANOM, 1Affpol 768, Bressoles to Platon, January 3, 1941.

24. ANOM, 1TEL 723, Nicol to Vichy, March 7, 1941.

25. ANOM, 1Affpol 768, Chot to Platon, February 21, 1942.

26. ANOM, 1TEL 807, telegram 61, Sorin to Vichy, March 19, 1941.

27. ANOM, 1Affpol 768, Platon to the Ministry of the Interior, January 8, 1941.

28. ANOM, 1TEL 722, telegram, Sorin to Platon, May 2, 1941.

29. ADG, INC 140, telegram from the president of the chamber of commerce of Basse-Terre to the governor, and his response (both dated March 4, 1941), kindly transmitted by Marie Touchelay.

30. ADM, 4M997, file "Israélites," report to Admiral Robert, April 22, 1941.

31. ANOM, 1Affpol 768, note de service, April 17, 1941.

32. ANOM, 1Affpol 768, telegram, Platon to Martinique, April 18, 1941.

33. ANOM, 1TEL 723, Robert to Platon, August 4, 1941.

34. ANOM, 1TEL 701, Platon to Martinique, March 11, 1941 (concerns 88 refugees); in the same carton, Platon to Martinique, March 15, 1941 (concerns 26 refugees), as well as Platon to Martinique, March 10, 1941 (concerns 21 refugees).

35. ANOM, 1Affpol 768, Darlan to Platon, May 29, 1941.

36. ANOM, 1Affpol 768, "Visa de transit."

37. CDJC, CCX VII–15, "Rapport d'activité de la HICEM en France pour 1941," 1942, p. 6.

38. SHMT, 18S 14, "Marine Antilles du 1ᵉʳ septembre 1939 à la fin des hostilités."

39. CDJC, AJDC 616 (France, emigration), confidential letter from Cuba, May 23, 1941; ADM 4M 997, "Israélites français et étrangers résidant à Fort-de-France." This figure is roughly corroborated by passenger testimonies, which refer to passenger totals, not refugee ones. Germaine Krull reckoned that the ship carried a total of 200; Victor Serge estimated 300; and Claude Lévi-Strauss guessed that some 350 people were on board. MF, Germaine Krull Archives, "Camp de concentration à la Martinique"; BLY, GEN MSS 238, box 4, folder 185, Victor Serge, "La guerre des océans," typescript, June 10, 1942; Lévi-Strauss, *Tristes tropiques,* 19.

40. CDJC, AJDC 616 (France, emigration), letter from Manuel Siegel, Havana, May 23, 1941.

41. Ibid.

42. "Der französische Dampfer *Ipanéma*," *Aufbau*, March 28, 1941, 2.

43. USNA, RG 84, box 5, "Movement of Merchant Vessels," January 30, 1941.

44. Léo Elisabeth, "Vichy aux Antilles et en Guyane, 1940–1943," *Outre-mers* 342–343 (2004): 161. Another source has the *Ipanema* leaving the Bordeaux region with 994 refugees, bound for Martinique and Veracruz via Sao Tomé, on June 12, 1940. However, this crossing did not find its way into Rouyer's list, either. Might this actually be the *Cuba*? Alba Martínez, *Andaluzas exiliadas en México tras la Guerra Civil (1939–1948)* (Almería, Spain: Universidad de Almería, 2015), 64.

45. MAE, Guerre, 1939–45, (Vichy) Continent Américain, dossier 182.

46. CDJC, AJDC 616 (France, emigration), HICEM activities in April and May 1941. On the course and timing of the vessels, see MAE, Guerre, 1939–45, (Vichy) Continent Américain, dossier 182.

47. SHMV, Marine TTE 32.

48. SHMV, Marine TTE 32, Benech to Malige, June 27, 1941.

49. MAE, Guerre, 1939–45, (Vichy) Continent Américain, dossier 182.

50. ANOM, 1Affpol 768, Platon (Gaston Joseph) to Darlan, May 23, 1941.

51. Caron, *Uneasy Asylum,* 336.

52. ANOM, 1Affpol 768, Platon to Darlan, May 15, 1941.

53. CDJC, CCX, VII–15, HICEM report for 1941, 24.

54. ADBDR, 255J5, Fry to Bénédite, December 25, 1941.

55. Fry, *Surrender on Demand,* 189.

56. Daniel Bénédite, *La filière marseillaise: Un chemin vers la liberté sous l'occupation* (Paris: Clancier Guénaud, 1984), 273.

57. USHM, ERC Archives, Herzog Files (3–9); Wilhelm Herzog, *Menschen, denen ich begegnete* (Bern, Switzerland: A. Francke Verlag, 1959), 285. On the infiltration of the German community at Sanary by an agent named Hans-Günther Von Dincklage, see Hal Vaughan, *Sleeping with the Enemy: Coco Chanel's Secret War* (New York: Vintage, 2012), 56–60. On Herzog leaving Germany in 1933, see Jean-Michel Palmier, *Weimar en Exil* (Paris: Payot, 1988), 1:139.

58. CDJC, AJDC 616 (France, emigration), HICEM report for April–May 1941.

59. Renée Poznanski, *Les juifs en France pendant la seconde guerre mondiale* (Paris: Hachette, 1997), 209–210.

60. Ibid., 211. On the Seghers-Radvanyi family making a similar cancelation of their Lisbon tickets for Martinique ones, see Anna Seghers to Bodo Uhse, June 1, 1941, in *Briefe, 1924–1952*, ed. Christiane Zehl Romero and Almut Giesecke (Berlin: Aufbau Verlag, 2008), 105.

61. "Via Martinique nach New York," *Aufbau*, March 7, 1941, 8.

62. "Ausreise aus Frankfreich," *Aufbau*, May 23, 1941.

63. "Schiffskarten, Marseille-Martinique-New York," *Aufbau*, May 30, 1941, 9.

64. ANOM, 1Affpol 1297, "Note de service," January 16, 1941.

65. Dominique Chathuant, "Un résistant? Maurice Satineau, un parlementaire colonial dans la tourmente, 1940–1945," *Outre-mers* 386–387 (June 2015): 136–139.

66. ANOM, 2 APOM 7, Rouyer to Devouton, March 7, 1941.

67. ANOM, 1TEL 701, Platon to Robert, April 18, 1941; ANOM, 1Affpol 1297, Platon to Marseille's colonial services, January 21, 1941.

68. ANOM, 1Affpol 1297, Satineau to Platon, March 6, 1941.

69. ANOM, 1Affpol 768, Fort-de-France to Vichy, July 8, 1942.

70. Frida Kahn, *Generation in Turmoil* (Great Neck, NY: Channel, 1960), 210, 170–171.

71. Helena Benitez, *Wifredo and Helena: My Life with Wifredo Lam, 1939–1950* (Lausanne: Acatos, 1999), 50.

3. Understanding the Martinique Route

1. Julie Boghardt, *Minna Flake: Macht und Ohnmacht der roten Frau: Von der Dichtermuse zur Sozialistin* (Frankfurt: Campus Verlag, 1997), 1–73. There is a discrepancy on her birth date, with Boghardt indicating 1886 and Flake's file at the Exil Archives in Frankfurt indicating 1887.

2. LBI, Renée (Renata) Barth, "A Born Refugee," unpublished manuscript, 1993, 13. Courtesy of the Leo Baeck Institute, New York.

3. GJECA, ERC Archives, box 1, folder 17, Flake biography; GJECA, Walter Friedlander Papers, box 7, folder 14, Friedlander letter of support for Renée Barth addressed to Margaret Bishop, March 14, 1949.

4. Barth, "Born Refugee," 38.

5. Ibid., 72.

6. GJECA, ERC Archives, box 1, folder 17, Flake application form, August 22, 1940.

7. Barth, "Born Refugee," 76.

8. On the rescue of Jews in predominantly Protestant areas of France, see Philippe Joutard, Jacques Poujol, and Patrick Cabanel, eds., *Cévennes, terre de refuge, 1940–1944* (Montpellier, France: Presses du Languedoc, 1987); Philip Hallie, *Lest Innocent Blood Be Shed* (New York: Harper, 1994); and Pierre Sauvage's documentary *Weapons of the Spirit* about the village of Le Chambon-sur-Lignon. On Protestant indignation at Jewish deportations in the Gard, see Robert Zaretsky, *Nîmes at War: Religion, Politics and Public Opinion in the Gard, 1938–1944* (University Park: Pennsylvania State University Press, 1995), 120–121. For the big picture, see Julian Jackson, *France, the Dark Years* (Oxford: Oxford University Press, 2003), 377, and Michael Bess, *Choices under Fire: Moral Dimensions of World War II* (New York: Knopf, 2006), 115–135.

9. GJECA, ERC Archives, box 1, folder 17, affidavit from the Brunswicks, August 21, 1940.

10. DEA, K. EB 73/21, ERC to Walter Friedlander, August 24, 1940.

11. Barth, "Born Refugee," 83, 87.

12. United States Holocaust Memorial Museum Photo Archives, http://digitalassets.ushmm.org/photoarchives/detail.aspx?id=1155267&search=&index=2; Friedrich Ebert Stifting, Archiv der sozialen Demokratie, https://www.fes.de/archiv/adsd_neu/inhalt/nachlass/nachlass_l/loewenstein-ku.htm.

13. Barth, "Born Refugee," 83.

14. DEA, K. EB 73/21.

15. Barth, "Born Refugee," 84–86

16. Ibid., 88.

17. Ibid., 90.

18. DEA, K. EB 73/21.

19. CCP, AG 90, 24/1, 1a, Breitenbach manuscript on the camps in France (untitled, Fall 1940).

20. Keith Holz and Wolfgang Schopf, *Im Auge des Exils: Josef Breitenbach und die Freie Deutsche Kultur in Paris, 1933–1941* (Berlin: Aufbau Verlag, 2001), 225–238.

21. CCP, AG 90, 4/23, S. Schott to Walter Friedlander, November 6, 1940.

22. CCP, AG 90, 12/10, 11.

23. Pierre Radvanyi, interview with the author, Paris, October 27, 2013; Susan E. Cernyak, "Anna Seghers: Between Judaism and Communism," in *Exile: The Writer's Experience,* ed. John M. Spalek and Robert F. Bell (Chapel Hill: University of North Carolina Press, 1982), 279.

24. Pierre Radvanyi, *Janseits des Stroms: Erinnerungen an Meine Mutter Anna Seghers* (Berlin: Aufbau Verlag, 2005), 48–51; Pierre Radvanyi, interview with the author, Paris, October 27, 2013. On foreign Jews crossing the demarcation line, see Eric Alary, "Les juifs et la ligne de démarcation, 1940–1943," *Les cahiers de la Shoah* 5 (2001): 13–49. On crossing the line, in both directions, see Robert Gildea, *Marianne in Chains: Daily Life in the Heart of France during the German Occupation* (New York: Picador, 2003), 142–143.

25. Radvanyi, *Janseits des Stroms,* 61, 64, 66; Pierre Radvanyi, interview with the author, Paris, October 27, 2013.

26. Frida Kahn, *Generation in Turmoil* (Great Neck, NY: Channel, 1960), 163.

27. Ibid., 171–173.

28. Limore Yagil, *Au nom de l'art, 1933–1945: Exils, solidarités et engagements* (Paris: Fayard, 2015), 314–315.

29. Kahn, *Generation in Turmoil,* 171–176.

30. Ibid., 178–180; NYPLA, Erich Itor Kahn Papers, box 6 (Huberman correspondence) and box 3 (Casals correspondence).

31. Kahn, *Generation in Turmoil,* 198–199.

32. NYPLA, Itor Kahn Papers, box 4, folder 2, Coyle to Kahn, November 29, 1940.

33. Richard Breitman and Alan Kraut, *American Refugee Policy and European Jewry, 1933–1945* (Bloomington: Indiana University Press, 1987) 134.

34. NYPLA, Itor Kahn Papers, box 3, folder 3, Lilly Patré (on a cure at Aix-en-Provence, staying at the Hôtel du Roi René) to Erich Itor Kahn, November 27, 1940.

35. NYPLA, Itor Kahn Papers, box 9, folder 9, Erich Kahn to Frida Kahn, April 8, 1941.

36. NYPLA, Itor Kahn Papers, box 9, folder 9, Frida Kahn to Erich Kahn, April 17, 1941. Chaminade was one of the few right-wing members of Fry's

entourage. Fry described him as a royalist admirer of and friend of Franco's. Bénédite suspected him of treason. Fry's depiction of him in his memoirs was hardly flattering: "Chaminade was certainly not very prepossessing in appearance. Short, bald, with big protruding eyes, he looked and acted like something left over from the court of Napoleon III. . . . Obsequious, luxury-loving, lazy, he gave the impression of a man who has learned to seep through life with a minimum of effort." Varian Fry, *Surrender on Demand* (Boulder, CO: Johnson Books, 1997), 102; Andy Marino, *American Pimpernel: The Story of Varian Fry* (London: Hutchinson, 1999), 214.

37. NYPLA, Itor Kahn Papers, box 9, folder 9, Erich Kahn to Frida Kahn, April 17, 1941.

38. NYPLA, Itor Kahn Papers, box 9, folder 9, Erich Kahn to Frida Kahn, April 19, 1941.

39. NYPLA, Itor Kahn Papers, box 52, folder 18, HICEM to Erich Kahn, April 30, 1941.

40. "Fernández Clérigo, Luis," in *El exilio español en México, 1939–1982* (Mexico City: Fondo de Cultura Económica, Salvat, 1982), 771.

41. Cátedra del Exilio, "Fernández Clérigo, Luis," September 17, 2012, http://exiliadosmexico.blogspot.fr/2012/09/fernandez-clerigo-luis.html.

42. "Todavía: La Resaca Roja," *ABC* (Madrid, Spain), no. 13.963 (January 24, 1941): 5, http://hemeroteca.abc.es/nav/Navigate.exe/hemeroteca/madrid/abc/1941/01/24/005.html.

43. Carlos Esplá to Mariano Gómez, Mexico, March 25, 1941, Archivo General de la Guerra Civil Española, Archivo Carlos Esplá, caja 11/9145, cited in Pascual Marzal Rodríguez, *Una historia sin justicia: Cátedra, política y magistratura en la vida de Mariano Gómez* (Valencia, Spain: Universidad de Valencia, 2009), 298. On Franco's "vindictive determination" to exact revenge on leading Spanish republicans, see Scott Soo, *The Routes to Exile: France and the Spanish Civil War Refugees, 1939–2009* (Manchester, UK: Manchester University Press, 2013), 157.

44. ANOM, 1Affpol 1297, Platon to the Embassy of Argentina, February 12, 1941; ANOM, 1Affpol 768, Marseille Office to Vichy, February 14, 1941.

45. Julián Calvo, Luis Fernández Clérigo, and Mariano Ruiz Funes, *Legislación soviética moderna*, rev. ed., trans. Miguel Luban (Mexico City: Hispano-Americana, 1947); Niccolo Machiavelli, *El príncipe*, ed. Luis Fernández Clérigo (Mexico City: Secretaría de Educación Pública, 1945); Carlos Martínez, *Crónica de una emigración (La de los Republicanos Españoles en 1939)* (Mexico City: Libro Mex, 1959), 85–86; "Fernández Clérigo, Luis," 771.

46. Bertrand Goldschmidt, *Pionniers de l'atome* (Paris: Stock, 1987), 122–123; Bertrand Goldschmidt, *Les rivalités atomiques, 1939–1966* (Paris: Fayard, 1967), 30. After the fall of France, Irène Joliot-Curie's husband, Frédéric, began negotiations with the Germans in a bid to continue using his Collège de France laboratory. Philippe Burrin explains the scientist's motives as follows: "In order to continue to work in his own laboratory, Joliot had chosen . . . the path of acceptance." Burrin adds that to Joliot "the best policy was to hold on and endure," even if that meant giving Germans access to his precious cyclotron, which helped

them with their nuclear program. Philippe Burrin, *France under the Germans: Collaboration and Compromise* (New York: New Press, 1996), 310–317.

47. Malicious rumor was a close cousin to the *bobard,* and it too enjoyed a golden era under the occupation. On the particular grip that it exerted over literary circles, see Gisèle Sapiro, *La guerre des écrivains* (Paris: Fayard, 1999), 28.

48. Michka Assayas, *Faute d'identité* (Paris: Grasset, 2011), 18, 121–124.

49. On the foundational nature of the obsession, see Tal Bruttmann, *Au Bureau des affaires juives* (Paris: La Découverte, 2006), 19.

50. Patrick Weil, *How to Be French* (Durham, NC: Duke University Press, 2008), 109–123; Claire Zalc, *Dénaturalisés: Les retraits de nationalité sous Vichy* (Paris: Le Seuil, 2016), 160–161, 170–174. The original *Habilitation à diriger des rercherches* thesis from which the book is derived contains more details on cases of Jews born in Istanbul. Claire Zalc, "Des relations de pouvoir ordinaries: Les dénaturalisations sous Vichy" (HDR for the Institut d'Etudes politiques de Paris, 2015), 228–229. Zalc accounts for the rather counterintuitive dip in denaturalization decisions in 1942 as follows: despite the denaturalization commission's having increased in numbers, it delegated and consulted far more after that point, and files were reviewed over a greater period of time, thereby slowing the denaturalization process.

51. Jacques Rémy, "Sur un cargo" (unpublished manuscript, kindly shared by his son Olivier Assayas).

52. Emmanuelle Loyer suggests that Lévi-Strauss never went through with the application, while Patrick Weil indicates that Lévi-Strauss' request for an exemption was denied by Vichy. See Emmanuelle Loyer, *Lévi-Strauss* (Paris: Flammarion, 2015), 245–247, and Weil, *How to Be French,* 89.

53. Loyer, *Lévi-Strauss,* 245–249.

54. William Smaldone, *Rudolf Hilferding: The Tragedy of a German Social Democrat* (De Kalb: Northern Illinois University Press, 2015), 185, 194–195, 200.

55. LBI, Kurt Kersten Archives, Kersten, "Das Ende Rudolf Breitscheids und Rudolf Hilferdings," 1957, 1.

56. ANF, 3W247, quoting a telegram dated August 30, 1940.

57. CRB, Varian Fry Papers, box 7, file "Breitscheid & Hilferding." Also see Fry, *Surrender on Demand,* 171–173; Marino, *American Pimpernel,* 262; and Smaldone, *Rudolf Hilferding,* 202–205. On the letter of introduction, see Daniel Bénédite, *La filière marseillaise: Un chemin vers la liberté sous l'occupation* (Paris: Clancier Guénaud, 1984), 183.

58. CRB, Fry Papers, box 7, file "Breitscheid & Hilferding"; Kersten, "Das Ende Rudolf Breitscheids und Rudolf Hilferdings," 1957, 13.

59. ANF, 3W12, Geissler, February 10, 1940, and, in the same file, note, Vichy, February 6, 1941. The latter document shows that Geissler received his orders to demand the handover of Hilferding and Breitscheid directly from Berlin, but that he had also obtained "agreement" on the matter from the armistice commission in Wiesbaden.

60. CRB, Fry Papers, box 7, file "Breitscheid & Hilferding"; Kersten, "Das Ende Rudolf Breitscheids und Rudolf Hilferdings," 13.

61. On Mehring's having translated Jean Giraudoux, Honoré de Balzac, François Villon, and Pierre de Ronsard into German, see GJECA, ERC Archives, box 2, folder 3, "Au sujet de M. Walter Mehring." On his socialist upbringing in a family that balanced Jewish traditions and secular ideals, see Hans-Peter Bayer-dörfer, "Jewish Cabaret Artists before 1933," in *Jews and the Making of Modern German Theatre,* ed. Jeanette Malkin and Freddie Rokem (Iowa City: University of Iowa Press, 2010), 143.

62. CRB, Fry Papers, box 4, Mehring to Fry, December 22, 1941.

63. GJECA, ERC Archives, box 2, folder 3, Mehring to Fry on Hôtel Beauvau letterhead, February 3, 1941.

64. ADBDR, 2M 41, Anna Esmiol file (107).

65. Pierre Radvanyi, e-mail exchange with the author, May 2016. He rightly noted that the photo was likely from well before 1940, rendering the identification exercise even more uncertain.

66. CRB, Fry Papers, box 4, Mehring to Fry, December 22, 1941.

67. Fry, *Surrender on Demand,* 174.

68. Alfred Kantorowicz, *Exil in Frankreich,* portion translated in Ulrike Voswinckel and Frank Beringer, *Exils méditerranéens: Écrivains allemands dans le sud de la France, 1933–1941* (Paris: Le Seuil, 2009), 245.

69. ANOM, 1Affpol 768, Platon to Fort-de-France, April 7, 1941.

70. ANOM, 1TEL 721, Robert to Ministry of the Colonies, March 2, 1941.

71. Richard Greeman, "The Victor Serge Affair and the French Literary Left," Encyclopedia of Trotskyism On-Line: Revolutionary History, vol. 5, no. 3, https://www.marxists.org/history/etol/revhist/backiss/vol5/no3/greeman.html.

72. Clive Bush, "Escape from Marseille: An American Story? Writing Victor Serge's, Laurette Séjourné's, Dwight and Nancy Macdonald's Balzacian Book," *Prospects* 28 (October 2004): 314.

73. Rosemary Sullivan, *Villa Air-Bel: World War II, Escape and a House in Marseille* (New York: Harper Collins, 2006), 310, 326.

74. All of the information on Lothar Popp was kindly provided by Klaus Kuhl, on the basis of his interviews with Popp's children. Unfortunately, Popp seems to have left no archives and penned no memoir.

75. Janet Biehl, *Ecology or Catastrophe: The Life of Murray Bookchin* (Oxford: Oxford University Press, 2014), 35–38.

76. "238 on Seized Ship Arrive in Port," *New York Times,* June 14, 1941, 8; Smaldone, *Rudolf Hilferding,* 200.

77. Marino, *American Pimpernel,* 275; Walter Friedlander, "Begegnungen mit Marie Juchacz in der Emigration," in *Marie Juchacz, Gründerin der Arbeiter-wohlfahrt, Leben und Werk* (Bonn, Germany: Selbstverlag, 1979), 120; Evelyne Heid, "Emil Kirschmann (1888–1949)," http://www.auswanderung-rlp.de/emigration-in-der-ns-zeit/emil-kirschmann.html.

78. Fry, *Surrender on Demand,* 188.

79. Simon Kitson, *Police and Politics in Marseille, 1936–1946* (Leiden: Brill, 2014), 111–112.

80. Jean-Marc Berlière, *Policiers français sous l'occupation* (Paris: Perrin, 2001), 31–32.

81. GJECA, ERC Archives, box 1, folder 42.

82. DEA, K. EB 73/21; copy in GJECA, ERC Archives, box 1, folder 42.

83. Anne Klein, "Conscience, Conflict and Politics: The Rescue of Political Refugees from Southern France to the United States, 1940–1942," *Leo Baeck Institute Yearbook* 43 (1998): 304.

84. GJECA, ERC Archives, box 1, folder 42, "Départ collectif d'émigrants pour les Etats-Unis," 1941.

85. Pierre Radvanyi, interview by Nicole Zand, *Le Monde,* March 19, 1991, 22. In my own interview with Pierre Radvanyi (October 27, 2013), he added that his mother was strongly persuaded of the complicity of the lady at the prefecture as well.

86. Anna Seghers, *Transit* (New York: New York Review of Books, 2013), 240.

87. Radvanyi, *Janseits des Stroms,* 66.

88. Fry, *Surrender on Demand,* 171.

89. Bénédite, *La filière marseillaise,* 182.

90. Pierre Ravanyi, e-mail to the author.

91. Victor Serge, *Mémoires d'un révolutionnaire, 1901–1941* (Paris: Le Seuil, 1978), 387.

92. MF, Germaine Krull Archives, "Camp de concentration à la Martinique," unpublished manuscript.

93. Bénédite, *La filière marseillaise,* 194.

94. Seghers, *Transit,* 195.

95. Obituary on Walter Mehring, containing long passages by him, and titled simply "Walter Mehring, 5.10.1981," held at the Friedrich-Ebert Stiftung, Bonn, Germany, kindly relayed by Alexander Boix.

96. R. M. Sallé, *70,000 kilomètres d'aventures: Notes d'un voyage Indochine-France et retour, 1940–1942* (Hanoi: Imprimerie d'Extrême-Orient, 1942), 108.

97. Bénédite, *La filière marseillaise,* 190.

98. Charles Maurras famously called the defeat of 1940 a "divine surprise," a pretext to refashion France.

99. Jackson, *France, the Dark Years,* 377. Simon Kitson suggests that many guards at Les Milles were secretly complicit with inmates. See Kitson, *Police and Politics in Marseille,* 121–122.

100. Krull, "Camp de concentration à la Martinique."

101. Victor Serge, *Carnets, 1936–1947* (Paris: Agone, 2012), 91.

102. Amos Reichman, "Jacques Schiffrin, aller sans retour: Itinéraire d'un éditeur en exil, 1940–1950" (master's II thesis, Université de Lyon/Columbia University, 2014), 13–14.

103. Ibid., 31–38.

104. André Gide and Jacques Schiffrin, *Correspondance, 1922–1950* (Paris: Gallimard, 2005), 164n1.

105. Ibid., 164–165.

106. Reichman, "Jacques Schiffrin," 51, 53, 55; Claude Lévi-Strauss, *Tristes tropiques* (Paris: Plon, 1955), 19. This was, alas, not an uncommon reaction to

seeing Jews escape France. In his journal, French chronicler Alfred Fabre-Luce railed with frightful violence against Jews escaping via Spain. Fabre-Luce, *Journal de la France, 1939–1944* (Paris: Fayard, 1969), 262.

107. On the ERC's involvement in his case, see Fry, *Surrender on Demand,* 188, and Bénédite, *La filière marseillaise,* 193.

108. Fry, *Surrender on Demand,* 177.

109. For this last example, see Diane Dosso, "Le plan de sauvetage des scientifiques français, New York, 1940–1942," *Revue de synthèse* 127, no. 2 (2006): 441.

110. Helena Benitez, *Wifredo and Helena: My Life with Wifredo Lam, 1939–1950* (Lausanne: Acatos, 1999), 53.

111. Kahn, *Generation in Turmoil,* 212.

112. Renée Poznanski, "Antisémitisme et sauvetage des juifs en France: Un duo insolite?," in *La Résistance aux genocides: De la pluralité des actes de sauvetage,* ed. Jacques Sémelin, Claire Andrieu, and Sarah Gensburger (Paris: Les Presses de Sciences Po, 2008), 99–116.

4. The Crossings

1. USHM, RG 50.030*0748, "Oral History with Diego Masson," March 12, 2014. The manifest of the *Carimaré* shows André Masson "travelling with his wife and three children" (this was an error; it should have read, "wife and two children"). USNA RG 84, box 3, "List of Passengers on the *Carimaré* Bound for the USA."

2. Jacqueline Chénieux-Gendron, *Surrealism* (New York: Columbia University Press, 1990), 2–3.

3. USHMM, RG 50.030*0748, "Oral History with Diego Masson."

4. GJECA, ERC Archives, box 1, folder 54, Warburg to George Warren, November 14, 1940.

5. GJECA, ERC Archives, box 1, folder 54, Fry to New York, April 8, 1941, and handwritten note dated March 25, 1941, beginning with "Théo va vous parler des Masson et de Lacan."

6. This was none other than German Jewish cinematographer Curt Courant, who worked with Jean Renoir on *La bête humaine,* with Alfred Hitchcock on *The Man Who Knew Too Much,* with Charles Chaplin on *Monsieur Verdoux,* with Fritz Lang on *Woman in the Moon,* and with Marcel Carné on *Le jour se lève.* Courant's presence on board is corroborated by Kay Weniger, *Lexikon der aus Deutschland und Österreich emigrierten Filmschaffenden, 1933 bis 1945* (Hamburg: Abacus Verlag, 2011), 46. On Courant in 1930s Paris, see Alastair Philips, *City of Darkness, City of Light: Emigré Filmmakers in Paris, 1929–1939* (Amsterdam: Amsterdam University Press, 2004), 46–50.

7. MF, Germaine Krull Archives, "Camp de concentration à la Martinique." On Krull, see Kim Sichel, *Germaine Krull: Photographer of Modernity* (Cambridge, MA: MIT Press, 1999), xvii–xxviii.

8. John Russell, preface to *Wifredo and Helena: My Life with Wifredo Lam, 1939–1950,* by Helena Benitez (Lausanne: Acatos, 1999), 15.

9. Daniel Bénédite, *La filière marseillaise: Un chemin vers la liberté sous l'occupation* (Paris: Clancier Guénaud, 1984), 192.

10. Richard Vinen, *The Unfree French: Life under the Occupation* (New Haven, CT: Yale University Press, 2006), 144.

11. BLY, GEN MSS 238, box 4, folder 215, "La Martinique" [1942?].

12. Victor Serge, *Memoirs of a Revolutionary*, trans. Peter Sedgick (Iowa City: University of Iowa Press, 2002), 366.

13. Nicol Smith, *Black Martinique, Red Guiana* (New York: Bobbs-Merrill, 1942), 46.

14. Walter Mehring, *Wir Müssen Weiter: Fragmente aus dem Exil* (Düsseldorf: Claassen Verlag, 1979), 94.

15. R. M. Sallé, *70,000 kilomètres d'aventures: Notes d'un voyage Indochine-France et retour, 1940–1942* (Hanoi: Imprimerie d'Extrême-Orient, 1942), 129.

16. André Breton, *Martinique, charmeuse de serpents* (Paris: 10/18, 1973), 57.

17. Jacques Rémy, "Sur un cargo" (unpublished manuscript, kindly shared by his son Olivier Assayas).

18. Ibid.

19. "French Ban Sailing of Spanish Refugees," *New York Times,* March 25, 1941, 5.

20. René Hauth to family on *Wyoming* letterhead, February 6, 1941. Document kindly shared by his family.

21. René Hauth to family on *Wyoming* letterhead, February 12, 1941.

22. Rémy, "Sur un cargo."

23. Claude Lévi-Strauss, *Tristes tropiques* (Paris: Plon, 1955), 19; Alba Romano Pace, *Jacqueline Lamba, peintre rebelle muse de l'amour fou* (Paris: Gallimard, 2010), 159.

24. Claude Lévi-Strauss, letter to the author, September 9, 1997.

25. Anna Seghers, *Transit* (New York: New York Review of Books, 2013), 234.

26. Walter Mehring, *The Lost Library: Autobiography of a Culture* (Indianapolis: Bobbs-Merrill, 1950), 266.

27. Claude Lévi-Strauss, letter to the author, September 9, 1997.

28. ADM, 2R 10491, Quenardel letter to Admiral Robert, January 3, 1941, and confidential note on the Parthos family, January 2, 1941.

29. Breton, *Martinique, charmeuse de serpents,* 67.

30. SHMV, TTD 790, "Chef de service de l'inscription maritime," May 17, 1941. Two months later, local Martinican employees of the Compagnie générale transatlantique went on strike. ADM, 5R 11691/B, Delpech report, July 12, 1941.

31. Bertrand Goldschmidt, *Pionniers de l'atome* (Paris: Stock, 1987), 123–124. Goldschmidt's presence aboard the *Carimaré* was also registered by the US consulate in Martinique. USNA, RG 84, box 3, list of *Carimaré* passengers bound for the United States.

32. Rémy, "Sur un cargo."

33. Victor Serge, *Carnets, 1936–1947* (Paris: Agone, 2012), 64–65, 82; Rémy, "Sur un cargo."

34. Serge, *Carnets,* 66.

35. Rémy, "Sur un cargo."

36. Lévi-Strauss, *Tristes tropiques,* 20; Emmanuelle Loyer, *Lévi-Strauss* (Paris: Flammarion, 2015), 257.

37. Serge, *Carnets,* 65.

38. Ibid., 71, 77, 78, 85; Benitez, *Wifredo and Helena,* 54.

39. Krull, "Camp de concentration à la Martinique."

40. Bernard Noël, *Marseille–New York, 1940–1945* (Marseille: André Dimanche, 1985), 54.

41. Pace, *Jacqueline Lamba,* 53, 94, 96, 105, 100–102, 110. From a slightly different vantage point, Breton's biographer makes the case that Lamba "felt smothered by Breton's expectations of her." Mark Polizzotti, *Revolution of the Mind: The Life of André Breton* (New York: Farrar, Straus and Giroux, 1995), 475.

42. LBI, Renée (Renata) Barth, "A Born Refugee," unpublished manuscript, 1993, 93.

43. Lévi-Strauss, *Tristes tropiques,* 22.

44. On Ylla and Lipnitzki, see Andy Marino, *American Pimpernel: The Story of Varian Fry* (London: Hutchinson, 1999), 284. On Leirens, see *Charles Leirens, 1888–1963* (Brussels: Monique Adam, 1978), 6–7. The complete list of photographers appears in an article by Fritz Neugass entitled "The Saga of the SS Winnipeg," source unknown, kindly forwarded by Peter Stein, as well as in Anne Egger, ed., *Portraits de l'exil: Paris-New York dans le sillage de Hannah Arendt* (Paris: Musée du Montparnasse, 2011), 45. On Lipnitzki's escape from Europe, see Françoise Denoyelle, *Boris Lipnitzki, le magnifique* (Paris: Nicolas Chaudun, 2013), 22.

45. My thanks to his son Peter Stein for this information. On Fred Stein and the Leica, see Dawn Feer, "Fred Stein (1909–1967): A Retrospective," in *"Escape to Life": German Intellectuals in New York: A Compendium on Exile after 1933,* ed. Eckart Goebel and Sigrid Weigel (Berlin: De Gruyter, 2012), 510–520.

46. Naomi Rosenblum, *A History of Women Photographers* (New York: Abbeville, 2000), 142–143, 310–311.

47. NGC, Ilse Bing Photographic Fonds, photos 2002.0196.39 (shows the busy deck), 2002.0196.40 (the boy with Notre-Dame de la Garde in the background), and 2002.0196.41 (the wolfhound with a luggage tag in front of the *Winnipeg* buoy).

48. Lévi-Strauss, *Tristes tropiques,* 22–24.

49. Ibid., 19.

50. Adolf Hoffmeister, *The Animals Are in Cages* (New York: Greenberg, 1941), 109–110.

51. BLY, GEN MSS 238, box 4, folder 215, "La Martinique" [1942?].

52. CRB, Varian Fry Papers, box 3, file "Jacqueline and André Breton," J. Breton [Lamba] to Fry, June 24, 1941. Note that Lamba was including her time in Martinique as part of her calculations of the voyage's length.

53. Anna Seghers to Nico Rost, February 20, 1946, in *Briefe, 1924–1952,* ed. Christiane Zehl Romero and Almut Giesecke (Berlin: Aufbau Verlag, 2008), 182.

54. GJECA, ERC Archives, box 2, folder 3, Mehring to Fry, "Thursday 6th, 1941."

55. Walter Mehring, *No Road Back* (New York: Samuel Curl, 1944), 147–149.

56. Lévi-Strauss, *Tristes tropiques*, 19.

57. Anna Pravdova, "Les artistes tchèques en France: De la fondation de la Tchécoslovaquie à la fin de la seconde guerre, quelques aspects" (PhD diss., University of Paris I/Charles University, 2004), 438, 473–475, 480–484. Also see Anna Pravdova and Tomas Winter, eds., *Senorita Franco a Krvavy pes: Malir, karikaturista a ilustrator Antonin Pelc (1895–1967)* (Prague: Narodni galerie, 2015). The dates of departure to Martinique are also recorded in NGP, Antonin Pelc Papers, calendar notebook; NGP, Drawings and Sketches Collection, K63695 IV/20, is part of the same series. The chaos in which the Czech refugees were released from the Bordeaux-area makeshift camp is recounted in Hoffmeister, *Animals Are in Cages*, 102.

58. Divis later wrote of finding inspiration from the graffiti of those who had preceded him in the cell, and of the prison's walls coming to life. Some of these sketches were terribly dark, such as Divis' piece titled "Confession of a Murderer Who Killed an Eight-Month Pregnant Woman with Eight Stabs of a Knife." Pravdova, "Les artistes tchèques en France," 476–477.

59. Alen Divis, *Kaleidoskop snů z vězení* (Prague: Kytice III, 1948).

60. On the influence of colonial-themed juvenile literature on Kafka, see John Zilkosky, *Kafka's Travels: Exoticism, Colonialism and the Traffic of Writing* (New York: Palgrave, 2003), 2, 105–111.

61. Rémy, "Sur un cargo."

62. Loyer, *Lévi-Strauss*, 255.

63. Victor Serge, *Mémoires d'un révolutionnaire, 1901–1941* (Paris: Le Seuil, 1978), 389–390.

64. Serge, *Carnets*, 66. On the Deux Magots and the Surrealists in 1939–1940, see Michel Fauré, *Histoire du surréalisme sous l'occupation* (Paris: La Table ronde, 1982), 42.

65. Benitez, *Wifredo and Helena*, 54.

66. Sallé, *70,000 kilomètres*, 112, 114, 123.

67. Ibid., 109.

68. Related by Bénédite in *La filière marseillaise*, 191, and taken up once more by Rosemary Sullivan in *Villa Air-Bel: World War II, Escape and a House in Marseille* (New York: Harper Collins, 2006), 326.

69. Bénédite, *La filière marseillaise*, 190.

70. FL, 1997 004 5180, "Rapport général de voyage du *Wyoming*," February to May 1938."

71. Lévi-Strauss, *Tristes tropiques*, 19; Loyer, *Lévi-Strauss*, 254.

72. FL, 1999 004 0911, "Plan du *Wyoming*"; SHMB, 4Q 436, "Annexe à la circulaire du 21 septembre 1939."

73. René Hauth letter to his family on *Wyoming* letterhead, February 6, 1941, and René Hauth to his cousins, card, February 6, 1941. The library comes up in his letter dated February 11, 1941.

74. FL, 1997 004 5854, "Plan du *Winnipeg.*"

75. FL, 1997 004 5174, "Rapport général de voyage du *Winnipeg*," January to May1940.

76. FL, 1997 004 6413, "Emménagement des passagers de cabines" December 23, 1941.

77. Breton, *Martinique, charmeuse de serpents,* 55–56.

78. Lévi-Strauss, *Tristes tropiques,* 19.

79. Pierre Radvanyi, *Janseits des Stroms: Erinnerungen an Meine Mutter Anna Seghers* (Berlin: Aufbau Verlag, 2005), 67.

80. Rémy, "Sur un cargo."

81. Barth, "Born Refugee," 91.

82. GJECA, ERC Archives, box 2, folder 3, Mehring to Fry, March 3, 1941.

83. Liselotte Salzburg Stein, interview transcript, kindly forwarded by Peter Stein.

84. Serge, *Carnets,* 82.

85. USHMM, RG 50.030*0748, "Oral History with Diego Masson." For the April 29 arrival date, see Chapter 2. For the April 2 departure, see Françoise Levaillant, ed., *André Masson, Correspondance, 1916–1942* (Paris: La Manufacture, 1990), 455.

86. Serge, *Carnets,* 86.

87. Krull, "Camp de concentration à la Martinique."

88. BJD, BRT 1006, Helene Holzer to Jacqueline Lamba, August 23, 1941. On the young Aube Breton's artistic skills, see Polizzotti, *Revolution of the Mind,* 489.

89. Barth, "Born Refugee," 92.

90. Serge, *Cahiers,* 85.

91. René Hauth to his loved ones on *Wyoming* letterhead, February 6, 1941; René Hauth to his cousins on *Wyoming* letterhead, February 24, 1941.

92. Serge, *Carnets,* 79–80; Rémy, "Sur un cargo."

93. FL, 1999 004 0796, Neptune-adorned certificate for passing the "tropiques."

94. On Fendler being on board, see Marino, *American Pimpernel,* 284. On the concert, see Sallé, *70,000 kilomètres,* 123, 129. On Wolff, who was also the spouse of photographer Ilse Bing, see Ruth Gillen, ed., *The Writings and Letters of Konrad Wolff* (Westport, CT: Greenwood, 2000), xxi–xxvi. On German musicians, including Fendler, Wolff, and Kahn, taking refuge in France in the 1930s, see Anna Langenbruch, *Topographien musikalischen Handelns im Pariser Exil* (New York: Georg Olms Verlag, 2014).

95. René Hauth to his wife, Marguerite, Martinique, April 19, 1941; Serge, *Carnets,* 80.

96. Rémy, "Sur un cargo."

97. Serge, *Carnets,* 80.

98. "238 on Seized Ship Arrive in Port," *New York Times,* June 14, 1941, 8.

99. Breton had been playing these games for some time, including at the Villa Air-Bel in Marseille. See Polizzotti, *Revolution of the Mind,* 447, 489, and Sullivan, *Villa Air-Bel,* 253.

100. Polizzotti, *Revolution of the Mind,* 502.

101. Serge, *Carnets,* 85.

102. Michael Miller, *Europe and the Maritime World: A Twentieth-Century History* (Cambridge: Cambridge University Press, 2012), 283.

103. Fitzroy Baptiste, *War, Cooperation and Conflict: The European Possessions in the Caribbean, 1939–1945* (Westport, CT: Greenwood, 1988), 64.

104. ANOM, 1TEL 701, Platon to Robert, January 29, 1941, announcing the German Armistice Commission's decision; Armand Nicolas, *Histoire de la Martinique,* vol. 3, *De 1939 à 1971* (Paris: L'Harmattan, 1998), 16.

105. ANOM, 1TEL 688, Bressoles to Bordeaux (where the French government had fled from Paris), June 17, 1940.

106. USNA, RG 59, box 5192, document 851B.00/12, Martinique to Secretary of State, July 27, 1940.

107. ANOM, 1TEL 682, Vichy to Admiral Robert, October 20, 1940.

108. "La flotte anglaise lève le blocus de la Martinique," *Le petit parisien,* November 24, 1940; "La Martinique n'est plus bloquée," *Le Réveil du Nord,* November 30, 1940.

109. FCDG, F22/18, dossier 3, "Liste des Français internés," May 16, 1941.

110. ANOM, 1Affpol 767, dossier 3, Lieutenant Bullier's report on postal intercepts for April 1941.

111. ANOM, 1TEL 682, Platon to Fort-de-France, September 10, 1940.

112. Barth, "Born Refugee," 90–93; Serge, *Carnets,* 57.

113. René Hauth, letters on *Wyoming* letterhead to his loved ones, February 6 and February 11, 1941.

114. René Hauth to his loved ones on *Wyoming* letterhead, February 24, 1941.

115. BLY, GEN MSS 238, box 4, folder 185, Victor Serge, "La guerre des océans," typescript, June 10, 1942.

116. ANOM, 1Affpol 768, telegrams on the arrival of the German submarine and the amputation of the sailor from Robert to Vichy dated February 17, 21, and 23, 1942 (Vichy was alerted of the submarine's arrival on February 17; von dem Borne was dropped off in Martinique on February 21 and amputated that same day.)

117. SHMV, TTE 33, Washington, February 28, 1942.

118. ANF, 40AJ/1265, movements of French commercial shipping, 1940–1941.

119. Sallé, *70,000 kilomètres,* 113.

120. Roger Jaffray, *La Compagnie générale transatlantique armateur au cabotage caraïbe* (Paris: Sciences, Techniques et Patrimoine, 2012), 21.

121. Miller, *Europe and the Maritime World,* 282.

122. This was the case of the set I perused in the University of Glasgow Archives and Special Collections (UGASC).

123. FL, 1999 004 0912, detailed report by commandant Paul Legrand on the sinking of the *Wyoming.*

124. Jean-Michel Guiraud, "La culture refuge," in *Varian Fry à Marseille, 1940–1941* (Arles: Actes Sud, 2000), 11.

125. Mehring, *Lost Library,* 11–18. Hoffmann was murdered at Auschwitz in 1944.

126. Lisa Moses Leff, *The Archive Thief: The Man Who Salvaged French Jewish History in the Wake of the Holocaust* (Oxford: Oxford University Press, 2015), 2–5, 10, 15, 21, 25, 49–51, 53, 55, 56–57, 61–62, 65–68, 71.

127. ANOM, 1TEL 701, Platon to Fort-de-France, January 30, 1941.

128. ANOM, 1TEL 721, Fort-de-France to Platon, January 22, 1941.

129. FCDG, F22/18, Pujol report, 9.

130. ANOM, 1TEL 701, Platon to Martinique and Guadeloupe, January 31, 1941.

131. ANOM, 1Affpol 767, contrôle postal, March 1941, 16.

132. ANOM, 1TEL 701, Platon to Robert, February 24, 1941.

133. BLY, GEN MSS 238, box 4, folder 215, "La Martinique" [1942?].

134. LBI, Kurt Kersten Archives, "Flucht aus Frankreich," 11–16.

135. Barth, "Born Refugee," 92.

136. Serge, *Carnets,* 60–61, 70.

137. Ibid.

138. Ibid., 87.

139. Lévi-Strauss, *Tristes tropiques,* 24.

5. Wartime Martinique

1. BLY, GEN MSS 238, box 4, folder 215, "La Martinique," [1942].

2. Along with Dakar, Saigon, and Diego-Suarez. See D. Suvélor, "La Martinique, un aspect de son équipement économique: Port et tourisme," *La revue des Ambassades,* July 1939, 25.

3. Théodore Baude, *Fragments d'histoire, ou Hier et aujourd'hui* (Fort-de-France: Imprimerie officielle, 1940), 31.

4. ANOM, AGEFOM 123, dossier 37, urbanisme, "L'urbanisme en Martinique," 6. The figure for 1940 appears in Baude, *Fragments d'histoire,* 14.

5. Pierre-Rodolphe Dareste, *Traité de droit colonial* (Paris: Imprimerie Robaudy, 1931), 2:559–560. My thanks to Yerri Urban for this lead.

6. Monique Milia-Marie-Luce, "L'immigration en Martinique pendant l'entre-deux-guerres," *Hommes et migrations* 1274 (July–August 2008): 36–46.

7. BLY, GEN MSS 238, box 4 folder 215, "La Martinique" [1942?].

8. See Eric Jennings, *Free French Africa in World War II: The African Resistance* (Cambridge: Cambridge University Press, 2015).

9. This power struggle is related in great detail by Rouyer in two documents contained in ANOM, 1Affpol 768: secret note, September 9, 1940, and "Extraits de carnets de notes du Capitaine Rouyer," October 20, 1940. On Robert's turnaround, his "eight days too late" comment, and the rumors of foul play, see Jean-Baptiste Bruneau, *La Marine de Vichy aux Antilles, juin 1940–juillet 1943* (Paris: Les Indes Savantes, 2014), 19–24. On Chomereau-Lamotte, see Armand Nicolas, *Histoire de la Martinique,* vol. 3, *De 1939 à 1971* (Paris: L'Harmattan, 1998), 23.

10. ANOM, 1Affpol 768, secret note, September 9, 1940.

11. ANOM, DAM 146, telegram 1766, Fort-de-France to Vichy, September 6, 1941.

12. Carrie Gibson, *Empire's Crossroads: A History of the Caribbean from Columbus to the Present Day* (New York: Atlantic Monthly Press, 2014), 258.

13. Kristen Stromberg Childers, *Seeking Imperialism's Embrace: National Identity, Decolonization and Assimilation in the French Caribbean* (Oxford: Oxford University Press, 2016), 13.

14. A stash of such requests, including one for projectors and ball bearings dated March 12, 1941, lies in ADM, 7R9100.

15. Humberto Garcia-Muñiz and Rebeca Campo, "French and American Imperial Accommodation in the Caribbean during World War II," in *Colonial Crucible: Empire in the Making of the Modern American State,* ed. Alfred McCoy and Francisco A. Scarano (Madison: University of Wisconsin Press, 2009), 448.

16. NAUK, FO 371-32017, Mack's January 22, 1942 annotations of a January 10, 1942 document titled "Trade with Martinique and Guadeloupe."

17. NAUK, FO 371-32058, document dated May 1942.

18. ANOM, 1TEL 721, Fort-de-France to Vichy, January 9, 1941, and, in the same carton, Robert to Darlan, April 12 and 26, 1941.

19. ANOM, 1TEL 721, Robert to Casablanca, April 11, 1941.

20. SHMV, TTE 33, "Historique et description de la crise de mai 1942 aux Antilles."

21. On this British-Dutch decision, see NAUK, FO 371-32058, Ministry of Economic Warfare, November 26, 1942.

22. SHMT, 18S 14, green notebook, 23.

23. See Léo Elisabeth, "Vichy aux Antilles et en Guyane, 1940–1943," *Outre-mers* 342–343 (2004): 155.

24. SHMT, 18S 14, green notebook, 39, 47.

25. Camille Chauvet, "La Martinique pendant la deuxième guerre mondiale" (PhD diss., University of Toulouse, Le Mirail, 1985), 134.

26. NAUK, FO 371, Downing Street, January 1942.

27. USNA, RG 59, box 5196 document FW 851B.24/164, L. Van Haecht to the Treasury Department, April 29, 1943.

28. SHMV, TTE 32, "Affaires économiques, rapport mensuel d'activité," February 10, 1941 (refers to a vain request to Indochina from December 1940).

29. SHMT, 18S 14, green notebook, 48.

30. USNA, RG 84, box 1, V. Harwood Blocker to the Secretary of State, October 19, 1940. On the dates of cruise liners (December–March), see ANOM, AGEFOM 123, dossier 32, port de Fort-de-France, document dated November 30, 1936.

31. "En vue d'un retour à la terre," *La Paix,* August 24, 1940, 1.

32. SHMV, TTE 32, "Programme de principe de Radio Martinique."

33. Ads in the January 24, 1942, issue of *Le Courrier des Antilles.*

34. Gibson, *Empire's Crossroads,* 262.

35. ANOM, 1Affpol 768, bulletin 4, contrôle postal.

36. ANOM, 1Affpol 767, contrôle postal, March 1941 report, 2. The topic comes up again in another report from that month, which mentions correspondents displaying "great prudence" in their written exchanges. ANOM, 1Affpol 2007, Secretary of State to the Colonies, March 3, 1941.

37. ANOM, 2 APOM 7, Devouton to Admiral Robert, April 19, 1941. On the housing crunch in metropolitan France during the war, and the tendency to blame refugees for it, see Shannon Fogg, *The Politics of Everyday Life in Vichy France: Foreigners, Undesirables and Strangers* (Cambridge: Cambridge University Press, 2009), 112. On massive increases in the cost of living in wartime mainland France, see Lynne Taylor, *Between Resistance and Collaboration: Popular Protest in Northern France, 1940–1945* (New York: St. Martin's, 2000), 43.

38. ADM, 1M3465, report on "massive purchases," signed Yven, May 6, 1941.

39. A large file in the Martinique archives contains the legal documents interning dozens of political prisoners, referring to this September 13, 1940, measure. ADM, 1R7187.

40. FCDG, F22/17, dossier 3, undated note by F. Augereau-Lara, the director of the newspaper *L'Action*; ADM, 1M3670, Bressoles, January 6, 1941; USNA, RG 59, box 5193, document 851B.00/48, January 8, 1941; ADM, 1M3670, internment of Jean Toulouse at Balata, document signed Bressoles, January 6, 1941. On the Gaullist material in Reynal's house, see ANOM, 1Affpol 767, Nicol to Platon, July 30, 1941, and ANOM, 1TEL 723, telegram 877, July 30, 1941. Also see Nicolas, *Histoire de la Martinique*, 66.

41. ANOM, DAM 269, "Extrait de l'avis general de la commission préparatoire d'épuration de la Martinique concernant des attentats aux libertés individuelles," signed H. Heimburger (n.d., p. 4). The record of Minatchy's internment in 1941 appears in ADM, 1M3670, Nicol's note on "internés administratifs," November 5, 1941.

42. Chauvet, "La Martinique," 92n9.

43. ANOM, 1Affpol 769, arrêté, June 5, 1941.

44. Dominique Julien, "Bug-Jargal: La Révolution et ses doubles," *Littérature* 139, no. 3 (2005): 78–92.

45. André Breton, "Début d'une conférence à la Martinique," in *Oeuvres completes* (Paris: Gallimard, 1999), 3:210.

46. SHMV, 1K518, Bouvil report, November 26, 1940.

47. Daniel Maximin, *L'isolé soleil* (Paris: Le Seuil, 1981), 152.

48. Frantz Fanon, *Pour la révolution africaine (écrits politiques)* (Paris: Maspero, 1964), 28, 32.

49. Ibid., 40.

50. USNA, RG 59, box 5192, document 851B.00/29, memo, November 13, 1940.

51. ANOM, 1Affpol 767, Devouton, April 11, 1941.

52. Dominique Chathuant, "La Guadeloupe dans l'obédiance de Vichy", *Bulletin de la Société d'Histoire de la Guadeloupe* 91 (1992): 22–25

53. ANOM, 2 APOM 7, Devouton, February 24, 1941.

54. Elisabeth, "Vichy aux Antilles," 164.

55. Chauvet, "La Martinique," 100.

56. ANOM, 1Affpol 767, decree, April 8, 1941, and correspondence from Nicol to Platon.

57. On Vichy's anti-Semitic measures in Guadeloupe, see Eric Jennings, *Vichy in the Tropics: Pétain's National Revolution in Madagascar, Guadeloupe and Indochina* (Stanford, CA: Stanford University Press, 2001), 95–96. On Martinique, see Eric Jennings and Sébastien Verney, "Vichy aux colonies: L'exportation des statuts des juifs dans l'empire," *Archives juives* 41 (Spring 2008): 111–113, and William F. S. Miles, "Caribbean Hybridity in Martinique," in *The Jewish Diaspora in Latin America and the Caribbean,* ed. Kristin Ruggiero (Eastborne: Sussex Academic, 2005), 140–143.

58. Jennings and Verney, "Vichy aux colonies," 112–113; Miles, "Caribbean Hybridity in Martinique," 143.

59. Fitzroy Baptiste, "Le régime de Vichy en Martinique," *Les cahiers du CERAG* (Cahiers du Centre d'études régionales Antilles-Guyane) 30 (November 1979): 17, 30n81.

60. ANOM, 1Affpol 767, Devouton, January 21, 1941.

61. SHMV, TTE 32, Battet, August 7, 1941.

62. SHMV, TTD 790, ronde, October 4, 1942.

63. Frantz Fanon, *Black Skin, White Masks,* (New York: Grove Press, 1994) ch. 2; Albert James Arnold, "Frantz Fanon, Lafcadio Hearn et la supercherie de Mayotte Capécia: De la parabole biblique à *Je suis Martiniquaise,*" *Revue de littérature comparée* 305 (2003): 35–48; Christiane Makward, *Mayotte Capécia, ou l'aliénation selon Fanon* (Paris: Karthala, 1999); Myriam Cottias and Madeleine Dobie, *Relire Mayotte Capécia: Une femme des Antilles dans l'espace colonial français (1916–1955)* (Paris: Armand Colin, 2012).

64. Mayotte Capécia, *La Négresse blanche,* in Cottias and Dobie, *Relire Mayotte Capécia,* 210.

65. Cottias and Dobie, *Relire Mayotte Capécia,* 25.

66. Mayotte Capécia, *Je suis Martiniquaise,* in Cottias and Dobie, *Relire Mayotte Capécia,* 139.

67. Ibid., 135. The breadfruit and avocado passage appears in the authors' introduction, ibid., 39.

68. Ibid., 140, 151.

69. Cottias and Dobie, *Relire Mayotte Capécia,* 17.

70. Eric Jennings, "La dissidence aux Antilles, 1940–1943," *Vingtième siècle* 68 (October–December 2000): 60; Richard Burton, "Vichysme et Vichystes à la Martinique," *Les cahiers du CERAG* (Cahiers du Centre d'études régionales Antilles-Guyane) 34 (February 1978): 1–101.

71. Elisabeth, "Vichy aux Antilles," 162.

72. SHDG, 972^{E}33, "rapport sur l'état d'esprit de la population," signed Delpech, March 9, 1942.

73. SHDG, 972^{E}33, Delpech, May 30, 1941.

74. FCDG, F22/18, dossier 3, Pujol journal, September 1940.

75. James Scott, *Weapons of the Weak: Everyday Forms of Peasant Resistance* (New Haven, CT: Yale University Press, 1985); James Scott, *Domination and the Arts of Resistance* (New Haven, CT: Yale University Press, 1990), xiii.

A case could be made that such oppositional practices persist to this day, for instance, the decapitation of the statue of Empress Josephine in Fort-de-France in 1991 (Josephine was the plantation-born wife of Napoleon I, who reestablished slavery in the French Caribbean). On this topic, see William F. S. Miles, "Schizophrenic Island, Fifty Years after Fanon: Martinique, the Pent-Up 'Paradise,'" *International Journal of Francophone Studies* 15, no. 1 (2002): 26–27.

76. SHDG, 972^{E}35, report signed Delpech, June 15, 1943. Other practices involved listening to Allied radio or ridiculing the symbols of the new regime. On the former, see Dennis McEnnerney, "Frantz Fanon, the Resistance and the Emergence of Identity Politics," in *The Color of Liberty: Histories of Race in France*, ed. Sue Peabody and Tyler Stovall (Durham, NC: Duke University Press, 2003), 261. On the latter, see Jennings, "La dissidence aux Antilles," 57–58

77. SHDG, 972^{E}42, report signed Eychenne, December 18, 1940, featuring a photo of Didnoit. Gachette's sentence to the penal colony of French Guiana is related in ADM, 1R7187, decision by Governor Nicol dated September 13, 1941.

78. SHMV, 1K518, "Martinique, Conditions There," police headquarters, Saint Lucia, November 2, 1940.

79. Matthew J. Smith, *Liberty, Fraternity, Exile: Haiti and Jamaica after Emancipation* (Chapel Hill: University of North Carolina Press, 2014).

80. SHMV, 1K518, des Etages report following his arrival in St. Lucia on February 9, 1941 (by canoe).

81. ANOM, 173 APOM 1, multiple reports on des Etages. On his internment aboard the warship, see ADM, 1R7187, decision by Governor Nicol, March 10, 1941.

82. FCDG, F22/17, dossier 3, Pujol report, 12.

83. SHDG, 972^{E}32, Captain Noël to the Gendarmerie, February 20, 1941.

84. Lucien-René Abenon and Henry Joseph, *Les dissidents des Antilles dans les Forces françaises libres combattantes, 1940–1945* (Fort-de-France: Désormeaux, 1999), 37–38.

85. ANOM, 173 APOM 1, General Henri Jacomy to Governor Ponton, December 17, 1943.

86. SHMV, 1K518, reimbursement claims for lodging refugees in St Lucia (among those listed: Elise Denis and child [February 1943], and Madame Lardeaux and child [May 1943]).

87. On deserting Vichy sailors, see Stromberg Childers, *Seeking Imperialism's Embrace*, 35.

88. ADM, 1M3670, General Picard report, July 19, 1940.

89. SHMV, TTE 32, Vanhuysen note, relayed by Castaing, June 1, 1941.

90. Jean Massip, "La Résistance aux Antilles," *Revue de Paris*, May 1945, 65.

91. ANOM, 1Affpol 2293, dossier 13, des Etages report, 1.

92. SHMV, 1K518, René Essen (spelling uncertain) testimony, February 3, 1941.

93. Chauvet, "La Martinique," 184.

94. LBI, Kurt Kersten Archives, "Der Tod auf der Insel," unpublished and undated manuscript, 23. Courtesy of the Leo Baeck Institute, New York.

95. Massip, "La Résistance aux Antilles," 65.

96. SHMV, 1K518, Joseph Paquemar file.

97. "Conditions in Martinique: Czechs Tell of Escapes," *Port-of-Spain Gazette,* January 26, 1941, 1.

98. Abenon and Joseph, *Les dissidents des Antilles,* 35.

99. SHMV, 1K518.

100. "Cadence Lypso Classics," mix by djeasy, https://www.youtube.com /watch?v=3cv2QVJfoEA. My thanks to Felix Germain for this link.

101. ADM, 1R10185, dossier 23, letter from General Jacomy, November 27, 1943. On Joseph's age, see Abenon and Joseph, *Les dissidents des Antilles,* 37.

102. Abenon and Joseph, *Les dissidents des Antilles,* 32–33.

103. David Macey, *Frantz Fanon: A Biography* (New York: Picador, 2000), 87; Alice Charki, *Frantz Fanon: Portrait* (Paris: Seuil, 2000), 21–23. Macey claims that Fanon was seventeen at the time of his departure, Charki eighteen.

104. Ibid.

105. ANOM, 173 APOM 1, confidential note for Lieutenant Noirel.

106. SHMT, 18S 14, green notebook, 51; ADM, 47 Isaac Alexandre Fontaine, *Le ralliement de la Martinique à la France libre,* 14.

107. Emmanuel Honorien, *Le ralliement des Antilles à la France combattante,* Martinique, (Fort-de-France: Imprimerie officielle, 1945), 7–16.

108. SHMT, 18S 14, green notebook, 54, 56.

109. Communiqué reproduced in Marie-Hélène Léotin, *La Martinique pendant la seconde guerre mondiale, 1939–1945* (Fort-de-France: Archives départementales, 1993), 102.

110. ADN, 378PO/C/2/127, Antilles, March 1946.

111. SHMT, 18S 14, green booklet, 55.

112. ANOM, 173 APOM 1, Jacommy to Ponton, December 28, 1943.

113. ANOM, 173 APOM 1, Ponton to the Ministry of the Colonies in Algiers, December 30, 1943.

114. "Légionnaires et volontaires," *Justice* (Fort-de-France), June 10, 1944, 2. Lucien-René Abenon noted a similar social diversity among friends of the Legion in Guadeloupe. See his *Petite histoire de la Guadeloupe* (Paris: L'Harmattan, 1992), 181–182.

6. Snake Charmers in a Viper's Nest

1. Claude Lévi-Strauss, *Tristes tropiques* (Paris: Plon, 1955), 24.

2. André Breton, *Martinique, charmeuse de serpents* (Paris: 10/18, 1973), 60.

3. MF, Germaine Krull Archives, "Camp de concentration à la Martinique."

4. LBI, Renée (Renata) Barth, "A Born Refugee," unpublished manuscript, 1993, 94. Courtesy of the Leo Baeck Institute, New York.

5. Frantz Fanon, *Pour la révolution africaine (écrits politiques)* (Paris: Maspero, 1964), 33.

6. Lévi-Strauss, *Tristes tropiques,* 23.

7. Breton, *Martinique, charmeuse de serpents,* 59.

8. ADG, SC 3974, "Contrôle des passagers en transit ou arrivant à la colonie," Robert to Sorin, March 23, 1941.

9. SHMV, TTE 32, Affaires coloniales.

10. Armand Nicolas, *Histoire de la Martinique*, vol. 3, *De 1939 à 1971* (Paris: L'Harmattan, 1998), 49.

11. SHMV, TTE 32, Affaires coloniales, form directed at incoming refugees.

12. ADM, 4N4590/A.

13. ANOM, 1TEL 688, telegrams, Bressoles, June 17 and July 16, 1940. In August 1940, an Italian national by the name of Annichiarico complained bitterly of having "suffered" at the Lazaret, adding that German nationals had received better treatment than Italian ones. ADM, 2R4858, intercepted letter from Annichiarico to Havana, August 28, 1940.

14. USNA, RG 84, French West Indies 1941, box 3800, US Consulate to US Secretary of State, Fort-de-France, March 21, 1941.

15. Ibid.

16. SHMV, TTE 32, Rear Admiral to the Governor of Martinique, April 24, 1941, regarding the arrival of foreigners.

17. Breton, *Martinique, charmeuse de serpents,* 60.

18. ADM, dossier de documentation 47, Isaac Alexandra Fontaine, 1981, 9.

19. Breton, *Martinique, charmeuse de serpents,* 62. On another such euphemism, see Max-Pol Fouchet, *Wifredo Lam* (New York: Rizzoli, 1976), 172.

20. SHMV, TTE 32, Pelliet note on the arrival of the *Winnipeg,* May 24, 1941.

21. ANOM, 1Affpol 767, postal control for April 1941, 4.

22. ADM, 1M3670, Governor Nicol's instructions, March 16, 1941.

23. Krull, "Camp de concentration à la Martinique."

24. Ibid.

25. Ibid., photo legends.

26. Gabrielle Saure, *Carl Heidenreich* (New York: Goethe-Institut, 2004), 64–65 (quote on 64).

27. The dates are from Pelc's notebook in NGP, Antonin Pelc Papers, calendar/notebook.

28. ADM, 5R11691/B, report on Bernard, May 28, 1941.

29. Krull, "Camp de concentration à la Martinique."

30. Pelc's experiences in these internment locales in France are detailed in NGP, Pelc Papers, calendar/notebook.

31. Barth, "Born Refugee," 95.

32. ADM, 4N4590/A, blueprint for the Lazaret, 1905.

33. Barth, "Born Refugee," 95.

34. Anna Seghers to F. C. Weiskopf, May 2, 1941, in *Briefe, 1924–1952,* ed. Christiane Zehl Romero and Almut Giesecke (Berlin: Aufbau Verlag, 2008), 467.

35. Victor Serge, *Carnets, 1936–1947* (Paris: Agone, 2012), 93.

36. Breton, *Martinique, charmeuse de serpents,* 60–61.

37. Nicol Smith, *Black Martinique, Red Guiana* (New York: Bobbs-Merrill, 1942), 31, 41 (quotation on 41).

38. Krull, "Camp de concentration à la Martinique."

39. Victor Serge, *Mémoires d'un révolutionnaire, 1901–1941* (Paris: Le Seuil, 1978), 366.

40. Krull, "Camp de concentration à la Martinique."

41. USNA, RG 84, French West Indies 1941, box 3800, US Consulate to US Secretary of State, Fort-de-France, March 21, 1941.

42. Barth, "Born Refugee," 96.

43. Krull, "Camp de concentration à la Martinique."

44. BLY, GEN MSS 238, box 4, folder 215, "La Martinique" [1942?].

45. Krull, "Camp de concentration à la Martinique"; Art Spiegelman, *Maus,* (New York: Pantheon Books, 1986) 2:98–100.

46. SHMV, TTD 790, "Accident de la vedette *Florida,*" May 28, 1941.

47. ADM, 1M3670, report on Balata, December 20, 1940.

48. Breton, *Martinique, charmeuse de serpents,* 61; Helena Benitez, *Wifredo and Helena: My Life with Wifredo Lam, 1939–1950* (Lausanne: Acatos, 1999), 54.

49. Breton, *Martinique, charmeuse de serpents,* 62.

50. Bertrand Goldschmidt, *Pionniers de l'atome* (Paris: Stock, 1987), 124.

51. Bertrand Goldschmidt, *Les rivalités atomiques, 1939–1966* (Paris: Fayard, 1967), 30.

52. Documents kindly shared by Jacques Rémy's son Olivier Assayas.

53. ANOM, 1TEL 701, Platon to Robert, April 15, 1941; ANOM, 1Affpol 768, Darlan to Platon, March 29, 1941.

54. ANOM, 1Affpol 768, Platon to Darlan, May 15, 1941.

55. Smith, *Black Martinique, Red Guiana,* 31. On the end of dancing and of the Carnaval, see Victor Saint-Cyr's testimony in *Les cahiers du CERAG* (Centre d'études régionales Antilles-Guyane) 30 (November 1979): 53, as well as Nicolas, *Histoire de la Martinique,* 45.

56. On the ban in metropolitan France, see Robert Gildea, *Marianne in Chains: Daily Life in the Heart of France during the German Occupation* (New York: Picador, 2003), 117.

57. Daphné Victor and Stéphane Dugast, *Paul-Emile Victor: J'ai toujours vécu demain* (Paris: Robert Laffont, 2015), 15–16.

58. Thierry Fournier, "Paul-Emile Victor, 1907–1995: Biographie d'un explorateur polaire" (thesis, Ecole des Chartes, 2001), chapter on the Second World War kindly made available by its author; see also Nicolas, *Histoire de la Martinique,* 36.

59. Fournier, "Paul-Emile Victor," chapter on the Second World War.

60. Nicolas, *Histoire de la Martinique,* 37.

61. Victor and Dugast, *Paul-Emile Victor,* 220.

62. Paul-Emile Victor to his parents, March 3, 1941. Text kindly forwarded by Victor biographer Thierry Fournier.

63. USNA, RG 84, box 3, Paul-Emile Victor file.

64. Paul-Emile Victor to his parents, January 24, 1941.

65. ANOM, 1Affpol 1297, Platon to Foreign Ministry, January 9, 1941.

66. Jean Mayer, "André Mayer, a Biographical Sketch," *Journal of Nutrition,* 99, no.1 (August 1969): 3–8.

67. Quoted in Diane Dosso, "Le plan de sauvetage des scientifiques français, New York, 1940–1942," *Revue de synthèse* 127, no. 2 (2006): 443.

68. Emmanuelle Loyer, *Paris à New York: Intellectuels et artistes français en exil, 1940–1947* (Paris: Grasset, 2005), 24.

69. Dosso, "Le plan," 443.

70. ANOM, DAM 269, "Extrait de l'avis de la commission préparatoire d'épuration de la Martinique concernant Mademoiselle Flament, dite Caron," signed Heimburger. Elements of Flament's application for a US visa are contained in USNA, RG 84, box 3, Malige to Fabrizi (Otis Elevator Co.), July 26, 1941.

71. ANOM, 1TEL 701, Platon to Fort-de-France, January 25, 1941.

72. On the alleged clandestine nature of their trip, see ANOM, 1Affpol 767, dossier 3, telegram, Governor Bressoles to Minister of the Colonies, Vichy. On their internment at the Fort Napoléon, see SHMV, TTE 32, Capitain Battet to Capitaine de frégate, transfer of administrative internees to Fort-Napoléon in Les Saintes, Fort-de-France, January 22, 1941.

73. ANOM, 2 APOM 7, Inspector Devouton, Fort-de-France, to Ministry of the Colonies, Vichy, May 3, 1941.

74. Fitzroy Baptiste, "Le régime de Vichy en Martinique," *Les cahiers du CERAG* (Centre d'études régionales Antilles-Guyane) 30 (November 1979): 17.

75. ANOM, 1TEL 701, Platon to Fort-de-France, February 12, 1941, telegram concerning Walter Ehrlich; ANOM, 1TEL 723, Nicol to Platon, February 15, 1941.

76. Thereafter, under Free French authority, the *Cuba* would transport troops and prisoners for the duration of the war, until it was sunk off Bambridge by a German submarine on April 6, 1945.

77. ADG SC 3974, Robert order on the expulsion of foreigners, March 11, 1941.

78. ANOM, 1Affpol 768, Platon to Robert, May 19, 1941; ANOM, 1TEL 701, Platon to Robert, May 19, 1941 (telegram 911).

79. Renzo Marinelli, "Montagnana Mario," in *Il movimento operaio italiano: Dizionario biografico, 1853–1953*, ed. Franco Andreucci and Tommaso Detti (Rome: Editori riuniti, 1977), 3:550–551; Giorgina Arian Levi and Manfredo Montagnana, *I Montagnana: Una famiglia ebraica piemontese e il movimento operaio (1914–1948)* (Florence: Editrice La Giuntina, 2000), 54–56; Claudio Rabaglino, "Montagnana, Mario," *Treccani biografico,* 2011, http://www.treccani.it/enciclopedia/mario-montagnana_(Dizionario_Biografico)/.

80. Levi and Montagnana, *I Montagnana,* 55–103; Rabaglino, "Montagnana, Mario."

81. Levi and Montagnana, *I Montagnana,* 104–108.

82. Mario Montagnana to Giorgina Levi and Enzo Arian, September 18, 1941, quoted in ibid., 108.

83. Ibid., 108–109.

84. USNA, RG 84, French West Indies, box 3, Otto Borchardt to the US Consulate in Marseille, March 22, 1941.

85. ANOM, 1Affpol 767, postal censorship for March 1941, 21, letter sent from the Dominican Republic on March 6, 1941.

86. ANOM, 173 APOM 1, Ponton to Algiers, December 24, 1944.

87. USNA, RG 84, French West Indies, box 1, Fort-de-France, Martinique, subject "Foreign Element, Martinique," December 19, 1940.

88. Ibid.

89. Ibid.

90. USNA, RG 84, French West Indies, box 3, document 811.11, Albert Steinem to Harwood Blocker, February 24, 1941.

91. USNA, RG 84, French West Indies, box 3, document 811.11, "Illegal Entry into the United States," April 4, 1941.

92. SHMV, TTD 790, passenger list for the New York–bound *Guadeloupe,* April 9, 1941.

93. USNA, RG 84, French West Indies, box 3, document 800, detention of Spanish refugees of SS *Wyoming* at Martinique, US consulate at Martinique to the Secretary of State, March 21, 1941.

94. USNA, RG 59, box 5193, document 851B.00/35, report from March 19, 1941.

95. USNA, RG 84, French West Indies, 1940–1941, box 1, Malige to Samuel Reber at the Department of State, July 12, 1941.

96. USNA, RG 84, French West Indies, box 3, 811.11, telegram, Malige to State Department, May 20, 1941.

97. Board of Immigration Appeals, Executive Office for Immigration Review, U.S. Department of Justice, 1 IN Dec. 154 (B.I.A. 1941), https://casetext.com/case/in-the-matter-of-w-1.

98. Anna Seghers to Bodo Uhse, June 1, 1941, in *Briefe,* 106–107.

99. US consul Marcel Malige referred to both men being "of the Jewish race" in his dispatch to the US State Department, January 28, 1942. USNA, RG 84, French West Indies 1941, box 6, 811.11. However, subsequent correspondence mentions only Breuer as Jewish.

100. LBI, Kurt Kersten Archives, correspondence file. On the ban by the Nazis, then the German Democratic Republic, see Jean Sigmann's (harsh) review in *Annales, histoire, sciences sociales* 12, no. 4 (October–December 1957): 702.

101. DEA, Nachlaß W. Stemfeld EB 75/177. The presence of Breuer and Kersten on board the *Dreyfus* is confirmed in USNA, RG 84, box 1, "Foreign Element, Martinique," December 19, 1940.

102. LBI, Kersten Archives, "Der Tod auf der Insel," manuscript, 2, 24, 39, 55. Courtesy of the Leo Baeck Institute, New York.

103. LBI, Kersten Archives, "Der Tod auf der Insel." The date of the transfer to Balata is indicated in ADM, 4M997, Friedlander file.

104. LBI, Kersten Archives, "Der Tod auf der Insel." The quinine shortage is described in ANOM, 1TEL 702, Platon to Fort-de-France, October 20, 1941.

105. LBI, Kersten Archives, "Der Tod auf der Insel," 137 (emphasis mine). Courtesy of the Leo Baeck Institute, New York.

106. USNA, RG 84, French West Indies, box 3, Friedlander file, letter from the Secretary of State, June 13, 1941.

107. USNA, RG 84, box 6, 811.11, Malige to US State Department, January 28, 1942.

108. USNA, RG 84, box 6, Pelliet to Robert, January 5, 1942.

109. LBI, Kersten Archives, "Der Tod auf der Insel," 122. Courtesy of the Leo Baeck Institute, New York.

110. Smith, *Black Martinique, Red Guiana,* 41.

111. LBI, Kersten Archives, "Der Tod auf der Insel," 26, 124.

112. Barth, "Born Refugee," 96–97.

113. LBI, Kersten Archives, "Der Tod auf der Insel," 17. Courtesy of the Leo Baeck Institute, New York.

114. SHDG, 972^E, 43, Police Commissioner Maurice, Fort-de-France, to Rear Admiral Battet, June 20, 1941.

115. SHDG, 972^E, 26–43, Police Commissioner Maurice to the Governor of Martinique, Fort-de-France, May 28, 1941 (for Keszler), Commissioner of Police Maurice to Inspector of the Colonies (Devouton), Fort-de-France, May 3, 1941.

116. ANOM, 2 APOM 7, Devouton to Platon, April 11, 1941.

117. David Macey, *Frantz Fanon: A Biography* (New York: Picador, 2000), 86.

118. FCDG, Félix Eboué Papers, F22/18, dossier 3, Pujol report, no date. On Pujol's role with respect to the passages to Saint Lucia, see ANOM, 1Affpol 2293, dossier 13, 17.

119. USNA, RG 59, box 5193, document 851B.00/13, intelligence report, April 9, 1945, 3.

120. Ibid.

121. JFC, "La vie secrète de René Hauth," *Les dernières nouvelles d'Alsace,* October 28, 2014, 4; René Hauth's Legion of Honor file, kindly forwarded by his family.

122. René Hauth to his cousins, card, February 6, 1941.

123. USNA, RG 84, box 4, Hauth file.

124. René Hauth to his wife, Marguerite, Martinique, April 19, 1941.

125. René Hauth, Legion of Honor file.

126. Information on René Hauth kindly provided by his family. Adrien Bosc, *Constellation* (Paris: Stock, 2014).

127. ANOM, 1Affpol 767, Nicol to Platon, May 29, 1941.

128. Encyclopedia entry by Mens Jbre on Jan Zemek in the online Internetova Encyklopedie Jedin BRNA, updated in 2016, http://encyklopedie.brna.cz/home -mmb/?acc=profil_osobnosti&load=6515; Michal Burian, Ales Knizek, Jiri Rajlich, and Eduard Stehlik, *Assassination: Operation Anthropoid, 1941–1942,* (Prague: 2002), 50, http://www.army.cz/images/id_7001_8000/7419/assassination -en.pdf both consulted in March 2016.

129. SHMV, 1K518, Von Leubuscher file.

130. Walter Leubuscher, *Der große Irrtum: Ein Beitrag zur Geschichte der nationalsozialistischen Bewegung in Österreich* (Basel, Switzerland: Tilly Verlag, 1937), 1.

131. SHMV, 1K518, Von Leubuscher file.

132. Database compiled by Free Frenchman Henri Ecochard, http://www .france-libre.net/liste-francais-libres/2013.

7. Surrealism Meets Negritude

1. André Breton, *Martinique, charmeuse de serpents* (Paris: 10/18, 1973), 76, 92–94; Alvan A. Ikoku, "Forêts del Sur and the Pretexts of Glissant's Tout-Monde," *Small Axe* 19, no. 2 (July 2015): 14.

2. Aimé Césaire, interview by Jacqueline Leiner, in the reedited version of *Tropiques* (Paris: Editions Jean-Michel Place, 1978), vii.

3. Jean-Claude Blachère, "Breton et Césaire: Flux et reflux d'une amitié," *Europe* 832–833 (August–September 1998): 149.

4. Helena Benitez, *Wifredo and Helena: My Life with Wifredo Lam, 1939–1950* (Lausanne: Acatos, 1999), 55–57

5. Ikoku, "Forêts del Sur," 18.

6. Breton, *Martinique, charmeuse de serpents,* 30–31.

7. BJD, BRT C 441, Suzanne Césaire to Breton, October 21, 1941, post-script; BJD, BRT C 442, Aimé Césaire to André Breton, April 10, 1942.

8. Benitez, *Wifredo and Helena,* 55–57. Diego Masson remembers having participated in these walks as a six-year-old. USHMM, RG 50.030*0748, "Oral History with Diego Masson," March 12, 2014.

9. Edouard Glissant, interview by Celia Britton, *L'esprit créateur* 47, no. 1 (2007): 100.

10. The pluperfect subjunctive appears in BJD, BRT C 1005, Lam to Breton, August 23, 1941. The mention of Benitez helping with Lam's French appears in the letter of Lam to Breton, September 24, 1941, held in BJD BRT 1006.

11. Benitez, *Wifredo and Helena,* 55–56.

12. Breton, *Martinique, charmeuse de serpents,* 65.

13. LBI, Kurt Kersten Archives, "Der Tod auf der Insel," manuscript, 21.

14. Seghers to Kersten, August 24, 1944, in *Briefe, 1924–1952,* ed. Christiane Zehl Romero and Almut Giesecke (Berlin: Aufbau Verlag, 2008), 152.

15. Anna Seghers, *Wiedereinführung der Sklaverei in Guadeloupe* (Frankfurt: Suhrkamp, 1966).

16. Aimé Césaire, interview by Leiner, vii.

17. BJD, BRT C 441, Suzanne Césaire to Breton and Lamba, October 21, 1941.

18. Laurence Proteau, "Entre poétique et politique: Aimé Césaire et la Négritude," *Sociétés contemporaines* 44 (2001): 26; Blachère, "Breton et Césaire," 147–148.

19. Maurice Nadeau, *Histoire du surréalisme* (Paris: Le Seuil, 1964), 180.

20. Ibid., 180, 187. On the limits of Surrealism, also see André Masson's text in *André Breton et le mouvement surréaliste* (Paris: Nouvelle revue française, 1967), 325.

21. Albert James Arnold, "Devenir Aimé Césaire, un itinéraire intellectuel et artistique," in *Aimé Césaire à l'œuvre,* ed. Marc Cheymol and Philippe Ollé-Laprune (Paris: Editions des archives contemporaines, 2010), 209.

22. Ikoku, "Forêts del Sur," 6, 16.

23. Mark Polizzotti, *Revolution of the Mind: The Life of André Breton* (New York: Farrar, Straus and Giroux, 1995), 495.

24. René Hénane, "Les armes miraculeuses: Avatars et metamorphoses," in Cheymol and Ollé-Laprune, *Aimé Césaire à l'œuvre*, 115.

25. Aimé Césaire, interview by Leiner, ix.

26. Blachère, "Breton et Césaire," 148.

27. Patrice Louis, *Aimé Césaire: Rencontre avec un Nègre fondamental* (Paris: Arléa, 2004), 41; Albert James Arnold, "Césaire Is Dead, Long Live Césaire! Recuperations and Reparations," *French Politics, Culture and Society* 27, no. 3 (2009): 14. I have quoted Albert James Arnold's translation of Césaire's interview with Patrice Louis with one change: I have opted to translate "Nègre fondamental" as "foundational" rather than "iconic."

28. J. Michael Dash, "Aimé Césaire: The Bearable Lightness of Becoming," *PMLA* 125, no. 3 (May 2010): 738.

29. Aimé Césaire, interview by Leiner, ix.

30. Ibid., vii.

31. ANOM, AGEFOM 124, "Bibliothèques officielles and liste des libraries."

32. ANOM, 1Affpol 2293, dossier 11, report to Henri Seyrig, August 17, 1944.

33. On the renaissance of Montreal's French-language publishing scene after 1940, see Marc Bergère, *Vichy au Canada: L'exil québécois de collaborateurs français* (Rennes, France: Presses universitaires de Rennes, 2015), 52–55. On Québec turning to Central America and the Caribbean for cultural contacts during the Second World War, see Sean Mills, *A Place in the Sun: Haiti, Haitians and the Remaking of Québec* (Montréal: McGill/Queen's University Press, 2016), 36.

34. Thomas Hale, "Les écrits d'Aimé Césaire," *Etudes françaises* 14, nos. 3–4 (1978): 229; Jennifer Boittin, *Colonial Metropolis* (Lincoln: University of Nebraska Press, 2010), 217.

35. René Ménil, "Tropiques, témoin de la vie culturelle," *Les cahiers du CERAG* (Cahiers du Centre d'études régionales Antilles-Guyane) 37 (November 1979): 146.

36. René Ménil, "For a Critical Reading of *Tropiques*," in *Refusal of the Shadow: Surrealism and the Caribbean,* ed. and trans. Michael Richardson and Krzysztof Fijalkowski (New York: Verso, 1996), 69 (first published in 1973).

37. Allan Stoekl, "What the Nazis Saw: *Les Mouches* in Occupied Paris," *SubStance* 102, no. 32 (2003): 78–91. There are also parallels here with the dilemma faced by the *Annales* under Vichy as to how to engage with scholarship on peasants and folklore at a time when the Vichy regime was celebrating both. See Natalie Zemon Davis, "Censorship, Silence and Resistance: The *Annales* during the German Occupation of France," *Historical Reflections* 24, no. 2 (Summer 1998): 363–365.

38. Aimé Césaire, interview by Leiner, viii, ix.

39. ADM, 2R4858, Hoppenot to Algiers, September 12, 1943, describes the "complete destruction of the naval police's archives" immediately before his arrival a few months earlier.

40. BJD, BRT C 442 and BRT C 444, Césaire to Breton, April 10, 1942, and August 3, 1943.

41. Alex Gil, "Migrant Textuality: On the Fields of Aimé Césaire and *Et les chiens se taisaient*" (PhD diss., University of Virginia, 2012), 73.

42. Daniel Maximin, introduction to *Le grand camouflage: Écrits de dissidence, 1941–1945,* by Suzanne Césaire (Paris: Le Seuil, 2009), 10–11.

43. A selection of removed articles, including from the Catholic *La Paix,* appears in ADM, 1M10144A.

44. ADM, 1M10630, Service d'information, Bayle to the press, September 18, 1941.

45. Aimé Césaire, interview in *Le nouvel observateur,* February 17–23, 1994, http://www.potomitan.info/cesaire/cri.php.

46. The May 10, 1943, letter from Lieutenant Bayle to Aimé Césaire is reproduced in the reedited version of *Tropiques* (1978), xxxviii.

47. See Anne-Marie Thiesse, *Ils apprenaient la France: L'exaltation des régions dans le discours patriotique* (Paris: Maison des Sciences de l'Homme, 1997). On Revert, see Louis, *Aimé Césaire,* 22.

48. Suzanne Césaire, "A Civilization's Discontent," trans. in Richardson and Fijalkowski, *Refusal of the Shadow,* 96 (first published in the April 1942 issue of *Tropiques*).

49. René Ménil, "Le dictateur," *Tropiques,* February 1943, reproduced in the reedited version of *Tropiques* (1978), 2:25–31.

50. Aimé Césaire and René Ménil, "An Introduction to Martiniquan Folklore," trans. in Richardson and Fijalkowski, *Refusal of the Shadow,* 101–103 (first published in the January 1942 issue of *Tropiques*).

51. Daniel Maximin, *L'isolé soleil* (Paris: Le Seuil, 1981), 192.

52. ADG, 2Mi 105R 226 (Depêches Ministérielles), Platon to the Governors of the Colonies, March 6, 1941.

53. Harry Gamble, *Contesting French West Africa: Battles over Schools and the Colonial Order, 1900–1950* (Lincoln: University of Nebraska Press, 2017), ch. 6. On the broader context of West Africa under Vichy, see Ruth Ginio, *French Colonialism Unmasked: The Vichy Years in French West Africa* (Lincoln: University of Nebraska Press, 2006). On similar phenomena in Indochina under Vichy, see Eric Jennings, "Conservative Confluences, 'Nativist' Synergy: Re-inscribing Vichy's National Revolution in Indochina," *French Historical Studies* 27, no. 3 (Summer 2004): 601–635.

54. René Ménil, "Birth of Our Art," trans. in Richardson and Fijalkowski, *Refusal of the Shadow,* 106, 108 (first published in the April 1941 issue of *Tropiques*).

55. On subsequent notions of Creoleness, authenticity, and post-Negritude, see Richard Price, *The Convict and the Colonel* (Boston: Beacon, 1998), 174–185.

56. Suzanne Césaire, "Civilization's Discontent," 98, 100. On the prescient nature of Suzanne Césaire's intervention, see Kristen Stromberg Childers, *Seeking Imperialism's Embrace: National Identity, Decolonization and Assimilation in the French Caribbean* (Oxford: Oxford University Press, 2016), 77–78.

57. Romuald Fonkoua, *Aimé Césaire* (Paris: Perrin, 2010), 71; Louis, *Aimé Césaire,* 36; Gary Wilder, *The French Imperial Nation State: Negritude and Colonial Humanism between the Two World Wars* (Chicago: University of Chicago Press, 2005), 279.

58. Fonkoua, *Aimé Césaire*, 71–72.

59. On this generation, and Brasillach in particular, see Alice Kaplan, *The Collaborator: The Trial and Execution of Robert Brasillach* (Chicago: University of Chicago Press, 2000).

60. Vincent Giroud, "Transition to Vichy: The Case of Georges Pelorson," *Modernism / Modernity* 7, no. 2 (April 2000): 221–248.

61. Hénane, "Les armes miraculeuses," 115.

62. Gil, "Migrant Textuality," 14. Maximin uses the same formula to determine the year 1941 in his novel *L'isolé soleil*, 271.

63. John Patrick Walsh, *Free and French in the Caribbean: Toussaint Louverture, Aimé Césaire and Narratives of Loyal Opposition* (Bloomington: University of Indiana Press, 2013), 124. On the calculations and ideals that drove Césaire to endorse departmentalization for Martinique in 1946, see Gary Wilder, "Untimely Vision: Aimé Césaire, Decolonization, Utopia," *Public Culture* 21, no. 1 (2009): 107–108.

64. Gil, "Migrant Textuality," 16. In his thesis, as well as in his article "La représentation en profondeur de *Et les chiens se taisaient* d'Aimé Césaire," Gil also focuses on the building blocks or "legos" that shifted in successive drafts of the manuscript between 1941 and 1956. Alex Gil, "La représentation en profondeur de *Et les chiens se taisaient* d'Aimé Césaire: Pour une édition génétique en ligne," *Genesis: Manuscrits, recherche, invention* 33 (2011): 67–76.

65. *Et les chiens se taisaient*, typescript from Saint-Dié-des-Vosges Library, kindly shared by Alex Gil, 11, blue (central) pagination. All pages cited use this pagination.

66. Ibid., 17, 20.

67. Ibid., 21, 27, 34, 61.

68. Laurent Dubois, *Avengers of the New World: The Story of the Haitian Revolution* (Cambridge, MA: Harvard University Press, 2004), 202, 232.

69. *Et les chiens se taisaient*, typescript, 31.

70. Ibid., 33.

71. Ibid., 60.

72. BJD, BRT C 449, Aimé Césaire to André Breton, April 4, 1944. Also cited in Gil, "Migrant Textuality," 126.

73. BJD, BRT C 444, Aimé Césaire to André Breton, August 3, 1944.

74. ANOM, 173 APOM 1, anonymous letter from a group of radio listeners.

75. ANOM, 173 APOM 1, report on the press in Martinique, August 12, 1944, 6.

76. Dimitri Béchacq, "L'ethnologie et les troupes folkloriques haïtiennes: Politique culturelle, tourisme et émigration, 1941–1986," in *Production du savoir et construction sociale: L'ethnologie en Haïti*, ed. Jhon P. Byron (Port-au-Prince, Haiti: l'Université d'État d'Haïti; Québec City, Québec: Presses de l'Université de Laval, 2014), 123–152. The bureau was inspired by the Musée de l'Homme in Paris, with which it had many contacts: Roumain had been a student of Paul Rivet's, and the Musée de l'Homme's Georges-Henri Rivière was also one of the leading figures involved in the founding of the bureau in Haiti in 1941. On these networks, see Alice Conklin, *In the Museum of Man: Race, Anthropology and Empire in France* (Ithaca, NY: Cornell University Press, 2013).

77. ANOM, 173 APOM 1, Kaminker report on Martinique's press, August 12, 1944, 6.

78. Aimé Césaire, "Lettre ouverte à Monseigneur Varin de la Brunelière," *Tropiques* 11 (May 1944): 104–116.

79. ANOM, Cab 57, dossier 377, Etiemble report, Algiers, April 23, 1944.

80. René Etiemble, "L'idéologie de Vichy contre la pensée française," *Tropiques* 11 (May 1944): 95–103.

81. ANOM, Cab 57, dossier 377, Etiemble report, Algiers, April 23, 1944.

82. On the conflict between Paris and the colonial lobby on the question of abolition, see Lawrence Jennings, *French Anti-slavery* (Cambridge: Cambridge University Press, 2006).

83. See Tyler Stovall, "Aimé Césaire and the Making of Black Paris," *French Politics, Culture and Society* 27, no. 3 (Winter 2009): 45.

84. ANOM, Cab 57, dossier 377, Etiemble report, Algiers, April 23, 1944; Etiemble, "L'idéologie de Vichy."

85. Lowery Stokes Sims, *Wifredo Lam and the International Avant-Garde, 1923–1982* (Austin: University of Texas Press, 2002), 10–25.

86. Ikoku, "Forêts del Sur," 19.

87. Pierre [Loeb], "Wifredo Lam," *Tropiques* 6–7 (February 1943): 61–62. On the fascination with the primitive in France, see Daniel Sherman, *French Primitivism and the Ends of Empire* (Chicago: University of Chicago Press, 2011).

88. Lou Laurin-Lam, "Une amitié caraïbe," *Europe* 832–833 (August–September 1998): 27.

89. Dash, "Aimé Césaire," 741.

90. Daniel Maximin, *Césaire et Lam, insolites bâtisseurs* (Paris: Musées nationaux, 2011), 15.

91. Pierre Mabille, "La jungle," *Tropiques* 12 (January 1945): 179.

92. Pierre Mabille, "The Jungle," trans. in Richardson and Fijalkowski, *Refusal of the Shadow,* 212 (first published in the January 1945 issue of *Tropiques*).

93. Sims, *Wifredo Lam,* 41–43.

94. Julia P. Herzberg, "Naissance d'un style et d'une vision du monde: Le séjour à la Havane, 1941–1952," in Dapper Museum, *Lam Métis* (Paris: Editions Dapper, 2001), 104.

95. On the rain, see Hénane, "Les armes miraculeuses," 115.

96. Benitez, *Wifredo and Helena,* 56.

97. Ménil, "Tropiques," 153.

98. André Breton, quoted in Daniel Maximin, *Césaire et Lam,* 7.

99. Sims, *Wifredo Lam,* 43.

100. Dominique Berthet, *Pratiques artistiques contemporaines en Martinique* (Paris: L'Harmattan, 2012), 9; Marie Louis, "L'art contemporain martiniquais de 1939 à nos jours" (PhD diss., University of Metz, 2009), 84–85, 87.

101. On Lam's poverty in the Dominican Republic, see BJD, BRT C 1004, Lam to Breton, August 1, 1941. On the shortage of brushes and paint in Cuba, see BJD, BRT C 1005, Lam to Breton, August 23, 1941.

102. BJD, BRT C 1005, Lam to Breton, August 23, 1941.

103. BJD, BRT C 1013, Lam to Breton, September 3, 1942.

104. BJD, BRT C 1015–16, Lam to Breton, April 9, 1943.

105. Ikoku, "Forêts del Sur," 19–21.

106. BJD, BRT C 1013, Lam to Breton, September 3, 1942.

107. BJD, BRT C 1015–16, Lam to Breton, April 9, 1943.

108. Vincent Bercker, "La période aixoise d'André Masson" (University of Nîmes, 1997), vol. 1.

109. Claude Miglietti and Stéphane Guégan, texts in *André Masson, de Marseille à l'exil américain,* exhibition catalog (Marseille: Lienart, 2015), 6, 27–29.

110. BJD, BRT C 1079, Mabille to Breton from Haiti, 1941 (no precise date).

111. Dash, "Aimé Césaire," 738.

112. BJD, BRT 1008, Lam to Breton, November 2, 1941.

113. Walter Mehring, *No Road Back,* trans. S. A. de Witt (New York: Samuel Curl, 1944), 147–149.

114. Ibid., 151.

115. George Cummins III, *Mahler Recomposed* (Bloomington: iUniverse, 2011), 155.

116. Mehring, *No Road Back,* 31.

117. Suzanne Césaire, "Surrealism and Us," trans. in Richardson and Fijalkowski, *Refusal of the Shadow,* 126 (first published in the October 1943 issue of *Tropiques*).

118. Glissant, interview by Britton, 101.

8. The Window Closes

1. ANOM, 1Affpol 767, report from the French legation in Havana, April 22, 1941.

2. Variations on such fears had abounded in the United States since the outbreak of war in Europe in 1939. See Richard Breitman and Alan Kraut, *American Refugee Policy and European Jewry, 1933–1945* (Bloomington: Indiana University Press, 1987), 112.

3. "Martinique: US May Take French Island," *Life,* September 15, 1941, 95.

4. USNA, RG 84, box 1, "Foreign Element, Martinique," document 800, Harwood Blocker to the Secretary of State, December 19, 1940.

5. USNA, RG 84 box 3, Robert to Malige, May 10, 1941.

6. SHMV, TTE 33, Benech report to the admiralty, October 22, 1940. This was not a vain threat. On December 12, 1941, the United States seized the legendary *Normandie* passenger vessel, which had languished in the docks of New York. While condemning the action, Vichy at least acknowledged that it received compensation from such seizures by the United States, contrary to ones by the United Kingdom. Jeffrey Mehlman, *Émigré New York: French Intellectuals in Wartime Manhattan, 1940–1944* (Baltimore: Johns Hopkins University Press, 2000), 198–199.

7. Peter Hayes, *Why? Explaining the Holocaust* (New York: W. W. Norton, 2017), 270–271.

8. USNA, RG 84 box 3, Robert to Malige, May 10, 1941.

9. ANOM, 1TEL 701, Secretary of State to the Colonies to Martinique, May 12, 1941.

10. SHMV, TTE 32, Robert to Nicol, May 17, 1941.

11. ANF, AJ40, 1265, "Délégation militaire auprès de la commission d'armistice, sous-commission Marine: Note pour la commission allemande d'Armisitice," Wiesbaden, November 30, 1940.

12. SHMT, 18S 14, entry for March 26, 1941; "Le blocus britannique," *La Paix* (Fort-de-France), April 26, 1941. The lifting of a previous ban in February 1941 is chronicled in ANOM, 1Affpol 1297, Admiral Platon to Darlan, February 17, 1941.

13. Carole Fink, *Marc Bloch, a Life in History* (Cambridge: Cambridge University Press, 1989), 255. On Bloch's efforts to reach New York, also see Emmanuelle Loyer, *Lévi-Strauss* (Paris: Flammarion, 2015), 249, and Aristide Zolberg, "The Ecole Libre at the New School, 1941–1946," *Social Research* 65, no. 4 (Winter 1998): 921–951.

14. ANOM, 1Affpol 1298, Captain Caron to Admiral Darlan concerning Marc Bloch, April 11, 1941, referring to an April 2 letter from the service des oeuvres.

15. Bloch to André Mazon, July 3, 1941, quoted in Agnès Graceffa, "De l'entraide universitaire sous l'occupation: La correspondance de Marc Bloch avec André Mazon," *Revue historique* 674 (2015): 409.

16. Fink, *Marc Bloch*, 306.

17. USNA, RG 84, box 4, document 820.02, Cordell Hull, US Secretary of State, Washington, to US Consul Malige Fort-de-France, Martinique, April 27, 1941.

18. Oscar Lansen, "Victims of Circumstance: Jewish Nationals in the Dutch West Indies, 1938–1947," *Holocaust and Genocide Studies* 113, no. 3 (Winter 1999): 437–458.

19. MAE, Guerre, 1939–45, Continent américain, dossier 182, *Alsina-Winnipeg*, Admiral Robert to Ministry of the Colonies, May 17, 1941.

20. ANOM, 1TEL 701, Secretary of State to the Colonies to Martinique, May 21, 1941.

21. USNA, RG 84, box 5, letter from *Arica* captain M. Raveau to the US consul in Martinique, June 26, 1941.

22. On the abruptness and consequences of this rupture, see ANOM, 2 APOM 7, Devouton, report to Platon, September 30, 1941.

23. ANOM, 1Affpol 767, dossier 3, Devouton to Platon, April 11, 1941.

24. NAUK, FO 837, Foreign Office to Washington, June 1, 1941. My thanks to Michael Dobbs for sending this folder.

25. Ibid.

26. ANOM, 1Affpol 768, Armistice Commission to Ministry of the Colonies, May 15, 1941.

27. On this diplomatic incident, see William Langer, *Our Vichy Gamble* (New York: Alfred Knopf, 1947), 236.

28. Allen Cronenberg, "French West Indies during World War II," *Proceedings of the Annual Meeting of the Western Society for French History* 18 (1991): 527–528.

29. David Wyman, *The Abandonment of the Jews: America and the Holocaust, 1941–1945* (New York: New Press, 2007); David Wyman, *Paper Walls: America and the Refugee Crisis, 1938–1941* (New York: Pantheon, 1985); Breitman and Kraut, *American Refugee Policy;* Henry Feingold, *Bearing Witness: How America and Its Jews Responded to the Holocaust* (Syracuse, NY: Syracuse University Press, 1995).

30. USNA, RG 84, box 3, telegram, C. Hull, June 5, 1941. Breitman and Kraut mention this measure in *American Refugee Policy,* 135.

31. Jacques Adélaïde-Merlande, "Va-t-on céder les Antilles françaises aux Etats-Unis?," in *Guadeloupe, Martinique et Guyane dans le monde américain,* ed. Maurice Burac (Paris: Karthala, 1994), 161–165.

32. NAN, Ministerie van Marine Archives for World War II, D27518, 167, 98.

33. NAN, Ministerie van Marine Archives for World War II, D27518, 98, entry for May 26, 1941.

34. "Nazis Destroy Papers as British Seize Martinique-Bound Ship," *Washington Post,* May 31, 1941; "Gestapo Rules Martinique, Refugees Say," *Washington Post,* June 14, 1941, 3; ANOM, 1Affpol 768, testimony of passenger Mrs. Marty, July 17, 1941; R. M. Sallé, *70,000 kilomètres d'aventures: Notes d'un voyage Indochine-France et retour, 1940–1942* (Hanoi: Imprimerie d'Extrême-Orient, 1942), 134, 137. A British report from May 30, 1941 notes that following the boarding of the *Winnipeg,* "several passengers sleeping on the upper deck were positive that two, three or even six sacks of boxes were thrown from the bridge into the Sea. The noise was unmistakable." NAUK, FO 837, contraband control services, Trinidad, May 30 1941.

35. Weekly intelligence report, UK admiralty, June 6, 1941, http://www. defence.gov.au/sydneyii/NAA/NAA.007.0115.pdf.

36. MAE, Guerre, 1939–45, Continent américain, dossier 182, telegram received in Havana on June 3, 1941.

37. MAE, Guerre, 1939–45, Continent américain, dossier 182, Foreign Ministry to Secretary of State to the Navy, June 6, 1941. The UK numbers are from NAUK, FO 837, Foreign Office to Washington, June 1, 1941.

38. "Gestapo Rules Martinique, Refugees Say," *Washington Post,* June 14, 1941, 3.

39. Ibid.

40. Sallé, *70,000 kilomètres d'aventures,* 140.

41. Ibid., 143, 150–151.

42. LBI, Yolla Niclas-Sachs, "Looking Back from New Horizons," unpublished memoir, 1974, 33–35. Courtesy of the Leo Baeck Institute, New York.

43. Sallé, *70,000 kilomètres d'aventures,* 170–171; ANOM, 1Affpol 768, testimony of passenger Mrs. Marty, July 17, 1941; SHDG, V972^E, police report, July 30, 1941.

44. SHDG, V972^E, police report, July 30, 1941.

45. USNA, RG 84, box 2, letter to the US Consulate, December 25, 1941.

46. MAE, Guerre, 1939–45, Continent américain, dossier 182, excerpts from dispatch N 116, November 6, 1941, from the American consulate at Martinique.

47. CDJC, Joint Distribution Committee Holdings, box 616, cable, May 26, 1941.

48. MAE, Guerre, 1939–45, Continent américain, dossier 182, Darlan to Foreign Ministry, June 8, 1941, *Alsina-Winnipeg.*

49. CDJC, Joint Distribution Committee Holdings, box 616.

50. MAE, Guerre, 1939–45, Continent américain, dossier 182.

51. CDJC, Joint Distribution Committee Holdings, box 616, memorandum, April 3, 1941, and note to all members of the *Alsina* committee regarding a meeting on April 23.

52. ANOM, 1Affpol 1298, Platon to Darlan, May 6, 1941.

53. ANOM, 1TEL 721, Admiralty to Martinique, May 10, 1941.

54. MAE, Guerre, 1939–45, Continent américain, dossier 182.

55. ANOM, 1Affpol 1298, Platon to the Minister of the Interior (Police des étrangers), May 16, 1941.

56. MAE, Guerre, 1939–45, Continent américain, dossier 182.

57. Ibid.

58. Mrs. Anita Sperling, correspondence with the author, October 2009, and copies of documents kindly sent by her.

59. Sarah Ogilvie and Scott Miller, *Refuge Denied: The St. Louis Passengers and the Holocaust* (Madison: University of Wisconsin Press, 2006).

60. MAE, Guerre, 1939–45, Continent américain, dossier 182, "Note pour la direction politique (Amérique)," May 30, 1941.

61. MAE, Guerre, 1939–45, Continent américain, dossier 182, Vichy to Rabat, June 4, 1941, and Darlan, July 1, 1941.

62. MAE, Guerre, 1939–45, Continent américain, dossier 182, Rabat to Vichy, June 6, 1941.

63. ANOM, 1Affpol 768, Fry to the Ministry of the Colonies, June 30, 1941.

64. CDJC, Joint Distribution Committee Holdings, box 616, JDC telegram from Lisbon to New York, June 24, 1941.

65. CDJC, Joint Distribution Committee Holdings, box 616, letter from A. Hirsch, June 6, 1941, and, in the same file, Lisbon, June 3, 1941.

66. MAE, Guerre, 1939–45, Continent américain, dossier 182, Vichy to the French Embassy in Lisbon, July 26, 1941.

67. CDJC, Joint Distribution Committee Holdings, box 616, "200 Refugees Rescued from Africa," press release by Roman Slobodin, JDC, May 8, 1941.

68. "One of 5," *New York Daily News*, September 25, 1941.

69. SHMV, TTE 33, "Historique et description de la crise de mai 1942 aux Antilles."

70. Ibid.

71. ANOM, 1TEL 723, Robert to Vichy, October 21, 1941.

72. ANOM, 1Affpol 768, note, December 13, 1941.

73. Wyman, *Abandonment of the Jews*, 113–116.

Epilogue

1. Gabrielle Sauré, *Carl Heidenreich* (New York: Goethe-Institut, 2004), 45–52.

2. MF, Germaine Krull Archives, "Camp de concentration à la Martinique," unpublished manuscript.

3. A third possible interpretation emerges from Frida Kahn's memoirs. She notes that she and Erich seldom quarreled, except over spelling and grammar, a field in which he felt himself superior. Frida had been fluent in Russian, French, and Yiddish before learning German (she also learned Hebrew after arriving in Germany in 1921). Consequently, the use of French probably placed her on better footing. However, this does not begin to explain why so many other refugees, such as Anna Seghers, and even Josef Breitenbach, whose French was sketchier, corresponded so extensively in French at this time. Frida Kahn, *Generation in Turmoil* (Great Neck, NY: Channel, 1960), 158–159.

4. LBI, Kurt Kersten Archives, René Hauth to Kurt Kersten, January 29, 1945.

5. See Anne Egger, ed., *Portraits de l'exil: Paris-New York dans le sillage de Hannah Arendt* (Paris: Musée du Montparnasse, 2011), 58, 81.

6. On nostalgia in the work of Seghers, see Susan E. Cernyak, "Anna Seghers: Between Judaism and Communism," in *Exile: The Writer's Experience*, ed. John M. Spalek and Robert F. Bell (Chapel Hill: University of North Carolina Press, 1982), 278–285.

7. GJECA, Walter Friedlander papers, GER 003, box 7, folder 14, Renée Barth to Friedlander, August 4, 1976.

8. GJECA, Walter Friedlander papers GER 003, box 7, folder 14, Friedlander to Renée Barth, December 10, 1970.

9. GJECA, Walter Friedlander papers GER 003, box 7, folder 14, Renée Barth to Friedlander, April 1, 1969.

10. GJECA, Walter Friedlander papers GER 003, box 7, folder 14, Renée Barth to Friedlander, May 29, 1972.

11. GJECA, Walter Friedlander papers GER 003, box 7, folder 14, Renée Barth to Friedlander, December 15, 1972.

12. Mark Polizzotti, *Revolution of the Mind: The Life of André Breton* (New York: Farrar, Straus and Giroux, 1995), 530.

13. Ibid., 532; Gérard Bloncourt and Michael Löwy, *Messagers de la tempête: André Breton et la Révolution de janvier 1946 à Haiti* (Pantin, France: Le temps des cerises, 2007).

14. André Breton Collection, Dossier de presse sur Haïti, http://www.andrebreton.fr/work/56600100917970. The version published in *La Ruche* reads instead "that I find myself in Haiti." It can be found at the Bibliothèque haïtienne des Frères de l'Instruction chrétienne (my thanks to Sean Mills for photographing it for me).

BIBLIOGRAPHY

Archival Collections

ADBDR: Archives départementales des Bouches-du-Rhône, Marseille, France

- Daniel Bénédite Papers (255J)
- 2M Personnel Files
- W Files (Justice)—consulted when these files were still located in Aix-en-Provence, at the annex of the departmental archives
- W Series (Prefecture)

ADG: Archives départementales de la Guadeloupe, Gourbeyre, Guadeloupe, France

- Microfilms (2Mi 105R)
- Série continue (SC)
- Série incendie (INC)

ADM: Archives de la Martinique, Fort-de-France, Martinique, France

- M Series
- N Series
- R Series

ADN: Archives diplomatiques, Nantes, France

- ADN 378PO/C/2/127, Antilles

ANF: Archives nationales (contemporary section), Pierrefitte, France

- AJ38
- AJ40
- AJ41
- 3W

ANOM: Archives nationales d'outre-mer, Aix-en-Provence, France

- Affaires politiques (1Affpol)
- Agence de la France d'outre-mer (AGEFOM)
- Cabinet (Cab)
- Département des affaires militaires (DAM)
- Emile Devouton Papers (2 APOM 7)
- Louis Ponton Papers (173 APOM)
- Télégrammes (TEL)

BJD: Bibliothèque littéraire Jacques Doucet, Paris, France

- André Breton Papers (BRT)

BLY: Beinecke Library and Archives, Yale University, New Haven, Connecticut, USA

- Victor Serge Archives (GEN MSS 238)

CCP: Center for Creative Photography, Archives, Tucson, Arizona, USA

- Josef Breitenbach Papers (AG 90)

CDJC: Centre de documentation juive contemporaine archives, Paris, France

- AJDC 616 (France, emigration)
- Joint Distribution Committee Holdings (copies)
- HICEM Archives (copies) (CCX VII–15)

CICR: Red Cross Archives, Geneva, Switzerland

- BG
- OCMS

CRB: Butler Rare Books Library and Archives, Columbia University, New York, New York, USA

- Varian Fry Papers

DEA: Deutsche Nationalbibliothek, Deutsches Exilarchiv, Frankfurt am Main, Germany

- Anna Seghers Papers (EB 2010.26x2)
- Harry Kriszhaber Papers (K. EB 73/21)
- Karl Heidenreich Papers
- Kurt Kersten Papers (American Guild, 39BL 22E).
- Minna Flake Papers (K. EB 73/21)
- Robert Breuer Material (Nachlaß W. Stemfeld EB 75/177)
- Walter Mehring Papers (American Guild EB 70/117)

FCDG: Fondation Charles de Gaulle Archives, Paris, France

- Félix Eboué Papers (F 22)

FL: French Lines (Compagnie générale transatlantique) Archives, Le Havre, France

- Series 1997
- Series 1999

GJECA: German Jewish Intellectual Émigré Collection, Albany, New York, USA

- Emergency Rescue Committee Archives (box 1, folder 17, Minna Flake; box 1, folder 42, Harry Kriszhaber; box 1, folder 54, André Masson; box 2, folder 3, Walter Mehring)
- Walter Friedlander Papers

LBI: Leo Baeck Institute, New York, New York USA (online holdings)

- Kurt Kersten Archives, including "Flucht aus Frankreich" and "Der Tod auf der Insel"
- Renée (Renata) Barth, "A Born Refugee," unpublished manuscript, 1993
- Yolla Niclas-Sachs, "Looking Back from New Horizons," unpublished manuscript 1974

MAE: Ministère des Affaires Etrangères Archives, La Courneuve, France

- Guerre, 1939–45

MF: Museum Folkwang, Essen, Germany

- Germaine Krull Archives, including photographs and the manuscript titled "Camp de concentration à la Martinique"

NAN: Nationaal Archief, Den Haag, Netherlands

- Ministerie van Marine Archives for World War II

NAUK: National Archives of the United Kingdom, Kew, England (formerly known as PRO)

- FO 371, French Caribbean
- FO 837, Economic warfare

NGC: National Gallery of Canada, Library and Archives, Ottawa, Canada

- Ilse Bing Photographic Fonds

NGP: Archives of the National Gallery, Prague, Czech Republic

- Antonin Pelc Papers

NYPLA: Archives of the New York Public Library, New York, New York, USA

- Erich Itor Kahn Papers

SHDG: Service historique de la Défense archives (Gendarmerie), Vincennes, France

- Martinique (972^{E})

SHMB: Service historique de la Défense archives (Marine), Brest, France

- 4Q Fonds (wartime cargo seizures)

SHMT: Service historique de la Défense archives (Marine), Toulon, France

- Admiral Rouyer Papers (18S 14)

SHMV: Service historique de la Défense archives (Marine), Vincennes, France

- TTD Series, World War II
- TTE Series, World War II
- Xavier Steiner Papers (1K518)

UGASC: University of Glasgow Archives and Special Collections, Glasgow, Scotland, UK

- Llyod's of London shipping registers for World War II

USHM: United States Holocaust Memorial Archives, Washington, DC, USA

- American Friends Service Committee Records Relating to Humanitarian Work in France
- Emergency Rescue Committee Archives
- Pyrénées orientales departmental archives, RG43.036
- "Oral History with Diego Masson" March 12, 2014, 50.030*0748

USNA: US National Archives, College Park, Maryland, USA

- RG 59, Martinique
- RG 84, Martinique

Private Papers and Correspondence

- Galina Yurkevich
- Raymond Assayas
- René Hauth
- Jacques Rémy

Primary Sources (Printed)

Assayas, Michka. *Faute d'identité*. Paris: Grasset, 2011.

Bénédite, Daniel. *La filière marseillaise: Un chemin vers la liberté sous l'occupation*. Paris: Clancier Guénaud, 1984.

Benitez, Helena. *Wifredo and Helena: My Life with Wifredo Lam, 1939–1950*. Lausanne: Acatos, 1999.

Breton, André. *Martinique, charmeuse de serpents*. Paris: 10/18, 1973.

———. *Oeuvres completes*. 3 vols. Paris: Gallimard, 1999.

Césaire, Suzanne. *Le grand camouflage: Écrits de dissidence, 1941–1945*. Paris: Le Seuil, 2009.

Crémieux-Brilhac, Jean-Louis. *L'Étrange victoire*. Paris: Gallimard, 2016.

Fabre-Luce, Alfred. *Journal de la France, 1939–1944*. Paris: Fayard, 1969.

Fanon, Frantz. *Pour la révolution africaine (écrits politiques)*. Paris: Maspero, 1964.

Feuchtwanger, Lion. *The Devil in France: My Encounter with Him in the Summer of 1940*. New York: Viking, 1941.

Gide, André, and Jacques Schiffrin. *Correspondance, 1922–1950*. Paris: Gallimard, 2005.

Gold, Mary Jayne. *Marseille année 40*. Paris: Phébus, 2001.

Goldschmidt, Bertrand. *Pionniers de l'atome*. Paris: Stock, 1987.

———. *Les Rivalités atomiques, 1939–1966*. Paris: Fayard, 1967.

Hoffmeister, Adolf. *The Animals Are in Cages*. New York: Greenberg, 1941.

Honorien, Emmanuel. *Le Ralliement des Antilles à la France combattante*. Martinique, Fort-de-France: Imprimerie officielle, 1945.

Kahn, Frida. *Generation in Turmoil*. Great Neck, NY: Channel, 1960.

Klarsfeld, Serge, ed. *Recueil de documents des archives du Comité international de la Croix Rouge sur le sort des juifs de France internés et déportés, 1939–1945*. 3 vols. Paris: Beate Klarsfled Foundation, 1999.

Langer, William. *Our Vichy Gamble*. New York: Alfred Knopf, 1947.

Lévi-Strauss, Claude. *Tristes tropiques*. Paris: Plon, 1955.

Louis, Patrice. *Aimé Césaire: Rencontre avec un Nègre fundamental*. Paris: Arléa, 2004.

Malaquais, Jean. *Journal du Métèque*. Paris: Phébus, 1997.

———. *Planète sans visa*. Paris: Phébus, 1999.

Massip, Jean. "La Résistance aux Antilles." *Revue de Paris*, May 1945, 64–71.

Maximin, Daniel. *L'isolé soleil*. Paris: Le Seuil, 1981.

Mehring, Walter. *The Lost Library: Autobiography of a Culture*. Indianapolis: Bobbs-Merrill, 1950.

———. *No Road Back*. Translated by S. A. de Witt. New York: Samuel Curl, 1944.

———. *Wir Müssen Weiter: Fragmente aus dem Exil*. Düsseldorf: Claassen Verlag, 1979.

Neruda, Pablo. *Memoirs*. New York: Farrar, Straus and Giroux, 1977.

Radvanyi, Pierre. *Janseits des Stroms: Erinnerungen an Meine Mutter Anna Seghers*. Berlin: Aufbau Verlag, 2005.

Sallé, R. M. *70,000 kilomètres d'aventures: Notes d'un voyage Indochine-France et retour, 1940–1942*. Hanoi: Imprimerie d'Extrême-Orient, 1942.

Seghers, Anna. *Briefe, 1924–1952*. Edited by Christiane Zehl Romero and Almut Giesecke. Berlin: Aufbau Verlag, 2008.

———. *Transit*. New York: New York Review of Books, 2013.

———. *Wiedereinführung der Sklaverei in Guadeloupe*. Frankfurt: Suhrkamp, 1966.

Serge, Victor. *Carnets, 1936–1947*. Paris: Agone, 2012.

———. *Mémoires d'un révolutionnaire, 1901–1941*. Paris: Le Seuil, 1978.

Smith, Nicol. *Black Martinique, Red Guiana*. New York: Bobbs-Merrill, 1942.

Voswinckel, Ulrike, and Frank Beringer. *Exils méditerranéens: Écrivains allemands dans le sud de la France, 1933–1941*. Paris: Le Seuil, 2009.

Secondary Sources

Abenon, Lucien-René. *Petite histoire de la Guadeloupe*. Paris: L'Harmattan, 1992.

Abenon, Lucien-René, and Henry Joseph. *Les Dissidents des Antilles dans les Forces françaises libres combattantes, 1940–1945*. Fort-de-France: Désormeaux, 1999.

Alroey, Gur. *Zionism without Zion: The Jewish Territorial Organization and Its Conflict with the Zionist Organization*. Detroit: Wayne State University Press, 2016.

Arnold, Albert James. "Césaire Is Dead, Long Live Césaire! Recuperations and Reparations." *French Politics, Culture and Society* 27, no. 3 (2009): 9–18.

———. "Frantz Fanon, Lafcadio Hearn et la supercherie de Mayotte Capécia: De la parabole biblique à *Je suis Martiniquaise*." *Revue de littérature comparée* 305 (2003): 35–48.

Azéma, Jean-Pierre, and Olivier Wieviorka. *Vichy, 1940–1944*. Paris: Perrin, 2000.

Baptiste, Fitzroy. *War, Cooperation and Conflict: The European Possessions in the Caribbean, 1939–1945*. Westport, CT: Greenwood, 1988.

Baruch, Marc Olivier. *Servir l'Etat français: L'administration en France de 1940 à 1944*. Paris: Fayard, 1997.

Béchacq, Dimitri. "L'ethnologie et les troupes folkloriques haïtiennes: Politique culturelle, tourisme et émigration, 1941–1986." In *Production du savoir et construction sociale: L'ethnologie en Haïti*, edited by Jhon P. Byron, 123–152. Port-au-Prince, Haiti: l'Université d'État d'Haïti; Québec City, Québec: Presses de l'Université de Laval, 2014.

Berlière, Jean-Marc. *Policiers français sous l'occupation*. Paris: Perrin, 2001.

Berthet, Dominique. *Pratiques artistiques contemporaines en Martinique*. Paris: L'Harmattan, 2012.

Bess, Michael. *Choices under Fire: Moral Dimensions of World War II*. New York: Knopf, 2006.

Blachère, Jean-Claude. "Breton et Césaire: Flux et reflux d'une amitié." *Europe* 832–833 (August–September 1998): 146–159.

Boghardt, Julie. *Minna Flake: Macht und Ohnmacht der roten Frau: Von der Dichtermuse zur Sozialistin*. Frankfurt: Campus Verlag, 1997.

Boittin, Jennifer Anne. *Colonial Metropolis: The Urban Grounds of Anti-imperialism and Feminism in Interwar Paris*. Lincoln: University of Nebraska Press, 2010.

Breitman, Richard, and Alan Kraut. *American Refugee Policy and European Jewry, 1933–1945*. Bloomington: Indiana University Press, 1987.

Browning, Christopher. *Nazi Policy, Jewish Workers, German Killers*. Cambridge: Cambridge University Press, 2000.

———. *The Path to Genocide*. Cambridge: Cambridge University Press, 1992.

Bruneau, Jean-Baptiste. *La Marine de Vichy aux Antilles, juin 1940–juillet 1943*. Paris: Les Indes Savantes, 2014.

Bruttmann, Tal. *Au Bureau des affaires juives*. Paris: La Découverte, 2006.

Burac, Maurice, ed. *Guadeloupe, Martinique et Guyane dans le monde américain.* Paris: Karthala, 1994.

Burrin, Philippe. *France under the Germans: Collaboration and Compromise.* New York: New Press, 1996.

Burton, Richard. "Vichysme et Vichystes à la Martinique." *Les cahiers du CERAG* (Cahiers du Centre d'études régionales Antilles-Guyane) 34 (February 1978): 1–101.

Bush, Clive. "Escape from Marseille: An American Story? Writing Victor Serge's, Laurette Séjourné's, Dwight and Nancy Macdonald's Balzacian Book." *Prospects* 28 (October 2004): 311–340.

Caron, Vicki. *Uneasy Asylum: France and the Jewish Refugee Crisis, 1933–1942.* Stanford, CA: Stanford University Press, 1999.

Cesarini, David. *Final Solution: The Fate of the Jews, 1933–1949.* New York: St. Martin's, 2016.

Charki, Alice. *Frantz Fanon: Portrait.* Paris: Seuil, 2000.

Chathuant, Dominique. "La Guadeloupe dans l'obédience de Vichy", *Bulletin de la Société d'Histoire de la Guadeloupe* 91 (1992): 3–40.

——— "Un résistant? Maurice Satineau, un parlementaire colonial dans la tourmente, 1940–1945." *Outre-mers* 386–387 (June 2015): 130–144.

Chauvet, Camille. "La Martinique pendant la deuxième guerre mondiale." PhD diss., University of Toulouse, Le Mirail, 1985.

Cheymol, Marc, and Philippe Ollé-Laprune, eds. *Aimé Césaire à l'œuvre.* Paris: Editions des archives contemporaines, 2010.

Conklin, Alice. *In the Museum of Man: Race, Anthropology and Empire in France.* Ithaca, NY: Cornell University Press, 2013.

Cottias, Myriam, and Madeleine Dobie. *Relire Mayotte Capécia: Une femme des Antilles dans l'espace colonial français (1916–1955).* Paris: Armand Colin, 2012.

Cronenberg, Allen. "French West Indies during World War II." *Proceedings of the Annual Meeting of the Western Society for French History* 18 (1991): 524–533.

Dapper Museum. *Lam métis.* Paris: Editions Dapper, 2001.

Dash, J. Michael. "Aimé Césaire: The Bearable Lightness of Becoming." *PMLA* 125, no. 3 (May 2010): 737–742.

Davis, Natalie Zemon. "Censorship, Silence and Resistance: The *Annales* during the German Occupation of France." *Historical Reflections* 24, no. 2 (Summer 1998): 351–374.

Dosso, Diane. "Le plan de sauvetage des scientifiques français, New York, 1940–1942." *Revue de synthèse* 127, no. 2 (2006): 429–451.

Dray-Bensousan, Renée. *Les juifs à Marseille, 1940–1944.* Paris: Les Belles Lettres, 2004.

Dubois, Laurent. *Avengers of the New World: The Story of the Haitian Revolution.* Cambridge, MA: Harvard University Press, 2004.

Dwork, Debórah, and Robert Jan Van Pelt. *Flight from the Reich: Refugee Jews, 1933–1946.* New York: W. W. Norton, 2009.

Elisabeth, Léo. "Vichy aux Antilles et en Guyane, 1940–1943." *Outre-mers* 342–343 (2004): 145–174.

Fauré, Michel. *Histoire du surréalisme sous l'occupation*. Paris: La Table ronde, 1982.

Fink, Carole. *Marc Bloch, a Life in History*. Cambridge: Cambridge University Press, 1989.

Fogg, Shannon. *The Politics of Everyday Life in Vichy France: Foreigners, Undesirables and Strangers*. Cambridge: Cambridge University Press, 2009.

Fonkoua, Romuald. *Aimé Césaire*. Paris: Perrin, 2010.

Fouchet, Max-Pol. *Wifredo Lam*. New York: Rizzoli, 1976.

Fournier, Thierry. "Paul-Emile Victor, 1907–1995: Biographie d'un explorateur polaire." Thesis, Ecole des Chartes, 2001.

Gamble, Harry. *Contesting French West Africa: Battles over Schools and the Colonial Order, 1900–1950*. Lincoln: University of Nebraska Press, 2017.

Gil, Alex. "Migrant Textuality: On the Fields of Aimé Césaire and *Et les chiens se taisaient*." PhD diss., University of Virginia, 2012.

———. "La représentation en profondeur de *Et les chiens se taisaient* d'Aimé Césaire: Pour une édition génétique en ligne." *Genesis: Manuscrits, recherche, invention* 33 (2011): 67–76.

Gildea, Robert. *Marianne in Chains: Daily Life in the Heart of France during the German Occupation*. New York: Picador, 2003.

Ginio, Ruth. *French Colonialism Unmasked: The Vichy Years in French West Africa*. Lincoln: University of Nebraska Press, 2006.

Giroud, Vincent. "Transition to Vichy: The Case of Georges Pelorson." *Modernism/Modernity* 7, no. 2 (April 2000): 221–248.

Graceffa, Agnès. "De l'entraide universitaire sous l'occupation: La correspondance de Marc Bloch avec André Mazon." *Revue historique* 674 (2015): 383–412.

Green, Nancy L. "The Politics of Exit: Reversing the Immigration Paradigm." *Journal of Modern History* 77, no. 2 (June 2005): 263–289.

Grynberg, Anne. "Les camps du sud de la France: De l'internement à la deportation." *Annales, economies, sociétés, civilisations* 48, no. 3 (1993): 557–665.

Guiraud, Jean-Michel. *La vie intellectuelle et artistique à Marseille à l'époque de Vichy et sous l'occupation, 1940–1944*. Gémenos, France: Editions Jeanne Laffitte, 1998.

Hayes, Peter. *Why? Explaining the Holocaust*. New York: W. W. Norton, 2017.

Holz, Keith, and Wolfgang Schopf. *Im Auge des Exils: Josef Breitenbach und die Freie Deutsche Kultur in Paris, 1933–1941*. Berlin: Aufbau Verlag, 2001.

Ikoku, Alvan A. "Forêts del Sur and the Pretexts of Glissant's Tout-Monde." *Small Axe* 19, no. 2 (July 2015): 1–28.

Isenberg, Noah. *We'll Always Have Casablanca*. New York: W. W. Norton, 2017.

Jackson, Julian. *France, the Dark Years*. Oxford: Oxford University Press, 2003.

Jennings, Eric. "Conservative Confluences, 'Nativist' Synergy: Re-inscribing Vichy's National Revolution in Indochina." *French Historical Studies* 27, no. 3 (Summer 2004): 601–635.

———. *Free French Africa in World War II: The African Resistance*. Cambridge: Cambridge University Press, 2015.

———. *Perspectives on French Colonial Madagascar*. New York: Palgrave, 2017.

————. *Vichy in the Tropics: Pétain's National Revolution in Madagascar, Guadeloupe and Indochina*. Stanford, CA: Stanford University Press, 2001.

Jennings, Lawrence. *French Anti-slavery*. Cambridge: Cambridge University Press, 2006

Joly, Laurent. *Vichy dans la "Solution finale," 1941–1944*. Paris: Grasset, 2006.

————. *Xavier Vallat*. Paris: Grasset, 2001.

Kaplan, Alice. *The Collaborator: The Trial and Execution of Robert Brasillach*. Chicago: University of Chicago Press, 2000.

Kitson, Simon. *Police and Politics in Marseille, 1936–1946*. Leiden: Brill, 2014.

Klarsfeld, Serge. *Vichy-Auschwitz: La "Solution Finale" de la question juive en France*. Paris: Fayard, 2001.

Klein, Anne. "Conscience, Conflict and Politics: The Rescue of Political Refugees from Southern France to the United States, 1940–1942." *Leo Baeck Institute Yearbook* 43 (1998): 287–311.

Langenbruch, Anna. *Topographien musikalischen Handelns im Pariser Exil*. New York: Georg Olms Verlag, 2014.

Laurin-Lam, Lou. "Une amitié caraïbe." *Europe* 832–833 (August–September 1998): 27–28.

Leff, Lisa Moses. *The Archive Thief: The Man Who Salvaged French Jewish History in the Wake of the Holocaust*. Oxford: Oxford University Press, 2015.

Lewis, Mary. *The Boundaries of the Republic: Migrant Rights and the Limits of Universalism in France, 1918–1940*. Stanford, CA: Stanford University Press, 2007.

Lise-Cohen, Monique, and Eric Malo, eds. *Les camps du sud-ouest de la France, 1939–1944*. Toulouse: Privat, 1994.

Louis, Marie. "L'art contemporain martiniquais de 1939 à nos jours." PhD diss., University of Metz, 2009.

Loyer, Emmanuelle. *Lévi-Strauss*. Paris: Flammarion, 2015.

————. *Paris à New York: Intellectuels et artistes français en exil, 1940–1947*. Paris: Grasset, 2005.

Macey, David. *Frantz Fanon: A Biography*. New York: Picador, 2000.

Maga, Timothy P. "Closing the Door: The French Government and Refugee Policy, 1933–1939." *French Historical Studies* 12, no. 3 (Spring 1982): 424–442.

Makward, Christiane. *Mayotte Capécia, ou l'aliénation selon Fanon*. Paris: Karthala, 1999.

Marino, Andy. *American Pimpernel: The Story of Varian Fry*. London: Hutchinson, 1999.

Marrus, Michael, and Robert Paxton. *Vichy France and the Jews*. New York: Schocken Books, 1983.

Maximin, Daniel. *Césaire et Lam, insolites bâtisseurs*. Paris: Musées nationaux, 2011.

Mehlman, Jeffrey. *Émigré New York: French Intellectuals in Wartime Manhattan, 1940–1944*. Baltimore: Johns Hopkins University Press, 2000.

Mencherini, Robert, ed. *Étrangers antifascistes à Marseille, 1940–1944: Homage au Consul du Mexique Gilberto Bosques*. Marseille: Gaussen, 2014.

———. *Provence-Auschwitz: De l'internement des étrangers à la déportation des juifs.* Aix-en-Provence: Presses Universitaires de Provence, 2008.

Mencherini, Robert, et al. *Mémoire du camp des Milles, 1939–1942.* Marseille: Le Bec en l'Air, 2013.

Miles, William F. S. "Caribbean Hybridity in Martinique." In *The Jewish Diaspora in Latin America and the Caribbean,* edited by Kristin Ruggiero, 139–162. Eastborne, UK: Sussex Academic, 2005.

———. "Schizophrenic Island, Fifty Years after Fanon: Martinique, the Pent-Up 'Paradise.' " *International Journal of Francophone Studies* 15, no. 1 (2002): 9–33.

Milia-Marie-Luce, Monique. "L'immigration en Martinique pendant l'entre-deux-guerres." *Hommes et migrations* 1274 (July–August 2008): 36–46.

Miller, Michael. *Europe and the Maritime World: A Twentieth-Century History.* Cambridge: Cambridge University Press, 2012.

Mills, Sean. *A Place in the Sun: Haiti, Haitians and the Remaking of Québec.* Montréal: McGill/Queen's University Press, 2016.

Nadeau, Maurice. *Histoire du surréalisme.* Paris: Le Seuil, 1964.

Nakach, Geneviève. *Malaquais rebelle.* Paris: Cherche Midi, 2011.

Nicolas, Armand. *Histoire de la Martinique.* Vol. 3, *De 1939 à 1971.* Paris: L'Harmattan, 1998.

Noël, Bernard. *Marseille–New York, 1940–1945.* Marseille: André Dimanche, 1985.

Nord, Philip. *France, 1940: Defending the Republic.* New Haven, CT: Yale University Press, 2015.

Pace, Alba Romano. *Jacqueline Lamba, peintre rebelle muse de l'amour fou.* Paris: Gallimard, 2010.

Palmier, Jean-Michel. *Weimar en Exil.* 2 vols. Paris: Payot, 1988.

Paxton, Robert. *Vichy France, Old Guard and New Order.* New York: Columbia University Press, 1982.

Peabody, Sue, and Tyler Stovall, eds. *The Color of Liberty: Histories of Race in France.* Durham, NC: Duke University Press, 2003.

Peschanski, Denis. *La France des camps.* Paris: Gallimard, 2002.

Polizzotti, Mark. *Revolution of the Mind: The Life of André Breton.* New York: Farrar, Straus and Giroux, 1995.

Poznanski, Renée. *Les juifs en France pendant la seconde guerre mondiale.* Paris: Hachette, 1997.

Pravdova, Anna. "Les Artistes tchèques en France: De la fondation de la Tchécoslovaquie à la fin de la seconde guerre, quelques aspects." PhD diss., University of Paris I/Charles University, 2004.

Price, Richard. *The Convict and the Colonel.* Boston: Beacon, 1998.

Reichman, Amos. "Jacques Schiffrin, aller sans retour: Itinéraire d'un éditeur en exil, 1940–1950." Master's II thesis, Université de Lyon/Columbia University, 2014.

Richardson, Michael, and Krzysztof Fijalkowski, eds. and trans. *Refusal of the Shadow: Surrealism and the Caribbean.* New York: Verso, 1996.

Rosenberg, Clifford. *Policing Paris: The Origins of Modern Immigration Control between the Wars.* Ithaca, NY: Cornell University Press, 2006.

Rothberg, Michael. *Multidirectional Memory: Remembering the Holocaust in the Age of Decolonization*. Stanford, CA: Stanford University Press, 2009.

Rovner, Adam. *In the Shadow of Zion: Promised Lands before Israel*. New York: New York University Press, 2014.

Ryan, Donna. *The Holocaust and the Jews of Marseille*. Urbana: University of Illinois Press, 1996.

Sapiro, Gisèle. *La guerre des écrivains*. Paris: Fayard, 1999.

Saure, Gabrielle. *Carl Heidenreich*. New York: Goethe-Institut, 2004.

Sémelin, Jacques, Claire Andrieu, and Sarah Gensburger. *La Résistance aux genocides: De la pluralité des actes de sauvetage*. Paris: Les Presses de Sciences Po, 2008.

Sherman, Daniel. *French Primitivism and the Ends of Empire*. Chicago: University of Chicago Press, 2011.

Sichel, Kim. *Germaine Krull: Photographer of Modernity*. Cambridge, MA: MIT Press, 1999.

Sims, Lowery Stokes. *Wifredo Lam and the International Avant-Garde, 1923–1982*. Austin: University of Texas Press, 2002.

Smaldone, William. *Rudolf Hilferding: The Tragedy of a German Social Democrat*. De Kalb: Northern Illinois University Press, 2015.

Smith, Matthew J. *Liberty, Fraternity, Exile: Haiti and Jamaica after Emancipation*. Chapel Hill: University of North Carolina Press, 2014.

Soo, Scott. *The Routes to Exile: France and the Spanish Civil War Refugees, 1939–2009*. Manchester: Manchester University Press, 2013.

Stovall, Tyler. "Aimé Césaire and the Making of Black Paris." *French Politics, Culture and Society* 27, no. 3 (Winter 2009): 44–46.

Stromberg Childers, Kristen. *Seeking Imperialism's Embrace: National Identity, Decolonization and Assimilation in the French Caribbean*. Oxford: Oxford University Press, 2016.

Sullivan, Rosemary. *Villa Air-Bel: World War II, Escape and a House in Marseille*. New York: HarperCollins, 2006.

Taylor, Lynne. *Between Resistance and Collaboration: Popular Protest in Northern France, 1940–1945*. New York: St. Martin's, 2000.

Thiesse, Anne-Marie. *Ils apprenaient la France: L'exaltation des régions dans le discours patriotique*. Paris: Maison des Sciences de l'Homme, 1997.

Varian Fry à Marseille, 1940–1941. Arles: Actes Sud, 2000.

Vinen, Richard. *The Unfree French: Life under the Occupation*. New Haven, CT: Yale University Press, 2006.

Walsh, John Patrick. *Free and French in the Caribbean: Toussaint Louverture, Aimé Césaire and Narratives of Loyal Opposition*. Bloomington: University of Indiana Press, 2013.

Weil, Patrick. *How to Be French*. Durham, NC: Duke University Press, 2008.

Wieviorka, Olivier. *Orphans of the Republic: The Nation's Legislators in Vichy France*. Cambridge, MA: Harvard University Press, 2009.

Wilder, Gary. *The French Imperial Nation State: Negritude and Colonial Humanism between the Two World Wars*. Chicago: University of Chicago Press, 2005.

———. "Untimely Vision: Aimé Césaire, Decolonization, Utopia." *Public Culture* 21, no. 1 (2009): 101–140.

Wyman, David. *The Abandonment of the Jews: America and the Holocaust, 1941–1945.* New York: New Press, 2007.

———. *Paper Walls: America and the Refugee Crisis, 1938–1941.* New York: Pantheon, 1985.

Zalc, Claire. *Dénaturalisés: Les retraits de nationalité sous Vichy.* Paris: Le Seuil, 2016.

Zaretsky, Robert. *Nîmes at War: Religion, Politics and Public Opinion in the Gard, 1938–1944.* University Park: Pennsylvania State University Press, 1995.

Zasloff, Tela. *A Rescuer's Story: Pastor Pierre-Charles Toureille in Vichy France.* Madison: University of Wisconsin Press, 2003.

Zilkosky, John. *Kafka's Travels: Exoticism, Colonialism and the Traffic of Writing.* New York: Palgrave, 2003.

Zolberg, Aristide. "The Ecole Libre at the New School, 1941–1946." *Social Research* 65, no. 4 (Winter 1998): 921–951.

Zuccotti, Susan. *The Holocaust, the French, and the Jews.* New York: Basic Books, 1993.

ACKNOWLEDGMENTS

This project received crucial and generous support from the John Simon Guggenheim Foundation and the Social Science and Humanities Research Council of Canada. They made possible years of archival digging on multiple continents, as well as providing research assistance and time off from teaching. A research grant from Victoria College made possible final research forays in Fort-de-France, Brest, and Ottawa. I also wish to thank the University of Toronto's History Department and the Faculty of Arts and Science for their ongoing support.

Short parts of Chapters 2 and 3 appeared in earlier form in "Last Exit from Vichy France: The Martinique Escape Route and the Ambiguities of Emigration," in the *Journal of Modern History*, Vol. 74, No. 2 (June 2002): 289–324 and "'The Best Avenue of Escape': The French Caribbean Route as Expulsion, Rescue, Trial, and Encounter," in *French Politics, Society and Culture*, Vol. 30, No. 2 (Summer 2012): 33–52. Brief portions of Chapter 5 appeared in "The French Caribbean in World War II: Upheavals, Repression and Resistance," in *World War II and the Caribbean*, Karen Eccles and Debbie McCollin, eds. (Kingston, Jamaica: University of the West Indies Press, 2017): 125–150. I wish to thank the University of Chicago Press, Berghahn Books, and the University of the West Indies Press, respectively, for permission to use this material.

Many of those linked to this story, either directly or through descent, shared invaluable information and displayed considerable trust in doing so. Pierre Radvanyi, who was aboard the *Paul Lemerle* in 1941, kindly agreed to an interview in Paris in 2013. Olivier and Michka Assayas allowed me to access their father Jacques Rémy's papers. René Hauth's daughters Marie-Claire Degott-Hauth and Eliane Degermann, as well as his grandson Matthieu Degott, did the same with Hauth's correspondence. Claude Lévi-Strauss graciously responded to my written inquiry in 1997. The estates of Victor Serge, Wifredo Lam, André Breton, and Aimé Césaire permitted me to consult their holdings at the Bibliothèque Jacques Doucet and the Beinecke Library (for Serge). Through Geneviève Nakach, Elisabeth Malaquais shared portions of Galina Yurkevich's diary. Anya Shiffrin led me to Amos Reichman's master's thesis on her grandfather. Peter Stein shared his mother's recollections of the *Winnipeg*. Anita Sperling spontaneously contacted me about her extraordinary experience aboard the *Alsina*.

Colleagues helped shape this project at every turn, of which there were many. Sean Mills uncovered useful André Breton and Wifredo Lam material in Haiti. Anna Pravdova welcomed me in Prague, where she helped me immensely with my sections on Czech artists Antonin Pelc and Alen Divis. Jiří Hůla provided provenance of a drawing by Divis. Alex Gil generously sent me a copy of the Aimé Césaire manuscript he uncovered in the Vosges. Gabrielle Saure, Richard Buxbaum, and Karla Lortz helped immeasurably with German painter Carl Heidenreich. Marie-Christine Touchelay forwarded a relevant document she unearthed in the Incendie collection at Guadeloupe's departmental archives. Anthony Glinoer introduced me to the Victor Serge academic community. Laurent Joly shared valuable materials on the Geissler bureau at Vichy and its role in the handover of Breitscheid and Hilferding. Klaus Kuhl revealed the results of his ongoing investigations into Lothar Popp's departure from Marseille in 1941. Ronald Pruessen assisted me with contacts in Cuba. Thierry Fournier passed along not only the relevant portions of his unpublished thesis on Paul Emile Victor but also his research notes from Victor's diary and correspondence. Yerri Urban guided me through relevant colonial legal texts. Alexander Boix kindly sent me Walter Mehring material from the Friedrich-Ebert-Stiftung in Bonn. William Miles shared insights on Martinique's Jewish community. Pierre Sauvage provided early leads relating to Varian Fry; Vincent Bercker, thoughts on André Masson; and Alain Paire, reflections on the intellectual scene in wartime Provence. Didier Schulmann and Alexandre Colliex put me in touch with Jacques Rémy's family. Dominique Chathuant kept me abreast of his work on Maurice Satineau. Michael Dobbs shared a file he uncovered in London. Felix Germain sent a reference to a Caribbean song that evokes part of this story. Patrick Weil provided outstanding suggestions on my first articles relating to the Martinique route. Richard Fogarty, Julia Clancy-Smith, Stefan Martens, Luca Somigli, and Gregory Mann all recommended remarkable and reliable students to help with specific research components.

I also received valuable feedback at venues where I presented drafts at the earliest, middle, and final stages: a talk at the New School for Social Research arranged in 2001 by Cliff Rosenberg and the late Aristide Zolberg; a conference at Columbia University's Maison française in 2011 spearheaded by Harriet Jackson, Robert Paxton, and Shanny Peer; a presentation for Alice Conklin's World War II seminar at Ohio State in 2014; a 2016 paper at the Parisian "Séminaire Empires," directed by Hélène Blais, Armelle Enders, Emmanuelle Sibeud, Pierre Sinagaravélou, and Sylvie Thénault; a presentation at the Université des Antilles at the invitation of Yerri Urban in December 2016; and a May 2017 presentation at the Musée d'Histoire de Marseille organized by Philippe San Marco and Sophie Deshayes. A special thank-you goes out to my patient and insightful readers, who considerably improved the manuscript as it evolved: Vicki Caron, Herrick Chapman, Alice Conklin, Tina Freris, Chantal and Larry Jennings, Laurent Joly, Derek Penslar, and the anonymous readers for Harvard University Press.

This project involved many leads and a fair share of wild goose chases (to give but one example, the 200E series in Marseille seemed promising until Olivier Gorse kindly sent me the list of boats included in it). As such, it required considerable travel and sleuthing, most of which I undertook myself. However, I also relied on an excellent team of student assistants at my institution and beyond to conduct a variety of important tasks. At the University of Toronto, Matthieu Vallières helped me compile a database and digitize material, and Christin Bohnke assisted with German texts. The translations of Kurt Kersten's manuscript and Anna Seghers' published letters are hers. Juan Carlos Mezo Gonzales pored over Spanish-language material relating to Luis Fernandez Clérigo. Francesca Facchi researched the biography of Mario Montagna; the translations of Italian-language materials relating to this leading Italian antifascist are hers.

At Frankfurt's Exil Archiv, Carla Reitter helped focus and accelerate my research with translation help. Columbia University's Devon Golaszewski photographed pertinent files in the Erich Itor Kahn Papers at the New York Public Library Archives; Evan Sullivan did the same with the German Jewish Intellectual Émigré Collection in Albany, New York, and Jaynie E. Adams with the Josef Breitenbach Papers at the Center for Creative Photography in Tucson, Arizona. My heartfelt thanks to all.

Last but certainly not least, I wish to thank Kathleen McDermott at Harvard University Press for her sage advice and her interest in the project, Ashley Moore for copyediting, and Celia Braves for indexing.

INDEX

Page numbers in italics refer to illustrations.